Bodies and Ruins

Social History, Popular Culture, and Politics in Germany
Kathleen Canning, Series Editor

Recent Titles

Marking Modern Movement: Dance and Gender in the Visual Imagery of the Weimar Republic
Susan Funkenstein

Anti-Heimat Cinema: The Jewish Invention of the German Landscape
Ofer Ashkenazi

Dispossession: Plundering German Jewry, 1933–1953
Christoph Kreutzmüller and Jonathan R. Zatlin, Editors

Sex between Body and Mind: Psychoanalysis and Sexology in the German-speaking World, 1890s–1930s
Katie Sutton

Imperial Fictions: German Literature Before and Beyond the Nation-State
Todd Kontje

White Rebels in Black: German Appropriation of Black Popular Culture
Priscilla Layne

Not Straight from Germany: Sexual Publics and Sexual Citizenship since Magnus Hirschfeld
Michael Thomas Taylor, Annette F. Timm, and Rainer Herrn, Editors

Passing Illusions: Jewish Visibility in Weimar Germany
Kerry Wallach

Cosmopolitanisms and the Jews
Cathy S. Gelbin and Sander L. Gilman

Bodies and Ruins: Imagining the Bombing of Germany, 1945 to the Present
David Crew

The Jazz Republic: Music, Race, and American Culture in Weimar Germany
Jonathan Wipplinger

The War in Their Minds: German Soldiers and Their Violent Pasts in West Germany
Svenja Goltermann

Three-Way Street: Jews, Germans, and the Transnational
Jay Howard Geller and Leslie Morris, Editors

Beyond the Bauhaus: Cultural Modernity in Breslau, 1918–33
Deborah Ascher Barnstone

Stop Reading! Look! Modern Vision and the Weimar Photographic Book
Pepper Stetler

The Corrigible and the Incorrigible: Science, Medicine, and the Convict in Twentieth-Century Germany
Greg Eghigian

An Emotional State: The Politics of Emotion in Postwar West German Culture
Anna M. Parkinson

Germany's Wild East: Constructing Poland as Colonial Space
Kristin Kopp

Beyond Berlin: Twelve German Cities Confront the Nazi Past
Gavriel D. Rosenfeld and Paul B. Jaskot, Editors

For a complete list of titles, please see www.press.umich.edu

Bodies and Ruins

Imagining the Bombing of Germany, 1945 to the Present

David F. Crew

University of Michigan Press
Ann Arbor

First paperback edition 2020

Published in the United States of America by the
University of Michigan Press
Manufactured in the United States of America
Printed on acid-free paper

First published in paperback August 2020

A CIP catalog record for this book is available from the British Library.

Library of Congress Cataloging-in-Publication Data

Names: Crew, David F., 1946– author.
Title: Bodies and ruins : imagining the bombing of Germany, 1945 to the present / David F. Crew.
Description: Ann Arbor : University of Michigan Press, 2017. | Series: Social history, popular culture, and politics in Germany | Includes bibliographical references and index.
Identifiers: LCCN 2016043290| ISBN 9780472130139 (hardcover : alk. paper) | ISBN 9780472122387 (e-book)
Subjects: LCSH: World War, 1939–1945—Destruction and pillage—Germany. | Bombing, Aerial—Germany—History—20th century. | World War, 1939–1945—Campaigns—Germany. | World War, 1939–1945—Aerial operations. | World War, 1939–1945—Influence.
Classification: LCC D810.D6 .C74 2017 | DDC 940.54/213—dc23
LC record available at https://lccn.loc.gov/2016043290

ISBN 978-0-472-03846-6 (pbk.)

Cover image: The Bavarian city of Nuremberg in ruins after the 1945 Allied bombing. Courtesy National Archives.

For my granddaughter, Maya

Acknowledgments

In the process of writing this book, I have accumulated debts to a number of institutions and individuals. It is a pleasure to be able, finally, to express my thanks in print. The financial assistance that made the research for this book possible was provided by The University of Texas at Austin (UT-Austin) in the form of a Faculty Research Assignment (Fall Semester, 2007) and by the Department of History at UT-Austin in the form of several Scholarly Activity Grants (SAG). As a Fellow of the Institute for Historical Studies in the History Department of The University of Texas at Austin during the academic years 2010–11 and 2013–14, I not only received valuable release time from teaching but also benefited greatly from the extraordinary intellectual exchange that took place in the Institute's weekly research seminars. I want to thank my colleague Julie Hardwick, the energetic first director, who has helped to make the Institute such a success.

The interlibrary loan service of Perry-Castaneda Library at UT-Austin deserves special thanks for its relentless pursuit of the large number of local publications that are the foundation of this study. I am also indebted to the staffs of the following archives in Germany for their patient and professional assistance: Sächsische Landesbibliothek-Staats- und Universitätsbibliothek Dresden, Bundesarchiv/Berlin-Lichterfelde, Bundesarchiv-Film Archiv/Berlin-Wilmersdorf, Bildarchiv preußischer Kulturbesitz-Berlin (BpK). At the BpK (now known as the Bildagentur für Kunst, Kultur und Geschichte), where I have been working for several summers on another related project, Norbert Ludwig and Hanns-Peter Frentz (the director) have been exceptionally welcoming and helpful.

The organizers and sponsors of several seminars, lectures, and conferences gave me the opportunity to present installments of my research and to benefit from thoughtful responses and criticisms. At an early stage in the development of this project, a workshop on "Memories of Catastrophe" at Virginia

Tech, Blacksburg, Virginia (March 30–31, 2007), gave me my first chance to air some preliminary ideas and arguments. A conference on "From Perpetrators to Victims? Constructions and Representations of German Wartime Suffering" at Leeds University, United Kingdom, June 29–July 1, 2007, helped me to move my thinking along, as did a lecture I was asked by Alf Lüdtke to present at the University of Erfurt, Germany, June 3, 2008. Finally, I want to thank Georg-Wagner Kyora and Axel Schildt for inviting me to the conference on "Wiederaufbau der Städte:Europa seit 1945/Rebuilding European Cities: Reconstruction Policy since 1945," in Hamburg, Germany, September 23–25, 2009, sponsored jointly by the Faculty of Philosophy of the Leibniz University Hanover, the Research Institute for Contemporary History–University of Hamburg, and the Deutsche Forschungsgemeinschaft, which gave me the opportunity to present an earlier version of chapter 4 of this book.

As I was writing this book, I enjoyed the exceptional good fortune of being able to turn for advice to four longtime colleagues. Each read the original manuscript closely and carefully, and each gave me many pages of suggestions about how to improve the final version. For more than a quarter of a century, Adelheid (Heidy) von Saldern has been an intellectual partner and a good friend. Whether at the dinner table in Göttingen or, more recently, on one of our trips to Poland, Lithuania, Ukraine, or Bulgaria, Heidy and I have talked endlessly about German history. I have profited immensely from these conversations. Heidy read every word of the manuscript of this book with great care, close attention to detail, and astute insight. So, too, did Uwe Lohalm in Hamburg, whom I first met in 1988 when I was working on the research for a previous book in the Hamburg Staatsarchiv. In Austin, Sabine Hake and Kirsten (Kit) Belgum were extremely generous with their time, knowledge, and insight. Both gave the book manuscript close and careful readings and made important suggestions that I have done my best to incorporate into the final product. I also want to thank the anonymous reader for the University of Michigan Press, whose astute comments encouraged me to look at the manuscript with different eyes.

Numerous other friends and colleagues on both sides of the Atlantic provided very necessary encouragement, support, and constructive criticism at every stage in the writing of this book. I want to thank three of my former graduate students, now established scholars: Rob Stephens and Heather Gumbert at Virginia Tech and David Imhoof at Susquehanna University, who continue to play an important part in my intellectual as well as personal life. In Austin, I have benefitted enormously from my many conversations with Joan Neuberger, who shares my interest in visual history and visual culture. I also want to thank Bob Abzug, Chris Ernst, Steve Hoelscher, Tatjana Lichtenstein, Neil Kamil, and Michael Stoff.

Two of my (now former) graduate students, Shannon Nagy and Michael Schmidt, took on the often frustrating task of hunting down reproduction permissions for pictures that originally appeared in obscure publications. I want to thank them both for their dogged detective work.

I am indebted to Geoff Eley, the past series editor, and Kathleen Canning, the current editor, who decided that this book belonged in the University of Michigan Press series on Social History, Popular Culture, and Politics in Germany. I also want to thank Ellen Bauerle (senior executive editor), LeAnn Fields (senior executive editor), Christopher Dreyer (editorial associate), and Kevin Rennells (production editor), who have shepherded this book into publication with enthusiasm, remarkable efficiency, and a keen understanding of what I was trying to accomplish.

Sharing everyday life with my wife, Sara, helped to make this book possible. For more than a quarter of a century, I have looked forward to seeing Sara at the end of our respective working days and to talking with her about the world, large and small, past and present. Since my last book was published, our daughter Kate has become the amazing mother of our wonderful granddaughter, Maya. Kate's wit and exceptional sense of humor cheered me on more than one occasion when the depressing subject of this book was beginning to get to me. My son-in-law, Aaron, has brought intelligence, patience, good humor, and a good heart into our now expanded family. This book is dedicated specifically to my granddaughter, Maya, but it is really meant for everyone in my family as well as for all of my colleagues, friends, and students who made it possible.

Material in chapters 4 and 5 has been previously published in part or in different versions in the following articles:

"Mourning, Denial, Celebration: The Visual Work of West German Reconstruction after 1945," in Georg Wagner-Kyora, editor, *Wiederaufbau europäischer Städte.Rekonstruktionen, die Moderne und die locale Identitätspolitik seit 1945/ Rebuilding German Cities.Reconstructions, Modernity and the Local Politics of Identity Construction since 1945* (Stuttgart: Franz Steiner Verlag, 2014). Used by permission of Georg-Wagner Kyora.

"Sleeping with the Enemy? A Fiction Film for German Television about the Bombing of Dresden," in *Central European History* 40 (2007). Used by permission of *Central European History*.

David F. Crew
Austin, Texas
July 2016

Contents

List of Illustrations xiii

Introduction 1

1 Local Stories: Narratives of the Bombing War, 1949–88 13

2 Picture Work 57

3 The Meanings of Ruins 87

4 Mourning, Denial, Celebration: The Visual Work of Picture Books 113

5 East Germany's Bombing War: Dresden 145

6 After the Cold War: The Multimedia Bombing War since the 1990s 169

Conclusion 213

Notes 219

Selected Bibliography 253

Illustration Credits 265

Index 269

Digital materials related to this title can be found on the Fulcrum platform via the following citable URL: https://doi.org/10.3998/mpub.340367

List of Illustrations

1.	Hamburg, damaged typewriter in a shop window after British firebombing	58
2.	Nuremberg, destruction caused by bombing	65
3.	Nuremberg, American soldiers at grounds where the Nazi Party held its rallies	67
4.	Stuttgart, dead Allied airman	69
5 & 6.	Aschaffenburg, Germans in air-raid shelters	73
7.	Hamburg, victim of firebombing	77
8.	Hamburg, dead bodies after the firebombing	78
9 & 10.	Hamburg, two female victims of the firebombing	79
11 & 12.	Nuremberg, priests and nuns in a Corpus Christi procession	82
13 & 14.	Frankfurt am Main, deportation of Jews	85
15 & 16.	Cologne, children and adult killed by Allied bombing	88–89
17 & 18.	Ludwigshafen, a main street before and after the bombing	93–94
19.	Berlin, a postman trying to deliver mail in the ruins	97
20.	Hanover, woman trying to clear a pile of ruins	101
21.	Freiburg, women smiling as they clear ruins	102
22.	Dresden, woman struggling to carry bricks from the ruins	103
23.	Bremen, old woman gathering firewood after an air raid	105
24.	Aschaffenburg, boy standing in ruins	107
25.	Bremen, a boy standing in ruins	108
26.	Photograph by Hilmar Pabel of the aftermath of a bombing raid	120
27.	Seven years later, survivors look at photos of this bombing raid	121
28.	Photograph by Hilmar Pabel of child survivor of bombing raid	122

29. Sharing this photo with the female survivor, seven years later 123
30. Heilbronn during a major air attack, December 4, 1944 126
31. Hitler Youth lined up in perfect rows 130
32. Mother searching for her children after an air raid on Berlin 131
33. Hanover, young children stealing food from bomb-damaged shops 134
34. Hanover, an armaments factory destroyed by Allied bombs 135
35. Bremen, man in a bomb-damaged building after the January 3, 1941, air raid 137
36. Bremen, corpse collection center after the air raid of January 1–2, 1941 138
37. Bremen, retrieving food from building after air raid of October 6, 1944 139
38. Bremen, woman at a "phosphorous cleaning station" 140
39. Bremen, street scene after the air raid of September 14, 1942 140
40. View from top of Dresden City Hall showing devastation of city 150
41. Corpse with Nazi uniform and swastika 153
42. Corpse of an air-raid warden whose gas mask did not save his life 154
43. A mummified woman in an air-raid cellar 155
44 & 45. Dresden shopping area, the Prager Strasse, in 1944 and 1984 159

Introduction

I became interested in the subject of this book in the late 1990s when the Allied bombing of German cities was gaining increasing prominence in German public discussions of World War II and the Nazi past. At that time, the claim was frequently made that this discussion was long overdue, that after 1945 the experience and suffering of German civilians during the Allied air war had been "off-limits," the subject only of private conversations around the family dinner table but never a major focus of public memory. Germans who had lived through the bombing were, it appeared, victims twice over—victimized by the bombing itself and then by the silence to which they were allegedly condemned after 1945. Now the time had come to talk openly and publicly about the 305,000 to 410,000 Germans, most of them women, children, and old people, who had been killed, sometimes in quite hideous ways, by Allied bombs.[1] Finally, it seemed possible to acknowledge the irredeemable loss of architectural treasures and cultural heritage. And, it now also seemed necessary—especially in view of the use of airpower in contemporary conflicts (Kosovo, Iraq, Afghanistan)—to pose difficult questions about the morality, legality, and military effectiveness of the Allied bombing of Germany during World War II.

What made this public attention to the bombing war possible in the 1990s? The end of the Cold War was a major factor. West Germany's Cold War alliance with the United States had made it difficult, if not impossible, to raise questions about the Allied bombing campaign.[2] In communist East Germany, the bombing war had always been an important component of Cold War anti-American propaganda. Now the GDR was gone and it was possible to raise questions about the air war without being accused of siding with the enemy in the Cold War. The bombing war was also one of the last common experiences shared by East and West Germans. After the fall of the Berlin Wall, talking about shared memories of the air war might help the newly unified nation in its search for a common identity. And, finally, big anniversaries of the end of

World War II—the 50th in 1995 and the 60th in 2005—drew media attention to the bombing war.

Two important books reflected and stimulated the growing public interest in the bombing war. In a series of lectures delivered in Zürich in 1997, subsequently published as *Luftkrieg und Literatur* (*Airwar and Literature*), the German author and literary critic, W. G. Sebald, argued that after 1945, Germans had pushed the bombing war to the margins of their historical consciousness.[3] Sebald faulted German writers in particular for not having made the air war a more central and significant focus of postwar literature. Sebald's provocative slim volume was followed in 2002 by Jörg Friedrich's massive (592 pages) book on the bombing war, *Der Brand. Deutschland im Bombenkrieg 1940–1945* (*The Fire. Germany in the Bombing War, 1940–1945*),[4] which generated intense discussion and quickly became a bestseller in Germany.[5] Descriptions and images of the bombing war were now to be found everywhere in the mass media—on the pages of German newspapers and magazines, on television, and on the Internet.[6] Forgotten novels about the bombing were reprinted.[7] And in March 2006, the German television network ZDF aired the first fiction film about the firebombing of Dresden. Shown in two parts on March 5 and March 6, 2006, this "most expensive German made-for-television production to date,"[8] at a cost of over 10 million Euros, drew an audience of 13 million viewers on the first evening it was broadcast.[9] At the beginning of the new millennium, German public interest in the bombing war had never been greater.[10]

The story Friedrich told his German readers was one many wanted to hear but may have felt they had been previously denied. His dense, often excruciatingly painful narrative focused on the details of German suffering during Allied air raids and the firestorms they sometimes produced. This emphasis on the painful experiences of the German victims was not complicated by any discussion of the identities of these Germans who had huddled together in the air-raid shelters. Friedrich did not ask whether these German victims might also have been accomplices and perpetrators. Had they denounced Jews to the Gestapo or profited from the plunder of Jewish property? Had they worked as foremen or managers overseeing Russian POWs or Soviet civilians deported from the occupied East to work for the war effort in Germany? Had some of these Germans even participated in Hitler's racial war of annihilation on the Eastern Front, as the photographs displayed in the controversial exhibition "Crimes of the Wehrmacht" seen by some 900,000 visitors had argued when it traveled to 34 cities in Germany and Austria between 1995 and 1999? What, in short, had these German victims of the bombing been doing before the day they found themselves in a bomb shelter or the ruins of a destroyed German city? And how might the answers to these questions complicate the image of Germans as innocent, suffering victims that Friedrich presented to his readers?

Friedrich also showed that the Allied bombing campaign destroyed large numbers of Germany's historic buildings, rare books, documents, and precious paintings. This was a loss of cultural heritage that could never be made good again. In Friedrich's extended lament for Germany's cultural losses as a result of the air war there was, however, no place for consideration of or comparison with the losses suffered by other European nations at the hands of the Germans. In 1939, 400 German planes destroyed the historic town center of Warsaw.[11] Then in 1944 German soldiers leveled Warsaw with dynamite, block-by-block, on Hitler's order as they retreated from the Red Army. Friedrich mentions Warsaw at eight different points in his book; none of these references talk about the destruction of the Polish capital's architectural heritage by the Germans. Friedrich suggests that such a comparison would be inappropriate because "the fate of German cities was different from that of Warsaw, Rotterdam, Coventry in the same way that a war is different from a battle."[12] But if the claim is to be made that the destruction caused by the bombing of German cities was somehow unique, a catastrophe "without historical precedent," as W. G. Sebald has suggested, then comparisons with the other "catastrophes" of World War II, including the murder of between five and six million Jews in the Holocaust and the eradication of many centuries of Jewish culture in Eastern Europe, would appear to be unavoidable.

Finally, Friedrich focused attention on the Allied politicians and military leaders whose decisions had produced the destruction of German cities. But instead of carefully examining the complicated and sometimes contradictory development of Allied strategy from the beginning of the war, Friedrich insisted that the bombing of German cities had no compelling military purpose, especially not in the final year of the war when, he argued, it became unrestrained revenge and destruction for its own sake. In his book, there is no considered assessment of the actual military effects of the bombing—did it, for example, help to shorten the war even if it did not achieve its major declared goals? Nor does Friedrich situate the Allied bombing campaign within the longer history going back to World War I of the theory and practice of air war developed by a number of different nations, including Germany itself.

Public interest in the bombing was sometimes stimulated by the claim that for the past 50 years open public discussion of the air war had been repressed by a "taboo" that insisted that Germans must be seen as perpetrators not victims.[13] One extreme version of this assertion insisted that for the German victims of the bombing war "no hours of remembrance are observed."[14] However, the flood of new research generated in response to Friedrich's bestseller and to Sebald's Zürich lectures has shown that these claims are quite simply untrue. Malte Thießen's book on Hamburg, Jörg Arnold's comparative study of Kassel and Magdeburg in the former GDR, Neil Gregor's work on Nuremberg, and Dietmar Süß's comparative analysis of the air war in Britain and Germany have all demonstrated that far from being marginalized in postwar historical consciousness, the bombing war was a central strand of German memory and identity from the 1940s to the present.[15] Along with the flight and mass expulsions of ethnic Germans from the East and the mass rapes of German women by Soviet soldiers, the bombing war allowed Germans to see themselves as victims at a time when the Allied liberation of the concentration camps and the Nuremberg trials presented Germans to the world as perpetrators, or at least as accomplices. The bombing war has continued to serve this function even as Germans have become more and more willing directly to confront the genocide of European Jews—which by the 1960s was beginning to be referred to as the Holocaust.[16] The history of German remembering of the air war supports Michael Rothberg's argument against viewing "the relation between memories of different historical events according to a . . . zero-sum logic of competition."[17] As the Holocaust became the object of greater public awareness, the bombing war did not become less important in German public consciousness. Indeed, heightened public interest in the genocide of European Jews at later points in German postwar history appears actually to have encouraged a resurgence of attention to the bombing war.[18] Dietmar Süß observes, for example, that "in the context of the legal reprocessing of German war crimes which became more intense from the end of the 1950s along with stronger media interest, the debates about the crime of the air war assumed a quite new significance, indeed they made it possible, at least indirectly, to balance off [Germany's] own blame for the murder of the Jews which could now no longer be denied against the crimes of the Allies and thereby to remain on an equal moral footing."[19] It was not coincidental, he suggests, that the first major book to deal with the air war at a national level, Hans Rumpf's *Das war der Bombenkrieg. Deutsche Städte im Feuersturm. Ein Dokumentarbericht* (*That was the Bombing War. German Cities in the Firestorm. A Documentary Report*), which appeared in 1961 after the 1958 Ulm Einsatzgruppen trial and the Eichmann trial in Jerusalem, "resonated so noticeably with a not inconsiderable segment of the German public."[20] In 1963, two years after it appeared in German, Rumpf's book was translated into English and published in New York by Holt, Rinehart and Winston.[21] A "Publisher's Note" at the beginning of the book warned readers that

> This book should be read with care. For, in the course of his study of aerial bombardment during World War II, Hans Rumpf has described in detail the horror and suffering that visited German civilians and German cities under Allied bombing attacks. But he has devoted no more than passing comment to the equally terrifying experiences inflicted by German aerial attacks on the people of London, Rotterdam, and Coventry. And he has made no mention at all of the millions who suffered and died in German concentration camps.
>
> Some will conclude from this that Herr Rumpf, by ignoring certain large moral questions, is asking for pity where none may be deserved. The publisher must strenuously disassociate himself from any such implied conclusion.[22]

The Centrality of the Local in Postwar Memory Cultures

Friedrich's book drew heavily upon the many local publications about the bombing that began to appear in the late 1940s and that have continued to the present. The very existence of this considerable body of local narratives disputes the claim that there was no significant public discussion of the bombing war until the late 1990s. Along with the local ceremonies and newspaper articles that commemorated the anniversaries of major air raids, local narratives of the bombing war had already established themselves as important "vectors of memory" in the late 1940s and early 1950s.[23] Not produced by professional historians and usually lacking any scholarly pretensions, these local publications are examples of the kind of "public history" that has been so influential in constructing and transmitting popular understandings of the past to successive generations of Germans since 1945.[24]

As I began to dig deeper into these local publications, I realized that Friedrich had not only drawn information from these books but that his own narrative in crucial ways replicated the patterns they established in the 1950s, which in turn owed a great deal to Nazi narratives of the air war. Nazi propaganda had demonized the Allies as "barbarians" who murdered innocent civilians and destroyed irreplaceable cultural treasures. To show that the German people had refused to be crushed by the "war crimes" committed by these Allied "air gangsters," Goebbels declared in August 1944 that German cities and communities must systematically preserve information and eyewitness reports about the experience of the air war. This archive would be used to create a "National Socialist memory of the history of the air-war" that demonstrated the collective will of the German people to survive and to win the war, as well as individual acts of courage and heroism.[25] After 1945, this same archive would serve as a "reservoir of memory" for many of the early local narratives of the air war.[26] This meant, however, that postwar local narratives often reproduced versions of the motifs that had characterized Nazi propaganda without, however, acknowledging (or questioning) their origins in the Nazi era. Continuities with Nazi narratives of the air war might also be reinforced by the fact that some of the authors had themselves been "activists in the National Socialist air defence, who continued in the histories they wrote from the 1950s onwards what National Socialist propaganda had begun."[27]

Most of the rapidly expanding research on the history of German remembering of the Nazi years has "conceptualized the German attempt to contend with the past in collective national terms."[28] Paul Jaskot and Gavriel Rosenfeld point out, however, that although "[t]his broad view is perfectly sensible for many reasons . . . it has largely overlooked the obvious fact that Germans have also confronted the legacy of the Nazi regime as the inhabitants of their respective localities. Ever since 1945, the process of *Vergangenheitsbewältigung* has unfolded within specific geographies and revolved around distinct sites with particular histories."[29] In this book, I want to argue that far from being peripheral or somehow marginal, local memory cultures have actually played a crucial role in the memory work done by Germans in the years since 1945.[30] Although discussion of the air war was entangled with national and even international debates about the war, it was, as Dietmar Süß concludes, "above all within the microcosm of the city that the consequences of the bombing had to be mastered and given meaning."[31]

The excellent local case studies by Thießen, Arnold, Gregor, and others mentioned above have reconstructed the development of individual local memory cultures in very rich detail. It is not yet clear, however, to what extent the findings of these case studies can be generalized. Do the similarities in the histories of specific local memory cultures outweigh the differences? Definitive answers to that question await additional local studies and comparative analysis. Instead of adding to this growing body of detailed local case studies, I decided that it was important to pursue a different approach by constructing as wide as possible a survey of the local publications written about many different German towns and cities in the period from 1945 to 1989. Hundreds of these local publications have appeared since 1945. Already by 1964, the bibliographical volume of *Dokumente Deutscher Kriegsschäden* (*Documents of German War Damage*), a multivolume investigation of the consequences of the air war published by the Bundesminister für Vertriebene, Flüchtlinge und

Kriegsgeschädigte (Federal Minister for Expellees, Refugees and Those Damaged by the War), could present some 27 pages of titles (over 600 publications) of local books and articles about dozens of cities ranging alphabetically from Aachen to Stuttgart.[32] This same bibliographical volume devoted some 77 pages to more than 2,200 local publications relevant to the postwar reconstruction of German cities. There is no doubt, then, that local publications were a crucial site of local memory work. Since 1990, the appearance of local publications has continued unabated. The Wartberg publishing house has developed an entire series devoted to "Deutsche Städte im Bombenkrieg." Cities such as Göttingen that had previously received little attention now also have a place in the ever-expanding local literature on the bombing war. Local publications have usually dealt with the bombing war at greater length and in much greater detail than annual commemorations and the newspaper articles that covered them. Yet historians have so far analyzed only a handful of the many local publications that have appeared since 1945. Examining how this important genre has developed over the entire period between 1945 and 1989, should, therefore, deepen our understanding of the changing parameters, limits, complexities, and contradictions of local memory work in a wide range of different German cities.

The second goal of this book, and what distinguishes it from the existing research even more than its wide perspective, is to engage in an extended investigation of the uses made of photography in local publications and in another important genre of local memory work, photo-books. Although they were normally quite "text-heavy," local publications almost always included a considerable number of images, usually photographs. The importance of the visual is even more evident in the many local photo-books that presented the bombing primarily in images, with words usually restricted to the function of captions. Photographs of German cities destroyed in the air war soon entered the national and even international visual memory of World War II. In 1958, the very first volume of *Dokumente deutscher Kriegsschäden* published photographs of the destruction caused by Allied bombs in Berlin, Braunschweig, Bremen, Frankfurt, Hamburg, Stuttgart, Hanover, Heilbronn, Kassel, Koblenz, Köln, Mainz, Munich, Nuremberg, Osnabrück, Pforzheim, Stuttgart, and Würzburg.[33] Hans Rumpf's 1963 book, mentioned above, began each chapter with a different photograph of a German city bombed by the Allies. Yet, despite its obvious importance, historians have paid very little attention to the visual representation of the bombing war.[34]

The authors of local publications and photo-books clearly believed that photographs could "offer immediate access to past realities." Julia Adeney

Thomas warns, however, that this assumption privileges intuitive and emotional responses to images.[35] She argues that this way of approaching photographs—which she calls "recognition"—can lead to a "Sensuous Muteness" that allows us only to know what we feel now about a photograph, not what that image may have meant in the past. Thomas suggests that the alternative to "recognition" is "excavation," which tries to understand photographs by locating them in the discursive and cultural contexts that produced them.[36] But "excavation" often lacks the information it needs about how people in the past actually gave meaning to specific images. "Excavation" can, therefore, run the risk of producing a "Blind Discourse." The dilemmas produced by both "recognition" and "excavation" lead Thomas to conclude that "there is no easy resolution, no middle ground to be found in the charged encounter with a photographic image."[37] A conference paper by Joan Neuberger suggests that understanding what photographs may have meant to Germans in the past is an even more difficult undertaking than Thomas has argued in her article. Neuberger points to the research in neurological science that shows that although language certainly plays a role in our perception of the visual, crucial brain processes are preverbal or nonverbal. Neuberger also argues that certain qualities of visual images cannot be grasped or communicated by language.[38] This means, however, that a significant element of the way Germans experienced the images they saw would not have been expressed in language and would not therefore have been preserved in the written texts upon which historians normally rely.

This all means that it is extremely difficult to find a way back to Germans' inevitably varied perceptions of these photographs at the time they were taken or to the new or different meanings they may have assumed as they were reproduced in later publications. I would not pretend to have discovered that path. My main goal has been to understand how authors of local publications tried to use pictures to create meanings and to tell stories.[39] But I recognize that examining what authors tried to do with images does not tell us how Germans who saw these pictures perceived and responded to them. The "imagining" in the subtitle of this book therefore refers, first and foremost, to the ways in which the authors of local publications and photo-books tried, in text and with images, to imagine the bombing war and to communicate what they thought was its meaning to their readers/viewers. It is much harder to say how these readers themselves understood and responded to what they read and saw. Each text and each image or series of images could be read/seen in a number of different ways. However, I am not sure that it is possible to retrieve the evidence that would tell us what those different responses actually were. That has not prevented me from making suggestions about the range of possible/plausible ways in which images might have been appropriated by the Germans who saw them. These suggestions should, however, be regarded as speculative.

Even though the published visual repertoire has expanded significantly from the 1940s to the 2010s, it has never included all of the different types of photographs that were taken and that could be considered as relevant to a visual history of the bombing war. Which of the photographs in this visual archive of the bombing war were used most commonly? Which others were published infrequently or not at all? How have the answers to these questions changed over the past seven decades? Photography "was rarely left to 'speak for itself' but usually integrated into narrative frames."[40] So, although I see this book as an experiment in visual history, this does not mean that I have concentrated on images at the expense of texts. To understand how photographs were used in local publications and photo-books, what meanings the authors wanted to convey, we have to pay attention to the relationships of individual photographs and other images not only to one another but also to the written texts in which these pictures were embedded. How have these relationships developed and changed since 1945?

The main aim of this book is to follow the search for what were considered to be the "right" stories and the "right" pictures of the bombing war in local publications and picture books from 1945 to the present.[41] In the immediate postwar years, authors could safely assume that most of their readers had actually lived through the experiences that local publications tried to describe. By the 1960s, however, authors faced the challenge of reaching postwar generations for whom the war might be only "an abstract monstrosity that exceeds their ability to comprehend."[42] What could descriptions and pictures of German cities destroyed by Allied bombs possibly mean to Germans born after 1945? The author of a book on Cologne published in 1970 admitted that it would indeed be difficult for these younger generations of Germans to imagine what that city had lost to the bombing: "What is the purpose of this publication at a time when only with great effort can one detect traces of the war in the cathedral city? . . . Those who are today younger than thirty . . . no longer know anything about the war: they only hear about rebuilding and prosperity."[43] The introduction to a book on the Mainz region published in 1988 noted that 70 percent of the citizens of Rheinland-Pfalz were simply too young to have had any direct experience of the war or even of the immediate postwar years. This was a very distant past about which they might know very little. But younger Germans' lack of knowledge (or, worse still, lack of interest) was not the only problem for the authors of local publications. By the 1970s, many younger

Germans were well aware that, however important the bombing had been to their parents and grandparents, it was not the only dimension of the Nazi past that deserved attention. A series of high profile trials that began at the end of the 1950s brought the genocide of the Jews back into national discussions. How did the authors of local publications respond to this challenge?

This book consists of six chapters. Chapter 1 begins by examining what I have called the local master narrative that was established in the late 1940s and 1950s. Although the way the story of the bombing war was told might vary considerably from one locality to another, local narratives shared one overriding priority, the desire to depict Germans as innocent, suffering victims but at the same time to praise the survivors' resilience and applaud the reconstruction of German cities after the war. The chapter shows, however, that as wider perspectives on the war and more frequent references to Germany's victims, including Jews, were introduced into local narratives, beginning in the 1960s, telling the story of the bombing war as a narrative of German suffering became increasingly more difficult than it was in the 1950s.

Chapter 2 examines the essential role played by images, primarily photographs, in these local publications. Images were used not simply to illustrate the written text but also to show aspects of the bombing war that the authors believed could not be communicated adequately in words. Yet the power of images was limited by the conditions under which they had been produced during and immediately after the war. Photographers had simply not been able to capture pictures of some of the most horrific experiences of the bombing. The images in the visual archive of the bombing available for postwar publication might gesture toward these horrors but they could not directly show them. The images that were used and the ways they were presented might also generate contradictions that could not be resolved visually. The early local publications established a fairly limited visual canon that relied primarily on pictures of ruins and (less frequently) dead German bodies to construct a visual argument that presented Germans as victims. But, as the repertoire of images expanded in the 1960s to include pictures of Allied air crews and of Jews or other victims of Germans, as well as photographs of the cities destroyed by German bombing, these other images made it more difficult to maintain an exclusive focus on German suffering. Moreover, images always relied on words for the production of specific meanings. Yet words could not freeze the meaning of images. Sometimes the images themselves included disruptive visual elements that complicated, even challenged the textual messages in which they were framed. And, as new generations of readers and viewers brought different questions to their contemplation of these same images, the meanings of these pictures could change.

Ludger Derenthal has argued that by the late 1940s, German photographers, publishers, and audiences had begun to tire of ruin pictures. Yet, pictures of ruins have remained the most common motif in publications about the bombing right up to the present.[44] Chapter 3 begins by asking why other shock photographs—especially pictures of dead German bodies—have not appeared in local publications as often as photos of ruins. This chapter then explores the complex and, at times, competing layers of meanings that ruin photos could produce. These qualities allowed images of ruins—which normally included much more than simply ruined buildings—to be read in a variety of different ways.

In chapter 4 I turn to postwar picture books that attempted to tell the story of the air war primarily with images rather than in words. This chapter explores the imaginative and emotional functions of these picture books that included mourning the irredeemable loss of the architectural and cultural heritage of German cities but also celebrating the achievements of postwar reconstruction. Picture books that focused on the everyday lives of German civilians during the bombing war tried to produce empathy for the suffering of those who lived through but also died during the bombing. These types of picture books also encouraged postwar viewers to acknowledge, perhaps even to admire, the resilience and resolve of the people who had survived the war and rebuilt their own lives as well as Germany's cities after 1945. However, pictures of Germans in the ruins also created spaces for viewers to ask unsettling questions about the biographies of the people they could see in these images: What had they felt about the Nazi regime before the bombs destroyed their cities? Had they supported the war when Hitler was still winning?

In chapter 5 we move to the other Germany—the GDR—and to the narratives of the bombing war constructed by the East German communist regime after 1945. Using the example of Dresden, this chapter shows how narratives and images of the bombing war were subordinated to the propaganda of the Cold War, which depicted the destruction of Dresden as an Allied war crime and as a prelude to an impending nuclear apocalypse. The Dresden narrative relied heavily upon Goebbel's last great propaganda success—the depiction of Dresden as a uniquely beautiful city with no significant military targets that became the innocent victim of senseless Allied terror. Of course, the GDR did not acknowledge the Nazi origins of this Dresden narrative, but its continuous use since 1945 has undoubtedly played an important role in anchoring the destruction of Dresden firmly in the German imagination and in transforming the Elbe metropolis into a "super-site" of German national memory after 1989.

In chapter 6, the final chapter of this book, I take the analysis into the recent present, examining the ways in which narratives and images of the bombing war have spread from the local publications that served as the primary "vectors of memory" for so many decades to national publications, film, television, and the Internet. Public discussion and debate have now expanded from the local into the national and even transnational public spheres. Has this proliferation of new actual and virtual spaces simply allowed the established range of narratives and visual repertoires to circulate to a wider audience or has it produced important new ways of knowing and seeing?

CHAPTER 1

Local Stories: Narratives of the Bombing War, 1949–88

Local communities developed their own distinctive forms of memory politics that, until well into the 1980s, paid little attention to the crimes committed under the Nazis in the locality or to the active participation of the city administration and the local population in the persecution of the Jews or other victims of the Nazi regime.[1] Local anniversary celebrations skimped on the Nazi years. Not until the 1980s and 1990s were local "History Workshops" (*Geschichtswerkstätten*) able to focus public attention more squarely on the "other" history of local communities in the Nazi period.[2] After 1945, the local memory of the war and the Nazi past was compressed into the experience of the bombing, especially in cities hit by particularly catastrophic air attacks such as those that devastated Hamburg at the end of July 1943; Kassel on October 22, 1943; Magdeburg on January 26, 1945; Dresden on February 13–14, 1945; or Pforzheim on February 23, 1945. The title of a book published in 1965 is symptomatic: *Frankfurt in the Firestorm: The History of the City in the Second World War* (*Frankfurt im Feuersturm.Die Geschichte der Stadt im Zweiten Weltkrieg*).[3] The subjects of local narratives were only those inhabitants present in the community during the bombing—the men and women who went off from Hanover, Kassel, Cologne, or any number of other German cities to fight in Hitler's wars or to participate in the brutal colonization of occupied territories in the East usually remained invisible.[4] And for many years, little was said about non-Germans—POWs or forced foreign laborers, for example—who were present in many German cities when they were destroyed by Allied bombs. Stefan Glienke also points out that, directly and indirectly, the air war affected not just the communities hit by bombs but the whole of German society. Fire fighters and emergency teams were recruited from areas hundreds of kilometers away to provide help after a heavy raid. Millions of evacuees from heavily bombed cities were sent to other parts of Germany considered to be less threatened. And, when Allied bombers approached Germany, no community could be entirely sure that it might not be a target.[5] Yet the popular narrative of the air war continues to be told largely as the story of specific communities directly hit by the bombs.

Local histories of the bombing of particular German cities written after 1945 "served local memory markets and . . . reflected the peculiarities of local memory cultures."[6] These books were (and still are) written primarily for the Germans who lived (or had once lived) in that particular locality. They were published by small local presses or appeared as volumes in local history series published by the municipal archive or a local "Art and History Society." Even the most successful did not reach huge numbers of readers. For example, Max Domarus's book on Würzburg, which first appeared in 1950, "was re-issued seven times by 1995 in versions that were expanded several times [but] the total number of copies printed was 27,000."[7] Important differences in authorship, content, style, and form distinguished these local publications from one another. There was no single model or template for writing a local narrative of the bombing war. One was a personal memoir, another a technical report, a third cobbled together a wide variety of different texts ranging from personal letters to newspaper articles to Nazi Party documents. Others took the form of diaries, even though they had clearly been written some time after the events they described. One of these books bore a very personal dedication: "To my relatives who fell victim to the bomb attack on 21 November 1944."[8] The authors of local publications came from different backgrounds and had experienced the bombing war in different ways. One was a municipal official, another a journalist. One had served in the fire brigades of a number of other German cities hit hard by air attacks, another, from a working-class background, had spent most of the war working for the Technical Emergency Aid ("Technische Nothilfe") saving people trapped in the cellars of collapsed houses or air-raid shelters, or removing corpses from air-raid bunkers. Yet, despite their differences, local publications exhibited "a surprisingly high degree of common basic assumptions and modes of representation."[9]

Local Narratives in the 1950s

In the 1950s, the authors of local publications in West Germany could write their narratives of the bombing war untroubled by critical or contentious national debates about the Nazi past. Under Konrad Adenauer, the signal sent from Bonn was that "the establishment of a functioning democracy required less memory and justice for the crimes of the Nazi era and more 'integration' of those who had gone astray."[10] In one of its first pieces of legislation, the Amnesty Law of 1949, the Bonn government made it clear that it planned to put an end to the denazification process initiated by the Allied occupiers. The persecution and extermination of European Jews was certainly not absent from national discussions of the Nazi past in the 1950s, but national memory was preoccupied with the problems and suffering of other victims—the German POWs still in Soviet captivity or the millions of ethnic German refugees from the East who had crowded into what became the territory of the Federal Republic.[11] It was certainly true that East Germany continued to confront West Germany and the world with the crimes committed under Nazism, but the Cold War made it possible to defuse if not completely dismiss these charges as propaganda.

Local narratives of the bombing written in the late 1940s and 1950s implicitly rejected the claim made by Allied atrocity reports in 1945 that Germany's real story was the story of the Jewish genocide. After liberating the concentration camps, the Western Allies tried to compel ordinary Germans to acknowledge their complicity in Nazi atrocities. In response, Germans insisted that they, too, were victims of the war. Yet, as a student at a Nuremberg Gymnasium complained in an essay written several years after the war, "one learns everything there is to know about the concentration camps, but what the German population lived through in the phosphorous rain, what horrors happened [then], no one talks about that anymore."[12] Local stories about the destruction of German cities by Allied bombing redressed this perceived imbalance. Yet it was important to ensure that descriptions of what Germans had experienced and lost in the bombing war did not promote unmitigated despair. While acknowledging German suffering, authors also tried to provide hope for the future. In the desperate postwar years, when many German cities had been reduced to fields of ruins, the past could serve as an important emotional resource. Some of the early local narratives of the bombing tried to reestablish continuity with a past that could no longer be seen in the streets of these destroyed towns, by reminding readers that their city had a long history reaching back hundreds of years. Describing the bombing as one of several catastrophes that a city had experienced in its longer history offered reassurance for the postwar future. If a city had recovered from a fire in the Middle Ages or from the destruction caused by the Thirty Years' War, then surely it would be able to rebuild again after 1945.

When it came to the Nazi years, however, the record of the past had to be carefully edited. It was important to avoid contaminating the history of the local community with any suggestion that ordinary Germans might have been responsible for their own suffering in the air war, that their support for Hitler and their enthusiasm for Hitler's Blitzkrieg had eventually led to the destruction of their own cities. If these local publications did discuss the Nazi years and the war in any detail, they made sure to draw a clear line between the ordinary Germans who were presented as the innocent victims of the Allied bombing raids and the Nazis whose cowardice and incompetence had only added to the suffering of their fellow citizens. Dieter Süß shows that in publications dealing with the consequences of the bombing war sponsored by the national government that began to appear in the late 1950s, "at most, National Socialism . . . played a role . . . at the periphery—and when it did, only as the cause of administrative chaos . . . the German 'People' stood on one side, Hitler, occasionally also Goebbels, on the other side."[13] Süß's conclusion provides an apt description of the early local publications about the bombing war; "and so, National Socialism disappeared from the history of the air war, the history of the victims and the losses dominated the stories and made the bombing into a fundamentally barbaric, failed Anglo-American act of transgression in the annihilationist struggle of 'total war.'"[14]

Neil Gregor argues "that civic memory politics were driven not only (and perhaps not even primarily) by an instrumentalist desire to suppress awkward truths about murdered others, but also by the need to address people who were trying to make sense of their own experiences of suffering."[15] This could mean, however, as Gregor acknowledges, that local memory work produced "[p]artial . . . and narcissistic" depictions of the Nazi past.[16] Local narratives of German suffering during the bombing war were usually silent about the suffering some of these Germans had inflicted upon their fellow citizens and that many other Germans had witnessed firsthand. In 2002, a project initiated by the Topography of Terror Foundation in Berlin published a book of photographs from local archives that confirmed visually what Michael Wildt had already established using documents from the archives, namely that local communities were deeply implicated in violence against Jews well before the nationwide pogrom in 1938.[17] Klaus-Michael Mallmann and Gerhard Paul have also shown that ordinary Germans played an active role in the construction of the Nazi apparatus of terror at the local level. Called on to fight an ever-expanding list of racial and other enemies, the understaffed Gestapo would have been virtually "blind" had it not been for the truly astonishing and frightening flood of denunciations made by ordinary Germans against their relatives, friends, and neighbors. These denunciations, usually made for quite banal reasons of greed or to settle old scores, "kept the machinery of terror going."[18] Mallman and Paul conclude that "[t]he concept of 'mass crime' therefore has a double meaning, these were crimes that affected masses of Germans, but a large part of the German population also participated in these crimes."[19]

Making the "bad" years when Allied bombs pulverized German cities the defining memory of the Nazi past also meant that local publications forgot the "good years" Germans had experienced under Nazi rule and could still remember fondly well into the 1960s. Ulrich Herbert has pointed out that as late as 1951 "almost half of those citizens of the Federal Republic of Germany questioned in a public opinion survey described the period between 1933 and 1939 as the one in which things had gone best for Germany."[20] Germans credited Hitler and the Nazi regime with "reduction of unemployment, economic boom, tranquility and order." When the *Wehrmacht* defeated France in June 1940, Hitler achieved unprecedented popularity. It was only after Stalingrad, when it became clear that Germany could not win the war, that ordinary Germans began to lose faith in the Führer. The continued success of the local narratives that equated the history of the war and the Nazi past with the history of the bombing depended on the ability of these narratives to insulate themselves from or simply ignore these other strands of local history.

In addition to "decontaminating" local history, some early postwar narratives created an important "foundation myth" for the Federal Republic. These narratives portrayed Germans not just as innocent victims but as determined, courageous survivors. These stories claimed that ordinary Germans, if not their Nazi leaders, had met the severe challenge of surviving the bombing war with exemplary courage, resourcefulness, and determination. And then in 1945, rather than sinking into despair at the overwhelming sight of the endless fields of ruins to which many German cities had been reduced, Germans energetically set about clearing away the rubble and rebuilding. Through this story of the Germans who had courageously "stuck it out" despite all the odds, the bombing war could function as a useful and popular "foundation myth" in postwar West Germany. The experience of the bombing war marked not only the beginning of the end of the Third Reich; it also cleared the path to the construction of a new democratic and prosperous Federal Republic.[21] Yet the story of the bombing was also a history of irretrievable, irredeemable destruction and loss—of the Germans who had been killed, of the historic buildings that had been destroyed, perhaps also of the individual city's historic identity that had been shattered. The mourning inspired by this negative narrative might threaten but could not be allowed to undermine celebration of the "will to stick it out" ("Durchhaltewillen") that had allowed most Germans to survive and rebuild. This was a difficult tightrope act that some bombing narratives performed more skillfully than others.

Local narratives might also argue that Germans' experience of the bombing war made them uniquely qualified to warn the world about the dangers of nuclear apocalypse.[22] These narratives claimed that Germans had already experienced the kind of unprecedented trauma that now threatened Europe and the rest of the world. In the 1963 translation into English of his book *The Bombing of Germany*, Hans Rumpf observed that contemporary discussions of Cold War nuclear strategy seemed to accept the idea that large numbers of civilians would be killed in any future war; "People are no longer shocked at the idea of the indiscriminate bombing of civilian objectives; in fact, nowadays it is accepted as part of the generally approved deterrent strategy."[23] As the victim of "the first unrestricted bombing war in history," Germany could, however, provide a "reliable contribution to the history of the bombing" that might encourage the rest of the world to think twice about these assumptions. The German experience of the air war thus gave Germans a new opportunity to speak with moral authority in the postwar world. Armin Schmid, author of a 1965 book on the bombing of Frankfurt am Main, believed that understanding what their parents had lived through during the war would help the younger generation to campaign against a potentially far more devastating nuclear conflict.[24]

Along with the growing number of local publications, a significant number of general discussions of the air war were also published in West Germany in the 1950s and 1960s. These general studies mirrored and reinforced the messages offered by the early local publications. The authors of these general books were not professional historians but military experts, experts in international law, or eyewitnesses. Many had been directly involved in the air war or in the Nazi regime. Hans Rumpf, whose book we have already encountered, had worked as the General Inspector of Fire Fighting Services. Like several of the other authors of these early general studies, Rumpf had a personal interest in presenting his own role in the air war in the best possible light.[25] Rumpf also wanted to disseminate a memory of the air war that would support his activities as a lobbyist for an active West German air defense policy in the darkest days of the early Cold War.[26] Until well into the 1970s, academic historians paid little serious attention to the air war: "This situation changed only when historians such as Olaf Groehler and Horst Boog published sound studies on this theme."[27] The research of these East and West German scholars challenged important elements of the popular narrative, but it also left intact one fundamental claim, namely that it was "the German civilians alone [who were] the victims of the [air] war."[28]

Narrative Trajectories

Local publications did not all begin or end at the same point in historical time. Some authors felt it was necessary to open their story in the city's distant past, starting with the Middle Ages or at least the Thirty Years' War and chronicling every previous catastrophe that had visited their city. The air war then became the most recent disaster but one that, like all the previous disasters, their city would overcome.[29] Max Braun-Rühling's 1953 book depicted the bombing of Kaiserslautern, a town in southwest Germany in the Palatinate with a population in 2011 of just under 100,000, as "the third great destruction" since the Thirty Years' War.[30] Before Dr. Rudolf Kiepke, the author of *Paderborn. Werden. Untergang. Wiedererstehen* (1949), arrived at the actual story of the bombing of this small Catholic town in present-day Rhineland-Westphalia late in World War II in the spring of 1945 he devoted more than 20 pages to the past thousand years of the city's history. This long-term view served two purposes. By reconstructing the many layers of the city's rich architectural heritage, accumulated over hundreds of years, Kiepke helped his readers understand what they had lost in a single night of Allied bombing.[31] Paderborn was the home of some of the most important religious buildings in northern Germany, and many of these buildings were also architectural treasures; "the technological advances that have been praised for decades took just 28 minutes to destroy what it had taken centuries to construct."[32] At the same time, however, Paderborn's long history taught that the city was no stranger to disaster. Fires had destroyed the city more than once in the Middle Ages. The Thirty Years' War had left Paderborn in ruins. After each of these previous catastrophes, Paderborn's citizens had rebuilt. They would do so again.[33]

History appeared to come to Paderborn from outside. Kiepke seldom depicted the city as an active agent in the changes that reshaped it and the German nation, whether these were the wars of unification, industrialization, railways, 1914, 1918, or the hyper-inflation of 1923. The Nazis were just one more of these outside forces. Kiepke claimed that the heavily Catholic population of Paderborn had steadfastly refused to vote for the Nazis before 1933, and even after the Nazis came to power Paderborn's Catholics retained their strong commitment to their faith.[34] During the war, Paderborn's citizens even deluded themselves into believing that they would not be attacked by Allied bombers because they were well-known to be "black" not "brown."[35] Kiepke did not deny that Paderborn had received some benefits from the Nazi regime. The rearmament drive had helped revive the economy of "the old garrison city,"[36] but rearmament also produced the devastating war that eventually destroyed the old Paderborn. When the war finally came, it was certainly not something that Paderborn's citizens wanted or from which they derived any benefit; in Kiepke's story, there is no hint of the jubilant enthusiasm with which many Germans greeted Hitler's early Blitzkrieg victories, nor of the tangible benefits for ordinary Germans offered by the growing Nazi racial empire. Kiepke mentions "the foreign workers who for the most part were forced to come here," yet only to make clear "that (German) workers retained a feeling for the suffering of these other fellow human beings. Even though they themselves lived frugally they still gave some of their bread to the hungry foreign work-comrades and, where it was possible, they made sure to lighten the heavy load in the workplace of these pitiable people."[37] If Paderborn's Catholics sympathized with the foreign slave laborers who were among the many victims of the Nazi regime, perhaps this reflected their own experience of persecution. Kiepke points to the Nazi campaign against the Catholic Church, as well as the Nazi euthanasia program. Paderborn Catholics, it appeared, were also victims of Nazism.

The war came home to Paderborn when the first bombs dropped on the city. From this point onward, Kiepke's story describes the slowly increasing frequency and intensity of Allied bombing raids with the clear suggestion that an apocalypse was now on the horizon.[38] Paderborners still continued to believe that they would be spared, that their city was too inconsequential to warrant serious attention from the RAF, but this illusion only intensified the bitterness of the story when the devastating air raid finally took place. The "big raid" hit Paderborn when the war was almost over. It was a tragic and sad irony that hundreds of Paderborners would die in the late winter and spring of 1945, when it was clear that Germany had already lost the war.[39] Blind luck decided who lived and who died, what would be destroyed and what would survive unscathed; the entire workforce of a local factory survived but the director and his wife were killed. Allied bombs did not spare even the dead; "17 January 1945 . . . in the Eastern Cemetery, gravestones and crosses were thrown in the air and from bomb craters shimmered the bones of those long since buried [it was like] a visionary flash of the final days . . . and the Last Judgement."[40] The entire population now lived in permanent fear of the next raid that would be even bigger, even more devastating than the previous one.

By March of 1945, fewer than 6,000 people were living in the ruins of Paderborn.[41] Those who remained were subjected to the terror of a firestorm created by Allied incendiaries. On March 27, in just 28 minutes, British bombers dropped some "60,000 stick incendiaries, 15,000 phosporous bombs, an enormous quantity of the means of destruction."[42] Many of the city's priceless architectural treasures and works of art did not survive this last major air raid of the war.

The Paderborn book paid a great deal of attention to the loss of the city's architectural and artistic treasures. Yet the loss of human life was certainly not ignored. The book presented gruesome verbal descriptions of the remains of those who had not been able to escape the firestorm, although, unlike some other later local publications, it included no pictures of corpses or body parts. "Many of the dead" could be found on the streets "some frightfully maimed . . . the carbonized, burned und shrunken corpses demonstrated in all of their gruesomeness what had happened to those who did not escape."[43] Relatives carried the unrecognizable remains of their loved ones to the city's two cemeteries "in cardboard packets or cigar boxes . . . or they pushed along a gruesome burden in small carts."[44]

Because so many bodies were still buried in the rubble and their decomposing corpses posed the threat of epidemics, the American troops closed the city off to the survivors who wanted to dig out of the ruins the few possessions that remained. Clearing the rubble and removing bodies from air-raid cellars was now the top priority; "it should be emphasized here that this work was not done on the order of the police or of the local authority. This sacrificial labor was performed in the spirit of Christian charity."[45] This was gruesome work; "often one could see helpers . . . forced by disgust and nausea to vomit on the ruins or on trees . . . every grave digger was given a litre of *Schnapps*. [Some of] the corpses had already begun to rot, others carbonized, still others completely desiccated and shrunken by the extreme heat in the glowing cellars." A Paderborn merchant reported that "I picked up people who would have weighed 150–180 pounds when they were alive, but now, completely desiccated, weighed only 30 pounds. They were like mummies."[46]

Overall, then, the book on Paderborn paid attention to both the human suffering and the architectural loss caused by the war; but this was suffering and loss experienced almost exclusively by Germans who were depicted as innocent victims, who bore no obvious responsibility for the war or for the crimes of the Nazis. Only one passage in the book made any reference to Jews—stuck in with discussion of the many buildings destroyed and rebuilt was a short description of the fate of "the Jewish orphanage which had already been confiscated by the National Socialist People's Welfare organization (NSV). It had been dismantled down to the external walls and still has not been rebuilt. At the beginning of 1945, only three men remained of the entire Jewish community, which had to suffer fiercely from the extermination policy unleashed against it. Some emigrated, but the largest number died in the camps and ghettos."[47] Forced foreign laborers and POWs appear in this story only as the objects of German sympathy or as willing helpers in the efforts to clean up after a bombing raid.[48] At the end of the war, however, POWs and forced laborers were depicted as plunderers, although the author admitted that Germans were also engaged in the theft of anything of value that still remained in the devastated city. An expert on the art and architecture of Paderborn had to admit that "it will forever remain a disgrace that Germans were also involved. . . . The museums suffered especially from this plague. Everything made of wood, fabric or metal was taken, regardless of its artistic value."[49]

The authors of other early local publications felt it was unnecessary to talk about any part of their city's history before the day on which the first major air attack announced the spiral into the abyss, even when that attack had not come until the last year of the war. The volume *Tod und Leben Hannovers 9 Oktober*, edited by the Heimatbund Niedersachsen in 1953, began its story immediately with a description of "Hanover's most difficult hour," when for "Forty minutes the Furies of War hammered; after these forty minutes Hanover was no more." This particular narrative variant heightened the tragedy and shock of the city's story of destruction so late in the war when it seemed to make no sense at all in military terms and the inhabitants had convinced themselves that they would be spared.

Published on the 10th anniversary of the bombing of Zweibrücken on March 14, 1945, Rudolf Wilms's short "Erinnerungsschift" also did not embed its narrative in the long history of this small town. Wilms did, however, take the reader back to the years before World War II, when Zweibrücken, a border city, was deeply affected by the construction of the Westwall, Germany's defensive installations on its western frontier. Zweibrücken was one of the smaller German towns (20,000 before the war) destroyed toward the very end of the war by a combination of Allied bombing and artillery fire. Wilms chronicled the evacuation at the beginning of the war of thousands of Germans who lived in the zone most threatened by France. In the summer of 1940, after the defeat of France, these evacuees were allowed to return to Zweibrücken and the surrounding area. In the fall of 1944, as the fighting in the ground war moved ever nearer to Zweibrücken after the Allied invasion of Normandy in June 1944, the inhabitants of the city had to deal with a second evacuation; "In contrast with the first evacuation, participation was voluntary. It also lacked the basic preparation and organization which characterized the first evacuation."[50] Under these circumstances, a substantial number of Zweibrücken's citizens decided to stay in the town, so that they could protect their property. Those who did leave, for southern Württemberg and the Allgäu, were able to escape the air attack of March 14, 1945. Had more stayed in the city, many of them would have been killed or wounded.

Zweibrücken was not well-prepared for a heavy bombing attack. The city did have air-raid shelters that had been built before the war, but most were in the cellars of people's homes and were not able to protect against "the penetrating power of modern bombs."[51] Fortunately, caves had already been excavated in nearby cliffs to serve as cool storage for local breweries. Along with disused mine shafts, these caves proved to be excellent air-raid shelters. In one location, a series of 26 caves was expanded so that this space could shelter some 15,000 people.[52] Initially, local citizens went to these shelters only when direct danger of an air attack threatened. By the end of the war, however, most of the citizens who had remained in Zweibrücken were living in these caves, day and night.[53]

On the night of March 14, 1945, British planes placed marker lights in the city to show the bombers where they should drop their loads. The attack lasted some 30 minutes: "In this short time what it had taken generations centuries to build was totally destroyed."[54] Most of the bombs fell on the core of the Altstadt. Because this big raid came virtually without warning, many locals had been unable to reach the large public shelters in the old beer and ice cellars of the breweries. In addition to this disaster, artillery fire started to come down on the city about 1 a.m. and lasted until 4 a.m., making it very difficult, sometimes impossible, for the rescue teams to save more people.

The author insists that it could not really have made a difference to the outcome of the war whether Zweibrücken was destroyed by bombing or not. He depicted the city as a helpless, innocent victim, incapable of posing any hindrance to the forward-march of the Allies. Certainly, rumors circulated after the war that, as part of the Westwall, Zweibrücken had been heavily fortified. Wilms claimed, however, that in reality "there were no soldiers in the city and no defensive installations had been built there."[55] The destruction of Zweibrücken this close to the end of the war appeared to Wilms to have made no more sense than the air attacks on Kaiserslautern and Pirmasens. All three unfortunate cities were simply crushed by the machinery of "total war."[56]

Wilms claimed that by the end of the war some 80 percent of all housing and other types of building had been damaged or destroyed.[57] One estimate suggested that it would require at least 67 million RM to reconstruct the city. Mobilizing the authority of the wartime enemy and current occupier, Wilms quoted a report in an American newspaper, published on July 3, 1945, that described postwar Zweibrücken as "[t]he once blossoming industrial city . . . [that is now just] the biggest pile of rubble. A few abandoned civilians, either too old, or too upset to leave are all that remain of the 20,000 inhabitants. More than a handful could in any case not live here, because Zweibrücken has ceased to exist."[58] Wilms then turned to the entry of American troops into Zweibrücken. In a description that might remind some readers of how the Red Army soldiers had behaved in eastern Germany, Wilms asserted that American soldiers were intent on claiming "souvenirs," which meant, in effect, stealing necklaces and bracelets from women, as well as rings and wrist and pocket watches. The Germans who were smart enough to see this coming hid their valuables.[59] Wilms depicts the American troops as being extremely nervous that they would be attacked by partisans and consequently trigger-happy, ready to shoot Germans at the slightest provocation.[60] Fearing that a *Werwolf* sniper had set himself up in a local church tower, the Americans destroyed the structure with their artillery. But the Americans were not the only problem: "After the city was captured, the population had to remain in the air-raid shelters for three days. The houses abandoned by their inhabitants were . . . plundered by Poles and foreign workers."[61]

Narratives of Catastrophe: Fate, God, or the Nazis?

"Catastrophe" was a keyword in the vocabulary used after 1945 to describe the bombing of German cities. One author of a local publication claimed that during the war, the Nazis had banned the term "catastrophe" from the official lexicon because it was thought to be too negative.[62] After 1945, the word resurfaced because now it could do different work. "Catastrophe" might be used to describe the cumulative effects of prolonged bombing over the course of the entire war, as in the case of Berlin. More often, however, catastrophe was used as a description of a single massive raid that destroyed a city and signaled the key turning point in that city's experience of the bombing war—the 1,000-plane raid on Cologne at the end of May 1942, for example, or the firestorm caused by the British bombing of Hamburg at the end of July 1943. After such a catastrophe, a city would never look the same again. In some instances, this catastrophe came very late in the war and was all the more devastating psychologically because the city's inhabitants had believed, or at least hoped, that they would survive the bombing without major damage and casualties. Dresden is a good example. Often described as the "Air Raid Shelter of the Reich," Dresden appeared to be a safe haven in the air war. Before the firebombing on February 13–14, 1945, it had not been the target of any major air raids. Other, smaller cities, such as Pforzheim, were also spared major air attacks until the very last months of the war. The destruction of Dresden or Pforzheim was presented as particularly cruel, precisely because their inhabitants had believed that their cities might escape major air attacks. Yet even if the inhabitants of a particular city did expect a major air raid, anticipating catastrophe did not make it any the more bearable when it finally came.[63]

Postwar narratives of catastrophe could be completely secular or they might be embedded in Christian perspectives and language. Interpreting catastrophe in Christian terms reinforced the churches' attempts to reclaim ground in the public commemoration of the war that before 1945 they had lost to the Nazis.[64] The religious language that shaped some of these postwar narratives was meant to provide spiritual consolation to the postwar Germans who had to live with the consequences of the bombing. Yet Christian rhetoric also constructed an indictment of secularization as the cause of the massive death and destruction produced by World War II. If not only the Germans but all the other nations involved in the war had retained their faith in the Christian God, they would have been spared such unprecedented violence. Yet, like Christ's sacrifice on the cross, the suffering of the German people during the war was a necessary step toward salvation. Returning to God after 1945 would make wartime suffering meaningful.

Max Domarus's book on Würzburg, which first appeared in 1950, insisted that the war had alienated his fellow-citizens from the Nazi Party.[65] From this early point in his story, Domarus's narrative became an extended homage to the role played by Catholic faith and the institutions of the Catholic Church in helping the citizens of Würzburg to survive the disaster that destroyed their city in 1945.[66] The very first photograph included in the book is not a picture of ruins or of dead bodies but a portrait of Matthias Ehrenfried (following page 24), Bishop of Würzburg, whom Domarus credited with providing indispensable spiritual leadership during the war. In early 1945, for example, the bishop issued a pastoral letter in which he equated the Allied bombing with crucifixion:

> Among those who bear the cross, I also see you who have suffered under the bombing. . . . All of you might break under the burden of this sacrifice. Think then of the saintly Bruno! He stood upright like a martyr carrying his cross. Like him, you must absorb all afflictions for the love of God! These sacrifices will then become rungs in the ladder leading you to heaven. Your salvation is the product of your sacrifice.[67]

Domarus's praise for the Catholic Church as a source of spiritual consolation to the citizens of Würzburg was matched by his scorn for the Nazi regime's failures. Before the war, Nazi authorities only managed to terrorize the population with "more or less scary lectures and articles" about the horrors of the coming air war that would leave the country attacked totally in ruins. The Nazi leadership saw gas attacks as the greatest threat and developed a relatively cheap "People's Gas Mask." They did not, however, pay adequate attention to the construction of air-raid shelters. When the anticipated air war did not immediately materialize after 1939, especially not in southern Germany, the panic subsided. The year 1942 marked a new stage in the intensity of Allied air attacks, but Würzburg still seemed to be safe, "far outside the danger zone."[68] Yet in that same year, Würzburg was bombed for the first time. Few people died and damage to the city's buildings was quite limited, yet Domarus saw this first raid as a warning of what was to come; "the danger had come significantly closer. . . . Würzburg sat right in the middle of a ring of favored targets for attack: Schweinfurt, Nuremberg, Stuttgart, Heilbronn, Aschaffenburg."[69] Despite the imminent threat, the Nazi authorities had still not provided Würzburg with "effective concrete bunkers."[70]

In early January 1945, Nuremberg was hit by a massive raid involving 1,000 planes, about 6,000 explosive bombs, and a million firebombs. Now there could no longer be any doubt that the main targets were not specific industrial plants but entire cities, especially their old and highly flammable city centers. Yet, although the citizens of Würzburg no longer had any reason to continue to think that they would be spared, they simply did not want to believe they would be hit by a large attack.[71] Rumors circulated that the British would not bomb Würzburg because Winston Churchill had studied there and had close personal ties with the bishop, who had been a fellow student. Churchill was even said to have fathered a child with a young German woman with whom he had been in love when he was a young man. Domarus informed his readers that Churchill had indeed once visited Würzburg, in September 1909, when he served as the British attaché during Imperial German Army war maneuvers but that all the other stories were no more than desperate fantasy. Similar tales had been told about several other German cities; but "the number of these 'Churchill'-cities became ever smaller, as more and more of them experienced the first heavy raid."[72]

Some of the early local publications about the bombing war insisted that the local inhabitants had experienced an almost tangible sense of impending doom. Each bombing raid served as a premonition of a catastrophic attack that was still to come. Domarus's book, on the other hand, presented a picture of local denial. Despite all of the evidence that should have suggested that Würzburg could not escape the bombing war unscathed, its citizens continued to believe they would be spared. Some citizens of Würzburg believed that their city would not be bombed because it had so many churches and cloisters; "no one could imagine that heaven would allow such a pious city with such a pious population to be exposed to destruction by squadrons of enemy bombers."[73] Domarus blamed the government authorities in Berlin for keeping this rumor alive. They continued to represent Würzburg as an "unassailable oasis" despite their own propaganda that the Allies were specifically targeting churches, hospitals, and cultural monuments.[74] By the second half of 1944, Würzburg was one of the few remaining large German cities that had not yet been struck by any major air raids. In all of these cities, the inhabitants clung to the belief that they could escape Allied bombing because their towns contained no major military targets. In September 1944, Darmstadt was the first of these large cities to be "suddenly ripped out of this dreamy illusion."[75] This "big raid" on Darmstadt made it very clear that the reason why it had been attacked—and why Würzburg would soon also be a target—was quite simply that both had prewar populations that qualified them as "Großstädte" and were therefore next on the list of Allied bombing targets.[76] In the 1920s and 1930s, many German cities had been eager to achieve the status of a "Großstadt." But if Würzburg had not incorporated Heidingfeld in 1930, perhaps it would never have become a target for Allied bombs.[77] In the end, however, Domarus argued that it was neither Hitler nor Churchill who had "passed the death sentence" on Würzburg. That judgment came "from a higher authority whose standards we do not know."[78] As a soldier would say, it was quite simply Würzburg's "turn." Perhaps Domarus honestly believed that it was unnecessary and futile to ask who was actually responsible for the destruction of Würzburg and many other German cities in the bombing war. Nevertheless, this way of approaching the bombing certainly did not challenge his readers to ask themselves whether their city would still have been standing in 1945 had Hitler not started World War II or to reflect on their own role in this war.

On the night of March 3, 1945, an RAF attack destroyed the Würzburg train station. Domarus suggested that the majority of citizens now breathed a collective sigh of relief; since the only site they considered to be a valid military target had been hit, they could now believe that the danger of further air raids was very small. But, Domarus observed sadly, "they did not understand the fundamental difference between the RAF night attacks and the American daytime bombing."[79] On March 16, 1945, American bombers launched a major raid that produced a firestorm in the city. This catastrophe was also a testing ground for the citizens of Würzburg. Their Christian faith gave the majority the strength they needed; "Almost all of them sought refuge in prayer . . . there were seldom any scenes of panic."[80] Domerus pointed out that this major air attack had taken place one day before *Passionstag* 1945. He clearly meant his readers to understand that just as Christ had suffered on the cross, so, too, now "Würzburg's Passion Week (*Passionszeit*) . . . had begun!"[81] Yet faith was not the only consolation. Domarus made it clear that it was "the charitable activities of the church offices" that helped the citizens of Würzburg deal with the aftermath of the raid and that this assistance "continued on not just for days, but for weeks and months, long after the state, the party and the Wehrmacht had collapsed."[82]

The progress that had been made since the war in reconstructing the city indicated to Domarus that "the work of the people of Würzburg was blessed anew." But he cautioned that despite the need for optimism and affirmation of life, it was important not to forget the warning that March 16, 1945, had brought to the city and that must be passed on to coming generations. This warning seemed, above all, to be that "all that is earthly is fleeting. . . . Against the workings of unfathomable, demonic powers, human understanding, human endeavor . . . can do nothing."[83]

Hitler and the Nazis

Few of the authors of these early local accounts felt that it was important to talk about the role Nazism had played in the city before the war began. Fritz Nadler's 1955 book on Nuremberg does not tell his readers, for example, that the city had figured centrally in the history of the Nazi movement since its earliest days. As the "City of the Reich Party Congresses," Nuremberg became a key site of Nazi propaganda. The annual Nazi Party rallies were held in the city from 1923 until 1938. The Nuremberg race laws that made the persecution of Germany's Jews legal were announced at the 1935 Nuremberg party rally. Nuremberg was also home to Julius Streicher and his rabidly anti-Semitic newspaper, *Der Stürmer.* Rather than commenting on Nuremberg's close association with the persecution of German Jews, Nadler actually included in his story a letter he claims to have received from a Jewish man, forced to emigrate from Nuremberg after Kristallnacht in 1938.The refugee wanted to know what had happened to Nuremberg during the war. Nadler described the destruction and the Jewish man responded by lamenting, "We read all about it and we all wept . . . for our beautiful Nuremberg."[84] When Nazi leaders do appear in Nadler's book, they figure only as the targets of popular scorn and resentment. Nuremberg's population grumbles about the Gauleiter Karl Holz, who is depicted as the "Number One War Monger" in the city, now that his mentor, Streicher, had been relegated to the sidelines. Nadler claims that local inhabitants were so angry about the air war that

> People complained without even bothering to use the "German look," that means, the cautious look over your own shoulder to see if any spies were listening. Even when police were nearby, everyone said what they felt.[85]

Nadler claimed that the "German Greeting" ("Heil Hitler") had almost completely disappeared from the streets of the city. "The Nuremberger have come back to the modest 'God's Greeting' ('Grüss Gott')."[86] In their suffering and anguish, the citizens of Nuremberg "curse the bombers, the war, the war mongers and the entire Hitlerism."[87]

The Technical Eye: Braunschweig, 1955

A distinctive type of postwar narrative viewed the air war with the cool technical eye of the expert firefighter. This technical perspective allowed authors such as Rudolf Prescher, who published a book on the bombing of Braunschweig in 1955, to create emotional distance from the horrors of the air war.[88] Prescher began working in the Dresden fire department in 1927. After the beginning of the air war against Germany, he worked in some of the most heavily bombed cities, including Leipzig, Berlin, Dortmund, Düsseldorf, Solingen, and Remscheid. In 1943, he became an officer in the Fire Protection Police (*Feuerschutzpolizei*) "in the city of Braunschweig which at that time was hardly damaged at all."[89] His professional training and experience as a fire engineer focused Prescher's attention on the development of air-raid defense measures.[90] The course the war took in its early years combined with Nazi propaganda misled the civilian population into a false sense of security.[91] From the fall of 1940, however, the top military leadership assumed that the air war against Germany would become more intense.[92]

The first major air raid against Braunschweig came on September 27, 1943. Prescher does not describe the physical or psychological impact of this raid but concentrates only on the lessons learned from this first experience that "served to further develop air defences . . . the danger of fire was a primary concern in Braunschweig."[93] A visitor to Braunschweig at the beginning of 1944 would see that even though the city had not yet been hit by a heavy air raid, it had already prepared itself for the worst; the city now had air-raid bunkers, emergency water supplies, artificial ponds, camouflage, flak installations on the roofs of factories, and air-raid warning sirens.[94] Braunschweig had also created a special agency to deal with the needs of citizens who lost their homes to bombing.[95] By 1944, however, German air defense authorities knew that they could not provide adequate protection against the next round of air raids. The undisputed superiority of Allied power in the air made the development of German air defenses "a feverish accommodation to the ever more horrible forms of the air war."[96] German air defense units confronted this increased threat with inadequate manpower; units had to rely on women and older men as the younger men were drafted into military service. In the spring of 1944, the frequency and intensity of Allied air raids increased. Braunschweig was the target of 11 air raids in the first three months that left the center of the city in ruins.[97]

At the end of May 1944, preparations for the invasion of Normandy gave Braunschweig the chance to catch its breath. Allied bombers now concentrated on destroying German military resources in northern France.[98] Then, beginning on October 15, 1944, the Allies targeted Braunschweig with a series of heavy air raids; "it soon became apparent that not just individual districts of Braunschweig were being hit, but the entire city. Several carpet bombing attacks took place. Fires were started to produce extensive destruction."[99] Confronted with fires wherever they turned, Braunschweig's air-defense units were overwhelmed. A firestorm soon began to develop. The winds were so strong that "[t]he storm carried off hats, caps, even light pieces of furniture, such as stools and tables. Gusty counter-currents stirred up the debris produced by the fire and whirled a thick rain of sparks through the burning streets. Anything that got in the way was singed, scorched or burned."[100] Some 23,000 people were trapped in bunkers. Although the thick concrete walls provided protection, it was unclear whether the fire would leave the people in the bunkers enough oxygen to stay alive. Prescher recounted the story of heroic firemen who managed to create an "alley of water" that allowed the people trapped inside a bunker to escape the flames all around them.[101] But other citizens of Braunschweig "who did not manage to leave this area before the big fire suffered a frightful fate."[102]

By the end of October, the damage done to Braunschweig "was appalling." Not only had the bombs destroyed or damaged the great majority of the city's historic buildings, housing, industrial and transport facilities but almost half of the population had been left homeless and unemployed.[103] Allied air attacks continued until the very end of the war. For a while Braunschweig was spared, but then on the morning of March 3, 1945, the city was hit by another heavy raid. This time the bombing was completely pointless. Prescher offers his readers a bizarre picture of bombs dropping on neighborhoods that had long since been turned into fields of ruins by earlier attacks.[104] We see all of this death and destruction with the same technical eye that Prescher has earlier focused on the city's air defenses. His descriptions retain a factual tone that keeps the reader at a distance from the horrors being detailed. Yet the cumulative effect of these descriptions of bombings that seem never to come to an end is devastating.

The bombings do eventually stop, but Prescher's discussion continues into the Cold War. As an expert on air defense programs, he concludes that the main lesson to be learned from the Allied bombing war is that "every means possible should be employed to reduce the city's vulnerability to fire."[105] As German cities are being rebuilt, efforts should be made to separate the neighborhoods where people lived from industrial plants and warehouses; "the key to preventing area fires and firestorms like those of the Second World War, lies . . . in the functional division of the city's buildings."[106] Prescher suggested that bunkers should be built in every urban neighborhood. He also warned that air-defense organizations needed clearer structures of command and better networks for transmitting information. He insisted that the work of air defense required younger men than had been used in World War II, and that civilians must be involved as auxiliaries. All of these measures seemed, however, to be hopelessly out of date. They scarcely took account of the very different destructive potential of a nuclear attack.

Communities of Suffering and Sacrifice

If the authors of early local publications saw any positive result of the bombing war, it was the sense of community—a community of suffering and sacrifice—that so many of them believed Germans experienced in the air-raid bunkers and cellars.[107] According to Max-Braun Rühling, the great majority of the citizens of Kaiserslautern had responded admirably to the challenges produced by the bombing:

> This was particularly the case in the rubble clearance actions ordered by the Lord Mayor months after the catastrophe, in which every citizen capable of working, including every strong girl and single young woman, was called upon to work in a regularly changing cycle. Alongside the street cleaners and day laborers, civil servants of both upper and lower

> grades hacked and shoveled for as long as they had the strength. Next to craftsmen and white collar workers there were artists as well as the available skilled and factory workers—and no one wanted to achieve any less than the other person. This was a prelude full of promise to the genuine, future democratic attitude that was so essential for all of us.[108]

What were the boundaries of this imagined "community of suffering and sacrifice"? Who was included, who was excluded? Immediately after the war, Allied interviews with "Social Democrats, industrialists and representatives of the churches" had revealed, surprisingly, that the bombing campaign had not seriously weakened the relationship between ethnic Germans and the Nazi Party.[109] However, many postwar publications about the bombing war engaged in a significant reworking of this relationship, arguing that, by and large, local Nazi leaders had excluded themselves from the *Volksgemeinschaft* by their attitudes and actions during the bombing. In this reshaped version of the past, ordinary Germans had become the victims not only of Allied bombs but of callous and selfish Nazi Party figures. Postwar authors pointed out that Nazi Party officials were frequently among the first to flee cities threatened by bombing.[110] Nadler depicted Nuremberg's Nazi leaders as cowards who each evening left the city to escape Allied bombing raids:

> Every evening, a long convoy of motor vehicles . . . secretly crept out of the shattered . . . city. It drove in a westerly direction. The (Nazi) big shots sat in the sleek automobiles and buses. They had no desire to risk their valuable lives in the rain of bombs. They descended at the Schwarzenberg castle near Oberscheinfeld where they spent their nights undisturbed by the howling (air-raid) sirens. . . . The farmers in the villages below the castle . . . complained quite openly that up there . . . despite the present hard times, orgies . . . took place.[111]

A joke that circulated among the inhabitants of Nuremberg's air-raid shelters claimed that "the Gauleiter's car is approaching the city—which means that we can soon expect to hear the all-clear siren . . . !"[112] Even if they did remain in the cities that were under Allied air attack, local Nazi leaders were kept firmly outside the boundaries of the imagined community of suffering. Indeed, Nazis were frequently depicted as causes of that suffering.

The thieves who took advantage of the chaos caused by air raids were clearly also excluded from the community of fate and suffering. In his book on

Kaiserslautern, Max Braun-Rühling observed that after the August 1944 raid on the city "thieving rabble/vermin emerged as if they had sprung up out of the ground and (they) engaged in plunder in many places."[113] Some authors insisted that only the foreign workers (*Fremdarbeiter*) had committed these crimes. The author of the 1949 book on Paderborn acknowledged, however, that "members of the so-called better classes (joined) this army of thieves, so that they could, as it was put quite unashamedly in those days, 'organize' something (or other). This expression, taken over from the soldier's life continues to serve as the common word for stealing."[114] Braun-Rühling also admitted that in Kaiserslautern "a certain under-class of the population and outsiders who had trickled in" had taken advantage of the chaos to plunder the ruins:

> The hunt for still usable building materials . . . set in. [Everything] from handcarts to lorries . . . showed up unabashedly in the ruins and were loaded up without disruption with bricks, beams, ovens, and iron supports.[115]

Moreover, theft continued for some time after the war: "These misdeeds did not stop altogether until . . . there was really not much more left to steal."[116]

Although many of the more than seven million foreign laborers forced to work for the German war effort were also trying to survive the bombing war, the early postwar publications did not pay much attention to these foreigners and clearly did not see them as integral members of a community of suffering and sacrifice.[117] The air-raid shelter ordinance issued on September 18, 1942, categorically excluded POWs and East European workers (*Ostarbeiter*) from air-raid shelters.[118] Other foreigners, Italians and French people, were only admitted if space was available. Forced laborers from the occupied East were only allowed access to slit trenches that they had to dig themselves, and which did not provide effective protection. Dietmar Süß concludes that as a result of this policy a "disproportionately large number of those killed in the air attacks were East European forced labourers, who . . . became a kind of double victim, first of German exploitation, second of the air war." A Reich Air Ministry decree of October 7, 1940, stated that Jews could not be excluded completely from air-raid shelters although this appears to have reflected the authorities' paranoid fear that Jews would steal the property left unguarded by the Aryans who were in shelters. Süß also shows that Germans policed the boundaries of the *Volksgemeinschaft* "from below." Even when the authorities in Berlin did not require certain categories of non-Aryans to be excluded, local party authorities or even simply ordinary German citizens made sure these people did not gain access to air-raid shelters or large bunkers. Postwar local publications paid little if any attention to this highly discriminatory politics of shelter inclusion and exclusion.

Sometimes, foreign laborers, POWs, and concentration camp prisoners were depicted helping to clean up the rubble after a bombing attack, although it was not made clear whether they had been forced to do this work. However, postwar local publications more commonly focused on the threat that foreign workers posed to the German population at the very end of the war. In his 1955 book on Nuremberg, Fritz Nadler complained that

> Our stomachs were growling—the foreigners ate their fill. The foreign workers and the prisoners who had been freed strolled through the streets that the citizens born in Nuremberg now avoided if at all possible. These foreigners held their heads a bit higher than before, whereas we now slinked around with our heads down. . . . Woe to the defeated . . . ! Some [of these foreigners] now looked quite different [having] "bought" new suits very cheaply from textile stores in the suburbs. . . . Many foreigners [now] came on bicycles.[119]

Wiederaufbau: The Reconstruction of German Cities after 1945

By no means did all of these early local narratives devote space to the period after 1945. The authors who did go beyond 1945 wanted to celebrate the collective postwar achievements of the Germans who had removed the rubble and started to rebuild Germany's cities. The Nazis had recognized the value of the promise of reconstruction to their attempts to mobilize the population; "reconstruction narratives . . . coupled rebuilding with 'Final Victory.'"[120] After 1945, reconstruction served a different political purpose by symbolically clearing the way for the construction of a new, modern, and democratic Germany.[121] In his introduction to Wilms's short book on Zweibrücken, for example, the city's Oberbürgermeister insisted that it was necessary to mourn their losses and to remind local citizens of "those horrible . . . painful events." Yet it was also important to commemorate "the pluck and the diligence with which everyone went to work to rebuild their city . . . after the disaster."[122]

The 1949 book on Paderborn acknowledged that destruction of "old" Paderborn was an irreplaceable loss, but it also provided new opportunities. As in most other German cities destroyed by bombing during the war, municipal authorities and city planners were well aware that their rebuilding plans must take account of the needs of modern traffic in an increasingly motorized society.[123] Rebuilding also gave the city the opportunity to provide much-needed green spaces in the area of the Innenstadt. This did not mean, however, that the rebuilt Altstadt would retain no architectural reminders of the past. Some noteworthy old buildings had been restored although it was impossible to reconstruct many others.[124] With a note of sadness, the book observed that the city that emerged from World War II would never be a replica of prewar Paderborn, even if certain significant architectural landmarks were rebuilt.

On the other hand, concerns about the loss of the architectural past did not trouble Braun-Rühling's appraisal in 1953 of the postwar rebuilding of Kaiserslautern:

> A new, practical building style celebrated its triumph, tasteful high-rise buildings soon pushed themselves up in the city-center and made clear that with this new building style a new spirit was beginning to stir in the people [who lived here]. Everywhere, huge blocks of houses grew up out of the ground. A new world was . . . taking shape inside as well as around us. It was simply a law of nature that anyone who was unable to get on board, must be left behind.[125]

Braun-Rühling congratulated his fellow citizens for the "astounding power of their will" with which they had begun to reconstruct Kaiserslautern and rebuild its industry. He also expressed thanks to the United States for the contribution its "generous and . . . truly humane intervention" had made to the economic recovery of West Germany. A significant US military base in Kaiserslautern channeled US dollars directly into the local economy.[126]

In Zweibrücken, the Americans had told the new *Bürgermeister* whom they had appointed after the war that it was "[n]onsense . . . to want to rebuild the city" where it stood.[127] Nevertheless, the locals began cleaning up the rubble; the first work was done by former members of the Nazi Party who had to start clearing the ruins under threat of losing their food ration cards. Reconstruction began to get underway seriously after the currency reform. At first "Zweibrücken's reconstruction program [was] somewhat halting, but later it accelerated to an almost American tempo."[128]

Some important historic buildings that had survived the bombing war did fall victim to indecision and inadequate finances; "Despite all the efforts made, it was not possible to preserve the interesting architecture of the archive building from demolition. Despite all the protests, it was torn down in 1953."[129]

Wilms concluded, rather sadly, that "it appears that there is little room for the old Zweibrücken to remain next to the new Zweibrücken. It will have its place (only) in memory." Against this loss of the architectural past, the citizens of Zweibrücken could, however, balance the achievement of reconstruction; "the reconstruction of our city will [never be] forgotten; [it] was achieved with . . . an incomparable speed, so that 10 years after the destruction of the city it had already grown out beyond its earlier extent."[130]

In the late 1940s and throughout the 1950s, descriptions of the air war frequently owed a generally unacknowledged debt to the narratives that the Nazis had already constructed before 1945 to make sense of the bombing. The postwar meanings of some of the key elements derived from the Nazi narrative might be transformed, yet lurking behind them were memories of what these terms had signified under the Nazis. After 1945, descriptions and pictures of ruins might function as a condemnation of war in general, or even of the war that the Nazis had started, but many Germans would have remembered that before 1945 the Nazis had used pictures of ruined churches and other architectural treasures not to condemn war in the abstract but to indict the Allies as the "barbarians, without culture who were alone guilty for escalating the air war into a weapon of 'terror' which transgressed the laws of war."[131] For the Germans who had lived through the war, it may therefore not have been necessary (or possible, given that West Germany was now allied to the former wartime enemy) explicitly to express anger at the Allies for the ruins with which they still lived; the responsibility of the Allies for these ruins had already been established verbally and visually by the Nazis. Pictures and descriptions of ruins could carry this previous layer of meaning into the postwar years, even when they did not explicitly condemn the Allies.

One essential element of the Nazi narrative was, however, missing from postwar local publications—the Nazis' insistence that it was the Jews who had unleashed the war against Germany and the Jews who were responsible for the bombing of German cities. Jeffrey Herf observes that "the air war over Germany . . . assumed a special place in Nazi anti-Semitic propaganda. Germany's devastated cities and civilian deaths became a primary piece of evidence to support official claims that the Jews were indeed trying to exterminate the Germans."[132] The Germans who wrote and read the first generation of postwar local narratives in the late 1940s and the 1950s would have remembered all too well that during the war even Germans who did not subscribe to Goebbels' propaganda might nonetheless believe that the Allied air attacks were "revenge for our treatment of the Jews."[133] Nicholas Stargardt observes that "[b]elief in the 'Jewish' bombing went beyond hardline Nazis, and was strengthened by more than just anti-Semitic propaganda. It was conditioned by the widespread knowledge of the mass shooting of Jews in the East."[134]

As the Allied air war spread across Germany, each new raid encouraged the circulation of rumors that Jews were orchestrating the air attacks.[135] In Heilbronn, for example, it was claimed that a Jewish former citizen, forced to emigrate before the war, had returned with a squadron of Mosquito bombers in 1944 to take revenge. In the Rhineland, a Jewish butcher who had also emigrated from Germany was supposed to have led an air attack on his former hometown, Oberlahnstein. A US Air Force lance corporal named Weinberg was said to be waging his own "private war" against his former hometown, Fulda.[136] A Security Service (SD) report of August 3, 1943, from Ochsenfurt, near Würzburg, mentioned the widespread rumor "that Würzburg would not be attacked by enemy planes because in Würzburg no synagogue had been set on fire. However, others say that now the planes would come to Würzburg, as a short while ago the last Jew had left Würzburg. Before his deportation he predicted that now Würzburg would be bombed."[137]

In a series of letters written to Goebbels between May and June 1944, some Germans suggested that the British and the Americans would stop the bombing if Germany held its remaining Jews hostage or simply executed them. One letter advised that "after every terror attack in which civilians are killed . . . ten times as many Jews and Jewesses and their children [be] shot."[138] Another proposed that instead of expelling all the Jews from Germany (this at a time when most of the remaining German Jews had already been deported to the East) "we should announce . . . that, with immediate effect, we are not going to attack any towns or cities in England any more and hence the enemies may also no longer attack our cities and towns. . . . Should our enemies nonetheless dare to attack even one of our towns or cities . . . then we shall have 10,000 or 20,000 or 30,000 Jews shot without mercy."[139] When Major Trapp was trying to motivate his Reserve Police Battalion to engage in its first mass shooting of Jews in July 1942 in the Polish village of Jozefow, it did not seem at all unreasonable for him to suggest that; "It might perhaps make their task easier . . . if they remembered that in Germany bombs were falling on the women and children."[140]

Well into the 1950s, some Germans were willing to talk about the murder of the Jews if this allowed them to insist that the killing of German civilians in air raids was a similar atrocity.[141] What the authors of local narratives did not want to do, however, was to remind their readers that during the war many of them had believed either that the bombing was Jewish retribution for German crimes against Jews or that the "Jewish air terror" justified murderous German retaliation against the Jews of occupied Europe.[142] Allowing room in local narratives for Germany's Jewish victims would certainly have made it more difficult to "decontaminate" local history.[143] In the late 1940s and the 1950s, leaving Jews out of local narratives was a fundamental precondition for talking about German suffering and about Germans as victims of the bombing war.[144]

Local Narratives in the 1960s: New Challenges?

From the late 1950s to the mid-1960s, the genocide of European Jews reentered national discussions of the Nazi past. At the end of 1959 and the beginning of 1960, the anti-Semitic graffiti that appeared on synagogues in Cologne and other West German cities raised questions about the persistence of anti-Semitism in the Federal Republic.[145] A series of high profile trials of SS perpetrators—the Ulm Einsatzgruppen trial in 1958, the Eichmann trial in Jerusalem in 1961, and the Frankfurt Auschwitz trials from 1963 to 1965—along with the parliamentary debates about the extension of the statute of limitations for murder "brought the annihilation of European Jewry to the forefront of public debates."[146] Nazi genocide shifted to the center of public perceptions of World War II for the first time since 1945. Pictures of the persecution and annihilation of European Jews also returned to the visual imagination of West Germany with the publication of Gerhard Schoenberner's *The Yellow Star* (1960), the first and still the best-known illustrated book on the destruction of the European Jews.[147]

Did these changes in national remembering create new challenges to the way local bombing narratives were written? If so, how did authors of these local narratives respond? The trials of SS perpetrators did bring public attention to the murder of European Jews. Marc von Miquel argues, however, that "many Germans were simply unwilling to accept the conclusion that could and should have been drawn from the trials—that the genocidal politics of the Third Reich had not been the actions of a few outsiders but instead had come from the mainstream of German society."[148] Schoenberner's book did make historical photographs and texts available to a broad public for the first time since the war, but it drew a clear line between the perpetrators and the broad mass of the German population. Here Germans were confronted with a picture gallery of sadistic Nazi murderers but never with their own reflections. Germans were not challenged to think about their own or their parents' complicity in the Holocaust but were encouraged instead to identify with the innocent Jewish victims of "inhuman, violent excesses" perpetrated by the brutal and sadistic mass murderers who followed Hitler's orders. Auschwitz was detached from the social and political context that had produced it.

The increasing presence of the Nazi past in 1960s West Germany did not therefore make it impossible or even very difficult for the authors of local publications to reproduce the basic elements of the local master narrative established during the 1950s. Jörg Arnold has found, for example, that "[i]n Kassel, shifts in the larger memory regime of the Federal Republic had local repercussions but a very limited influence on the historiography of the air war."[149] The more serious challenge for the authors of local publications—at least in their own minds—was that they now had to address a new generation of readers born after 1945, who had no direct experience of the bombing and who could no longer see the traces of destruction in the urban landscape. Armin Schmid began his 1965 book on the bombing of Frankfurt am Main by reminding his readers that just 20 years ago "the last bombs fell on our city's landscape of ruins, low-flying planes strafed civilians, drum-head court martials murdered, old men and half grown boys were sent to the front in the *Volkssturm* while the party big shots and the high level officers 'withdrew.'"[150] Schmid thought it was unfortunate that the memory of these events was already beginning "to crumble away."[151] He believed that his book might help two kinds of young people. As an educator he had encountered those who were "alert, open-minded young people, who had to bear the continuing burden of the past. They wanted to know the truth, to orient themselves in the confusion of all the different opinions."[152] But there were also those who were inclined to "express their rebelliousness against adults by reproaching them with the Nazi years, which they had not lived through themselves."[153] He thought that his book might help these rebellious youths to comprehend "what the older generation had suffered through and how . . . [these Germans] had actively helped one another."[154]

Schmid's book is an assemblage of a wide variety of different texts ranging from contemporary newspaper reports to Nazi Party documents to personal letters. Schmid did insert himself into the story by claiming the authority of an eyewitness:

> During the heaviest attack on Nuremberg, I, as a soldier, was put to work clearing the rubble and digging out the bodies. So, I know this time from my own experience.[155]

Yet he clearly wanted to construct a narrative not in his own words but through the documents he had chosen and by the way in which he put these different excerpts together. Schmid did not present this material as an unproblematic, factual documentation of the bombing war. He warned the reader to be critical of some of these sources. In response to a report in one of the local newspapers on October 9–10, 1943, describing the effects of the "big raid" on October 4, Schmid insisted, for example, that

> The newspaper reports about the attack, give an impression of those days. But they are also documents of Nazi language and propaganda. They show with what means the regulation of language from above was meant to fill the people with fanatical hate and will to resist, how the deeds of the party functionaries were made heroic and cleverly linked to ordinary people so as to impose the sense of ideological unity. . . . The way in which an event is depicted also belongs to the picture of the time.[156]

Schmid also criticized the rhetoric used by the Nazis in their official ceremonies of mourning for those killed in the bombing raids: "It is . . . an example of the . . . phraseology of those days, [which tried] to convert the unspeakable suffering of those affected into hatred and desire for revenge."[157] Schmid juxtaposed the hyperbole of Nazi burial ceremonies that insisted that all bombing victims were heroes with documents that revealed the gruesome realities of retrieving corpses from the ruins and interring large numbers of dead bodies. One document reported, for example, that local authorities decided to give rescue teams alcohol and tobacco to counteract the stench of rotting corpses.[158] Another document showed that when there were not enough coffins for all of the dead, local authorities had to bury bombing victims in paper bags.[159]

Few of the local publications that appeared in the 1950s had asked their readers to see the bombing as a result of the war that Hitler had started. Most of the early narratives preferred to draw a clear distinction between the Nazi leaders who were responsible for the war and the ordinary, innocent Germans who were depicted as its final victims. The bombing war was frequently presented as a disaster that came to the individual German city from an ill-defined elsewhere. Schmid's book broke with these conventions by insisting that postwar Germans "must recognize and confess that the bombing terror was a consequence of Hitler's war and of the bestial crimes on the German side."[160] At the same time, he also insisted that the British and American people must acknowledge their own responsibility for the "calamity caused by the British and American air forces," although he conceded that "dealing with this guilt is these people's own affair."[161]

Unlike the authors of many of the previous books on the bombing war,

Schmid acknowledged Germans' enthusiasm for Hitler's Blitzkrieg, so long as the *Wehrmacht* was winning: "The popular mood was in general very good . . . and people accepted the discomforts of the air defense measures."[162] However, news of the military "catastrophe" at Stalingrad in 1943, combined with "the stress caused to the population by the air raid alarms," produced a downturn in the mood of the German public.[163] Schmid also made his book about Frankfurt noticeably different from most previous local publications by including descriptions of the persecution of the Jews. As early as page 21, for example, readers were told that on January 30, 1941, eight local cinemas showed the anti-Semitic film *The Eternal Jew*, and that on September 19, 1941, Frankfurt's Jews were forced to wear the Yellow Star and that "the deportations increased."[164] Schmid also included a story about a Jewish man, who had not yet been deported because he was married to a non-Jewish woman. When a heavy air raid began, the couple tried to go down into the coal cellar of their house even though "Air Raid Warden W., a fanatical Jew-hater, had already driven the S. couple out of the coal cellar once before with the words 'Get out, Jews, go to the dung heap.' This time, however, the humanity of the other inhabitants of the house triumphed and the S. couple were able to find refuge in the . . . air raid shelter."[165] When incendiaries set the house above them on fire, the Jewish man, Herr S., escaped with the other tenants into the courtyard of the building. Finding that here they were surrounded by fire, they fought their way "to a large cellar in the same street which was already jam-packed with other people seeking refuge. A few women who knew Herr S. concealed him and another Jewish citizen by placing them in the darkest corner of the cellar at the air pump which was worked by hand. For two hours they pumped the air, their backs to the crowd, while their wives covered them from view as well as they could."[166]

In the testimony of eyewitnesses used to depict the experience and effects of the "big raid" of October 4, 1943, Schmid included a report written by Herr S, "a long-established, Jewish citizen of Frankfurt, married to a non-Jewish woman, who fought in the war of 1914 to 1918, won the Iron Cross Second Class, the Hessian Medal for Bravery and a badge recognizing that he had been wounded who was sent temporarily to Buchenwald by the Gestapo."[167] After two weeks in the camp, Herr S. was released. He was then forced to work in a brickworks and at one of the city's cemeteries. The administrator of the cemetery secretly gave Herr S. food to supplement the low rations he was allowed as a Jew. Schmid claimed that other ordinary Frankfurt citizens had helped Jews, even though this meant they ran the risk of being sent to a concentration camp. With this laudable, if improbable, record of assistance to Frankfurt's

Jews to their credit, the ordinary citizens of Frankfurt could scarcely have deserved the "big raid" of March 1944 in which "Old Frankfurt, as the world knew and loved it, was leveled to the ground."[168]

Yet despite his attempts to tell the story of the bombing in a different way, Schmid still at times fell back on some of the well-established conventions for this type of narrative. So, for example, the description he included of the first bombs that fell on Frankfurt resembled earlier publications that portrayed local citizens as being completely unaware of the disaster that would eventually destroy their city.[169] Construction of air-raid bunkers did begin to unsettle the Frankfurt population and to fuel rumors that the enemy might use gas attacks against civilians. But the impact of these anxieties was defused to a certain degree by the inclusion of a jingle popular at the time: "No meat, no fat, in bed at eight, the arse scarcely warm, air-raid alarm."[170]

It is not at all clear how Schmid wanted to present the reactions of Frankfurt's population to the bombings. As in other local publications, Nazi Party officials are certainly depicted as cowardly, rescue workers as heroic, and the German *Volk* as suffering victims. Certainly, Schmid suggested that the bombing war alienated many Germans from the regime, citing the example of a banner, now illicitly hung above the ruins that earlier in the Third Reich had adorned new buildings; the banner read, "For this, too, we can thank the *Führer*."[171] Yet he also included a report from the Frankfurt police (*Schutzpolizei*) that concluded:

> The mood of the population was not only as one would expect after terror attacks, but also angry. Over and over again, one heard people say "When will we finally have revenge on England?" The mass of the population was however not moved to insults of any kind [against the regime].[172]

In general, however, Schmid presents the ordinary citizens of Frankfurt as simply trying to carry on until the war was over, sometimes assisted by a touch of "gallows humor."[173]

Putting the Allies in the Air War

Many Germans, including most of the authors of the earliest local publications, may have felt that the bombing of German cities was militarily unjustified, morally wrong, even a war crime.[174] These sentiments could not, however, be openly expressed without drawing criticism, especially from outside Germany, that presenting the bombing as an Allied atrocity was simply an apologetic attempt to draw illegitimate moral equivalences between the Allies and the Germans. This concern perhaps helps to explain why the first generation of local publications seldom paid much attention to the American and British air crews who had dropped bombs on German cities. The early local publications constructed narratives that allowed them to present Germans as victims without explicitly stating who had caused their suffering. In his 1961 book on the bombing of Schweinfurt, Ludwig Wiener did take the unusual step of including a contribution from a former American airman, Budd J. Peaslee.[175] But Heinz Bardua's *Stuttgart im Luftkrieg, 1939–1945*, originally published in 1967/68 and reissued in 1986, was one of the first local narratives to insist that writing the story of the air war required discussion not only of the Germans who have experienced "its horrors in the cellars, bunkers, tunnels and burning canyons of the city streets" but also of "the fates of the men, who as soldiers under orders flew British and American bombers against Stuttgart."[176] Bardua justified this argument in three ways. First, "History includes the fate of all mankind; it includes everything that happens to or is done by human beings, whether friend or foe (how changeable are such concepts in any case!)"[177] Second, and more concretely, Bardua argued that the very nature of air war demanded a different perspective than the merely local or the German side; "the essence of a strategic air war, which plays itself out in three-dimensional space, does not allow an all-too-narrow local demarcation. The events in the sky above Stuttgart must therefore always be seen in a larger context."[178] Finally, Bardua urged German readers to realize that "the situation of the Allied bomber crews . . . was scarcely more pleasant than that of their victims in the cellars and tunnels of the city."[179] Bardua refused, however, simply to equate the suffering of Allied bombing crews with that of the Germans on whom they had dropped their bombs: "An essential difference consisted of the fact that it was soldiers who sat in these planes while in the cellars and tunnels . . . after the men fit to serve had been drafted—it was primarily women, children and older men who had to fear for their lives."[180]

The introduction to Bardua's book, written by the Oberbürgermeister of Stuttgart, presents this publication as a scholarly and objective analysis, based on years of research not only in German but also in Allied archives. These claims to be "scientific" were reinforced by the fact that the book was published as part of a series sponsored by the city archive of Stuttgart. Bardua was not a professional historian. He said that he had combined his own experiences and observations as a member of a fire brigade in Stuttgart up to the spring of 1944 and then as a soldier in the Luftwaffe, with pertinent German, British, and

American documents.[181] Local citizens had supplied descriptions of their own personal experiences in response to an appeal included in a series of short articles on the air war, published between November 10, 1966, and January 19, 1967, by a local newspaper, *Stuttgarter Wochenblatt*, which reached most Stuttgart households.[182] In February 1967, Bardua had also managed to publish a notice in the newsletter of the Royal Air Forces Association in London (*Air Mail*), which produced "valuable connections to former officers and men of the Royal Air Force, who flew in bombers over Stuttgart."[183]

Bardua's true purpose in drawing attention to the experiences of Allied air crews was to show that both they and the German civilians killed by the bombing had been victims of their political and military leaders "who wanted . . . the bombing war in this form without any consideration for the victims it would produce on both sides."[184] Bardua's book paints Churchill and the civilian and military leaders who supported his policies in the air war as the real perpetrators. The head of Bomber Command, Air Marshall Harris, had worked out the plan for the "annihilation attack of 28 March 1942 against Lübeck."[185] Then he had planned the first thousand-plane raid against Cologne.[186] Later in the book, Bardua depicts Harris as bent on achieving the total annihilation of Stuttgart.[187] After the war, Harris claimed that continuing the bombing had been necessary to prepare the way for the defeat of Germany. But Bardua argued that any effect the bombing may have had on German morale was insignificant and in no way proportional to the intensity of the bombing.[188] Describing the 35th raid on Stuttgart on November 26, 1944, Bardua also insisted that "in the meantime, the Allies must have seen that the destruction of industrial installations and workers' housing in the cities was not able to cripple German war industry. Through decentralization of the most important plants . . . in underground spaces around the country, the Germans managed to parry the first, heavy blows against their main industries concentrated in the cities."[189]

Bardua claimed that ordinary airmen sometimes questioned the necessity and morality of the Allied bombing campaign. He quoted David Irving's description of a navigator who was outraged in December 1940 when he received the order to bomb residential neighborhoods in the center of Mannheim. But what could these men do? In "the Bomber Command of the RAF, there must also have been cases of being compelled to execute orders that were illegal or immoral."[190] Here Bardua draws an obvious parallel with the defense commonly used after 1945 by Germans charged with war crimes that they would have risked their own execution had they not followed orders to kill civilians.[191] Like ordinary German soldiers, Allied airmen were simply "following orders" with which they often might not agree. Bardua claims that "[i]n the photographs which show the air crews as they climb into their huge, black birds, it is hard to detect any very happy expressions. One has the impression that these men are not enthused about their trade."[192] The young men who sat in the Allied bombers and the German civilians on whom these planes dropped their deadly cargo only wanted to survive long enough to see the end of the war. During the war, these Allied air men had not been able to see the destruction their bombs had produced. Today, many of them were emotionally devastated when they learned the details of "the other end of the air war" down on the streets of the German cities they had bombed. One British veteran, who had been a 19-year-old rear gunner on a Lancaster Bomber that attacked Stuttgart, told Bardua, "How impersonal it seemed then and how frighteningly personal it is now, 17 years later, as we look at the city together with a Stuttgart friend."[193]

Bardua emphasized that the missions these young men had flown over Germany were extremely dangerous, that many planes were shot down, that many airmen did not make it past the 20th raid.[194] He argued, however, that the men in charge of Bomber Command were quite prepared to sacrifice the lives of their air crews so that the planes could drop ever larger loads of bombs on German cities. Describing the technical details of the Lancaster, Bardua remarked that "in the course of the war, the amount of armor plate . . . that would have given the crew a better chance to withstand a hit uninjured so that they could then jump out with a parachute was increasingly cut back so that the planes could carry more bombs."[195] It appeared that even the Germans who were the victims of the Allied bombing campaign displayed greater respect for Allied airmen than their own leaders. When one Allied plane was shot down, the German authorities accorded the six dead Canadian crew members the honors of a full military funeral. Bardua does not mention, however, that some downed Allied airmen were beaten up and even murdered by irate Germans.[196]

Like the young airmen who had died in the air war, ordinary German citizens had also become the victims of their leaders. The devastating British attacks on Hamburg at the end of July 1943 made it clear that Germany needed more and better air defenses. Yet Hitler clung to the idea that attack was the only defense and ordered that German war industry build more bombers than fighters.[197] Germany might have regained air superiority, at least during the day, with the new German jet fighter, the Me 262, but Hitler ordered that it be redesigned as a high-speed bomber.[198]

Because the Allies had won the war, they had been able to claim that their policies were justified. Yet, today, even people in Britain understood clearly that it had not been possible to bring Germany to its knees in World War II "by air terror alone. The brutal attacks upon cities aroused feelings of hatred and anxiety in the inhabitants concerned as well as their relatives at the front, which clever Nazi propaganda exploited to stiffen their resolve to resist. The Allies could not have wanted this."[199] Bardua did not deny that in the long run Allied bombing had made the population "irritable and nervous . . . occasionally it was also possible to detect the first signs of a disintegration of morale."[200] He also admitted that the Allied air attacks, which were spread out all over Nazi Germany, had tied down significant numbers of military personnel that the Germans badly needed on the Eastern Front. In 1942, flak batteries were manned by some 439,000 Germans; in 1943, that number rose to 600,000 and in 1945, 900,000.[201] But Bardua insisted that the air war's contribution to Allied victory was meager.[202] The larger lesson Bardua wanted his readers to learn was, however, that "[a]ll those who participated in the Second World War, need to request forgiveness and also to forgive themselves. There would scarcely be one of them who would want to live through another war."[203]

A book published 13 years later than Bardua's, in 1970, showed the tenacity of key strands of the local master narrative constructed in the 1940s and 1950s. At the same time, however, this book also demonstrated the possibilities of opening up this narrative in new directions. Like some of the earlier local publications, *Köln '39–'45. Der Leidensweg einer Stadt. Miterlebt von Josef Fischer* described the destruction of Cologne's architectural and artistic treasures. Josef Fischer, the author, emphasized that the bombing made the city unrecognizable even to longtime inhabitants: "Overnight, the city's appearance was transformed. Deep furrows had been dug into its cheerful face, ennobled by the works of many centuries. Streets were missing. Hospitals, museums, monuments and businesses were transformed into ruins."[204] After the 1,000-plane raid during the night of May 30–31, 1942, Cologne's citizens were forced to acknowledge that life could never be the same again: "Now they recognized that they confronted the unalterable necessity of taking leave forever of their cherished habits and their possessions, acquired by their strenuous labor over many years, decades, perhaps even generations."[205]

Fischer's description of the ways that Germans on the ground experienced and responded to the bombing certainly included some hopeful stories of survival, of life defeating death even in the most extreme of circumstances.[206] Very soon, however, this section of the book began to depart from the conventions that had governed the writing of most local narratives. Fischer argued that the repeated bombing of Cologne "had long since burst the limit of anything human beings could endure."[207] In just one month the city was subjected to "an unbroken series of big attacks lasting several days at a time . . . twenty-eight large scale attacks rolled over the city in this month and plowed up the ruins over and over again."[208] This unprecedented wave of violence transformed the inhabitants of the cathedral city into passive objects, deprived of any possibility of influencing their own fates.[209] Everyone now confronted a simple, brutal truth: "Every night, when the sirens howled, it was time to die." Waiting for a death that appeared inevitable, the most that the living could do was to "organize" food, water, and shelter, but this drive for survival in the short-term produced "the dissolution of any concept of law, it signified latent anarchy . . . now human beings are full of dangerous forces."[210] In Fischer's book there was no trace of the "Community of Suffering and Sacrifice" that was such an important element of early local narratives. The bombing had radically fragmented local society. Fischer insisted that eventually all that was important was one's own house, one's own family.[211] By the end of the war, the ruins themselves had become a surreal landscape, where "[d]eserters and foreign workers on the run, had crept into the rubble and defended their skins (against) the military police chasing them with machine pistols. What we hear is shots being fired, hand grenades."[212] Overall, this is a dark, despairing picture of what the bombing had done to the minds as well as the bodies of Cologne's citizens. Nor was the unrelenting gloom of Fischer's narrative relieved by any expression of hope that Cologne would be "reborn" after the war. These were simply not Fischer's concerns. At the end of the war, his only priority was that "we have to hold on to the roof over our heads. When the war ends, a roof, a place to stay will mean the world."[213]

What makes Fischer's narrative even more unusual is that he devoted considerable space to the German air war against British cities. Fischer reproduced an account of a German air attack written by an official Propaganda Company reporter who went along in one of the Luftwaffe planes. The rhetoric is typical of these types of reports that Germans would have been able to read in newspapers and illustrated magazines. The reporter tells his readers that the RAF fighter planes ensured that flying over England "was certainly no bloody stroll."[214] But the "steel-hard determination" of the German air crews "was richly repaid."[215] After they reached their targets and dropped their bombs, the reporter could see down on the ground that "[a] gigantic flame flickered against the heavens, a new torch of destruction on British soil. That same evening, British radio had to acknowledge this catastrophe." Nazi propaganda claimed that German planes attacked only British military targets. Fischer insisted, however, that the truth of the word "catastrophe" in this official report was that German planes were also killing women and children.

Fischer contrasted another official report about the bombing of London with his own experience of listening to a Radio London broadcast. The British report described how a huge bomb fell on Peckam, a poor district of south London; "[h]ere the Luftwaffe had altered the geography: a new market square for Peckham! the complete defiance of the people who heard their houses and furniture whir away in a few seconds was visible: they had stuck little British flags into the ruins. Churchill was there. People came running from everywhere. Thousands stumbled over the ruins and pushed their way around him."[216] Fischer turned up the volume so that he could hear what the British crowd was saying; "[a]nd once again, over and over: 'Pay them back!'" At this point, Fischer's wife covered her ears; "she pressed the flat of her hands hard against her head, and it was in just this same way that later, sitting on a chest down in the cellar, she cowered when . . . the plaster fell from the ceiling and the ground swayed and the English air mines falling above us swept the earth clear. Pay them back. We had to think about that often in 1942, 1943, and October 1944 when the tide had turned."[217]

Earlier in this section, Fischer had suggested that some Germans may have seen the air war against Britain as "revenge." As the war continued, however, the British took their revenge on Germany. After the Luftwaffe destroyed Coventry "a new word was born . . . Coventrate!"[218] Just a year and a half later, however, "this word was exchanged for another in the inferno of Cologne; the new word was 'Kolonisiert.' [It] described no clearly defined condition, as did 'Coventrate' (but rather) a stage of the bombing war, [it] meant the progressive annihilation of a large German city, demonstrated with the example of Cologne."[219] The official OKW report insisted that German civilians were the main target of the British attack on Cologne. Fischer claimed, however, that "227 factories were hit."[220] The air war "had become, on both sides, the schizophrenic fury of the 20th century."[221] Although the Germans lost this apocalyptic competition, their deployment of V-1 and V-2 rockets toward the end of the war ensured that "the destruction continues without interruption." The despairing, perhaps even cynical lesson that Fischer draws from this comparison of German destruction of British cities and the Allied bombing of Germany is that "[t]he survivors will be the ones who dispose of the most planes the longest and who can carry the heaviest bombs through the air."[222] The reason why Cologne makes Coventry look like "child's play" is the morally agnostic conclusion that "the Germans have in the meantime become decidedly weaker in this business of destruction."[223] In its tone as well as its content, Fischer's book was an unusually dark reframing of the local narrative. It was certainly not imitated by many other local publications before 1989.

Local Narratives in the 1980s

On four consecutive evenings in January 1979, West German television aired the American miniseries *Holocaust*. This soap opera traced the stories of two fictitious families during the Third Reich, one Jewish and one German. Over half of the adult population of West Germany (some 20 million viewers) watched the film.[224] *Holocaust* did not give viewers any historical information that was not already known to professional scholars. But the film generated an unprecedented (and unexpected) flood of emotional responses.[225] The network that screened *Holocaust* set up phone banks manned by experts to answer viewers' questions. The thousands of viewers who called in asked emotionally charged questions that these experts found difficult to answer. Some callers cried over the phone. Viewers wanted to know how ordinary Germans had allowed "this" to happen? With the screening of *Holocaust*, troubling moral questions about the responsibility of ordinary Germans for the Jewish genocide were now being asked in millions of German households for the first time since 1945.

Edgar Reitz's 16-hour film *Heimat* was a direct response to the American *Holocaust* miniseries.[226] Reitz complained that Hollywood films like *Holocaust* prevented Germans from "taking narrative possession of our past. . . . The Americans have stolen our history through *Holocaust*."[227] *Heimat* would rescue German history from the grasp of Hollywood film. No fewer than 25 million West Germans saw at least one of the eleven episodes aired in the fall of 1984.[228] *Heimat* invented stories and images about the lives of ordinary Germans in "the Hunsrück region, a rural area in the southern part of the Rhineland" from the 1920s to the 1980s.[229] This was history "from below," the history of "'simple people' [who] either knew nothing or preferred to know nothing."[230] Reitz's film did not exclude Nazism from the history of the local community; "more narrative time is granted in *Heimat* to the exploration and visualization of the causes, progress, and consequences of German fascism than in most full-length feature films or documentaries on National Socialism."[231] Yet, "the annihilation of the Jews is almost completely excluded from the plot."[232] Gertrud Koch has observed that "in order to tell the myth of 'Heimat,' the trauma of Auschwitz had to be shut out of the story."[233] The generally positive reception of Reitz's film in West Germany indicated that despite the earlier impact of the American miniseries *Holocaust*, national memory culture had certainly not become inhospitable to the continued production of the kinds of local narratives of the bombing war that had established themselves in the 1950s.

Nor did a major controversy about Nazism that raged from the summer of

1986 to January 1987 pose a direct challenge to these local narratives. Ernst Nolte argued that Nazi atrocities lost their uniqueness when seen in the wider context of the 20th century. When it came to mass murder, it was, Nolte claimed, the Soviet Union that showed the way, starting with the Civil War, moving through Stalin's purges and forced industrialization, and ending with the rampaging of the Red Army as it advanced through eastern Germany to Berlin. Nolte argued that Hitler learned from the Soviets and that in many ways the Holocaust was a response to the "Asiatic Deed" that the communists had pioneered.[234] Jürgen Habermas immediately and sharply rejected this attempt to "relativize" the Holocaust.

One development in the German memory work of this period did have the potential to disrupt established patterns of writing local air war narratives. In the 1980s, the History Workshop movement and other popular initiatives to explore the history of everyday life during the Third Reich started to bring Nazism more and more into local history. The 50th anniversary in 1983 of the National Socialist "seizure of power" provided the impulse for a number of projects on the local history of the Nazi movement and the Third Reich. Local History Workshops began to unearth parts of the local past that had been forgotten, repressed, or quite literally erased from the physical landscape of the community. In the small town of Achim in Lower Saxony, for example, the local *Geschichtswerkstatt* had to go to the Land Registry Office to establish the exact location of the synagogue there that was destroyed in 1938.[235] This archaeology of the local Nazi past sometimes met with disapproval and frequently provoked controversy. The local *Heimat Verein* in Achim refused to cooperate with the History Workshop when it wanted to investigate the town's Nazi history. By the 1980s, many inhabitants of local communities were ready to acknowledge the "negative inheritance" of local Nazi history. Yet others refused to accept these new understandings of the local past. The new critical culture of local history that the History Workshops had helped create may have influenced some of the authors of local air war narratives. But it would appear that if most of the authors of local air war narratives paid any attention at all to the new perspectives, it was only to reject them and to (re)assert that the German experience of the air war was the most important local story of World War II.

Frankfurt Revisited (1983)

The development that did produce a discernible effect upon the writing of some local narratives was the flaring up of the Second Cold War in the late

1970s and early 1980s. In 1979, the "NATO-Doppelbeschluss" that American midrange missiles should be stationed in West Germany renewed the threat of nuclear war and revived the peace movement.[236] A second book on Frankfurt, published by Karl Krämer in 1983, supported the peace movement's belief that the destruction of German cities in World War II should serve as "a pacifist parable in the atomic age."[237] From a working-class background, trained as a roofer, Krämer had served in World War I as a sapper. During the German Revolution he joined the SPD, then moved further left to the more radical USPD. In the Weimar Republic, he was an active trade unionist. During the Great Depression, after eleven months of unemployment, he started his own roofing firm. Afraid when the Nazis came to power that he would be arrested, he slept with a loaded revolver to protect himself. But the Nazis ignored him and he was able to devote his energies to building up his firm's business. When the war started, he was drafted and served until the end of 1940 in a bridge-building battalion. Released from active duty, he returned to Frankfurt and signed up to work in the Technical Emergency Service ("Teno"), "an organization that withdrew him from the further grasp of the party and the army. He found his niche and his shelter in the Teno."[238] But the author of the introduction to Krämer's book insisted that he was no shirker, trying to sit out the war quietly; Krämer volunteered for every dangerous job. Certainly, thrill-seeking was a part of his character—after the war, he took up mountain climbing. But he worked for the Teno not "in order to take senseless risks . . . but he saw the chance to occupy one of the few places within the framework of a dangerous machinery of destruction where lives could be saved."[239] In the 1950s, Krämer entered local politics. By the 1980s, he had become involved with the peace movement that, as Gerhard Beier explained in his introduction,

> had again developed into a mass movement. Drawing on his own experience, Krämer repeatedly stood up in meetings to warn emphatically against any trivialization of modern weapons of mass destruction. That is also the goal of his book. From this unvarnished depiction of those days of horror, the reader should receive the most tangible possible sense of the true consequences of a war.[240]

Unlike Schmid's 1963 book on Frankfurt, Krämer's book spoke with one voice—his. He wrote primarily about his own, often extremely harrowing experiences working on a rescue team in the Teno that dug out people who were still alive as well as corpses from the rubble of destroyed buildings. The book draws primarily on Krämer's own personal memories, but it also relies on documents and photographs that the author consulted in the municipal archive. Yet the book is not simply a documentary record. It includes clearly fictional components. Krämer invented conversations to dramatize certain incidents and even made up some of the stories he recounts. For the sake of confidentiality, he occasionally changed some names and places. Krämer insisted that these fictional elements helped the book to produce "the realistic picture of a Frankfurt empire of death, which never before has been reported so vividly."[241]

Like the inhabitants of several other German towns, the citizens of Frankfurt tried to delude themselves into believing that their city would be spared the worst of the bombing. One bizarre rumor claimed that "[t]he Rothschilds would not permit that the city of Goethe should be smashed up. [This rumor] completely overlooked the fact that Jews from Frankfurt had also been sent to camps . . . only a few people knew these were extermination camps."[242] People in Frankfurt continued to insist that the bombs that had already fallen on the city were only dropped as an emergency measure by Allied planes damaged by flak or night fighters. No one in the city could imagine the effects of a heavy raid, even though other German cities had long since suffered this kind of destruction. If Frankfurt were to become the target of heavier raids, most citizens believed they would be safe in the air-raid bunkers that the city was beginning to construct. Few bothered to ask whether there were enough places in these bunkers to protect everyone.

The graphic horror of the stories presented in Krämer's book is counterbalanced and to an extent redeemed by other tales of heroic rescue and by the manly comradeship that sustains his team, along with generous rations of alcohol, tobacco, "cynicism and gallows humor."[243] Despite the fact that each one of them eventually loses their own home to the bombs (Krämer himself is bombed out three times), these men continue to devote themselves selflessly to helping other victims of the bombing war.[244] The air war is a testing ground for their manliness and teamwork that has nothing at all to do with the Nazi regime. In a confrontation with a pompous—and drunk—Nazi Party official, Krämer makes it very clear that he and his men have only contempt for the Nazi movement. Between Krämer's men and frontline soldiers in the *Wehrmacht*, however, there is mutal respect: "a frontline soldier is never one of the whiners; even from a distance, he can see what the men in the grey work uniforms (of the *Teno*) are up to. The only people who have an instinct for blood, death and decay are those who must stick themselves far enough in to them, whether in frontline fighting or in a bombed out cellar."[245] Like frontline soldiers, Krämer's team really had no desire or need to talk about the horrors they had seen.[246]

Krämer was one of the few authors to suggest that Germans might have felt any solidarity with foreign laborers who were also exposed to the bombing. Describing the 26th attack on Frankfurt am Main on September 10, 1944, which killed 28 and wounded 113, he observed that "the victims were overwhelmingly . . . foreign workers who had to suffer to the same degree as the Germans under the Allied air attacks."[247] However, this observation says more about his own personal relationship with a brigade of French POWs he was supervising than about the attitudes of other Germans.[248] He allowed these French POWS to work without a guard and to wear civilian clothes, so that they did not stand out. Nevertheless, only Krämer's intervention during an impending air raid convinced other Germans that they must allow these French POWs to join them in a shelter.[249] Krämer's patriarchal concern for his own men did not prevent him from depicting other foreign laborers and POWs as dangerous. The increasing chaos in Frankfurt at the end of the war allowed thousands of them "to run around . . . in gangs, venting their rage for years of slave labor and tyranny by robbing and plundering—although they now took revenge on innocent [Germans]."[250]

The 1980s campaign against deployment of American Pershing missiles in Germany may also have facilitated the unrestrained condemnation of the Allied air war between 1939 and 1945 that is the centerpiece of a book about the Mainz region published in 1988.[251] But this book is also in many ways a reiteration of the basic arguments offered by Schmid's volume on Frankfurt 25 years earlier. The book on the air war in the Mainz region presented itself as the objective result of extensive research in German, American, British, and even French archives. It was published in an officially sponsored series of regional histories. The author's goal was, as the introduction by the president of Rheinland-Pfalz observed, to make a contribution to a wider current discussion "above all in England, about the ethical judgement of the air-war against the civilian population."[252] The author, Dieter Busch, acknowledged the differences, at least in theory, between American and British strategies; whereas British air raids were directed against German civilians, the Americans focused primarily on military targets. After more than 300 pages, Busch came to the conclusion that despite these differences, the effects of British and American air attacks were basically the same. Because the targets attacked by American bombers were located in heavily populated urban areas, "losses among the civilian population were predetermined." Busch did not argue that the USAF command had intentionally planned to kill so many German civilians, but "such losses were consciously and unscrupulously taken into account."[253]

In the RAF, Air Marshal ("Bomber") Harris was the driving force. Busch depicts Harris as having been obsessed with the idea that "area bombing" would bring the Germans to their knees.[254] On the basis of the RAF's experience in the first part of the war, Harris was convinced that bombers were incapable of destroying specific targets. In late autumn 1944, the leadership of the RAF rethought its strategy and wanted to give oil and transport targets higher priority, but "Air Marshall Harris stuck . . . stubbornly to area attacks against city-centers."[255] On December 22, 1944, the air crews of 4 Group were able to demonstrate to Harris "that he was proceeding on the basis of completely false prerequisites and under-estimating the possibilities of his weapons in a completely grotesque manner."[256] With the aid of highly developed Pathfinder tactics, 4 Group severely damaged the Bingerbrück railway marshaling yards without killing any German civilians. Yet Harris would not change his mind. Area bombing continued. Ironically, the same 4 Group air crews that had demonstrated that they could bomb military targets with great accuracy were now ordered to participate in the "terror attacks against Mainz" on February 1 and 27, 1945, which reduced residential neighborhoods "to rubble and ashes." From the "hectic activity of the British bomber weapon, which reduced a German city to rubble whenever the weather permitted, one could gain the impression that Air Marshal Harris was worried that the war might come to an end too soon." By the time in March 1945 that the British political leadership decided to restrain Harris it was already too late for Mainz and most other German cities.[257]

Busch argued that it made absolutely no difference to ordinary Germans whether their relatives or friends "were killed by an American 'precision attack' that went wrong or by a 'successful' British area attack. It makes no difference whether a lifetime's work was destroyed by an intentional attack on a residential neighborhood or by a mistake." Unable to understand what was happening to them, German civilians were easy targets for Nazi propaganda that systematically stirred up hatred of the allied "air gangsters" and encouraged "acts of brutal vigilante justice." Without explaining exactly what he meant, Busch argued that during the war uncertainty and anxiety had generated rumors and legends "that sadly have been given new life by the local press over and over again and shape the public image of the air war right up to the present day."[258]

Conclusion

The examples I have discussed in this chapter show that even though the writing of local narratives changed in important ways between 1949 and 1988, the central motifs established between the late 1940s and the 1960s exhibited remarkable staying power. The early postwar local publications reproduced many of the components of the bombing narrative that the Nazis had already established during the war without of course acknowledging their original source. Nazi propaganda depicted the Allied bombing campaign as the barbarous destruction of German architectural treasures and cultural heritage with absolutely no military justification. It condemned the Allied "terror bombers" and "air gangsters" who did not hesitate to murder innocent German women and children but also praised the resilience of German civilians and their refusal to be broken by the massive violence visited upon them from the air.[259] Postwar local publications did make two important changes in this Nazi narrative. First, they dropped all direct reference to the Nazi claim that it was the Jews who were behind the bombing war. Second, they depicted Germans as the innocent victims of not only the Allied bombing but of the Nazis as well.

Since the 1960s, West German discussions of the Nazi past have paid increasing attention to the genocide of European Jews and other Nazi crimes, yet these reorientations of national memory debates do not appear to have encouraged major rethinking of local narratives about the bombing. Until the 1980s, it was still possible to see the local history of the war as the history of the bombing and to claim untroubled status as innocent victims for the inhabitants of local communities. In the 1980s and 1990s, History Workshops began to focus the attention of local publics on their own particular city's involvement in the Nazi regime and Nazi crimes. The authors of local narratives of the bombing seldom felt, however, that these changes in local memory cultures had very much to do with the stories they wanted to tell. In their minds, the air war was a different story that they clearly believed they could continue to describe within the basic parameters they had inherited from the earliest local narratives of the bombing war. Changes did occur. Some local publications paid greater attention to the Allied planning and conduct of the air war. Others tried to show how Germany's experience of the bombing war was relevant to the antiwar/antinuclear campaigns of the 1960s and then, again, of the 1980s. In the 1980s, as critiques of postwar urban planning became more pronounced (it was sometimes described as a "second destruction" that deprived German cities of "more buildings worth keeping" than the air war itself[260]), celebration of the achievements of postwar reconstruction became less common. None of these shifts in emphasis fundamentally challenged, disrupted, or altered the basic message of local bombing narratives.

Few authors of local publications situated their narratives within wider historical contexts that included the German air war against Britain or the genocidal German land war in the East. Fischer's comparison in 1970 of Luftwaffe attacks on London and Coventry with the Allied destruction of his own city, Cologne, anticipated the wider perspectives that some local narratives would adopt after the end of the Cold War. But his example was not widely imitated before 1989. And even to the present day, some authors have continued to write local narratives of the bombing that do not differ in essentials from the books published in the 1940s, 1950s, and 1960s. The difference between the early 21st century and the period before 1989 is that these local narratives now have to compete with a wider range of other ways of telling the story of the bombing, especially, as we will see in chapter 6, in the national and international mass media.

CHAPTER 2

Picture Work

Words and Images: A Division of Labor?

A photograph taken by Erich Andres provides a vivid, if probably unintended, comment on the immense challenge that language faced in any attempt to describe the experience of the firestorm produced by the massive British and American air raids on Hamburg at the end of July 1943. The picture (fig. 1) shows a battered typewriter, perched on the ledge of what had probably once been the display window of a local shop. The badly damaged machine could no longer be used to type the words that might attempt to describe what had happened. Andres's picture appeared to suggest that the firestorm had quite literally rendered impossible the texts that this typewriter would normally have produced.

Authors of local publications readily admitted that normal language might not be capable of adequately describing the air war's horrors.[1] A report on the firestorm that destroyed the center of Hamburg in July 1943, written immediately after the event and published in 1960, insisted that "language fails in the face of the enormity of the horror that for ten long days and nights rocked human beings and whose indelible traces were written in the face of the city and the people."[2] Allied air attacks, particularly those that produced firestorms, created unbelievable sights: the mutilated corpses of the dead, sometimes "burned beyond recognition,"[3] or the uncanny panorama of an entire city reduced in a matter of minutes to a sea of ruins. Yet the starkly visual nature of Germans' experiences of the bombing war provided no guarantee that they would be rendered with images rather than in words. Gruesome "shock" pictures of mutilated corpses were published in some of these local publications. Yet the work of helping readers imagine the hideous ways of dying that had produced these dead bodies was frequently performed by words rather than pictures. The book on Paderborn published in 1949 presented grisly verbal descriptions of the remains of those who had not been able to escape the firestorm, but it included no pictures of these corpses or body parts. A 1964 book on Darmstadt pre-

Fig. 1

sented no images other than ruin pictures. Yet eyewitness accounts of the bombing that constituted the bulk of the text in this book were packed with horrible descriptions of what had happened to human bodies during the firestorm. On the other hand, the work of trying to help readers imagine a sea of ruins left behind by the bombing war was performed almost entirely by photographs. This was a visual spectacle that authors apparently found difficult to render in words. Most would probably have agreed with the observation made after the war by a local official in Cologne that "words cannot depict the shocking condition of our city nearly as well as good photographs."[4] Yet what these ruins meant to those who had survived the war could only be described in language. Local publications thus reveal an unpredictable relationship between visuality and textuality.[5] Some experiences that we might think were intrinsically visual were frequently made available to readers in words, rather than or at least more commonly than with pictures. Others were conveyed primarily in pictures. Still others were represented by both images and words together.

The Visual Archive

The picture work that could be done in postwar publications was of course limited by the actual photographs available. What could be published depended heavily on what had been photographed during and immediately after the war. Who took these pictures? How did the conditions under which these photographers had to operate determine what types of photographs could and could not be taken?[6] In their study of photographs of the bombing taken in Cologne before 1945, Thomas Deres and Martin Rüther have shown that these pictures were produced by a wide range of photographers. Only two types of photographers had official permission: those who worked for the local authorities documenting the destruction, so that these pictures could be used to make claims against the Allies for reparations when Germany finally won the war, and those who were taking pictures to be used in German propaganda to stiffen the resolve of the German population to keep on fighting through to victory.[7] In Bremen, "[a]n official picture reporter, the photographer Cüppers," took a large number of photographs of bomb-damaged buildings.[8] In Nuremberg, photographers working for the city documented the damage after each raid.[9] In Leipzig, Paul Kröber obtained an official permit to take pictures.[10] In Hamburg, a professional photographer, Hugo Schmidt-Luchs, had a special permit to photograph buildings hit by bombs, especially churches and public buildings because, at the beginning of the air war, "Hitler had the deranged idea someday as the victor to present the defeated with a bill for all the damage."[11] As the air war continued, the Propaganda Ministry lost interest in photographing the devastation, but Schmidt-Luchs continued to take photographs in the ruins even though the work was often dangerous; "duds, time delay bombs and collapsing walls repeatedly put his life at risk."[12] Other photographers working for the municipal authorities took additional pictures of ruins after the war.[13]

Photographs taken with the permission of the authorities concentrated on the material destruction caused by the bombing. In Bremen, "Cüppers captured property damage and damage to houses; the everyday life of people in the bombing war found its way into the pictures . . . only more or less by accident."[14] People appeared more often in Schmidt-Luchs's pictures of destroyed or damaged Hamburg buildings, but buildings were still the main subject. Pictures of dead bodies could be found in the authorized visual record of the bombing war but they appear often to have taken the form of film footage rather than photographs. As early as May 1942, Goebbels had come to the conclusion that it was important for the German newsreels to depict the war as realistically as possible, so that the German people could be prepared for the difficult problems still to come. However, Hitler wanted to ensure that the moving images shown in public would produce faith in the German military leadership and in ultimate victory. As a result, images of Germans killed by Allied bombs were usually not shown in the Nazi newsreels.[15] After the war, however, stills taken from these films could be used in publications about the bombing war.

Unauthorized photographs were taken by professional photographers, and by amateurs or "snap-shot" picture takers (*Knipser*). The professional photographer, Erich Andres, who served from 1939 in a Luftwaffe propaganda company, was in Hamburg on leave in July 1943 when the city was hit by the massive British air raids known as Operation Gomorrah. Andres took unauthorized photographs immediately after the raids that he hid until the war was over.[16] Hans Brunswig, a Hamburg fire department officer, took private color film footage of burning buildings during the air raids, of firemen fighting the fires, of smoking ruins, of refugees trying to flee the city, and of dead bodies in the streets.[17] In Hamburg-Wilhelmsburg, Ewald Rüffer and an unnamed photographer in the Lauritzen family took private photos of the bomb damage in their neighborhood.[18] Another amateur photographer in the Kunde family took a series of pictures of neighbors inside Hamburg air-raid shelters.[19] In Leipzig, a number of photographs were also taken by amateurs.[20] The Nuremberg architect, Hermann Weber, took pictures during or immediately after air raids. Even some of the forced foreign laborers working in the German war industry in Berlin took pictures of the effects of the bombing.[21]

What moved these private photographers to take pictures? In Cologne, some said that they were simply interested in creating private visual memories of what the bombs had done to their own immediate neighborhoods. One local photographer told Martin Rüther that he had taken some pictures for his wife who had already been evacuated to the Hunsrück, "so that she could show the family she was staying with: 'Here, this is how it looks in Cologne. This is why we had to get out of Cologne.'"[22] Other picture takers roamed the entire city, looking for opportunities to capture images of an event that they understood to be unprecedented; "most of them were aware that they were documenting with photographs something . . . previously unimaginable."[23] Several of these photographers focused their attention on the destruction of buildings and other urban landmarks with important symbolic meaning not just for them personally but for many of their fellow-citizens.[24] Photographers might also focus on a particular subject or site because they found it visually interesting or aesthetically compelling, regardless of its significance.

Almost all of these private photographers shared the belief that they were doing something that was "forbidden," if not explicitly "illegal." The author of a book on Heilbronn claimed that "taking private photographs was unthinkable . . . from August 1943 this was officially forbidden."[25] In Hamburg, even though Schmidt-Luchs wore a red armband to show that he had an official commission, "he was frequently apprehended by distrustful contemporaries and interrogated by subordinate officials."[26] The photographers interviewed by Deres and Rüther in Cologne said that they were well aware of the danger of being denounced to the Gestapo by fellow citizens for taking pictures of corpses, smoking ruins, or even simply for being spotted with a camera around one's neck or in one's hand. In Frankfurt am Main "it was known that in individual cases . . . the Gestapo pursued Frankfurt citizens who took private photographs after air attacks and destroyed the film."[27] The Gestapo was probably concerned about the challenge these illicit photographs could pose to the Nazis' own propaganda, "whose pictures were supposed to stimulate the will to carry on, hatred of the enemy, and unshakeable belief in the Final Victory."[28]

The conditions under which these private, unofficial photos were taken imposed important restraints on the form as well as the content of the images. To reduce the risk, some photographers devised ingenious methods of taking photos unobserved, such as photographing from a moving bicycle or through the window of a car, or even through the buttonhole of the coat that the photographer was wearing.[29] This meant that it was seldom possible to compose a shot; "in these situations they frequently photographed without putting the camera to their eye."[30] One of the photographers interviewed in Cologne claimed that "it was all luck, from A to Z."[31] People are seldom to be seen in these unofficial photographs. Fear of detection encouraged some photographers to take their pictures when other Germans were not in the streets. Others took pictures from the safety of their rooms through open windows.[32] As a result, most of these photos show "destroyed apartment buildings and businesses, churches as well as empty streets and squares displaying traces of the destruction."[33] If people did appear in these unofficial pictures, they were normally shown at a safe distance from or with their backs to the photographer. When people looked directly into the camera, and realized that their picture was being taken, they often appeared to be either anxious or angry.[34]

Inevitably, an aura of secrecy and danger was attached to these unofficial photographs. They seemed to convey forbidden knowledge. It is hard to know, however, to what extent this dangerous quality is a postwar accretion of meaning intended to make these particular photos more valuable and perhaps also to distance the photographer from any association with the Nazi regime.[35] Some of the photographers interviewed by Deres and Rüther portrayed their unofficial picture taking as acts of resistance, although others dismissed such claims.[36] Many of the photographers interviewed took precautions even after they had finished photographing the ruins. One sent his exposed film to his father who was working for the German railway system in Posen to have it developed.[37] Others only made contact sheets from their negatives and some of the exposed film was not developed until many years afterwards.

Despite the risks involved, some professional and amateur photographers did take illicit photographs of dead bodies. Andres's unauthorized pictures of the results of the firebombing of Hamburg included a gruesome scene of charred human bodies. He hid the negatives of these photographs until after the war.[38] Amateur photographs taken by the architect Hermann Weber in Nuremberg included pictures of "horribly mangled victims."[39] In Dresden, Heinz Kröbel, a building engineer from Leipzig, took a series of photographs in the town center after the February 1945 raids that included pictures of the corpses still on the streets before many of the people who had been killed were cremated in huge piles on the Altmarkt on February 20, 1945.[40] Kröbel offered his photographs to the city of Dresden, but they were not published until 1994 when they appeared in an exhibition catalog.[41]

After 1945, photographers could operate more freely, but certain subjects had now become harder to photograph.[42] Dead bodies had been removed from the streets. Other corpses still lay buried in the rubble, but few photographers followed the example of Richard Peter in Dresden, who accompanied recovery teams into the air-raid shelters submerged under mounds of rubble, where he was able to take pictures of bodies and other human remains.[43] This was a gruesome task. In his memoirs, Peter described the conditions under which he worked:

> The rescue squads always kept me up to date . . . so that I missed scarcely any opportunity to take photographs of the indescribable horror in the air raid shelters cleared of rubble, [which were] more shocking and more convincing than the best written description. . . . When I got into the streetcar, after spending many hours in these pestilential holes, I had to get out again at the next stop. . . . I waited for the next tram in the vague hope that perhaps this time I would encounter other passengers with less sensitive noses. After making numerous changes, I had to scamper swiftly into the bath and clean myself. From the soles of my shoes to the tips of my hair.[44]

At least 30 professional photographers took pictures of Dresden and Berlin after 1945, but they concentrated on the material devastation of these cities and on the attempts of postwar Germans to survive in the ruins and to rebuild their everyday lives.[45] In Berlin, Friedrich Seidenstücker, Fritz Eschen, Henry Ries, and Horst Urbschat all took major photo series between 1945 and 1950.

Working for the East Berlin Building Administration (Bauverwaltung) between September 1948 and January 1953, Emil Tiedemann took a series of unusual panoramic photographs of buildings.[46] Even Hitler's personal cameraman, Walter Frentz, took still color photographs of ruins in Dresden and Berlin (as well as in Nuremberg, Munich, Stuttgart, Freiburg, Paderborn, Ulm, Cologne, and Heilbronn), both before and after the end of the war.[47] American, British, and Russian military and civilian photographers also took pictures of Berlin after 1945. So, too, did Jewish photographers such as Henry Ries[48] or Abraham Pisarek,[49] both of whom had survived the Holocaust. Several American photographers who came to take pictures of the Nuremberg trials also photographed the ruins of that city.[50]

The Picture Work of Local Publications, 1949–67

The images that appeared in local publications after the war certainly reflected "contemporary understandings about which photographs do a particular kind of work."[51] Yet the decision to publish some photographic images and not others was also influenced by quite practical considerations of access, time, and money. For his 1967 book on the bombing of Stuttgart, Franz Bardua used images from a wide range of sources: the Stuttgart city archive, the Federal State Picture Service (Landesbildstelle) in Stuttgart, pictures taken by official German Army Propaganda Company photographers during the war, the *NS-Kurier* newspaper, the *Württembergische Zeitung* newspaper, and his own private collection. Thirteen of the 67 images reproduced in the book came from foreign sources: the Imperial War Museum London (9 pictures) and *Life* magazine (4 pictures). Bardua had been able to devote years to the research, had probably traveled to foreign archives, and had also been able to pay the fees required to reproduce certain images. Most of the authors of local publications had neither the time nor the funding that made Bardua's book possible. Lacking these resources, they were considerably more constrained in their use of images, restricting their choices to the most readily available and affordable pictures from public archives and commercial picture libraries. Although large numbers of photographs were deposited in these public institutions, many images remained in private hands for decades and were seldom available, or even known, to the authors of local publications. Archives had limited space and did not take all the photographs that might be offered to them.[52] The organization of the images that had been deposited in public archives also reflected archivists' assumptions about which photographs were relevant to the bombing war and which were not. Certain pictures might remain invisible because of the way they had been catalogued. Where, for example, might one come across photographs of Germans physically abusing, even lynching downed Allied airmen?[53] Or pictures of the auction and distribution to Germans who had been "bombed out" of furniture and other household items stolen from Jews all over Europe when they were deported to their deaths in Eastern Europe? It took 30,000 freight cars to haul into Germany the requisitioned goods of West European Jews. Most of this was destined for cities that had been bombed. Frank Bajohr estimates that 30,000 Jewish households in Germany and Western Europe were broken up into 100,000 Aryan homes in Hamburg alone.[54]

Between the late 1940s and the 1960s, the authors of local publications established a visual repertoire that focused heavily on certain motifs, primarily ruins (which I will explore in greater detail in the following chapter) but also postwar reconstruction. The images used in the 1949 Paderborn book, which included numerous drawings, were meant to show "the beauty of the city before the great doom smashed it [to pieces]," as well as the ruins of the city after the bombing. Most of the photographs included in the 1953 book on Kaiserslautern were repetitive scenes of ruins that might be found in almost any German city at the end of the war. Human subjects were present in only a few of these pictures. Wilms's short book on Zweibrücken (1955), just 49 pages long, included 13 images; 12 of these were photographs, while one was a map showing the building plans for the city center. These images were quite conventional and restrained, showing two destroyed churches, the heavily damaged Pestalozzischule, the ruins of the castle, and the state court prison. Other ruin pictures showed the remains of the city's high street (Hauptstrasse) immediately after the bombing and later, after cleanup work had already begun. Wilms's book included no pictures of dead bodies and no juxtapositions that showed how buildings had looked before they were destroyed. Only one pair of photographs compared the old festival hall after it was destroyed with the postwar reconstruction of the same building. In the 1953 book on Hanover, photographs of ruins greatly outnumbered images of buildings before the bombing. The book included 27 photos of individual ruined buildings and one high-angle panoramic shot of the ruins in the city center, probably taken from one of the remaining church towers. Five photographs showed people in the ruins. The captions that accompany these photographs were extremely terse ("The Dead City," "Destroyed Industrial Works," and so on). In Nadler's 1955 book on Nuremberg, the captions did more of the picture work than in many of the other local publications. The caption attached to a photograph of the destruction in the center of the city (fig. 2) reads, for example: "A picture of horror—seen from the train station. This once was old Nuremberg . . . !

Fig. 2

Nuremberg's glory as an Imperial city lies buried under the piles of rubble. In this valley of sorrow, there are no more places to live. Only naked chimneys rise accusingly out of these ruins. In the background, the landmark of Nuremberg, the castle. . . . People believe it is undamaged. But that is only how it appears. . . ."

Like some of the other authors of local publications, Nadler used before-and-after pictures to give his readers a sense of what had been lost to the bombing. In one of these juxtapositions, however, the "before" picture is a genre painting rather than a photograph that exaggerates the visual contrast between the two images.

Some local publications also showed the new buildings constructed since 1945. The 1953 book on Hanover combined the past and the present in a single frame by showing new postwar housing that had been built in the area near a destroyed church that also appeared in the photo. Two pictures included near the end of the book turned the reader's attention toward the city's postwar economic recovery. The first shows Hanover's new "Trade Fair Building." Launched in 1947, the Hanover Export Trade Fair soon became an important symbol of the Cold War competition between West and East Germany. The Hanover Fair was intended as a direct competitor with the Leipzig Fair, "traditionally the most important fair in Germany."[55] The fair in Hanover soon became a symbol of Germany's export-led "Economic Miracle." In its very first year, the Hanover Trade Fair "was successful in closing export deals totaling 31.58 Million US Dollars" and made Hanover an important site of West Germany's vital international commerce.[56] No less important than the building in this photograph of the site of the Hanover Trade Fair are the rows of new cars filling the large parking lot. Many are Volkswagens, which had also become important symbols of West Germany's export-driven "Economic Miracle."[57]

Occasionally, there were surprises. One of the more curious photographs included in Nadler's book shows a monkey in the Nuremberg Zoo. The caption tells the reader that the sad animal seems to be thinking that "[h]uman beings are beasts." The monkey did not experience the end of the war and the pitiless carnage (Nadler had earlier described how forced foreign workers senselessly tortured and slaughtered animals in the zoo) because he had already succumbed due to a lack of bananas.

Hitler and the Nazis

Only one of these early postwar publications—Nadler's volume on Nuremberg—paid visual attention to Hitler and the Nazis. Nuremberg was intimately associated with the Nazi movement.[58] Although this key fact is not discussed in Nadler's text, some of the images in the book do refer to this connection. Yet the choice of pictures is strange because they are not drawn directly from the Nazi visual archive but from Allied propaganda during and after the war. The only images of Hitler in Nadler's book are photographs taken during one of Hitler's speeches that were incorporated into Allied propaganda brochures dropped over the city at night. The only picture of the site where the Nazi party rallies were staged is a photograph (fig. 3) taken by the Americans after Nuremberg was occupied.

Showing the Enemy

In the 1960s, two local publications expanded their visual repertoire by including photographs of Allied bombers and their crews. The images in a 10-page section of Herman Hasenclever's 1964 book on the bombing of Remscheid presented the bombing war, as the title of this section put it, from "The other side." The very first image was a map that showed the approach routes to Rem-

Fig. 3

scheid of Allied bombers. The map presents Remscheid as the abstraction it undoubtedly was to the Allied airmen who bombed it, one among a very large number of potential targets with nothing to distinguish it from all the many other German towns and villages in this section of the map than the spelling of its name. The map is covered with dozens of other place names. It was followed by a clipping from an unidentified German newspaper that published "[t]hree laconic sentences from the Armed Forces Report (*Wehrmachtsbericht*) of 31.7.1943 about the attack on Remscheid."[59] The caption makes no comment on the Nazi language used in the news story that identifies the raids as "[t]error attacks on Kassel and Remscheid." Juxtaposing the newspaper clipping and headline suggests that designating Allied air raids as "Terrorangriffe" is an appropriate description, from which Hasenclever makes no effort to distance himself in the caption.

The seven images that follow visually trace each of the important stages in the mounting of an Allied air raid. The photographs used were taken by the Allies. They appear in Hasenclever's book with captions in both English and German. Hasenclever clearly wanted his readers to understand that the planes shown in these individual photographs were only components of a much larger air armada sent to destroy the city. This message was difficult to convey visually, so the German caption attempted to point toward the larger picture: "they formed themselves into a stream of bombers." The overall impression these pictures and their captions tried to convey was that the British had mobilized large numbers of machines and men for the single, and "senseless," task of destroying German cities.[60]

Heinz Bardua's 1967 book on Stuttgart also included photographs of the enemy in the air war. No fewer than 18 of the 67 images in this book depicted Allied planes in the air attacking Stuttgart or other German cities or on the ground shot down by German flak or fighters. On the same page, Bardua paired two pictures of dead bodies. The top photograph, taken by a Propaganda Company (PK) photographer, showed the dead bodies of two "fallen Allied fliers" lying next to the wreckage of their plane. Below this, a picture (fig. 4) from the Municipal Historical Collection showed "[o]ne of 4,562 Stuttgart victims of the bombing."[61] This pairing could be interpreted as a visual confirmation of a statement by a "neutral observer" quoted by Bardua at the very beginning of his book, which suggested that both Allied airmen and German civilians should be seen as victims of the bombing; one definition of the air war was that "some people die in the sky while others burn to death in the cellars."[62] Yet this visual pairing might also lead viewers to question the validity of such an equation between the deaths of Allied airmen and those of Stuttgart's citizens when the number of German civilians killed was so much greater. This pairing might even have allowed some German viewers to see the bodies of the Allied airmen as signs of retribution for the hundreds of thousands of Germans killed by the bombs the Allies had dropped on Germany.

Other photographs showed that German fighters had indeed made the Allied bombers pay a heavy price for their attacks on German cities.[63] Bardua quoted a Swedish newspaper that reported that "these fighters . . . turn Allied bomb attacks against Germany into an inferno, in which the British and American fliers in their machines have to bear the same horrors and the same fear, as that which the German civilian population undergoes in the air raid shelters."[64] Bardua complained, however, that "Hitler gave preference to an intensification of the air attacks against Great Britain rather than the urgently necessary strengthening of defense of the Reich."[65] Night fighters were not the only weapons that Germany could deploy against the Allied bombers. Plates 9, 10, 11, and 12 showed the antiaircraft guns that also claimed considerable numbers of downed Allied planes: "the clout of the alert German air defense managed to hinder bombs being dropped on Stuttgart for almost a year after the war began."[66] In both the text of his book and these pictures, Bardua paid attention to an experience shared by hundreds of thousands of young men and women during the war, which previous postwar publications had seldom discussed or pictured—service at one of the many flak installations defending German cit-

Fig. 4

ies. Fifteen- and 16-year-old schoolboys were increasingly drafted into service at these flak installations, so that older men could be sent to the front. Many of these young boys were still in school; they continued to be given lessons at the site of the flak battery. Some of these young boys had already won medals before they turned 17 and were drafted into the Reich labor service or the army. Many of the postwar Germans who read Bardua's book and looked at these photographs would themselves have been members of this "flak helper generation" (*Flakhelfergeneration*).[67]

The Limits of Representation

The words and the images in local publications faced their most severe test when it came to depicting two extreme experiences of the bombing war—living and dying in the air-raid shelters and surviving a firestorm.[68] As the Allied bombing of German cities intensified, millions of German men, women, and children spent increasing amounts of their time in air-raid cellars and bunkers. In his 1970 book on Cologne, Fischer made clear to his readers that as the air war continued life was reduced to sitting in a shelter or a bunker:

> We eat, we drink, just as we did before. New, however, is the thesis and the anti-thesis. The thesis, that is the ruins. The anti-thesis, that is above all the concrete, the bunker, our air raid cellar. . . . These alone have become the realities of our lives.[69]

Air-raid shelters became sites of anxiety, fear, and sometimes death. Descriptions of life in air-raid cellars and bunkers tried to convey the fear felt by the ethnic Germans for whom the air-raid shelters and bunkers were reserved. Nadler's 1955 book on Nuremberg described a typical scene in a shelter during a raid:

> With their teeth chattering, a dozen people sit jammed together in the air raid shelter and do not say a word. As if responding to a command, they all buckle forward together every time that heavy bombs scream down in a particularly horrible way. As if responding to another order, they all breathe a sigh of relief, when they are still alive after the explosion and they know that the bomb had not hit their roof.[70]

In his book on Würzburg, Domarus observed that some people refused to leave the air-raid cellars during a firestorm because they believed that the burning streets were too dangerous or because they had been told to wait until the fire was under control; "[m]ost of them were suffocated by fire gas that pushed its way in or they died of the intense heat."[71] Domarus insisted, however, that under other circumstances deciding to stay in the cellar might have been the right decision—there was no real way of knowing; "there were also the opposite cases in which people survived the fire by staying in the cellar, while others who went outside were hit by falling beams or shrapnel from time delay bombs. It was all a question of fate."[72]

Descriptions of life in the air-raid shelters and bunkers included numerous horror stories of what happened when the people inside could not escape a firestorm or when a bomb hit the shelter directly. Fischer described the effects of a direct hit on an air-raid cellar in a Cologne hotel:

> Thirty-eight soldiers crouched in the cellar. . . . The Red Room and the White Room collapsed above their heads. That is the last thing they heard in this life. Then it was their turn. What remained was a pile of bricks, debris, dust . . . dirt, some scraps of their uniforms and of something that was once called a human being. Direct hit. Dead. Done. In Cologne, no

> one needs to break off the identity disks. Perhaps out there, on the frontline that still needs to be done by the medic or the pastor. But the medics and the pastors are with those others who are . . . partially carbonized.[73]

Although horror stories like this one dominated many of these local accounts, they were sometimes counterbalanced with tales of hope, of miraculous survivals and rescues. Fischer's book on Cologne also told the story of a woman and her 11-year-old daughter who were trapped for 36 hours in the rubble of a bombed house:

> The police approached the property from several different sides . . . finally they succeeded in finding a way in to undertake a rescue, meanwhile the mother had given birth to a child in the pitch black. They were all alive, the newborn the mother and the eleven year-old. Many others, who likewise confronted the higher power of fate were also saved.[74]

As much as they might focus on the horrors experienced in the air-raid cellars and bunkers, punctuated from time to time by stories of rescue and survival, few authors believed that it was really possible to convey what people had felt when they died. A report on the firebombing of Hamburg, published in a 1960 volume, insisted that "[n]ot even the most fantastic imagination could ever manage to fathom and to describe the scenes of horror and terror that were played out in numerous air raid shelters."[75] Bardua's 1967 book on the destruction of Stuttgart included a statement by an eyewitness that "indescribable scenes must have played themselves out here."[76] But if words were unable to convey the full horror of being trapped in a cellar or a bunker during an air raid, images do not appear to have compensated for this deficit. One type of bunker photograph shows these buildings under construction. Some of these images are Nazi-era propaganda photos meant to reassure Germans that they would be protected from the intensifying force of Allied air attacks. In these pictures, bunkers appear massive and unassailable. Other pictures show people lining up to be allowed into these huge bunkers, or running to get inside a bunker before the bombs hit the ground.

Photos also showed people leaving bunkers when an air raid was over—one shows people who had been trapped in a bunker by fire but who managed to escape because firemen created a path through the flames with the water from their hoses. Another photo shows people emerging from a bunker after the very last raid of the war. An aerial view demonstrates that a bunker is the only structure left standing in a vast sea of ruins. Other photographs taken after raids showed, however, that bunkers could be severely damaged by large Allied bombs or by direct hits and that the people sheltering in them would be killed.

Some photographs showed people being rescued from air-raid shelters after being buried alive. However, Germans seldom saw the remains of people who had died in the air-raid shelters. Even these gruesome images could only allude to the suffering experienced by German civilians as they suffocated or were incinerated in these bomb shelters.[77] That some Germans thought it was important to visualize scenes not captured in any photograph may be inferred from the fact that one postwar publication included drawings by an artist who tried (although not very convincingly) to imagine the death-throes of German civilians trapped in bomb shelters.[78] The need to show and to see what Germans had suffered in the air-raid shelters might, in part, have been a reaction to the strict censorship under the Nazi regime that resolutely refused to allow photographs to be published that depicted the most traumatic experiences of the civilian population during the war.[79] In Hamburg, official Nazi propaganda transformed the air-raid bunker into "an idyllic village community."[80] This depiction in the local press of the "community" that was allegedly produced at the site of bunkers could only have appeared as a cynical attempt to obscure the actual "tearing apart of families and entire urban neighborhoods."[81]

The growing gap between official propaganda and everyday experience may have encouraged some Germans to take their own pictures.[82] Yet these private photographs also tended to "play-down the traumatic bunker-experience . . . denial and trivialization of the consequences of the war for the (civilian) population remained central."[83] A series of private photographs taken in a Hamburg air-raid cellar shows Germans smiling as they sit on the stairs smoking cigarettes or as they continue a birthday party that has been interrupted by an air-raid warning. These particular private pictures laid claim to a semblance of normality in a historical context that had made extreme violence an everyday experience. In other photographs, the atmosphere inside the air-raid shelter was distinctly less convivial. Two photographs included in a book on Aschaffenburg, published in 1970, show that these shelters were very overcrowded. In the top photograph (fig. 5) there was scarcely room to move. People were piled up four high on bunk beds. Those sitting on benches looked uncomfortable and no one was smiling. In the bottom photograph (fig.6), only the young child in the center-foreground smiled. Most of the adults seemed to be either bored or anxious.

After the war, the Allied occupiers blew up some of the major bunkers in German cities. Photographs of the bunkers that remained reminded Germans

Fig. 5

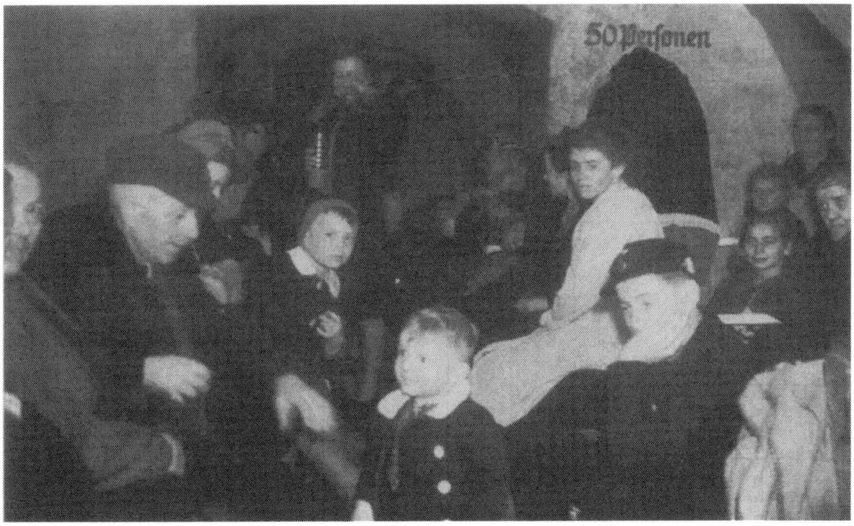

Fig. 6

not only of the wartime trauma of the bombing but also took on additional layers of meaning, drawing attention, initially, to Germany's postwar housing crisis. A picture of a woman being evicted from a bunker, showed, for example, that well into the 1950s some bunkers were still being used as emergency housing for people who had been bombed out or who were refugees. By the 1960s, the construction of new housing meant that most of the Germans made homeless by the war no longer had to be sheltered in bunkers. In Hamburg, bunkers were converted into hotels, exhibition halls, workshops, even film and television studios.[84] A photograph on page 85 of Schmid-Luchs's 1967 picture book shows the Wielandstrasse in postwar Hamburg. In 1941, the authorities had authorized construction of a bunker on this street. Residents of the neighborhood started to use the bunker in 1943 "even though the concrete had not yet properly dried."[85] During the massive British air raids in July 1943, an explosive bomb broke through the concrete and ripped open the air shaft of the bunker. That same night, the entire Wielandstrasse was reduced to rubble; only two houses remained undamaged. The postwar photograph shows that after the war new houses had been built in this street to replace those destroyed in the bombing. The bunker remains as an imposing physical reminder of the bombing war. Too massive to be destroyed and removed after the war, the bunker "today acts . . . as an alien body between the neat rows of houses built in the 1950s. It serves as a warehouse. And as a reminder of a time that people would like to forget."[86] At the same time, however, this photograph shows that Hamburg has overcome the postwar housing crisis. Photographs of bunkers like this one now became symbols of "the rise of the Phoenix from the ashes, the happy metaphor used to describe Hamburg's reconstruction into the 1960s."[87]

Firestorms

How did images and words respond to the challenge of depicting the most novel and frightening experience of the bombing war—a firestorm? A report by the Hamburg Police president published in a 1960s collection of materials about the damage to German cities caused by the Allied bombing offensive concluded that,

> Fire storms were the cause of the . . . heavy damage, [and] the exceptionally high number of dead victims by comparison with earlier attacks. As a result of [these firestorms], primarily during the second big attack on the night of 27–28 July, a situation was produced which must be described in every respect as new and unimaginable.[88]

Firestorms might be produced when bombers dropped explosives followed by huge numbers of incendiaries that set fire to the house materials destroyed by the explosives.[89] A second installment of explosives drove the firefighters back into the shelters with the result that fires were able to spread unhindered. Large numbers of small fires quickly joined together to form huge area conflagrations. And this produced a firestorm that could heat the air to 600, 800, or even 1,000 degrees. The heated air rose rapidly, sucking in cooler air from all around the fire that in turn fueled the fire itself. Clouds of glowing sparks blew across wide areas starting fires outside the radius of the original fire. The reports written soon after the Hamburg firestorm that were published in 1960 emphasized the futility of trying to escape from the "unprecedented hurricane of fire."[90] The speed with which the firestorm developed "defeats every intention and every plan for creating a defense of the population . . . [before] the necessity of taking flight can be recognized, the path to safety has often been cut off."[91]

The descriptions of firestorms that appeared in postwar publications fell into two basic categories: eyewitness reports and technical explanations. Eyewitnesses struggled to find a language to convey their unprecedented experience. Sometimes they lapsed into clichés, describing what they had experienced as an "apocalypse," "hell," or an "inferno." But eyewitnesses also reported details of the firestorm's effects on human bodies that functioned as the kind of shock images photographers were seldom able to capture in a picture. One eyewitness reported, for example, that "the people caught in the open by waves of embers and showers of sparks were thrown to the ground and burned up. Others, transformed into living torches, jumped from tree to tree in the 44 meter wide boulevard, screaming horribly. . . . This morning at 2 am there were still burning corpses on the melted asphalt of the sidewalks. All of those, primarily women and children who had managed to escape from the alleys of the lower Old City into the boulevard in the hope of finding protection under the double rows of linden trees, were asphyxiated by the dense smoke, their bodies burned and carbonized there."[92] Another eyewitness described how during the five hours that he and his wife had been laying on the ground in one of the city's squares, seeking to escape showers of sparks, he had seen "many people burning like torches. Just five meters away from us a woman caught on fire and brought us also into danger . . . my wife got up and tried to extinguish the fire. . . . She tried to pull the apparently dead woman away to another place; but she was not strong enough. Moreover, the [dead woman's] skin stuck to my wife's hands. We managed slowly to put out the fire, by throwing stones at the body."[93] A woman who was trapped along with her husband in public toilets during the raid could not escape because the fire was at the entrance; "[t]hree soldiers shot themselves to death. Because the flames from the burning bodies threatened to reach us, I told my husband to use our rug (which, along with our [important personal] papers was the only item we had saved) to beat out the flames. . . . Quickly but carefully, so that we did not slip on the bodies, we escaped outside."[94]

Trying to grasp what they had experienced, the survivors of a firestorm fastened upon particular details and images. They were stunned, for example, to discover that people could quite literally be incinerated by the firestorm:

> The destruction . . . is so radical that there is quite literally nothing left of many people. From a loose layer of ashes in a large air raid shelter, the doctors could only estimate the number of people who died here as between 250 and 300.[95]

Eyewitnesses were clearly horrified yet at the same time quite fascinated by macabre details of what had happened to the bodies of those killed in the firestorm:

> The Hammerland street was full of people. They squatted on the steps of the embankment stairs, they sat leaning against trees, they lay on the pavement with outstretched arms, pleading for help. Dead people, only dead people. The heat had forced many of them into surreal, mind-boggling positions. Slowly . . . one's gaze moved from the dislocated limbs to the no longer human faces whose horrific nature made them threatening. Mouths ripped wide open, protuberating eyes—faces from which in a final . . . convulsion, an enormous, powerful scream rose up as an anguished . . . accusation.[96]

The second main approach to a firestorm was to focus on the technical and scientific dimensions of its production and consequences. In 1978, Hans Brunswig published one of the most important books in this genre, *Feuersturm über Hamburg* (*Firestorm over Hamburg*). By 1994, the book had been reprinted in 10 new editions. In 2003, it was published as a special edition.[97] During the war, Brunswig had been a fire brigade captain and member of the Hamburg "Fire Extinguishing and Detoxification Services of the Air Protection Police."[98] He approached firestorms as a scientific problem. He was very concerned to get all the technical details right and to correct any false impressions created by the eyewitness reports. Firestorms could, he observed, be divided into two types—thermal and atmospheric. The Berlin Fire Department

Fig. 7

encountered the thermal variety during the Reichstag fire in 1933.[99] The second version was completely unknown until 1943. Both types occurred in Hamburg during the 1943 raids. The key here was the way that large numbers of separate, individual fires joined together to form a large area fire.[100]

Further in his book, Brunswig overwhelmed his readers with details of temperature increases, air currents, cloud formations, and the results of all of the various studies done after the war, including by American scientists, to explain what particular conditions, including building density, had contributed to the Hamburg firestorm.[101] Brunswig's language creates distance between the reader and the actual horrors of this particular form of destruction. The photographic images in this book have quite the opposite effect. They are among the most arresting to be found in any postwar publication. The first photograph (taken by Erich Andres) shows 25–30 people burned to death at the corner of Campestrasse and Bullerdeich: "They were probably caught by a vortex of fire, which raced around the street corner—from which there was no escape."[102] Another photograph (fig. 7) shows the little that was left of a bicycle messenger for the Air Defense Police who was unfortunate enough to have been caught in the open by the firestorm at the corner of Ausschläger-Weg and Hammerdeich.

Fig. 8

The next photograph (fig. 8) shows a line of dead bodies, some without clothes, killed on a street in Hamburg. Two other photographs (figs. 9 and 10) show the burned remains of two women on a staircase and the mummified corpse of a woman that was found in the toilet of an air-raid shelter.

Photography's "Reality Effect"

In his unusual book *In 1926. Living at the Edge of Time*, which experiments with ways of writing that attempt "to fulfill the desire for direct experience of the past" and "enhance the illusion of being-in-a-past-world," Hans Ulrich Gumbrecht decided not to "include photographs and other visual documents . . . For they produce an effect of immediacy which easily overwhelms any that can be provided by a text."[103] The authors of postwar publications on the bombing were not troubled by Gumbrecht's concern about this possible relationship between words and images. Indeed, they were eager to take advantage of the widely held belief—a belief they shared—that photographic images offered a peculiarly immediate and direct connection to the past.[104] Their big-

Fig. 9

Fig. 10

gest problem was not that they felt images might overpower words, but rather that photographs of the bombing war could not show everything. Although many of the photographs in the visual archive were horrifying, certain horrors remained beyond the photographer's grasp. Joachim Paech reminds us that "wars stipulate the form in which they can be observed and hence also remembered."[105] In World War I, it had been impossible to take real photographs of soldiers going "over the top" during actual combat—the photographer would have been killed in the attempt. The "combat" photos to be found in the visual archive of the First World War are "staged" images, usually taken behind the lines during training exercises.[106] How Germans could visualize the bombing war after 1945 was also determined by the conditions under which the available photographs (or, more rarely, film footage) had originally been taken.[107] There are, for example, no photographs of people on fire during a bombing raid. Any photographer close enough to take such a picture would probably also have been consumed by the flames.[108] Words might stand in for the photographs that could not be taken, but even eyewitness testimony could only tell readers what those who survived had seen and felt. It could not retrieve the experiences of those who had been killed.

The massive destructive force of Allied explosive and firebombs could at best be imagined with the photographic record of the traces of the violence that had been delivered from the air. A survivor of the 1943 Hamburg firebombing insisted, for example, that

> The impression produced by looking at a burned-out city neighborhood is colorless in comparison with the fire itself, the howling of the firestorm, the wailing and screaming of the people who are dying and the bangs made by the . . . bombs. To be able to depict exactly this seems important because the calamity is as much to be seen in the course of the destruction itself as in the facts this destruction realizes.[109]

The remarks of this eyewitness remind us that senses other than sight were intensely engaged during and after an air raid. Eyewitnesses insisted on the importance of noises such as the uncanny howling and the actual physical experience of hurricane force winds. Interviewing Germans after the war, James Stern concluded that "a striking number . . . had been temporarily or permanently deafened by continual bombardment."[110] Smells were also vital elements of this experience, especially afterwards—the smell of burnt and rotting flesh (as well as the buzzing of tens of thousands of flies); "[t]he heat of a summer day lay over the 'dead city.' A burnt smell mixed heavily with the sickly sweet odor of decay. . . . The smell of decay clung to us and we carried it with us on our clothes and in our hearts as well."[111] Yet neither words nor images were capable of fully capturing and conveying what people had heard and smelled.

The authors of local publications were well aware that photography had been unable to document all the realities of the air war. But they also knew that the popular belief that photography was a documentary medium—that it reproduced reality—might allow them to use photographs to stimulate emotions and to engage their viewers' imaginations. Photographs could be manipulated to create perceptions that differed in significant ways from the historical realities. Although based on photographs of real people or events, visual myths might be created that could significantly influence Germans' understandings and memories of the bombing war and its aftermath.[112] One good example would be the iconic "Women of the Rubble" (*Trümmerfrauen*) photographs that have circulated so widely since 1945. Photographs of *Trümmerfrauen* were used to create a powerful myth about the role women had played in clearing the ruins and beginning to rebuild German cities. "[W]omen of the rubble became a central symbol of the era . . . [they] came to personify West Germany's reconstruction."[113] Marita Krauss and Leonie Treiber have shown, however, that the historical reality was not what these images suggest. In most German cities, "removing the rubble was . . . organized differently from the beginning: it was in the hands of professional construction companies who employed overwhelmingly men."[114] The Allied occupying powers sometimes also supplied trucks, heavy equipment, and manpower to help with the cleanup.

Physical manipulation of photographic prints could also shape readers' perceptions of ruined cities. Two remarkably similar sets of photographs taken after the war in Nuremberg and Cologne illustrate the subtle but important differences that could be achieved by retouching the original images. Nadler's book on Nuremberg included two photographs of priests and nuns moving through the city's ruined streets during a Corpus Christi procession right after the war (figs. 11 and 12). Like the very similar but better-known photographs taken by Hermann Claasen in 1946 in Cologne, the Nuremberg pictures show signs of the renewal of religious faith in the devastated city. Unlike Claasen's Cologne pictures, the images from Nuremberg and the captions that accompany them also draw attention to the evidence of material recovery that can already be seen in the ruins (the rails for wagons carrying rubble out of the ruins).

The caption of one of Nadler's photographs reads: "Shocking and at the same time accusatory picture documents, realistically captured by the photographer Ludwig Harren. This was old Nuremberg . . . ! Even someone who knew

Fig. 11

Fig. 12

the *Altstadt* well could scarcely guess, that this picture was taken from the Kaiserstrasse over the Pegnitz and beyond. In this bleak gray on gray, the white choir robes of the priests have as enlivening an effect as the narrow white panels on the hoods of the nuns taking part in the Corpus Christi procession, who pass by the ruins of the glory of the Imperial city murmuring prayers. . . . Scarcely a simple dandelion sprouted on this rubbish heap on this pretty summer day.—'Here, once stood Nuremberg . . . !' But in the foreground a ray of hope—the rails [for the wagons that will remove the rubble . . .]".

Claasen, on the other hand, wanted his readers to see only the symbols of religious renewal. Through extensive retouching of the two photographs he had used to create a panorama, Claasen got rid of any signs in the ruins suggesting that Cologne was beginning to recover from the bombing such as an advertisement for a fish dealer and an electric cable running across the picture. He also created a somber mood by rendering the printed version of the photo darker than the original. The endless rows of nuns crossing in front of the ruins in their dark habits were meant to provide a convincing manifestation of the renewal of faith caused by the catastrophe. This message was not to be combined, as in the two Nuremberg photographs, with any reference to signs of material recovery.

Photographs might at times even be used to deny reality. A comparison of two picture books on Nuremberg published in 1947 and 1953 reveals an unexpected irony; the collection of photographs *Unvergängliches Nürnberg* (1953) is actually less "truthful" than the portfolio of drawings, *Nürnberg. Bilddokumente* (1947). Although photographs were culturally coded as a documentary medium, the photographs in *Unvergängliches Nürnberg* consistently engaged in visual denial of the destruction. The way this 1953 book is structured, it would be hard to tell simply from looking at the photographic images that anything at all had been destroyed in Nuremberg. All of the 126 pictures included in this book show the city's historic buildings or exterior and interior details of specific structures. It is possible to detect traces of war damage in only one of these photographs.[115] The publishers of the 1947 portfolio of drawings clearly thought, on the other hand, that it was important to show the ruins that the 1953 book ignored. The introduction to *Nürnberg. Bilddokumente* explained that the Nazis lacked all respect for the hallowed tradition of Nuremberg and had robbed the city of its cultural-historical significance. Then they had plunged Germany into a war that consigned Nuremberg to destruction. In 1945, "[o]ne of the most beautiful cities in the world lay in ruins—but its ruins insistently urged the living to engage in thoughtful planning and creative redevelopment. May the honorable memory of our great masters and the dirge of the somber ruins unite all those of good will to (engage) in collective creation and construction. Everyone should know that great things succeed only as the result of energetic commitment."[116]

These examples remind us of the importance of the relationship between images and words. Photography's ability to stimulate viewers' imaginations and to engage their emotions depended to no small degree on the connection between the images and the texts in which these pictures were embedded.[117] This did not mean, however, that the power of an image was ever completely subordinated to the text. Although the choices made by the photographer might delimit what viewers could see in a single photograph or series of photographic images, photographs "always capture something more and something different than . . . the photographer consciously wanted to picture."[118] Christopher Pinney argues that because "[t]he photographer can never fully control the resulting photograph . . . that lack of control and the resulting *excess* . . . permits recoding."[119] Whether the words that accompanied a photograph could actually stabilize the meanings of the image might also depend on the wider universe of images and everyday visual experiences that Germans brought to their contemplation of any specific picture. Alf Lüdtke suggests that these other "pictures in their heads" could encourage "self-assertive ways of looking" that allowed viewers to recode the meanings of the images offered them. In 1965, for example, Armin Schmid's book on the firebombing of Frankfurt became one of the first local publications to include any direct visual references to the persecution of German Jews. Two photographs (figs. 13 and 14) showed the deportation of Frankfurt Jews to Theresienstadt in the autumn of 1943.[120]

Schmid tried to control the effects of these two pictures. Acknowledging that the extermination of the Jewish citizens of Frankfurt was one of the "most terrible chapters" of the city's history, he nevertheless placed most of the blame on Nazi officials. The local Gauleiter Springer was depicted as a "fanatical Jew-hater" who delighted in beating up Jews—including women and children—as they were waiting at the Great Market Hall to be deported to the East.[121] Ordinary citizens of Frankfurt do not seem, in Schmid's story, to have been involved in the persecution of the Jews that began with Kristallnacht in 1938. Schmid insisted that many ordinary Germans continued to be "friendly" toward Frankfurt's Jews, providing them with food and taking care of their valuables when they were deported so that these goods would not be confiscated by the Fiscal Office. He also claimed that ordinary Germans had employed Jews in their businesses and hid them from the Gestapo: "For doing this, some of these brave citizens had to go to prison or a concentration camp."[122] The images Schmid used also helped because they spared readers the full horror of the Holocaust. They showed Jews being deported from Frankfurt

Fig. 13

Fig. 14

to the East but not the ghettos and mass shootings that awaited them once they arrived. And because these photographs were taken by the Gestapo or by municipal authorities who wanted to compile a visual record of their own efficiency and "correct" behavior, they hid the very real physical violence (which Schmid does describe in his text) that accompanied the deportation of Jews from German cities.[123] Yet Schmid's remarks might not have prevented some of his readers/viewers from asking what had happened to these Frankfurt Jews after these photographs were taken, especially if these readers/viewers had already seen some of the pictures published five years earlier in Gerhard Schoenberner's *The Yellow Star*, the first and still the best known illustrated book on the destruction of the European Jews.[124]

CHAPTER 3

The Meanings of Ruins

"Shock Pictures": Pictures of Bodies/Photographs of Ruins

Jörg Arnold has suggested that during the Allied air war against Germany hundreds of thousands, perhaps even millions, of Germans must have seen the dead and mutilated bodies of their relatives, neighbors, and friends in the now-ruined streets and buildings that had once been the normal context of their everyday lives. Germans carried these images of extreme violence in their heads, but they also preserved them in writing and in photographs. Throughout the war, photographers took pictures of Germans killed by Allied bombs. We would expect that the Nazis would have been eager to exploit these photographs of dead Germans in their propaganda against the Allies. Yet, surprisingly, Arnold has found only one publication that showed dead German children after the bombing of Freiburg on May 10, 1940 (which, after the war, was shown to have been the result of a mistake made by the Luftwaffe). Thereafter, pictures of dead German bodies were not displayed publicly. Even Goebbels's last big propaganda campaign about the bombing of Dresden did not use any of the horrific photographs of German bodies taken after the destruction of the city. Arnold concludes that "the gap between what was captured on film and what was shown publicly opened up more and more."[1] This visual body politics was specific to Nazi propaganda about the bombing. Goebbels did not hesitate to use photographs of the bodies of Germans who, it was alleged, were murdered and mutilated by the advancing Red Army in the east of Germany.

Arnold argues that after the war, even when such "horror pictures" (*Schreckensbilder*) were available, they were seldom shown publicly. Of course, the West Germans who had lived through the bombing war remembered what they had seen and the photographs of dead bodies published by the GDR ensured that these shock images were never totally absent from the public sphere. Arnold finds, however, that at the local level, which was decisive for the development of a postwar culture of remembrance, photos of the German dead were generally

Fig. 15

not exhibited in public. In their place, West Germans were shown images of ruins and of the cities as they had looked before they were destroyed.[2]

In this chapter I want, first of all, to scrutinize Arnold's argument by examining the full range of ruin and body photographs used in postwar local publications about the bombing war from 1945 to 1989. My main argument is that it was never simply a question of whether or not pictures of bodies or of ruins would be used in these postwar local publications but rather which kinds, in what ways, and in what relationship to each other? It is certainly true that photographs of ruins appeared far more frequently than pictures of dead bodies. Yet the visual restraint Arnold postulates was never quite as complete as he suggests. Photographs of the often gruesomely mutilated bodies of Germans killed by the bombing were rare but had certainly not become "[p]hotos that are not to be shown."[3] Well into the 1970s and beyond, some local publications continued to exhibit pictures of dead Germans. When local publications did not show photographs of corpses, graphic textual descriptions tried to help readers imagine what they did not see in images. I want also to show that the range of

Fig. 16

ruin photographs that appeared in local publications was more extensive and complex than Arnold suggests; many ruin photos were not simply "deserted."[4] They showed not only ruined buildings but also the Germans who had survived the air raids. What these Germans were doing and how they looked communicated complex, at times contradictory, messages to postwar viewers.

The pictures of corpses that were actually published put German suffering on display, yet some were definitely more gruesome than others. The dead bodies might show no traces of physical violence, they might even look as if the dead were simply asleep. Or they might be unrecognizable as human beings—charred clumps of flesh, for example. What remained to be photographed showed the ways in which these Germans had died.[5] If their bodies were unmarked, then they had probably died of carbon monoxide poisoning. On the other hand, people might have been burned to death or their already dead bodies might have been mummified by extreme heat when fire reached the air-raid shelter in which they had died. Others were killed by the intense concussion produced by the explosion of large bombs or air mines. People could also be killed by drowning when water mains burst and flooded cellars or even boiled alive by super-heated water.[6] Josef Fischer's 1970 book on Cologne brought two different types of pictures together on the same page (figs. 15 and 16).

Armin Schmid's 1965 book on Frankfurt included three photographs of dead bodies. One showed dead children laid out on the floor in a corner of a building. The children's bodies were not visibly mutilated. The caption to this photograph told the viewer that "a direct hit by a bomb killed 90 children and 16 women on the hospital staff."[7] Another photograph showing what looked like a death mask was described as the face of a "person trapped in the rubble in the Carmelite Church." It was followed by a photograph of corpses retrieved from that same church. These bodies had been covered over with sheets of cardboard but it was still possible to see their feet protruding out from the edges of this covering.[8] We have already seen that in 1978 Hans Brunswig published a series of gruesome photographs of Germans killed in the firebombing of Hamburg in July 1943.

Arnold begins his article with a statement made by Cardinal Michael von Faulhaber in June 1945 that if people around the world could see photographs of the bodies of Germans killed in Allied air raids they would be no less enraged than they had been by the shock pictures of concentration camp victims taken by the Allies when they liberated the camps.[9] Foreign observers at the time viewed claims such as this one as "strategies of denial and apologetics" meant to transform Germans from perpetrators and accomplices into victims by suggesting that these two forms of violence were in some way equivalent.[10] Arnold insists, however, that "well into the late 1950s, these pictures were shown less often than a consistent strategy of claiming equivalence would have suggested . . . [instead] the allied air war entered the visual memory of the nation through ruin and rubble photographs."[11] He argues that photographs of dead German bodies were not published more often because Germans who had survived the air war did not need these types of shock pictures to imagine the deaths the bombing had caused—they still carried around in their heads the gruesome sights of the mangled corpses of their relatives, neighbors, and friends. While this may be a valid suggestion about the attitudes of the Germans who had actually lived through the bombing, it is hard to see how it can apply to the younger generation born after the war. Nor does Arnold's argument explain why Germans appear to have needed pictures of ruins even though they were still living in the rubble after 1945.

I agree with Arnold's contention that photographs of Germans killed by Allied bombs were seldom used in local publications directly to equate German with Jewish suffering. But does this mean that Germans saw no other connections between these two types of shock pictures? I think it is reasonable to suggest that the postwar use of photographs of the bodies of Germans killed by Allied bombs might have been inhibited by visual associations with Allied photographs from the camps, and by the uncomfortable questions about German involvement in the genocide of the Jews that such associations could produce. Habbo Knoch argues that the German confrontation with the Allied photos of the liberation of the concentration camps in 1945 imposed lasting aftereffects on the West German culture of remembering "because defense against the visual shock was inscribed in the genesis of [West Germany's] own picture memory."[12] The piles of bodies and half-dead inmates that the Allies had discovered became negative reference points against which "visual taboo zones" were constructed in the Federal Republic.[13] Certain photographs of Germans killed in the bombing war might, on the other hand, challenge these taboos by reminding Germans of those other pictures of Jewish suffering and death in the Nazi camps; "photographs," as Susan Sontag puts it, "echo photographs."[14] Heinz-Peter Preußer suggests, for example, that "[a]s a German, when looking at the piles of bodies to be burnt in Dresden, one simultaneously recognizes Auschwitz."[15] One of the reasons that ruin photos became the primary visual signifiers of death and destruction in the air war may have been that they did not run the risk of conjuring up these associations with the bodies of dead Jews.

Ruin Pictures

Some scholars have suggested that pictures of the ruins of German cities offered a visual antidote to the photographs of piles of dead bodies in the liberated concentration camps with which the Allies confronted the Germans in 1945.[16] Yet ruin photos functioned as more than simply counterimages, a type of "photographic revanchism" designed to regain the visual and symbolic territory lost to the Allied pictures of the camps in 1945.[17] Anne Fuchs has recently suggested that "the prevailing interpretation of German rubble photography as a revisionist genre misses its central affective function for postwar Germans. The visual narrative unfolding in German rubble photography is more complex and nuanced than the binary between Allied concentration camp photography and German rubble photography would suggest."[18] Fuchs's analysis of Richard Peter's 1949 picture book, *Dresden, Eine Kamera klagt an! (Dresden. A Camera Accuses)*, claims that his ruin photos "provided postwar Germans with an iconic narrative that allowed them to contemplate and mourn a collective loss."[19] Yet the widespread use of ruin pictures in postwar publications also perpetuated Nazi visual strategies that, "[i]nstead of reporting the suffering of the civil population, . . . concentrated on . . . the destruction of German cultural and architectural monuments."[20]

Before and After Pictures

One of the key problems faced by the authors of local publications was that pictures of ruined buildings could all start to look the same. The 1953 book on Kaiserslautern appears to have been defeated by the problem that confronted all attempts to use ruin pictures to convey the fate of an individual town: their lack of specificity. Most of the photographs included in this book were repetitive scenes of ruins that might be found in almost any German city at the end of the war. Little distinguished these images from other photos of urban ruins. Only the captions anchored these images to a specific place and time.

One way to display an individual city's distinctive architectural and cultural loss was to juxtapose "before" and "after" pictures that contrasted the way the city had looked before it was destroyed with pictures of the same sites in ruins. The very first book about the firebombing of Dresden performed its "work of memory" exclusively by comparing images of well-known Dresden buildings before and after their destruction in February 1945.[21] Several of the books about other German cities published after the war claimed that the "old city" ("die alte Stadt"), the result of hundreds of years of cultural and architectural history, had quite simply been "killed" by the bombing raids. These books presented the bombing as the "downfall" or "death" of "die alte Stadt."[22]

Placing two photographs of a city, one before and one after its destruction, on the same page could produce a visual shock that might help readers perceive what Germans had felt when they first saw the fields of ruins left behind by Allied planes (figs. 17 and 18). Even lifelong inhabitants of a particular town or city no longer recognized locations that before the bombing they had known very well. In Hamburg, one eyewitness asked, "What actually remained of Hamm, Hammerbrook and Rothenburgsort[?] In the morning, there was much that I could not recognize, what I could see was a picture of total destruction."[23]

The iconography established by German romanticism aestheticized ruins. The extent and the rapidity of the destruction caused by Allied bombs made it difficult (if not completely impossible) to make these particular ruins romantic. Anne Fuchs observes, for example, that "the scale of the destruction of Dresden points to an excessive violence that unhinges the notion of a gradually passing time which is implied in the Romantic notion of decay."[24] Contemporaries were astonished by the speed with which these ruins had been produced.[25] Unlike the romantic ruins created by slow decay that had inspired poets in the 19th century, these were "premature ruins"; "the relationship of places that had been destroyed by bombs to romantic ruins was like that between an unexpected death in an emergency room and a dignified passing away at home at a ripe old age."[26] Two photographs of the same street in Ludwigshafen before (fig. 17) and after (fig. 18) a bombing attack demonstrate the shock effect of this sudden destruction.[27]

Other types of before-and-after pictures contrasted the city in ruins after the bombing with the reconstructed city after the war. W. G. Sebald argues that these before-and-after pictures

> make it look as if the image of total destruction was not the horrifying end of a collective aberration, but something more like the first stage of a brave new world. . . . From the outset, the . . . legendary and in some respects genuinely admirable reconstruction of the country after the devastation wrought by Germany's wartime enemies, a reconstruction tantamount to a second liquidation in successive phases of the nation's own past history, prohibited any look backward.[28]

Yet even in these photographs of reconstruction, viewers were expected to look backwards as well as toward the future; only the contrast with what cities had suffered and lost during the war made the postwar achievements meaningful.

Fig. 17

Fig. 18

By the 1960s, when most West (although not East) German cities had been rebuilt, the architectural and cultural losses produced by the bombing were compounded by a growing loss of visual memory.[29] "Before-and-after" pictures were the only way that the younger generation of Germans could see how the prewar cities or their postwar ruins had looked.

Ruined Churches

Ruined churches and religious buildings figured prominently in the visual record of the bombing. The ruins of churches might convey a variety of different meanings: loss, certainly, but also survival and the persistence of religious faith and hope. Damaged or destroyed churches might stand as surrogates for the mutilated bodies of Germans killed or wounded in the bombing, especially when the photographs of a ruined church focused on statues or icons of Christ on the cross. Some churches were important local landmarks and key symbols of local identity; their destruction by bombing signified cultural loss. Pictures of ruined churches might also implicitly indict the Allies for destroying German cultural patrimony.[30]

When they took pictures of churches, photographers focused on destruction, but they also paid attention to survival. The survival of the Cologne cathedral was presented as something of a miracle, because it sat right next to the city's main train station, "crossroads of the West. The Hohenzollern Bridge was its direct extension, a three-star [target] in the General Staff's Baedecker."[31] In his picture book *Gesang im Feuerofen, Köln, Überreste einer alten deutschen Stadt* published in 1947, for example, Hermann Claasen communicated the irony of the cathedral's survival by taking a picture of its still standing towers through the crumpled remains of the important railway bridge that led across the Rhine to the main train station.[32] Both Claasen and an unnamed photographer made the same point from a greater distance—a long shot of the Cathedral that showed it as the only intact structure in a field of ruins.

Ruined churches could function as war memorials. The Aegidienkirche was, for example, left as a ruin to serve as "the central site of remembrance for the dead which the city of Hanover had lost in the war and the frightful destruction."[33] A photograph of this ruined church was included in the 1953 book on Hanover.[34] In Darmstadt, Hamburg, Dresden, and Berlin, important churches were also left as ruins to remind local citizens and visitors about the air war.[35] Probably the best known of these is the Kaiser Wilhelm Memorial Church (Gedächtniskirche) on the Kurfürstendamm (Ku'damm), an important commercial avenue in West Berlin. Constructed between 1891 and 1895, the Gedächtniskirche was severely damaged by Allied air raids in 1943. Only the ruins of the old tower were left standing. After the war, some Germans wanted to rebuild the church. Others insisted that the ruins be completely demolished. In 1957, an architectural prize committee finally approved a design for a new building on this site that also preserved the damaged tower.[36] Since 1945, images of the ruined Gedächtniskirche have appeared in illustrated magazines, guidebooks, and picture-postcards, allowing even Germans who have never visited Berlin visual access to this important site of memory. Postcards for tourists identified the ruins of the Kaiser Wilhelm Memorial Church as an unmistakable emblem of West Berlin in the Cold War. Although these postcard images might still have reminded the viewer of the destruction caused by the Allied bombing, their main concern was to present the Gedächtniskirche not as a site of memory and mourning but as one of the many tourist attractions that a visitor to Berlin simply must see.

Photographers of cities in which distinctive landmarks were still intact—whether these were religious or secular buildings—could use photos of these recognizable structures to distinguish their ruins from those of other cities destroyed by the bombing. Pictures of Cologne's cathedral certainly served this purpose, as did photos of the Brandenburg gate or the Reichstag in Berlin. Pictures of important individual buildings that had survived the war helped establish the unique identity of a particular city. Smaller provincial cities that lacked similar landmarks were at a disadvantage. The tendency to equate German cities with their medieval and early modern buildings and neighborhoods made it difficult for cities that did not possess the same architectural heritage to claim special significance for their ruins. A book on Schweinfurt published in 1961 acknowledged that "[o]ur city . . . cannot claim to be an architectural pearl" but insisted that the city had also suffered architectural loss: "in the first four decades of this century [Schweinfurt] had grown into a clean, light industrial city (which now, however) looked like a witch's cauldron. Housing blocks became torches and huge bomb craters gaped out of the streets."[37]

Panoramas and Aerial Overviews

Ruins produced, quite literally, a loss of direction. Several of the authors of local publications commented on their sense of disorientation in the ruins of their own city—even someone who had lived in the same place their entire lives could no longer find their way in the ruins:

> I have had enough of this self-guided tour, want to go home. But which direction will take me there . . . ? Do I have to keep left or go right? My sense of orientation is on strike in this vale of sorrow, where every street looks like every other, every ruin, every pile of rubble looks like every other, just as one egg resembles another.[38]

A photograph by Horst Urbschat (fig. 19) emphasizes the unique problem of finding one's bearings in a city whose topography has been rendered unrecognizable by the bombing. The caption accompanying this photograph reads: "The large areas of destruction in Berlin made it difficult for postmen to find the addresses for their deliveries. At the old addresses, there were often notes such as 'we are still alive, are now in the Wilmersdorfer Street. . . .' Postmen in postwar Berlin therefore often had to cover long distances."[39]

In their attempts to convey the enormity of the destruction, postwar pub-

Fig. 19

lications sometimes included aerial perspectives. Aerial photographs tried to give viewers an overview of the "sea of ruins" that was virtually unintelligible at street level. Only an aerial view could begin to provide a sense of the immensity of the destruction. Yet the attempt to offer a view of the whole might be emotionally problematic because most of these aerial pictures had been taken by Allied air reconnaissance flights to survey the damage done by Allied bombers and to demonstrate the destructive power of Allied air raids to politicians, military leaders, and the Soviets.[40] German viewers had to be prepared to look at their city from the point of view of the planners of these air raids and of the Allied bomber crews rather than that of the German victims.

People in the Ruins: Signs of Life?

Ruin pictures were seldom simply the urban landscapes devoid of all human beings that Arnold suggests may have functioned as counterimages to photographs of dead bodies. They showed not only ruined buildings but also the Germans who had survived the air raids. Pictures of ruins taken immediately after the bombing could show firemen or Hitler Youth suppressing the remains of fires still smoldering in the ruins. Other photographs showed rescue teams trying to pull people out of the ruins. Looking at these pictures after the war, Germans may have found signs of hope—some people had after all managed to survive the horrors of being trapped in the cellar of a house reduced to rubble by the bombing. Postwar viewers may also have praised the bravery of the rescue workers who risked their own lives to save other Germans. Yet ruin pictures might also signify the loss of family members or friends who had not been rescued and whose bodies had never been recovered from the ruins. Postwar publications sometimes used pictures of the grave markers that had been placed in the ruins by relatives. These photographs reminded the survivors and the postwar generations that Germany's reconstructed cities had been built on the bodies of the dead.[41]

Buried in the ruins were not only the bodies of dead relatives and friends but also the family possessions and furniture that Germans had not been able to save. A picture book published by Hugo Schmidt-Luchs and his son, Werner, in 1967 observed that as the rubble was removed from Hamburg after the war,

> one snatches away from so many citizens the property accumulated through the diligence and parsimoniousness of entire generations which used to be set up in their own houses but which now is heartlessly, pitilessly shaken out into huge hollows at the periphery of the city. Eyes tear up at the sight of this sorrowful burial. Even after years have passed, many mourners cannot get over this . . . each day, they stand mourning at the ruins of their happiness, their property, their familial pride. They know how to judge and to value what the ancestors were required to deny themselves in their lives, so as finally to be able to build their own longed-for homes.[42]

Some photographs taken during the war showed German civilians desperately trying to save their furniture, household items, and personal belongings from bomb-damaged buildings. The caption to a picture taken by Schmidt-Luchs in Hamburg reads:

> In the middle of smashed up, burned out ruins of houses, a couple of people try to recover what is left of their belongings. Only with effort is it possible to pull and push the two-wheeled handcart through the rubble. This [visual] document could have emerged in any German city, it is universal.[43]

The caption for another photograph by Schmidt-Luchs told readers, "In June of 1944, thousands would have been happy with a mattress, a blanket, a wash basket full of clothing. Wealth was a full suitcase, an intact place to live was a fortune."[44]

Other photographs showed furniture on the streets but without the individuals or families to whom these items belonged. What has happened to the owners at the moment that these pictures were taken? Have they gone off to rescue other household goods? Are they looking for missing relatives or friends? Are some of them dead? These photographs could suggest that as long as furniture and personal items had been saved, family life might continue. Yet these images could also remind postwar viewers that by the end of the bombing war, large numbers of Germans had lost everything. And, finally, these photographs might also remind some Germans that during the war the Nazis had replaced furniture destroyed by Allied bombers with furniture stolen from Jews deported to the East.[45] In his book on Cologne, Josef Fischer observed that "[f] urniture was supposed to be taken out of Holland, Belgium, and Alsace,"[46] without explaining who had previously owned this furniture. Germans reading Fischer's book, which was published in 1970, might however have been aware that in 1971 the West German parliament passed a Federal Restitution Law that constructed a new legal framework for dealing with claims about several types of property confiscated from Jews during the war, including "the spoils of large-scale 'furniture operations' in which occupation authorities in France, the Netherlands, Luxembourg, and Belgium had shipped off furniture belonging to deported Jews for distribution to Germans who had lost their household possessions during air raids."[47] Between 1943 and August 1944, the German national railway system delivered at least 2,699 freight cars to the city and Gau of Hamburg alone, which were "packed with furniture, household items and clothing. The freight cars came from France, Holland and Belgium and contained the possessions of deported Jews."[48]

The Gender of German Suffering: Women, Men, and Children in the Ruins

Jörg Bernig reminds us that "the bombing war was above all an experience of women, children and old people."[49] Yet local publications seldom paid much direct attention to the experiences and activities of women. Only in the 1980s and 1990s did women's history and oral history projects begin to reconstruct the gendered dimensions of the bombing war.[50] Women did, however, figure prominently in the postwar visual record of the bombing, although the women pictured in postwar publications were frequently not the women who, along with their children, had been the primary victims of the Allied air raids. They were the semimythical "women of the ruins" (*Trümmerfrauen*) who, so it was claimed, had begun to rebuild Germany's devastated cities after 1945 with their own two hands.[51]

Pictures of *Trümmerfrauen* dominated the images of women presented in early postwar publications. One of these pictures, included in the 1953 volume on Hanover, showed a woman working on her own in a way that emphasized the magnitude of the task that confronted her (fig. 20). The picture is taken from below. The low-angle of the shot emphasizes and probably exaggerates the size of the pile of rubble that this woman had to clear before rebuilding could begin.

Trümmerfrauen were also photographed working in groups. An unknown photographer took a picture of three women pushing a heavy wagon filled with rubble (fig. 21). What remains of the skyline of Dresden can be seen in the background. In another photograph, women in Berlin push a heavily loaded cart along rails that lead in the direction of the ruined Reichstag. Both pictures convey a sense of the physical exertion required of women to clear the ruins and the cooperation that made this possible. Both pictures suggest that women had, quite literally, to pull together in order to begin the reconstruction of German cities. What Allied men in the sky had destroyed, German women would rebuild.

Photographs of "rubble women" were, as Marita Krauss puts it, "Part of an iconography of hope . . . they stood . . . for the new beginning. It was mostly younger women who were photographed with firmly knotted head scarves and aprons, sometimes wearing trousers: these women conform to the type of 'Female Work Comrade' from the [Nazi] League of German Girls and the Labor Service."[52] Despite the effort their work required, the women clearing the rubble can often be seen smiling in these photographs; "the work appears to be fun for these women."[53]

Asking about these women's histories under Nazism did not serve the myth that these photographs tried to construct. Krauss shows that in Munich the women in one of these photos had been compelled to do the work because they were members of the Nazi party. Only by ignoring or denying "the active role of women during the Nazi years"[54] could all women working in the ruins be depicted as selfless volunteers, untainted by the Nazi past, giving Germany a fresh start.

Some photographs could, however, undercut the general visual celebra-

Fig. 20

Fig. 21

tion of the role played by "rubble women." These pictures showed women who were exhausted, perhaps even crushed by their labors. A photo published in 1965 (fig. 22) shows a woman working in Dresden who is almost buckling under the weight of the five bricks that she is carrying from the ruins.

In some photographs, the "rubble women" are actually men. One of the very first postwar picture books on the destruction of Dresden, put together by Kurt Schaarschuch in late 1945, ended with a photograph of a male worker using a jackhammer to break up the rubble. Braun-Rühling's book on Kaiserslautern included two photographs showing adult males and young children collecting and stacking bricks from the rubble. Another photo, bearing the caption "so the clearing of the ruins began," showed six teenaged males as they worked in the ruins, passing bricks from one to the other.

Some photographs of postwar reconstruction concentrated on the machinery that was being used to clear the rubble, rather than on the people doing the work. The book on Paderborn published in 1949 included a photograph of "[t]he mechanical shovel, the powerful helper." Other photographs showed the immediate product of all of this work, male and female, hand and machine—endless piles of recovered bricks that transformed ruins into useful building materials.

Self-Help in the Ruins

Photographers were also interested in the efforts of ordinary Germans to find water, food, fuel for heating and cooking, and other necessities of everyday

Fig. 22

life after Allied bombs had disrupted or destroyed the normal sources of supply. Women figured centrally in these photographs. Women are the focus of attention in a photograph taken in Bremen after an air raid on November 26, 1943. The women in the picture have lined up to get water from the pump in the street when the bombing disrupted the normal water supply by damaging the underground water pipes. Around the women at the pump, a small group of young children has formed a perimeter. Only one man appears at the edge of this circle. The other men in the picture stand slightly away from the women at the pump.

If this photograph can be seen as a tribute to women's ability to overcome adversity, other pictures emphasized the exhaustion produced by trying to survive in the ruins. A photograph taken in Stuttgart after a major air raid in 1944 offers a different version of this same motif. In this picture, the woman drawing water from the "only source," the fire hydrant on the Leonhardsplatz, is alone and anonymous (we see her only from behind) and her body seems painfully bent forward to pick up the bucket.[55]

Pictures of old women in the ruins conveyed the uncomfortable message that some were struggling to survive both physically and mentally. Another picture taken in Bremen after the November 26, 1943, air raid (fig. 23) shows an old women supporting herself with a cane, painfully reaching down to gather a piece of firewood.

Even though they sometimes emphasized the huge difficulties of trying to survive in the primitive conditions created by the destruction of German cities, most of the pictures of "rubble women" could be integrated into a visual narrative that ended with a comforting conclusion—the reconstruction of German cities. On the other hand, images of women taken during or immediately after the bombing might evoke traumatic memories of the fear, anxiety, and suffering women (and children) had experienced while the air raids were actually taking place.[56] These photographs of women and children might also raise uncomfortable questions about the longer-term residue of wartime trauma in their lives after 1945. In interviews with German women about their experiences during the war, Margarete Dörr has found that "air attacks occupy the central place in their memories."[57] Germans who had been children during the war remembered the fear that gripped them when they heard the sound of air-raid sirens or as they sat with their mothers in the shelters while the bombs exploded above them.[58] It is perhaps not surprising, then, that pictures such as one that showed women and their children running to the nearest air-raid shelter in Hamburg during an attack were not published until much later.[59]

Nor does there appear to have been a great deal of space in the early post-

Fig. 23

war publications for pictures of women in the ruins after 1945 that could not convey as positive a message as images of the *Trümmerfrauen*, such as the picture of a young, homeless women in the ruins of Cologne, taken by an American photographer, John Florea. The woman is going somewhere with all her remaining possessions, which include a dog. At the moment that Florea took this picture, the young woman was taking a break to rest and to smoke a cigarette. The sullen expression on her face may suggest her annoyance with the photographer who wants to document her plight. Another type of picture of women in the ruins occupied an ambivalent status—photographs of stylish, well-dressed young women taken against a background of destruction. A photograph, also taken by an American photographer in July 1945 on the Ku-Damm in Berlin with the Gedächtniskirche in the background, shows a young, well-dressed woman holding the hand of a smiling young child as she walks along the avenue; several other well-dressed women are also on the sidewalk. The caption reads: "Defeated but smart." Germans who saw fashionably dressed women promenading in postwar Berlin might have regarded them as hopeful expressions of a commendable desire to return to normal life. But perhaps they would instead have drawn an unfavorable contrast with the "rubble women" in work clothes and trousers hard at work in the ruins.

Children in the Ruins

Below are two photographs taken during the bombing war, one in Aschaffenberg, the other in Bremen. The first picture (fig. 24) shows a young boy standing in the ruins of a building. The caption tells us that "[e]ven children save their last possessions from the ruins."[60] With these words, the child becomes another victim of the bombing war who, like the adult men and women we see in so many other photographs, tries to save what he can from his bombed-out home. The picture shows us that the Allied bombing war is cruel, since it makes no distinctions between men, women, and children. Children are not exempted from its destructive force. Pictures of children as victims of the bombing war could provide an indirect condemnation of the Allies who had planned and executed the destruction of German cities. Christoph Hamann observes in a different context that "[c]hildren are a symbol of innocence, weaker than adults [they are] powerless and unable to defend themselves. At the same time, they embody potential, the future, hope and survival. Whoever threatens children puts themselves in the wrong and risks the future."[61]

The boy in the first picture may have been posed in this location. He appears to be proud that he has managed to retrieve a jug and some other item (in his left hand). He props up a picture that he has also saved so that we can see it, but the photographer was too far away to allow us to discern what the picture shows, indeed whether it is a photograph or a print of a drawing, or something else. Nonetheless, it seems important to this boy—or to the photographer who posed him in these ruins—that he has managed to save an image from his life before the bombing.

Fig. 24

Fig. 25

In a second photograph taken in Bremen with a very similar motif, a boy has been posed standing in a bomb crater (fig. 25). We are given more information about this picture—it was taken in 1941, after the air raid on March 18, and the location is Togostrasse 17, Gröpelingen. The caption tells us that the child has been positioned in the bomb crater to give us an idea of just how big the hole in the ground is.[62]

In these two photographs, children are pictured—and in these particular instances have probably quite literally been posed—for different purposes. Although the subject and the composition of the two pictures are quite similar, I think they are meant to be read in two different ways. In the first picture, the child is a victim of the bombing; in the second, the child's body serves only as a measure of the destructive force of a single bomb. The first picture explicitly allocates this child (and by extension other German children) a place in the community of suffering and loss created by the bombing. In the second picture, the child's relationship to that community is not as clear. The same tension between depicting children as historical subjects and using their bodies as signs of something else runs through many of the pictures of children in the ruins, both during and after the war, which was an important motif for some photographers.

After the war, several photographers took pictures of children playing in the ruins. A photograph taken by Friedrich Seidenstücker in 1946, for example, showed a young boy in Berlin smiling as he sat on a "slide" he had made from two iron girders supported by rubble.[63] A series of Berlin photographs by Horst Urbschat showed children happily appropriating ruins for their own fun. Urbschat was, however, well aware that the ruins were not only a "huge adventure playground" but also a potentially deadly danger zone for children: "Many young boys and girls died in these years as the result of accidents when they were buried in debris . . . as they played in cellars."[64] Years after the war was over the ruins were still dangerous. Children who had escaped death during the bombing war might still be buried alive, and thus killed, by rubble—as many other children had been before 1945.

Conclusion

Ruin pictures appeared in a quite surprising array of different manifestations. The wide spectrum of pictures of ruins used in postwar publications could convey a considerable range of different and even competing messages. Perhaps this explains why ruin pictures have remained such a central element of the bombing war's visual repertoire since 1945. Ruin pictures displayed the utterly unprecedented destruction of German cites by Allied bombing, yet they also showed that certain key architectural symbols of local identity survived. When coupled with photographs showing how a city had looked before the bombing, ruin pictures played a melancholy role, emphasizing the irredeemable architectural loss. However, when paired with pictures of postwar buildings, ruin pictures celebrated the achievements of reconstruction. Pictures of people in the ruins might display the exhaustion and despair inscribed in the faces and on the bodies of the Germans who had survived the bombing. Ruin pictures also showed that many Germans had not survived, and some of these photographs drew attention to the horrific ways in which these people had been killed. But photographs also showed Germans who were determined to rescue relatives, friends, and other people trapped in the rubble; to save what they could of their furniture and household goods; to clear away the ruins; and, once the war had ended, to rebuild their cities.

Yet ruin pictures remained in crucial ways silent, unable to tell postwar readers all that they might want to know about the bombing and the people who had experienced it. Ruin pictures could not, for example, show the actual moment of destruction, but rather what this violence from the air had left behind. As in World War I, "in the absence of better picture motifs, which could intensely display action, ruin pictures often only provided a stop-gap solution . . . the concrete event itself remained hidden from the observer. [The ruin picture] perceived only the effects."[65] Ruin pictures therefore drew attention to what they did not and could not show.[66] The use of ruin pictures after the war also depended on not showing other pictures. At least until the 1980s, most of the published ruin pictures Germans encountered did not suggest any connection between Germany's ruined cities and the genocidal war Germans had fought for Hitler. Pictures of how these ruined buildings had looked before the war seldom confronted the reader with symbols of the Nazi regime, such as swastika flags. And pictures of the buildings destroyed by the bombing seldom included "the local ruins of Nazi residences, agencies or other offices of the regime."[67]

Photographs of people in the ruins invited viewers to imagine what these individuals had experienced and felt.[68] Ruin pictures might create sympathy for the suffering they showed but they also encouraged admiration for ordinary Germans' defiant resolve to carry on with their everyday lives, despite the violence and destruction that had been directed at them from the air. In Hermann Hasenclever's 1964 book on the bombing of Remscheid, we can see men and women walking through the ruins with apparent purpose and direction; men carry briefcases on their way to work, women carry bags of groceries or push baby carriages along streets that have been cleared of rubble. The architectural fabric of the city has been destroyed by the bombing, rendering the cityscape through which these people move surreal and unreadable.[69] Yet the coordinates of their everyday lives seem still to be in place.[70]

How readers might respond to these pictures would depend on what they were able to know about the people they saw in the photographs. The less said in the captions or texts that accompanied the pictures, the easier it might be for readers to react emotionally to what they saw—these images could produce dismay and sorrow for the suffering they depicted but also, perhaps, some measure of pride in the behavior of the Germans who had refused to be beaten down by the bombing.[71] Sparse captions might indicate that the authors of these books believed certain photographs were capable of exerting a strong emotional impact without a great deal of textual guidance. At the same time, however, it might have been easier for readers to feel sympathy or admiration for the Germans they saw in these photographs if they knew that these people had not eagerly supported the Nazi regime and participated in Hitler's racial war of annihilation. In most instances, the authors of these books could not provide concrete and precise knowledge. The Germans in the pictures could only be identified in the most general terms as a man, a woman, a child. Yet if readers could not be given information that proved, as these photographs appeared to claim, that these Germans were innocent victims, then they might wonder whether some of the people in the pictures had also been perpetrators or accomplices. Asking those questions could complicate readers' emotional responses and moral evaluations.

Some of the pictures of Germans in the ruins displayed certain affinities with iconic British images of the Blitz—for example, the London milkman still delivering the daily bottles of milk even though he has to walk over the rubble created by the previous night's bombing. These British images became symbols of the indomitable British refusal to be broken by the bombing of London and other cities in the south of England. They were used to construct a myth of the spirit of the Blitz that had helped Britain continue fighting, even though it was all alone, and which eventually led to victory over Nazi Germany.[72] German versions of these photographs that showed people "carrying on" despite the bombing of German cities could not serve the same function—after all Germany had lost the war. But they could be used after 1945 to show that the Allied air war was senseless because it had not destroyed German morale. Yet these photographs might also raise questions they were not prepared to answer. Did the determination to continue with normal life, to refuse to be shattered by the bombing, to integrate the destruction into everyday life that we can see in many of these photographs allow the Nazi regime to keep on fighting the war to the bitter end? Hitler had always feared a repetition of November 1918, the revolution that had overthrown the monarchy and ended World War I. Pictures of Germans "carrying on" in the ruins of their cities showed that he did not need to worry.

The genre of ruin pictures has changed since 1945. Ruin pictures now routinely include photographs of cities bombed by the Germans—Guernica, Warsaw, Rotterdam, London, Stalingrad.[73] Pictures of forced foreign laborers, Russian POWs, and even Jews in the ruins draw attention to Nazi racism and genocide. The important question is, however, not whether but how these pictures of Germany's victims have entered the visual world of the bombing war. Are they presented in ways that require readers to look at the suffering caused by Germany while still allowing them to empathize with the German victims of the bombing? Or do they seriously disrupt the ability of photographs of Germans in the ruins to elicit the sympathy of contemporary readers/viewers? Or do pictures of Germany's victims, when they are set side-by-side with images of Germans as victims, show readers that World War II turned ordinary people on all sides into victims and created a European-wide community of suffering?

Chapter 4

Mourning, Denial, Celebration: The Visual Work of Picture Books

Jörn Glasenapp reminds us that photography is a relatively "lazy," even "incompetent" and "niggardly" medium that cannot be made to work unless the fragments of history—the snapshots in time—that it produces are given a past and a future that help viewers understand the wider historical context.[1] Picture books attempted to construct a broader narrative visually. Some individual photographs could certainly present elements that pointed to what had come before and what might come next. Most did not. Photo books assembled photographs in a sequence that was meant to show what could not be communicated in a single picture. Picture books were an important genre of postwar visual engagement with the destruction of German cities by Allied bombers. In most of the books that I have discussed so far, the work done by pictures was secondary to that performed by words. These images were not necessarily simple illustrations of the written text, but they did not create a sustained and separate storyline by themselves. In picture books, images were supposed to play a much more important role. Picture books tried to shift "the task of signification to photographs," to have photographs play the role in the construction of a narrative that had previously been reserved for words.[2] What kinds of stories did these publications try to tell in pictures?

Picture books came in two main types. The first drew upon a prewar genre of urban picture volumes that provided scenic visual tours of individual cities. In this genre, the city's buildings, not its people, figured as the main characters. Images were used not only to document and celebrate the physical rebuilding of postwar German cities but also to mourn the loss of architectural heritage and to construct for German viewers a virtual city that no longer existed in reality. The tension between these documentary and imaginary functions of images generated a sense of permanent loss that always threatened to undermine any attempt merely to celebrate the undeniable achievements of postwar reconstruction.[3]

In the second type of picture book, people played more prominent roles. By showing that Germans had survived the bombing and rebuilt their lives after 1945, photographs could be used to construct stories with happy endings. But pictures of the Germans who had survived might also draw attention to those who had not. And visual allusions to the mass death Germans had suffered might encourage viewers to imagine the mass death that Germans had inflicted on others during World War II.

Mourning, Loss, Denial

The bombing war destroyed buildings and killed people, but it also damaged the distinctive sense of local identity that in Germany has usually been described as *Heimat*.[4] German feelings of *Heimat* were deeply attached to an intense sense of place and of the uniqueness of each individual *Heimat*. When that *Heimat* was a town or city, place was identified by, among other things, specific historical buildings and architectural landmarks. The ruins left behind by the bombs deprived German cities of the visual differences that had made them unique before the war. What might be done to retain and communicate the distinctiveness of any given location, even in the face of this dreary sameness of ruins?

One route of visual escape from the ruins led backwards to historic images of the city that no longer existed in reality. With its very cover (a painting of an old house front), a 1950 publication on Heilbronn signaled the visual flight into the past of "Old Heilbronn, as we knew and loved it," which dominated the first 56 of the small book's 82 pictures. The introduction written by the city's lord mayor (Oberbürgermeister) informed readers that "on December 4, 1944, as the city of Heilbronn was reduced to a huge pile of rubble, thousands lost their lives and their *Heimat*. On that evening, the city also lost the face it had taken centuries to form."[5] In this first section, the book presented images of the city's major landmarks.

Like the second part of this book's title—*Ein Bildband der Erinnerung (A Picture Book of Memory)*—Oberbürgermeister Paul Meyle's introduction made clear that the purpose of the images that followed would be not to show Heilbronn's destruction but rather to counter the visual effects of this destruction on the memories of postwar citizens of Heilbronn: "The destruction was so complete, that the [city's] once so familiar features . . . threatened to become blurred in our memories. I am thus very pleased if, with [this] book, what has been forgotten can be revived and what was destroyed can be retained."[6] Meyle insisted that in the pictures that followed "the old Heilbronn that we were so proud of, just as a child is proud of its father, lives once more. The precious old sites, with which so many memories are connected, will once again emit their magic."[7]

In his own preface, Werner Gauss, editor of the volume, also emphasized the importance of the images that followed. Showing Heilbronn as it had once been was a crucial aid to the reconstitution of the identities of Heilbronn's citizens after the war. Their previous experiences, their hopes, joys, and memories could not be separated from the physical and architectural surroundings of Heilbronn in which local citizens had lived out their everyday lives before the bombing.[8] Place and identity could not be separated from each other.

Other cities destroyed by the war had already recognized and responded to these visual needs of their citizens with their own "memory books . . . which . . . captured in a picture that which had been lost."[9] Now, fortunately, it was time that "a monument in the form of an image . . . be dedicated to dear old Heilbronn."[10] Restoring "Alt Heilbronn," at least visually in the form of a picture book, would recuperate its distinctive individuality that had been erased by the bombs and the war.[11] The pictures of the "Alt Heilbronn" that followed were—"with the exception of those on pages 42 and 43—exclusively views from historic Heilbronn inside the old city walls."[12] All of these buildings had been destroyed or damaged by the air raid of December 4, 1944, "together with large areas of housing and industry, because the attack extended to the periphery of the city."[13] However, the book included no photographs of these devastated residential and industrial districts. Heilbronn was to be identified visually with its medieval and early modern old town, not with the city it had become by the time the war began.

Roland Barthes has drawn attention to the morbid aspect of photography. Because the people in photographs taken in the past are often already dead when we see them, these pictures point toward the mortality of their own subjects.[14] The photographic images in the 1950 picture book on Heilbronn performed a quite different function; they visually resurrected the "Alte Stadt" that was now "dead," killed by Allied bombs. Yet in his contribution to the 1953 book on Hanover, Hermann Deckert doubted that photographs could really serve this purpose. Deckert acknowledged that pictures of buildings as they had looked before the war might provide later generations with some knowledge of the extent of individual losses. But he thought it would be impossible to understand from these photographs what the larger architectural ensembles had actually meant to those who had lived with them.[15] Reversing the usual relationship between image and reality, the 1949 book on Paderborn suggested that the handful of historic buildings that had survived the bombing resembled "the remaining, colorful pages of a once exquisite picture book, callously torn apart by ignorant hands. . . . The next generation will be deprived forever of the familiar sight of the city with all its unique characteristics, created by successive phases of history over the past thousand years. From books, they can pick out only fragments of what for us was a reality filled with life."[16] If one of the ways in which the distinctive German concept of *Heimat* was transmitted from one generation to the next was through the buildings in which people lived and worked, then the destruction of a city's architectural fabric by the Allied bombing was a severe rupture in *Heimat* history. This was a permanent loss to which it was impossible ever to become reconciled.

The second path of visual escape from the ruins took viewers into the postwar reconstructed city.[17] It is not surprising that local publications increasingly offered pictures of the new buildings that, by the 1950s, had begun to replace the fields of ruins Germans were left with in 1945.[18] In East Germany, pictures of new buildings were meant to demonstrate that the GDR was building a new socialist state on German soil. In West Germany, photographs of new buildings symbolized the Federal Republic's embrace of modernity. Another small picture book on Heilbronn published in 1954 gave the viewer 35 photographs, some in color.[19] Less than half of these pictures (14) showed the city as it had been before the war or showed the viewer the ruins after the bombing. Some of the prewar images were accompanied by nostalgic captions, but one picture of a street in the Altstadt was described as having been "just as unhealthy as it was picturesque. Even without the war, it probably would not be there anymore."[20]

All of the remaining photographs were devoted to the new face of Heilbronn embodied in such structures as the ultra-modern interior of a new church, the entrance to the new train station, rows of new housing, and the new building for the county savings bank. A picture of the new home of a local newspaper commended local citizens for their "openness to new ways of building." The caption attached to a picture of the Theodor-Heuss-Gymnasium expressed local pride in an institution that was not only named for a native son but that also "combined modern style with humanistic tradition." The book did include pictures of some old buildings that had been reconstructed, but in general the visual emphasis focused on the new Heilbronn.

A similar affirmation of postwar reconstruction and modernity can be found in a 1967 picture book, *Hamburg. Phönix aus der Asche.Ein dokumentarischer Bildband* (*Hamburg. Phoenix from the Ashes. A documentary picture book*), by the Hamburg photographer Hugo Schmidt-Luchs and his son, Werner Schmidt-Luchs.[21] This book shows how Hamburg's unique qualities as a hardheaded port and commercial center gave it the strength, the drive, and the direction needed to rebuild after the devastation of the bombing war. The two photographers begin their story with a photo of the "Ruins-Express," which shows a small locomotive pulling open cars filled with rubble from left to right.[22] The train is presented as a symbol of progress into a future that "would in any case be better than the dark present, which was scarcely to be endured with no roof and with inadequate food." In 1945, no German had any idea "at what surprising stations the train of time would . . . arrive. Who would have dared to predict that the lumbering "Rubble Express" one day would become an elegant, comfortable "Europa-Express."

Opening with this photograph let readers know where they were going—the present was the destination—a present that the postwar generation of Germans might take for granted. But younger Germans needed to be reminded about what had to be overcome. The authors might also have chosen to begin their book with this picture of the "Rubble Express" because they recognized the emotional effect it could have on viewers. Here they were confronted not simply with ruins, as on the second page ("This picture captures the entirely hopeless and oppressive atmosphere of March 1945"[23]), but with a symbol of hope for the future quite literally emerging from these ruins.

The postwar city would be a very different metropolis: a modern urban center shaped by the needs of the automobile. The prewar urban past is gone, destroyed by the bombs but also rejected by postwar city planners. Hamburg has paved over the fields of ruins to construct new, wide streets that meet the needs of a motorized postwar Germany; "familiar streets disappeared without a trace, in their place, imposing skyscrapers grew up along the new rows of streets."[24] In most of this book, the emphasis is on the modernity of postwar Hamburg, forward-looking, dynamic, not nostalgic about its past. Occasionally, a note of regret intrudes upon this optimism, regret that in a city that had done little enough before the war to preserve the architectural reminders of its historical past, the few remaining architectural monuments had been wiped out by the Allied bombing. In general, however, the tone of *Phönix aus der Asche* with regard to the postwar architectural transformation of Hamburg is approving. The caption for one picture suggests that "in this sober city there is no room for melancholy reminiscing. The old must give way to the new—and perhaps in this posture lies some small part of the secret upon which the success of this vital, tough, impressive—and beautiful—city is based."[25]

In the 1950s, the Germans who had lived through the bombing war would have seen ruin pictures, especially when paired with photographs of the city as it had once looked, as very immediate reflections of their own suffering and loss. When juxtaposed with pictures of new buildings, ruin pictures might provide visual confirmation of this generation's postwar achievements. At the very least, photographs of new buildings served as a promise to Germans that a better future awaited them once the ruins had been cleared away. In that sense, photographic images played an active role in reconstruction; they were not simply documenting what had happened but helping Germans to imagine the future.[26]

The work of imagination performed by photographs became even more important as the bombing war receded into the historical past. By the late 1960s, when West German cities had been rebuilt, the authors of local publications realized that they had to address a new generation of readers/viewers born after 1945, who had no direct experience of the bombing. The younger generation of Germans might not know how the prewar cities or their postwar ruins had looked even though they could at times actually be standing on some of the rubble that had been incorporated into the physical fabric of the postwar city; "who among the football fans who cheer on the HSV [Hamburg Sport Club] in the People's Park Stadium (Volksparkstadion) ever thinks that they are standing on Hamburg's rubble? The entire, enormous oval of the spectator tiers consists of debris from West Hamburg."[27] Photographs were supposed to help these younger Germans imagine the unthinkable horrors of the bombing war so that they could appreciate the achievements of reconstruction.

Yet time can significantly alter the meaning of a photograph. By the 1960s, the flight into the future offered by pictures of new postwar buildings was threatening to become a depressing journey. In 1965, Alexander Mitscherlich complained, for example, that "after the war, we threw away the chance to build cleverly thought-out, really new cities."[28] Mitscherlich felt that German postwar cities exhibited a depressing uniformity; "someone only knows whether they have in front of them the housing silos of Ludwigshafen or Dortmund because they know that they traveled to one or the other of these cities."[29] Lacking a unique identity, the rebuilt German city could never become a genuine *Heimat* for the postwar Germans who lived and worked in it.[30] Pictures that confronted Germans with what Mitscherlich called *Die Unwirtlichkeit unserer Städte* (*Our Inhospitable Cities*) in his book by the same name would no longer be able to serve their original purpose of celebrating the achievements of postwar reconstruction.[31]

Rebuilding Lives

Many of the Germans who survived the bombing war had lost everything—the roof over their heads, their furniture and household goods, sometimes also relatives and friends. These survivors had to rebuild not only their cities but also their own lives. Yet the early postwar picture books seldom used photographs of these people to tell their stories. One exception is the 1954 picture book *Jahre unseres Lebens. Deutsche Schicksalsbilder* (*Years of Our Lives. Pictures of the Fates of Germans*) by the West German photographer Hilmar Pabel, which included a short sequence of photographs on the air war. During or immediately after Allied air attacks, Pabel had taken photographs of individual Germans. In the early 1950s, he returned to the locations of these wartime photos to find his original subjects. In two of the three cases, he actually showed these same people the pictures he had taken of them during the war. All of the subjects of Pabel's photos were happy that they had survived, but they also found it very difficult to believe that what the photos depicted had actually happened to them just a few years earlier.[32] The message of this sequence of photographs is summarized by the captions that tell the story of a young girl rescued from an air-raid shelter (figs. 26–29). When Pabel finds the girl after the war, he is glad to learn that "the unbelievable is reality: the sobbing young girl . . . has become a young mother, who can today smile happily" (fig. 29). After Pabel took his wartime photograph, the young girl was reunited with her parents who had been buried in the rubble of the same bomb shelter. Their story is the subject of two other pictures in this sequence (figs. 27 and 28). The last part of the caption explaining figure 29 assures us that "[s]he will certainly never forget the terrible days of her childhood—but the memory is no longer painful."

Fig. 26

The caption reads: “Did we really experience this? Here a women is rescued from the ruins of a house that a bomb crushed like a box of matches. Who was this woman? Perhaps a mother—and where were her children? Back then, when I took this picture, I did not know anything about her. She was one of the millions of nameless victims of the air war. Perhaps, she had not even survived the next hour. And now I sat before her. For some time, I delayed showing her the frightful picture.”

Fig. 27

The caption reads: "Oh, God—this woman on the stretcher, was that me? Shaken, the married couple looked at the pictures of a terrible time. "Do you know what, father? When they pulled me out, you were still down there . . . it was mid-night before they found you . . .", and her eyes filled with tears: her youngest child remained there, with seventeen others of the dead, underneath the rubble. How could she bear this pain? But life must go on, because there were two other children, who needed the father and the mother."

Fig. 28

The caption reads: "That is our girl, our Elly . . ." At that time (the woman's) daughter was a child. A child, who trembled for the life of her mother: "No, no, I will not leave—my mother is definitely under there, Mum, Mum, where are you?" Helpless, the fourteen year-old clenched her fingers together. Her entire body was trembling. She was one of the very first to be rescued by the helpers from the collapsed cellar of her parents' house"

Fig. 29

The caption reads: Seven years later: "Unbelievable—that is supposed to be me?" the young woman asked and showed her husband the picture from back then . . ."

The story Pabel tells depends not only on the pictures he took during the war but on the material presence of these wartime photographs in the postwar encounters he documents photographically. Pabel clearly assumed that the intervention in the present of visual artifacts from the past would allow these Germans to reimagine what they had lived through, what it had felt like and meant. Yet this assumption was challenged at the outset by the reactions of the people to whom Pabel showed these photographs. Even though these were pictures from their own lives, the subjects reacted with disbelief. Could that really be me? Did this really happen? Did we (collectively as Germans) really live through such horrible times? These reactions exhibit more than the normal sense of distance Germans might feel when they looked at photographs of themselves taken when they were much younger and looked quite different.

The "estrangement effect" in this particular historical situation was probably extreme—because Germans were being asked to look back from the vantage point of a reconstructed Germany to a Germany in ruins. The farther Germany moved away from these ruins and the experience that had produced them, the more difficult it would become to imagine this past, even with the aid of photographs that showed that it had indeed "happened." At the same time, documenting this estrangement reinforced the overall message of this picture sequence: this is a past that now seems very far away.

In Pabel's picture sequence, the captions play a crucial yet also contradictory role. On the one hand, the text supports the visual narrative, guiding the reader/viewer toward the "happy end" shown in the pictures of the parents who survived and were reunited with their child, Elly, who by the 1950s had herself become a young, happy mother with her own small baby, and whose life is now so removed from wartime tragedy that she scarcely believes the photograph of her wartime self that Pabel shows her. Yet the captions also give the reader other, much less comforting information that produces tension with the message of the pictures; we learn, for example, that although Elly survived, her youngest sibling and 17 other people in the bomb shelter did not.

Like Pabel's short sequence of photographs, a book on Heilbronn by Wilhelm Steinhilber, published in 1961, told its story primarily with pictures of the men, women, and children who had experienced the bombing war. Unlike Pabel, Steinhilber gave his readers very few postwar images that would have allowed them the consolation of being able to see that the people who had survived the bombing had managed to rebuild their lives. Instead, the book ends on a bitter note: for the generation who lived through it, the war is not yet fully over, but the postwar generation knows little and appears to care even less about the bombing. Steinhilber shows Heilbronn as an unsuspecting city that lives out the war in relative normality until one day, disaster strikes. The book creates a slow visual build up to the catastrophic attack. The first bomb damage, even the first death, seems still to be a curiosity that only temporarily disturbs the deceptive normality of the home front. Then the air war comes home with a vengeance on an unsuspecting population. What is shocking about the destruction is its speed.[33]

Steinhilber tried to convey this central message in a sequence of three very unusual pictures. The three images are actually stills taken from film footage shot in September 1944 by an unidentified film director who happened to be on the roof of a building looking down across the square in front of the Rathaus on September 10, 1944, when a daylight air raid hit the city. In the first still, taken "[m]inutes before the daytime attack," we see several men standing with a horse and cart in the square. The scene is peaceful, the square sunny and undisturbed, with the outline of the shadow of another building at the lower right-hand side. In the next shot, taken just a few minutes later, the square is completely obscured by smoke and dust; we no longer see the men and the horse and do not know whether they were able to escape the attack or have been killed by Allied bombs. All we can see now in the space occupied by the square in the previous picture is a number of lights, the product of the "hail-storm of firebombs" that has fallen on the square. In the final shot, we see the square again, blackened and covered with soot and debris. The city hall, still intact in the first two pictures, has been heavily damaged, its roof has been completely destroyed by a fire that is still burning; so, too, the roof and gable of the adjacent building on the left-hand side of the picture. Smoke from the fire still obscures the upper left-hand side of the picture. The last of these four pictures looks up to the sky to show us the cause of this destruction, the "27 Flying Fortresses, with their fighter escorts."[34]

The other unusual photographs in this book were taken during the night of the major attack on Heilbronn, on December 4, 1944, which produced a firestorm in the city.[35] All of these photographs were taken on the streets of the city while the buildings all around the photographer were consumed by flames. Six of the nine photographs show people in these streets as the buildings around them burn. Some of these figures are firefighters, others are civilians trying to escape or find shelter. The two pictures on page 68 show figures moving away from the camera along the Rosskampfstrasse. The caption for the top picture explains, "The fire begins to jump out from the house." In the bottom picture, which is a closer-in shot of the same street scene, we see "the same house a little later as a single glowing oven." Now there are only four figures in view. It is not clear what has happened to the two men in the top picture who were standing nearer the building, one of whom appeared to be wearing a helmet and was pointing toward the fire. But close to where they were standing, the fire has burst out onto the street. Two of the figures in the bottom picture are clearly women; one holds the hand of a small child and carries a bag in her other hand. The woman on the left-hand side of the photo is alone and carrying a larger bag, presumably containing possessions she has been able to save from the destruction. It is not clear whether the figure in the center of the picture is male or female because this person appears to be covered in a blanket or large piece of cloth presumably wetted to combat the effects of the extreme heat.

The caption for the next picture claims that it shows "someone trying to escape with a blanket hung around them [who] runs for their life through the firestorm in the Weststrasse at the Hotel Fatherland." On the next page, another

Fig. 30

photograph (fig. 30) shows two figures "[i]n a rain of sparks and glowing embers."[36] These pictures allow the reader the rare opportunity to imagine what it must have been like to have been out on the streets during the early stages of a firestorm. At the same time, however, it is unlikely that even the photograph on page 71 was taken at the height of the firestorm; all the available eyewitness descriptions we have indicate that the winds would have been so intense that the photographer would have been concentrating on protecting him/herself rather than taking pictures. This means that what actually distinguished a firestorm from the other types of destruction caused by Allied bombing raids still remained outside the frames of any of these individual photographs. Joachim Paech observes that "the media conditions of its genesis figure in every photograph depicting war . . . the technical-operative possibilities . . . permit certain observer positions and thus certain perceptions, which define in the final analysis what will be remembered visually as war."[37] What we see, even in these unusual photographs from Heilbronn, is the perspective of the observer who was standing far enough away from the heart of the firestorm to have survived. In these pictures, the experience of being inside a firestorm may be intimated, but it cannot be shown directly. Even the picture on page 71 arrests the intense movement of sparks and debris that eyewitnesses agree was one of the most terrifying aspects of a firestorm. At the height of a firestorm, the air was filled with fast-moving fragments of destroyed buildings that could seriously injure or even kill people who were still out on the streets. Quickly moving showers of sparks not only set other buildings alight but also ignited the clothing on people's bodies.[38]

At the end of this book, Steinhilber shows us two contemporary photographs of Heilbronn. One is a street scene with numbers of young women dressed for cold weather in front of a modern building. The picture next to it shows a café at night with tables outside. The caption reads: "resurrected from the ruins, Heilbronn leads the life of a big city today: young people know nothing about this hard time."[39] The juxtaposition of these two pictures with the one next to them suggests that this statement is not merely an observation but, in part at least, a recrimination; although the younger generation may not know or care about the bombing war, the older generation certainly does. In this next photograph, we see a large crowd of men and women who are taking part in the annual commemoration of the December 4 air attack on Heilbronn and honoring the victims at the Cemetery of Honor. Four older women, closer to the camera, sit on a bench at the left-hand side of the picture and look toward the crowd of participants, who are in turn facing a huge cross behind which we can see another row of participants. The caption reads: "Every year on the 4th December, during the hour of commemoration at the Cemetery of Honor, earnest faces remember the horrors of the war."[40] Steinhilber's book ends with the visual suggestion that despite the disinterest of the younger generation the bombing war might in fact not be completely over for the Germans. Two pictures show men at work retrieving potentially dangerous remnants of the air war that could still be found buried in the ground, many years later: "it must be assumed that unexploded bombs remain as a dangerous inheritance—from quite normal bombs to air mines weighing several tons."[41]

When Pabel published his picture sequence of the bombing war, he could reasonably assume that most of his adult readers could see their own recent lives in his photographs. These were experiences that were still fresh in the memories of millions of Germans. Pabel's job was to construct a visual narrative that gave these wartime experiences a "happy end" by showing that those who had survived had been able to rebuild their lives after 1945. By the time Steinhilber published his picture book in 1961, many Germans were too young to have experienced the war directly. Steinhilber's priority was to implant in their minds powerful images of the bombing war. He was clearly much less concerned than Pabel with using these images to construct a narrative that offered his readers the consolation of seeing what Germans had been able to achieve after 1945. Indeed, his final images drew attention to the gulf in historical memory that had begun to open up between the generation that lived through the war and those who grew up after the destruction.

Subversive Juxtapositions: Richard Errell's *Bilderbuch für Nachdenkliche* (1961)

Early picture books often used the juxtaposition of images as a central device in the construction of their visual narratives. Richard Errell's unorthodox 1961 picture book, *Bilderbuch für Nachdenkliche* (*Picture Book for the Thoughtful*), showed that by pairing different photographs than those normally used in postwar publications a subversive visual argument could be developed that did not allow viewers to ignore the Nazi past.[42] Errell's juxtapositions insisted that the real cause of German suffering and loss during the war was German support for Hitler and participation in the Nazi regime. Even in an apparently conventional visual pairing that contrasted the historic Römer district in Frankfurt am Main before the bombing with its postwar ruins, viewers were not allowed simply to lament the loss of this once beautiful and unique historic neighborhood. The caption to the second photograph, a quotation from Bertold Brecht's *Kriegsfibel* (*A Primer of War*), argues that Germans had brought this destruction upon themselves because they supported Hitler and the Nazis so enthusiastically. It also reminded readers that German cities were not the only towns destroyed in the war: "These are the cities, where we roared our 'Heil' back to the destroyers of the world. And our cities are only some of all of the cities which we destroyed."

In another juxtaposition, Errell took advantage of the characteristic openness of photography to suggest a range of possible meanings. The first image in this pairing shows a view from the main guard tower and entrance to Sachsenhausen concentration camp. It is winter. The camera looks down upon hundreds of prisoners lined up for roll-call. On the right-hand side of the picture, we see the barrel of a machine gun, but no guards are in view. Rather than guiding the viewer to a preferred interpretation of this image, the terse caption, "Work-creation program" ("Arbeitsbeschaffungsprogramm"), poses at least two questions without answering them. Does the image simply illustrate the official Nazi propaganda that insisted that concentration camps provided work for the unidentified inmates so as to rehabilitate them and reintegrate them into the "racial community"? Or did the Nazi concentration camps create "work" for the SS guards who are not seen in this photograph?

The second picture in this pairing is an aerial view of part of the Krupp armament factories in Essen in 1945 probably taken by Allied reconnaissance. Rows of factory buildings lay completely in ruins; the workshops that once produced armaments are now mere shells with no roofs. The pairing of this second photograph with the first suggests that the type of dictatorship that incarcerated hundreds of thousands in concentration camps also unleashed a massively destructive war that eventually took work away from millions of Germans by destroying factories like the one we see in this second picture. This connection is reinforced by the visual parallel between the rows of devastated workshops in the second photograph and the rows of concentration camp inmates in the first.

A quintessential theme of Nazi visual propaganda—the disciplined, organized masses—introduces another juxtaposition. This first image shows long rows of Hitler Youth in uniform (fig. 31). In the top section of the picture, the rows of *Hitlerjugend* (*HJ*) boys who are farthest away from the camera hold large banners erect that stretch off into the distance beyond the upper frame of the picture. The title of the picture, "Hard as Krupp Steel," is drawn from one of Hitler's speeches but also refers back to the earlier pairing that showed long rows of Krupp workshops destroyed by the war. Errell matches the photograph of the Hitler Youth with a picture of a woman looking for her children or relatives after a bombing raid (fig. 32). The photograph shows the woman in profile in the foreground with a pile of dead bodies in the center background. Errell's caption reads: "After an air attack on Berlin. A mother looks for her child." This image had already appeared in at least one earlier publication and it would be published several times again after Errell used it in his 1961 book. But Errell was the only author to make a statement about the political causes that he thinks produced the dead bodies we see in this picture. His message is that the indoctrination and military drilling of young people by the Nazis shown in the first picture has led to the rows of children's corpses pictured in the second image. As with some of Errell's other juxtapositions, this set of pictures is shaped by a bitter visual symmetry: rows of bodies disciplined by the Nazis generate rows of bodies killed in the war. The connection between these two sets of bodies is emphasized visually by the way the woman looks toward not only the corpses of dead children in the background but also to the disciplined bodies of the Hitler Youth on the other page.[43]

Errell posited a similar connection between disciplined and dead German bodies in another pairing. The first picture shows an impressive display of military equipment and soldiers at an army parade in 1936, shortly after Nazi Germany began to rearm. The caption quotes Generaloberst von Blomberg: "The *Wehrmacht* protects the German people and its living space. It serves the Führer

Fig. 31

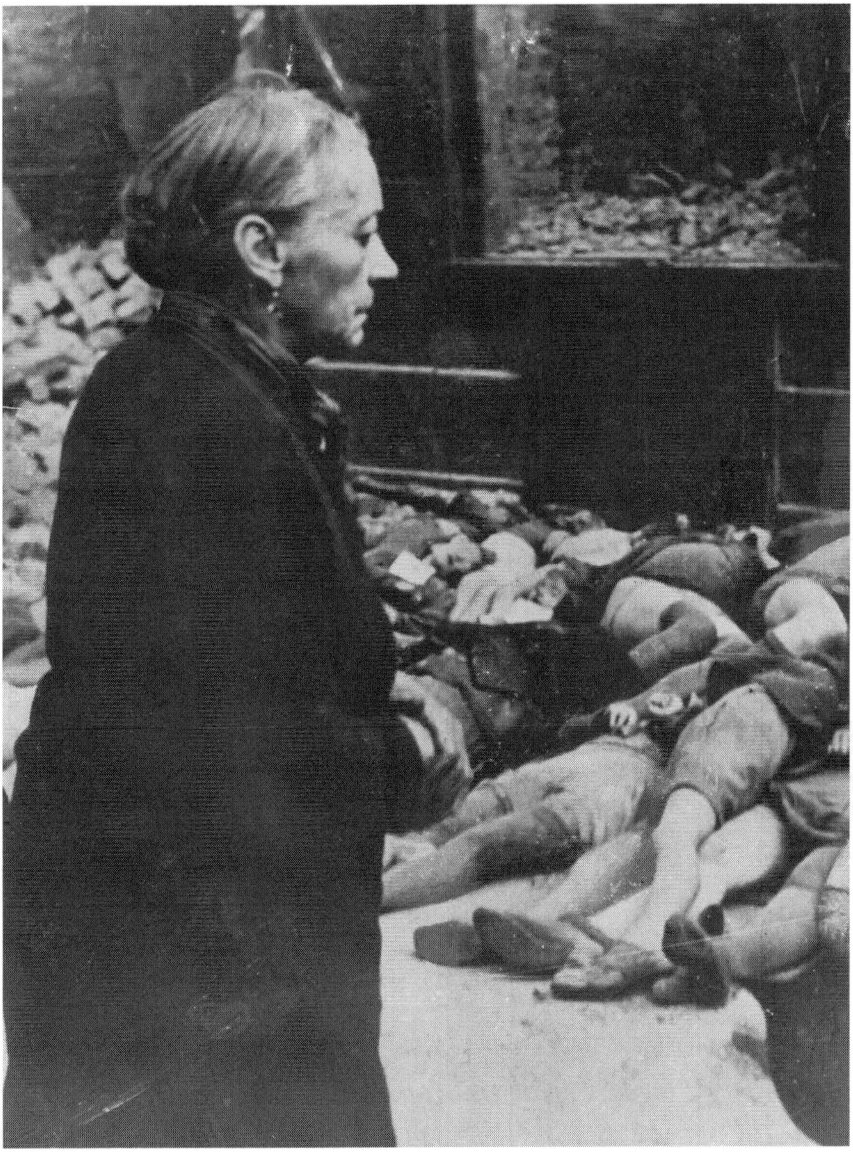

Fig. 32

with unstinting trust and obedience, the state through its readiness for action, the people through its enthusiastic submission to the National Socialist idea, to which Germany owes its rebirth." The second picture shows this claim is untrue. Identified as "After an air-attack upon Berlin," the picture shows two long rows of the dead bodies of civilians killed in the air raid that have been pulled out of the ruins of bombed-out buildings by the men in the emergency services who can be seen standing in the left and center background of the picture. The visual message of the two pictures is that the rows of soldiers and military equipment have not only been unable to prevent rows of civilian corpses but have actually produced them, "In Reih und Glied" ("in rank and file").

In the 1960s, Errell's picture book stood virtually alone as a challenge to the visual narratives constructed by mainstream publications.[44] Later picture books did begin to move beyond the conventions established in the 1950s and 1960s, although they were by no means prepared to go as far as Errell had done. The main innovation of two picture books published in the 1980s, for example, was to focus their readers' attention on the everyday lives of ordinary Germans *during* the bombing war. This perspective was certainly compatible with a visual argument that Germans had been innocent, unsuspecting victims of the bombing. Yet it could also open up space for viewers to ask questions about the participation of these ordinary Germans in the Nazi regime and Hitler's war.

We can begin with a book on Hanover, published in 1983.[45] The major concern of this book was to return its readers—in both words and images—to the lived experience of the bombing war. The book conveys the experiences of ordinary Germans with direct quotes from the oral testimony of eyewitnesses. Fifty-five of the photographs in this book were loaned from the collections of private individuals.[46] The 1983 book deals with topics not usually discussed or pictured in earlier publications about the bombing of German cities—such as the persecution of Hanover's Jews and the German attack on the Soviet Union. Yet even though this book talks about and shows the wider war, it does not examine ordinary Germans' involvement in that war—their war is still the bombing war.

The 1983 Hanover volume makes extensive use not only of photographs but also of reproductions of Nazi documents and other artifacts of the bombing war. The status of these Nazi materials is ambiguous. On the one hand, these contemporary documents and images create the impression of authenticity—this is what we (they) saw, this is how it looked! Yet some of these artifacts might also convey the message that ordinary Germans were victims of their Nazi leaders, such as the playful cartoon figures that were used to communicate information about what to do in an air raid that, though certainly comical, did not prepare Germans for the horrors they would eventually experience by making it all seem relatively harmless and unthreatening. And, in the postwar viewing context, pictures taken during the early stages of the air war to provide ordinary Germans with reassurance that they would be adequately protected from the bombing were transformed into cruel jokes played by the regime upon its unsuspecting, naive subjects.

By 1943, at the latest, dealing with the bombing war dominated everyday life.[47] Daily life under the conditions of prolonged emergency is shown to be provisional, often lived out-of-doors, even in winter. When the buildings housing public agencies were hit by bombs, the authorities continued to provide services as best they could. A photograph shows citizens of Hanover using an emergency mail center that consists simply of a table set up outdoors because the main post office was destroyed in a bombing raid. In another picture, a woman carrying two shopping bags walks away from a table set up outside near the Café Kröpcke to provide IDs to people who have been bombed out and to *Wehrmacht* dependents.[48] An earlier picture shows us that the Kröpcke café itself no longer exists; in it we see a woman walking toward a wooden barracks that has been set up as a temporary Café Kröpcke.[49]

Children and young people figure prominently in the visual representation of *Kriegsalltag* and life in the postwar ruins. One of the earliest pictures in the book shows a smiling young child looking at the camera as she/he (?) stands in front of a slit trench that is supposed to protect people caught in the streets during an air raid from bomb fragments.[50] The preparations for an air attack are presented here as interesting curiosities worth a photograph. There is no hint in this picture of anxiety about the destruction that an air raid could bring to Hanover. Another photograph shows a young boy, dressed in winter clothes, standing on a stepladder that has been set up so that people can examine a downed British bomber put on display next to the opera house. The boy is smiling and looking at the camera. The plane is a trophy but also an assurance that German air defenses will protect the boy, his family, and the other inhabitants of Hanover from Allied bombing raids. In both pictures, the smiles on these children's faces suggest that their spirits are still high. The air war is still a curiosity, perhaps even a welcome diversion from everyday routine.

There are also smiles on the faces of the teenage boys and the men in the picture on page 55; "*Flak* helpers and soldiers in the Leinehaufen position, 1943." One of the boys leans against the barrel of the flak cannon. The boy on his left raises his arm in a kind of salute. The boys appear to be enthusiastic; the older men less so. The air war is still an adventure for the younger males.

Fig. 33

On page 119, a photograph shows several young boys, probably all members of the one school class, who have just finished an air-raid drill and are leaving the entrance of a bunker. Two older youths stand in front of the bunker; they wear uniforms, steel helmets, and gas masks. At the time that the photograph was taken, this exercise might still seem like a game; but the caption warns: "Soon this will be bitterly serious."[51]

These pictures present children and young people as unsuspecting targets of the bombing war that will soon turn them into helpless victims of massive violence over which they have no control. However, one final and rather unique photograph, taken at the end of the war, shows children actively asserting themselves against the extreme conditions of *Kriegsalltag*. The photo that appears on page 209 shows three children stealing food from a store in April 1945 (fig. 33).

The volume certainly includes photographs of ruins and bomb-damaged buildings, including one that appeared in the 1953 publication, a view from the still-standing tower of the Rathaus that showed the swath of devastation in the center of the city. Yet the 1983 Hanover volume also showed a different type of ruin: destroyed industrial plants that had been producing military goods for the German war effort. These images echoed other pictures of local industry shown in a 1951 picture book on Hanover; but whereas the 1951

Fig. 34

volume ignored the role local industry played during the war, the 1983 picture book included photographs that showed that local industry was working for the Nazi war machine.[52] These pictures also contradicted the argument that Allied bombing raids had devastated the buildings in which Germans lived, destroyed architectural treasures, and killed many civilians but had been relatively ineffective in damaging Germany's ability to produce armaments and war materiel. That German war industry had also been severely affected by the bombing—whether or not the damage done significantly shortened the war—was made quite forcefully, for example, in a photograph that showed a factory that had been making tanks for the *Wehrmacht* destroyed by Allied bombs (fig. 34). The large muzzle of an unfinished tank juts up out of the twisted wreckage. Several other tanks that never left this factory in Hanover-Linden can be seen in the background.[53]

Another picture in this same volume shows the refinery in Misberg (which also appears rebuilt in the 1951 book) in April 1945. It has been completely leveled by Allied bombing. The text in which these pictures have been embedded observes that "within 12 minutes, more than 1000 high explosive bombs transformed the refinery and large areas of this locality into a field of ruins . . . the mayor of Misburg . . . reported . . . that the refinery and the cement works were put completely out of commission."[54]

In the 1983 book on Hanover, photographs of *Kriegsalltag* encouraged viewers to identify and sympathize with the ordinary Germans who had lived through and sometimes died in the bombing war. Pictures of children who were too young to be held responsible for Hitler's genocidal war may have made it easier for postwar viewers to see ordinary Germans as unsuspecting, innocent victims. However, pictures of weapons and other war materiel destroyed by the bombing demonstrated that Hanover had contributed to the Nazi war machine, and these images may have encouraged viewers to ask what role adult civilians in Hanover had played in Hitler's racial war of annihilation.

Bremen

The first few pictures in a book published in Bremen in the same year, 1983, show the effects of the bombing and give us a taste of what is to come in 1941 and 1944.[55] Here we are taken back to the more "innocent" phase of the early 1930s when Germans were anticipating the air war to come. Photographs of children learning to put on gas masks, of an orderly row of utensils and equipment necessary to fight fires and to dig one's way out of a collapsed air-raid shelter hint at possible dangers but also suggest that, no matter how difficult an actual attack might be, the bombings could still be mastered and dealt with by adequate training and preparation.

The photographs begin to trace the trajectory of escalating violence and destruction from the air. These pictures show that before Germans became the targets of Allied air raids, the Luftwaffe had devastated Guernica and Warsaw. The first bombs do not drop on Bremen until May 18, 1940.[56] Initially, bomb damage is slight. These early air raids cause few deaths and the victims are not anonymous; a picture shows the corpse of a single person killed by a bomb, Reichsbahnbeamter K., 46 years of age, who has been laid out on a table in the morgue.[57] Bombs do serious damage to some buildings; but one photo shows that even in the spring of 1941 a guest in the train station hotel was still able to go back to his room to look for his luggage after an air raid. Yet these pictures also demonstrate that the bombing has become serious enough to warrant the

Fig. 35

construction of bunkers in Bremen. A photo depicts one being built at the Domshof in September 1940. The caption reads, "The city digs itself in."[58] By 1941, air raids on Bremen do more damage; a photograph shows an entire street of houses, though still standing, seriously damaged by British bombs. The people who lived in these houses have been "bombed out" and have to find a place to stay elsewhere.[59] Bombs are no longer curiosities; they have begun to intrude into everyday life. A photo from 1940 shows the front garden of someone's house in Bremen where a sign has been posted on the fence, next to the gate, saying, "Unexploded bomb, deadly peril!"[60] Occasionally, oddities attracted the attention of the photographers who took these pictures; one photograph captures a man in uniform standing in a building (fig. 35). A bomb has apparently blown off the roof and all the windows, because there is a layer of snow on top of the debris that litters the floor. But a bust on a short pedestal has survived the attack. The man in uniform points to the bust as he looks at the camera and smiles.[61]

A photograph taken in April 1941 shows that the destructive force of Allied air raids has increased substantially: civil defense leader (Luftschutzleiter) Major Klatte and his staff make a special inspection of the site where the first air mine was dropped on Bremen. The entire block has been completely flattened; not a single building is left standing in the area where the mine ex-

Fig. 36

ploded. Death becomes more common and more ugly; a picture taken after an air raid in January 1941 shows six corpses at a body collection site (fig. 36). One corpse has no clothes, while the three bodies on the floor are bloodied, their clothes torn.[62]

The last picture in this section depicts two survivors (fig. 37). We can see only the top half of the man's body as he is standing on the ledge of a basement window. A woman stands on the sidewalk bending forward to pick up the containers of food that the man is passing up to her from the cellar. The building is still standing but is filled with rubble. In this instance, a cellar, where many Germans were killed during air raids, has become a source of survival.[63] Not so the air-raid bunker being inspected by three uniformed officials on page 119. A direct hit has blasted a hole in the reinforced concrete of the bunker that had previously been designated as "secure against bombs." The threat of death from bombing has been brought visually much closer.

The Bremen book pays attention to aspects of the air war that were either marginalized or not pictured at all in earlier publications. A series of photographs shows, for example, the use of prisoners, foreign workers, and even Jews to clean up bomb damage. A photograph on page 126 shows penitentiary prisoners who are clearing rubble from the interior of a municipal hospital; the

Fig. 37

caption points out, "They work with their bare hands and without rescue equipment."[64] On page 194, a photograph displays POWs under guard filling in a bomb crater after the May 9, 1941, raid. A Hitler Youth watches them. A series of photographs on pages 210, 213, 214, 215, and 222 show POWs who have been set to work cleaning up more serious bomb damage. Two other pictures depict POWs and foreign workers as victims of the bombing. Page 219 displays a photograph of bomb damage to a POW camp. A picture on page 166 shows the site where an earth bunker collapsed under a bomb, killing the people inside, most of whom were foreign laborers employed in a hospital laundry service. On pages 222–27, concentration camp prisoners are shown working in the rubble and bomb-damaged buildings. The picture on page 241 is unique. It shows that, after the October 6, 1944, air attack, even Hungarian Jewish women were forced to clean up bomb damage.

The Bremen book also includes photographs of experiences during the bombing war that were seldom, if ever, pictured in other books. On pages 128 and 129, for example, we see Germans having phosphorous removed from their shoes after the June 26, 1942, raid. The first picture demonstrates that a "phosphorous cleaning station" had been set up in the street to perform this task. Draw-

Fig. 38

Fig. 39

ing a connection between the Allied bombing of Germany and the Vietnam War, the caption of this first photograph tells us that "phosphorous bombs" were the "precursors to napalm." The picture on the next page (129) shows a man in uniform cleaning a woman's shoes with a stout brush (fig. 38). The woman holds on to a bicycle and looks directly into the camera. The caption explains that "if phosphorous is tracked into a house on shoes it can ignite itself."

People are present in almost every photograph in the 1983 Bremen book. Some of these pictures are interesting not only because of what they show but how they show it. One picture of two men looking through the rescued inventory of a store is particularly striking (fig. 39). The soldier on the left is looking directly at the camera, engaging the photographer, while the other man on the right appears to be completely absorbed in adjusting his scarf or tie. The mirror reflects the images of several other men in uniform who are not visible in the photograph itself, thus bringing into the frame of the picture what is actually outside it. The caption reads: "At home on leave—rescued inventory: a hair dresser's commode, books, plates and dishes, a [typically kitsch] porcelain figure of a bellowing deer raised up on its hind legs."[65]

The 1983 Bremen book also tries visually to connect the experience of the bombing war with fears of and protest against a nuclear war—fears that were reactivated by the second Cold War confrontations in the 1980s. The photograph on page 325 echoes the one at the beginning of the book. By showing neatly ordered tools hanging on the wall of a reactivated air-raid bunker during the Cold War, this second image seems to be saying that it is all happening again—and with predictably similar results for German civilians.

Conclusion

Anton Holzer has observed that photographs "record separate, small excerpts" from the past.[66] Picture books tried to put these fragments of the past together in a sequence that would tell a coherent story. Yet the ways viewers might respond to these pictures could complicate, even thwart this project. The first type of picture book, which showed photographs of historic buildings, then pictures of melancholy "premature ruins,"[67] and then finally the new buildings constructed after the war was supposed to move the reader visually (but also emotionally) from mourning to celebration.[68] However, the power of individual images in such before-and-after sequences might threaten to unravel the visual narrative they were supposed collectively to construct. Ghostly pictures of "die Alte Stadt" before its destruction could haunt the minds of readers and create an "imaginary parallel reality" that made it hard for them to celebrate the new postwar future, because they continued to mourn the loss of their city's past.[69] Perhaps this is why one local publication tried to reassure its readers in 1955 "that despite the great losses, the innermost essence of the city remains intact . . . a great deal of what connects us to the past was saved and what has been achieved in the ten years since the 22 March [the date of the major attack] through the unbelievably tough, untiring work of reconstruction . . . is beginning to join the old with the new."[70] Still, the power of individual pictures could trap the viewer in a past moment of unmitigated, unredeemed violence and destruction that, in the instant of viewing, seemed all too present. Unlike films, picture books could not make the individual images seem to disappear by creating the illusion of movement.[71] Picture books might give viewers the feeling that they were moving through time as they turned the pages, but they could not control how the viewer looked at the images. Confronted with the desolation of ruins or the horror of mutilated or incinerated dead bodies, viewers might be overwhelmed and not know how or whether to move forward. Even in the picture books that tried to show a "happy end," viewers might still become absorbed in and linger over certain individual pictures longer than others. And they might not even view the pictures in the sequence in which they had been presented. The use of images demanded a very delicate balancing act: images should promote horror but not generate despair.

Secondly, changes in the ways that Germans dealt with the Nazi past could significantly affect how they looked at photographs and which pictures they wanted to see. Until the early 1960s, local publications seldom included photographs that would have complicated the dominant narrative of German suffering.[72] Readers were normally not allowed or encouraged to see the bombing as a result of the war that Hitler had started and that they had supported as long as Hitler was winning. Photographs of European cities bombed by the Germans, or of the suffering that Germans had inflicted on others—Jews, concentration camp inmates, Russian POWs—were stranded on the periphery of contemporary visual representation in rare, critical publications, such as Richard Errell's *Bilderbuch für Nachdenkliche* (1961). By the 1960s, however, it was becoming increasingly clear that the visual repertoire established in the 1950s no longer satisfied the visual needs and desires of younger Germans.[73] New debates about the Nazi past and the return to public consciousness of the pictures of dead and dying Jews in the liberated concentration camps may have stimulated younger Germans' desire to see beyond what the established visual canon allowed.[74]

Some picture books began to reflect these new visual priorities. But when they included photographs of Jews, of slave laborers, or Russian POWs, or of cities that the Germans had bombed, they may have planted questions in their readers' minds that the picture books themselves could not answer. Looking at the photographs of concentration camp prisoners, foreign workers, and Hungarian Jewish women forced to clean up bomb damage that appeared in the 1983 book on Bremen, readers might wonder what happened to these other victims of the war after 1945.[75] Had Soviet POWs and forced laborers been able, like the German subjects of Pabel's picture sequence, to pick up the threads of their shattered lives and rebuild their families when they returned home? Or had Stalin's secret police shipped them off to the Gulags or simply executed them when they were repatriated?[76] If the Hungarian Jews in these pictures had survived the war at all, did they return home only to find that all the other members of their extended families had been murdered?[77] Asking about the pain of others—pain frequently inflicted by Germans—might in turn lead the Germans who had been moved by these pictures to reassess the meaning of the suffering that they, or their parents, had endured during the bombing war.

And yet (finally), knowing what happened after a photograph was taken might make it difficult to understand what the picture originally showed. When we look at photographs of Holocaust victims who are still alive in the Lodz ghetto, for example, we already know that they will soon be murdered. Ulrich Baer argues, however, that at the time these photographs were taken, most of the victims probably did not know their fate. Life in the ghetto was seen as a gamble with the future, a desperate attempt to stay alive long enough for the war to end, for the Red Army to arrive.[78] We know that this gamble would not succeed. The Jews in these photographs did not. This "tension between two temporal orders marked in every photograph" also structures our relationship to photographs of German cities devastated by Allied bombing.[79] Looking at the "then" preserved in these photographs, from the vantage point of our "now," we know that these "dead cities" would eventually come back to life.[80] However, the Germans pictured in these photographs did not know that the horror would end, that their cities would be rebuilt. Only in retrospect, from the comfortable vantage point of the West German Economic Miracle (*Wirtschaftswunder*), has it been possible to integrate this unmitigated violence and destruction into a redemptive narrative in which the end of the war in May 1945—*Stunde Null*—serves as the prelude to postwar reconstruction and renewal. In his 1998 novel, *In der Erinnerung*, Dieter Forte suggests another possibility. Living in the ruins of an unnamed German city at the end of the war, his characters have absolutely no sense of a future. For them, time stands still; "Zero hour, as everyone called it, no man's time in no man's land, was born out of people's feeling that life was meaningless. . . . In this shadowless landscape of stone nothing changed. . . . One froze in summer as in winter, the body reacted differently than before."[81] Framing photographs in a narrative that ends with reconstruction and the *Wirtschaftswunder* can make it difficult for us to see that for the Germans who appear in these photographic images, 1945 may not have felt like the beginning of anything at all.

CHAPTER 5

East Germany's Bombing War: Dresden

How did East German narratives and images of the bombing war compare to those circulating in West Germany after 1945? Many of the types of images used by East German publications—ruin pictures, for example—were the same as those that appeared in the West. But the meanings of these East German pictures were different because they were embedded in and explained by a different view of Germany's history and by different narratives of the bombing war. Architectural remnants of Germany's previous history could not be revered or mourned in quite the same ways that they were in the West. They symbolized a past whose class inequities and conflicts the communist regime promised to overcome by building a better, fairer, peaceful socialist society.[1] When framed by the right political narrative, ruin pictures could, however, be quite useful to the GDR. This sometimes meant using ruin pictures to show the misery that Hitler and the Nazis, or German militarism more generally, had inflicted on the German people. More often, ruin pictures were exploited by Cold War propaganda as indictments of the "barbarism" of the American former ally, now Cold War enemy. This use of ruin pictures was particularly pronounced in the official representations of the devastation of Dresden by Allied bombing in February 1945. Dresden became a focal point of East German visual and textual representations of the air war and its aftermath. The bombing of Dresden not only functioned as a local traumatic memory but was staged by the regime as a national tragedy. The political instrumentalization of the destruction of Dresden by the SED regime required other East German cities, such as Magdeburg, which had also been devastated by Allied bombs, to take a back seat to the metropolis on the Elbe.[2]

The Dresden Narrative

"Operation Thunderclap," the code name for the Anglo-American bombing of Dresden on February 13–14, 1945, was the largest air raid of the war. It was intended to be so devastating that the Third Reich would collapse under the shock. The systematic destruction of one of the few large German cities still virtually untouched by the Allied bombing campaign was supposed to "bomb the population into understanding" that it was pointless to continue fighting. On the night of February 13, 1945, British Lancasters dropped 3,000 tons of bombs on Dresden, concentrating on the city's historic center. On the following day, American planes attacked the still-burning city. Incendiaries produced a firestorm with temperatures that reached 1,000 degrees centigrade. A huge area of Dresden was turned into a wasteland. The city was filled with refugees from the East, so it has never been possible to establish the number of victims precisely. The best recent estimates suggest that between 18,000 and 25,000 people perished in the attacks.[3]

The crucial components of the Dresden narrative were established by Goebbels's propaganda machine immediately after the devastating raid. Goebbels presented the destruction of Dresden so late in the war as a militarily senseless and barbaric attack on an "innocent city" that had wiped from the face of the earth a singularly beautiful architectural and cultural treasure. The architectural loss was matched by the human suffering, but "the collective memory of the unique Dresden was above all a memory of the beauty of its buildings and of the architectural ensemble."[4] The official East German narrative, virtually unchanged until 1989, adopted these key elements of Goebbels's wartime propaganda but depicted the firebombing of Dresden as the opening round of the Cold War.[5] Immediately after the war, official statements had still blamed the Nazis for starting the war that eventually resulted in the destruction of Dresden. In 1948, on the third anniversary of the bombing, the *Sächsische Zeitung* (*SZ*) signaled "an impending shift in the attribution of guilt," mentioning, for the first time since the war, that it was "Anglo-American planes" that had killed so many of Dresden's citizens "at a point in time when the Nazi war had already reached its end."[6] In September 1948, Minister President Max Seydewitz gave a speech at the reopening of the State Theater in which he castigated the Nazis for the bombing but also accused the Western Allies of the senseless destruction of the city at a time when the outcome of the war was already obvious.[7] By the 1950s, the Dresden narrative had been reworked to serve the propaganda requirements of the Cold War. The SED regime charged that the Western Allies had dropped their bombs on Dresden to demonstrate their military might to the Soviets and to devastate a city that would soon be taken by the Red Army and would serve as an important center of the Soviet Occupation.[8] From the 1960s onward, the SED regime claimed that the Allies had actually planned to drop the first atomic bomb on Dresden. Only German capitulation in May 1945 had stopped them.[9]

This, however, was no more than a temporary reprieve. In 1965, the *Sächsische Zeitung* insisted that the Bonn government was planning to build a line of atomic mines along the entire length of the border between East and West Germany and along the common frontier with Czechoslovakia.[10] The newspaper insisted that a single thread of "imperialist policy" connected this most recent atomic threat with "the fascist extermination camps Auschwitz, Buchenwald, the massacre in the Congo, the most recent terror attacks of the USA against peaceful North Viet Nam—actions of unimaginable horror."[11] All were symptoms of the aggressive appetites of American "dollar imperialism" that had already demonstrated its affinity with Nazism in the destruction of Dresden.[12] The *SZ* attempted to emphasize the connection between the firebombing of Dresden and the threat of nuclear war by drawing attention to a recent telegram sent by the mayor of Hiroshima on the occasion of the 20th anniversary of the firebombing of Dresden. The *SZ* wanted its readers to conclude that Hiroshima and Dresden recognized each other as victims of the same monopoly capitalist imperialism.[13]

In 1965, David Irving's book *The Destruction of Dresden*, which described the bombing as the "biggest bloodbath in European history," reinforced this Dresden "code" (*Chiffre*).[14] His narrative was gripping, full of shocking details and illustrated with photographs not previously seen. Irving claimed that 135,000 people had been killed in the Dresden raid, more than by the atomic bomb dropped on Hiroshima. Irving influenced another project by Walter Weidauer, the communist mayor of Dresden between 1945 and 1948 who was beginning to write his own history of the bombing now that he had retired.[15] In return for help given with his research in Dresden, Irving donated copies of documentary materials from British and American archives to the Dresden city archive. This helped give Weidauer's work the appearance of an objective investigation, which was even supported by documents from the Western Allies. In 1965, Weidauer published his book, *Inferno Dresden. Lügen und Legenden um die Aktion "Donnerschlag"* (*Inferno Dresden. Lies and Legends about the Action "Thunder Clap"*). The key claim in this book was that Dresden was supposed to have been the target of the first American atomic bomb; only the swift advance of the Red Army prevented this from happening. Weidauer's book, which appeared in nine editions to 1990, became the basis for GDR propaganda, popular histories, and an exhibit at the Dresden city museum. The official GDR history of World War II became frozen—the bombing and antifascist resistance were the only two topics discussed. In the period after the construction of the Berlin Wall, détente required that the emphasis shift from the United States to West Germany as the main threat to peace. Praise of the GDR's own successes in rebuilding came to occupy center stage. In the second half of the 1960s, the Vietnam War reinvigorated the propagandistic confrontation with the United States; "what is going on in Viet Nam today is essentially the same crime perpetrated against Dresden on 13 February 1945—terror, blind-raging destruction and genocide."[16] At the high point of the Vietnam War, Kurt Vonnegut's bestselling novel *Slaughterhouse 5*, published in 1969, reasserted and transmitted to the next generation the established collective narrative of the innocent, unique city and its senseless, unparalleled destruction.[17] Vonnegut's book helped spread around the globe the image of Dresden as a universal symbol of military violence against civilians. The phrase "like Dresden after the bombing" now became an ultimate description of destruction.[18]

In 1975, the *SZ* returned to the argument that the bombing of Dresden was a prelude to the Cold War. The newspaper now claimed that the Allies had ordered the attack so as to terrify Stalin with a demonstration of the horrific destructive power they could unleash against the Soviet Union.[19] An article by the East German historian, Olaf Groehler, repeated this assertion in 1985. Groehler insisted that the Allies had decided to bomb Dresden because it was still largely intact. Air raids on this city would give the Russians a clear demonstration of the devastation that Anglo-American bombers could produce. Hiroshima and Nagasaki were the next stage of this attempt to intimidate the Soviet Union and its allies. It was claimed that by November 1945, the United States had already targeted 20 Soviet cities for nuclear attack. Groehler insisted that ever since Hiroshima and Nagasaki, America had threatened the very existence of humanity on a global scale. Only the consistent pursuit of peace by the Soviet Union had prevented a nuclear apocalypse.[20]

Picture Work

Several photographers and artists worked in the ruins of Dresden after the February 13–14, 1945, bombing: Kurt Schaarschuch, Richard Peter, Erich Höhne, Walter Hahn, and Wilhelm Rudolph.[21] This meant that there was an abundance of different images of the same sites in Dresden. As early as December 1945, the Dresden city council published Schaarschuch's picture book *Bilddokument Dresden. 1933–1945* (40,000 copies),[22] which contrasted photographs of important architectural sites in the city center before the bombing with their ruins after the attack.[23] Schaarschuch tried to take his pictures of the ruins from the same standpoint as the prewar images.[24] His "before" and "after" pictures were well-suited to present the architectural and cultural losses produced by the bombing. But what they ignored was as important as what they showed. Schaarschuch "did not complain with his photographs about the dead killed by the bomb attacks, nor about the destruction of factories and residential neighborhoods and he did not devote one picture to the strenuous life in the ruins."[25] By setting up the contrast between 1933 and 1945, Schaarschuch's book also simply ignored the Nazi years and the war that had come in between. The book ends with a picture of a building worker with a compressed air hammer in the ruins of Dresden that conveys the message that despite all the devastation, the city would rebuild. Both the image and the message are out of place, tacked on to provide an incongruous closure to a visual journey whose endpoint is really the ruins shown in so many of the previous pictures, not the rebuilt city, which still lies in the future: "the all-too-often recurring schema of 'before-after' bestows upon these pictures a comprehensive finality which cannot be overturned by this one photograph."[26]

Richard Peter's *Dresden. Eine Kamera klagt an* achieved much greater recognition than Schaarschuch's book. Along with Hermann Claasen's picture book on Cologne, *Gesang im Feurofen*, it became one of the classic "rubble photo books."[27] Peter was not in Dresden during the bombing. He returned to the city in September 1945, after he was released from an American POW camp. In 1946, he became picture editor for *Zeit im Bild*. In his free time, he took thousands of photographs of the devastated city with a borrowed Leica. After four years of taking pictures, Peter offered the state government of Saxony 200 images as a foundation for an official picture archive. The authorities decided instead to ask Peter to put together a picture book on the destruction of Dresden. The book was published in a first run of 50,000 copies. Peter remembered that they sold out very quickly. A poem by Max Zimmering included in the book blamed "Wallstreet" for the destruction of Dresden, presented the Red Army as the city's saviors, and sang the praises of the men and women who had set about clearing the ruins and rebuilding the city.[28] The first three images are pictures of Dresden taken at night before the war. Then a panoramic view of the center of the city on the Elbe was juxtaposed with the first and undoubtedly the most famous of Peter's ruin pictures (fig. 40). If any photograph of the bombing war qualifies for iconic status, it is this picture taken in 1945 from the top of the Dresden City Hall tower. In the foreground, the photograph shows a sculpture on the tower roof (normally misidentified as an angel but in reality an

Fig. 40

allegorical figure of good government). Behind the statue, we see the endless, jagged ruins of buildings that stretch away to the top of the photograph and apparently to the very horizon of the city. The figure stands, slightly bent, with outstretched right hand, as if pointing sadly to the ruined buildings. In the course of the past six decades, this photograph has become an unmistakable emblem of the air war.

Michael Neumann's explanation of the power of this one photograph focuses on its internal composition.[29] He argues that the gesture of the sculpture locates both it and the viewer outside the destruction to which it also draws attention. The viewer is invited to adopt a distanced, aesthetic stance toward the ruined city. Yet this aesthetic appropriation of the image collides with the moral and emotional effects (horror, sadness, anger) produced by seeing the destruction. A powerful fusion of aesthetics, emotion, and moral response is the result, allowing the image to serve as an accusation but also as an affirmation of German collective identity. Confrontation with Dresden's "sacrifice" reminds Germans of their identity and of their duty to rebuild the nation. The photograph transcends history by giving the destruction of Dresden a mythical status that bestows meaning on this meaningless historical event. More recently, Anne Fuchs has offered a somewhat different reading of the aesthetic qualities of this photograph that suggests that "the allegorical rendition of the picture . . . lent itself to a much broader reception as a generalised icon of the gratuitous destruction of warfare."[30] These analyses are convincing as far as they go. What they do not take into account is the fact that three other photographers—by Willy Rossner, Erich Andres, and Ernst Schmidt—took very similar pictures at the same location between 1945 and 1947. Neither Neumann's nor Fuch's analyses helps us understand why only Peter's photograph became such a powerful icon.

After 1947, photographers continued to take pictures from this same vantage point at the top of the city hall. In these subsequent photographs, what we can see of the city behind the sculpture predictably changes. The views offered by Hilmar Pabel in 1955 and by Dietmar Alex show us the immense, uncanny empty space in the very center of Dresden left after the ruins had been cleared, which is now traversed by just a few lonely streets; "because of the slow reconstruction, the war and its consequences were thus present as extensive areas of wasteland."[31] By 1969, however, when Richard Peter returned to take another photograph from the same tower, this urban void had been filled in with socialist housing and public buildings. The fact that photographers kept returning to this site, even though ruins were no longer to be seen in the background, suggests that it is the location itself that has become iconic. In that location, the one constant element is the figure of the "angel." Do the later photographs that depict the new socialist housing in the background "work" because the image of the "angel" reminds viewers of the earlier photographs of destruction taken at this same location? Over the years, has the "angel" in fact become the iconic element of all these photographs?

The general impression created by Peter's book is of the complete devastation that has affected all areas of the city's life.[32] A long section of ruin photos, which constitutes more than half of all the images in the book, ends with a photo of a skeleton that had been used for instruction in anatomical drawing at the Dresden Academy of Art. The figure is pictured as it "grasps with its claw over the ruins of the Frauenkirche and the City Hall Tower."[33] The picture on the very next page shows messages written in chalk on the remaining walls of buildings by people looking for missing relatives and friends. This is the first direct reference to the human victims of the bombing. In this entire first section of the book, there are no pictures of dead bodies, although one picture of a Christ figure and effigies of saints lying in the ruins may serve as indirect allusions to the human beings killed in the raid. The section of the book that follows moves from ruined buildings to pictures of dead bodies in these ruins, which Peter had taken when he accompanied cleanup details into basements and air-raid shelters.

Of the three corpse pictures taken by Peter that are published in his book, two are of men in uniform. One of the dead men was a Nazi Party official (fig. 41). The message was that some of those who died in the bombing were indeed perpetrators *but* it was precisely these Nazis who had brought the bombs down on everyone else, including the woman who is the subject of the third picture. This visual strategy also uses gender to establish categories of guilt and innocence; the guilty male figures (perhaps also representing fascism in the broadest sense as a violent and aggressive masculine political aberration) are the cause of the suffering and death of the innocent female victim. On the page following the picture of the dead air-raid warden, Peter included two pictures of corpses being burned on the Altmarkt by another photographer who was in Dresden at the time of the raid and who had official permission to take pictures.[34]

Fig. 41

It is unclear whether the swastika on this Nazi Party official's uniform did in fact survive the bombing or was placed on the corpse afterward. At the very least it would appear that the corpse's arm has been rearranged to make the swastika visible.

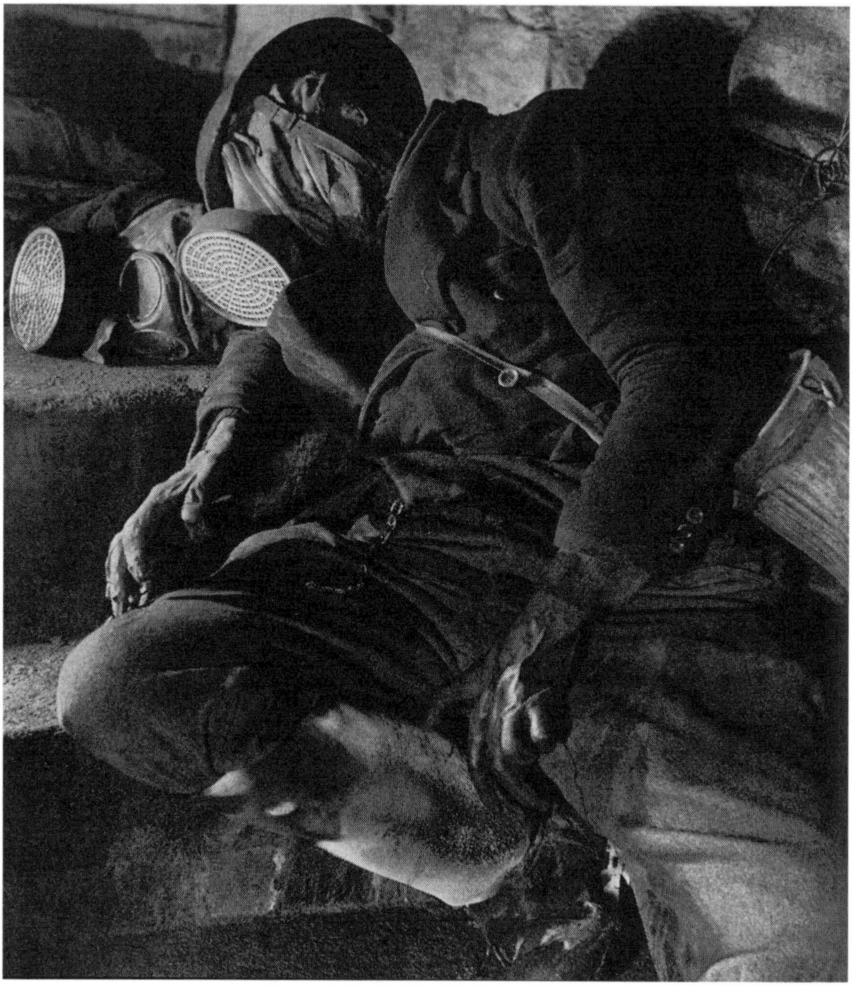

Fig. 42

Corpse of an air-raid warden whose gas mask has not helped save his life. This male figure seems to occupy a position somewhere between perpetrator and victim. Obviously, he is implicated in the Nazi dictatorship by his uniform and function, but was he forced into this job or simply duped?

Fig. 43

A mummified woman in an air-raid cellar.

The next section of Peter's book shows that there was also life in these ruins: refugees from the East, a returning soldier, children, but above all workers helping to clean up the ruins. The following section moves the visual narrative into the postwar period. We see workers building a bridge across the Elbe to reconnect the Alt-und Neustadt.[35] Other workers construct new buildings, reconstruct factories, and build streets. In these pictures, men and women work together, and Dresden citizens volunteer their free hours to help with the cleanup. We see new hospitals, clinics, apartment houses, and homes for old people under construction. One picture shows the new Rathaus, another shows workers back at the drawing boards and work benches of a rebuilt factory. The book ends with a picture of a mason, carrying a load of mortar on his back and climbing a ladder to the top of a building under construction. In his memoir, Peter wrote about this section of the book, saying, "It was not enough for me [to document the destruction]. Along with the destructive, the constructive . . . had to be made visible, which with all its strength started the removal of the material and spiritual rubble, which with bare hands and empty stomachs bored into the piles of rubble and, sorting methodically, retrieved from the disastrous legacy that which was still usable."[36]

As in other East German cities, the SED authorities in Dresden wanted to focus less on the city's past than on its socialist future. Ruin pictures were combined with photographs of new buildings to show, as one contributor to the *SZ* put it in 1975, that "from the Residenzstadt which was destroyed has come a new socialist city."[37] Still, the prewar image of Dresden as the "Florence on the Elbe" was too powerful to resist. Susanne Vees-Gulani argues that a distinctive "visual archive," compiled over the course of the previous two centuries, shaped the way that postwar Germans could see and understand the destruction of Dresden. Since the 18th century, Dresden had been presented visually in paintings, photographs, and mass circulation postcards as a unique architectural and cultural treasure. On a visit to Dresden in 1956, the president of the GDR, Wilhelm Pieck, emphasized the importance of reclaiming Dresden's architectural heritage: "Dresden was and is a pearl among the cities of Europe. It is an honorable obligation for our Republic to care for Dresden and its reputation."[38] Visual and textual representations of postwar Dresden tried to show that the SED's rebuilding program had achieved a balanced combination of new socialist housing and painstaking reconstructions of historically important structures.[39] To demonstrate how the "old and the new have grown together to form a harmonious unity," the *SZ* printed a story in 1985, accompanied by several photographs, about the rebuilding of the "Street of Liberation" between 1975 and 1979.[40] Here a "loving" synthesis had been achieved by making the new buildings gesture architecturally to the old. Such concessions were not required of the old buildings. In fact, this was a particularly purist restoration that got rid of the 19th-century "disfigurements" of the *Bürgerhäuser* to reveal their original baroque forms.[41]

Of course, it may have been difficult to explain to the ordinary citizens of Dresden why scarce building materials and skilled labor were being diverted to the reconstruction of historic buildings when so many people still needed roofs over their heads. In his novel *Phosphorus and Lilacs* (*Phosphor und Flieder*), published in 1954, Max Zimmering, a Jewish communist émigré who spent the Hitler years in Czechoslovakia, Palestine, and England, tried to address this apparent contradiction by invoking the authority of Lenin.[42] In a painfully artificial scene (one of many thinly disguised political manifestos in the novel) set in the years right after the war, Wulf-Dieter Bergius, grandson of a "bourgeois" former art professor and son of a *Wehrmacht* veteran and ex-Nazi Party member, until recently a prisoner of war, has just started to work on the restoration of the Zwinger.[43] During a break, the young man goes out to the Brühlsche Terrasse, a historic architectural ensemble. As Wulf-Dieter sits on a bench reading a book, an old man starts to talk with him:

> "You must be working nearby? In the Art Academy?"
>
> "No, in the Zwinger."
>
> "It is good that the Zwinger will be rebuilt. If you put your shoulder into it, I may perhaps still be alive to experience the completion of the reconstruction. . . . I am eighty-one, at my age one's time horizon is a bit shorter. . . ." "How long will you need until you are finished with the Zwinger?" the old man asked.
>
> "Perhaps five years, perhaps six or seven. It depends upon the delivery/supply of building materials."
>
> With a sigh, the old man observed that "It took just one night to destroy it."[44]

Realizing that this stranger is old enough to have been alive during Marx and Engel's time, Wulf-Dieter asks him whether he ever met the two leaders. The old man regrets that he did not but says that he did know Lenin and even spent time with him when he visited Dresden before the Russian Revolution. Lenin, it turns out, was an expert on Dresden's architectural treasures. The two of them stood in exactly this same spot on the *Terrasse* many years ago, as Lenin pointed out each of the important buildings in Dresden's exceptional urban panorama. Lenin, the old man feels sure, would have heartily approved of the restoration of the Zwinger: "Above all, he had great respect for these achievements. At that time, I did not quite understand why exactly a Russian revolutionary would display such high regard for the buildings of the past."[45]

Yet the SED regime's claims to have retrieved the most important architectural heritage of Dresden while at the same time moving ahead with the construction of a new "socialist" city were challenged by what citizens could see around them in their everyday lives. The Frauenkirche, which "[f[or many . . . represented the center of Dresden's cultural reputation and the city's true soul," was intentionally left as a ruin.[46] Large areas of ruins, which could have been salvaged, were torn down and cleared away, leaving "immense amounts of empty space."[47] By the beginning of the 1950s "only the ground plan of the old city remained, its streets and underground network of utilities."[48] The authorities may have wanted to present this radical restructuring of urban space as a necessary first step in the construction of a new "socialist" Dresden. But the vast emptiness of the city center in the immediate postwar years can only have intensified the feelings of cultural loss encouraged by the official rhetoric that depicted the Allied bombing as a crime that deprived Dresden of its unique cultural and architectural history.

When new buildings eventually began to fill in this empty urban space, they contrasted visibly with the prewar structures that had been destroyed, not only by the bombing but also by the radical postwar removal of ruins (see figs. 44 and 45). In 1984, for example, an East German publication showed the famous Dresden shopping area, the Prager Strasse, as it had appeared before the bombing and as it now looked with its new "socialist" structures. Whatever Dresden residents may have felt about the aesthetic merits of socialist construction, it could not be denied that postwar building had radically altered the face of much of the city.[49]

Until the very end of the SED regime in 1989, the GDR nevertheless continued to trumpet its achievements in restoring the architectural treasures of Dresden. The reopening of the Semperoper in 1985, for example, was televised and broadcast to 19 different countries, East and West.[50] Tourists no doubt appreciated this revival of historic Dresden. The *Sächsische Zeitung* claimed that by 1975, over three million of them were visiting the city each year.[51] Yet the visual traces of the city's baroque past in its "socialist" present may have made it difficult for Dresden's citizens to reconcile the old with the new. The SED regime exploited photographs of the many historic buildings that had been destroyed as well as the limited number that it had restored to reinforce its political message that the Allied bombers' destruction of this "unique city" was an unparalleled crime. By continuing to insist that what had been lost was irreplaceable, the official narrative of the bombing ensured that "Dresden before the destruction continued to exist as an imaginary parallel reality."[52] It is hard to see how Dresdners could be convinced that they could both mourn the loss of their city's past and yet at the same time celebrate the new socialist future: "no 'New Dresden' could replace the unique city of the collective narrative."[53] It is not surprising that after the end of the GDR "Dresden residents have un-

Fig. 44

Fig. 45

dertaken popular initiatives to ensure the rebuilding of almost all parts of the historic city center the way they looked before the firebombing in 1945, even if this means the destruction of buildings erected during East German times."[54]

Peace and Socialism

The GDR frequently used the example of Dresden as an argument for its official "peace movement." Apart from Hiroshima and Nagasaki, Dresden provided the clearest possible warning against the horrors of a nuclear war. If this kind of devastation had been produced by the firebombing of one German city, what might be in store for the victims of a nuclear attack? The bombing of Dresden was presented as a conversion experience. In the ashes of the Elbe metropolis, East Germans had come to realize that they must embrace socialism if they were ever to have peace again. Monopoly capitalism (here meaning the United States) was already preparing the next war before the last fires in the ruins of Dresden had died out. In 1955, West Germany joined NATO and in 1956 the Federal Republic introduced conscription and began to build up a new army. These steps were depicted by the East German regime as the prelude to the next war. Because the 10th anniversary in 1955 of the bombing of Dresden coincided with the campaign against the Paris Treaties that made possible West Germany's entry into NATO, the East German authorities were able to use this commemoration to draw attention to the threat they claimed NATO posed to peace.[55] From the middle of January, one month before the actual anniversary date, the National Front organization in Dresden staged "enlightenment weeks" to explain the reasons for "the senseless incineration of their city" in 1945 and to encourage Dresden citizens to fight against the Paris Treaties. Local "enlightenment centers" offered exhibitions and lectures with slides that pictured Dresden as it was before the bombing and immediately after the attack. Images of the destruction of the old Dresden were contrasted with pictures of the new "city of art and culture" that was under construction in 1955. East Germans were exhorted to prevent another February 13, 1945, that would destroy what had been achieved in the past 10 years. Who knew better than the citizens of Dresden how important it was "to dedicate all their strength to the preservation of peace?"[56]

The struggle for world peace was not meant to be an exclusively East German concern. Although condemning the West German political leaders who wanted to "rearm German militarism,"[57] the *SZ* insisted that ordinary Germans, especially those who had suffered through the Allied bombing of other cities, wanted peace regardless of whether they lived in West or East Germany. When the 10th anniversary of the destruction of Dresden was officially commemorated, the *SZ* reported that "numerous people from the West of our homeland will also spend some time in Dresden." The newspaper drew attention to "a particularly strong delegation from Pforzheim . . . the city which was also heavily destroyed during the Second World War."[58] East Germans met with these and other West Germans to discuss the problems of peace and Dresden citizens were encouraged to write letters to West Germans asking them to protest against ratification of the Paris Treaties by the Bundestag.[59]

In addition to West German visitors, delegations from Czechoslovakia, France, England, and Japan came to Dresden for the commemoration of the 10th anniversary of the city's destruction by English and American bombs.[60] Oberbürgermeister Weidauer described this international participation as the "obligation of the entire German people to strengthen its struggle against the remilitarization of West Germany and also against a new, frightful 13 February 1945."[61] To emphasize its argument that "it is up to all of us to prevent a new war,"[62] the *SZ* drew its readers' attention to the individual partnership agreements Dresden had signed with several other cities that had also been devastated by World War II.[63] Why, however, these particular cities should be "partnered" with Dresden was by no means self-evident. After all, German air raids had devastated Coventry. Stalingrad was destroyed by German bombing and by house-to-house fighting between German and Red Army troops that claimed close to a million lives before it was finished. German soldiers had leveled Warsaw with dynamite, block-by-block, on Hitler's order as they retreated from the Red Army. But from the point of view of SED propaganda, "there was no longer a difference between the 'imperialist' German *Wehrmacht* and the equally 'imperialistic' American air fleet."[64]

Max Zimmering's novel showed how Dresden and Warsaw (and by implication all the other cities in the *Sächsische Zeitung* story above) could be seen as "partners" in the fight for world peace. Toward the end of the book, a delegation of visitors from Poland, who have just attended the 1951 Third World Festival of Youth and Students in East Berlin, visit Dresden as part of their tour of East German cities. Their host and guide is Erich Reichhold, an antifascist imprisoned by the Nazis who, ironically, was able to escape from prison when the Allied bombers attacked Dresden. Now, six years later, he is an important official in the local administration. During the tour of Dresden, Reichhold points out the "Blue Wonder," a famous bridge over the Elbe. One of the Polish visitors, an architect from Warsaw, makes a note so that he can give a full report to his colleagues at home; "the visitors from Warsaw wanted to know everything . . . and they especially wanted to hear about Dresden . . . because a community of fate connected [the two cities]." This remark makes Reichhold uncomfortable. He begins to apologize for the crimes committed in Warsaw by the Germans but his guest interrupts the apology with the simple assertion that "Fascism is always and everywhere barbarous."[65] All of these cities, then, share a history of suffering inflicted by "fascists." Whether it was Germans or Americans who caused the destruction appeared not to matter. By 1965, this international brotherhood of the victims of fascism included Leningrad, Wroclaw, Coventry, Strasbourg, and Vietnam, all of whom sent delegations to that year's commemoration ceremonies that were attended by 100,000 citizens of Dresden.[66] Organizers continued to try to achieve international prominence by inviting foreign delegations, especially from symbolically important cities such as Coventry or Leningrad, Warsaw or Lidice.[67]

That same year, Max Jaap's documentary film for East German television, *Dresden—Remembering and Warning*, restated the argument that there was a direct link between the bombing of Dresden and the threat of nuclear war. The film opened with scenes of New York, London, and Paris. What would these world metropolises look like, the commentator asked, if they became the targets of atomic bombs? Pictures of ruins in Nagasaki, Coventry, and Dresden provided the answer. The film blamed Hitler for the destruction of Germany, but by bombing Dresden the Americans and the British had sunk to the same level of barbarism as the Nazis. Pictures of demonstrations against nuclear rearmament made it clear that the postwar generation of East Germans would not accept the threat of nuclear war. It had already devoted too much energy to building a new Dresden and a new Germany. Like other visual representations of postwar Dresden, Jaap's film presented images of both the restored Zwinger and of modern postwar apartment buildings. The film also depicted the new industries and factories that the GDR had built in Dresden since the end of the war. The new Dresden would be both a "City of Technology" and a "City of Art."[68] Images of young people, studying, working, dancing, or visiting museums, reinforced the film's central message that this postwar generation was committed to constructing a "new more just, better world" than the one that had produced the destruction of Dresden.[69]

The Russian "Friends"

Demonizing the American "imperialists" who had sent their "air pirates" to destroy Dresden in 1945 and who continued, with the support of their West

German "fascist" allies, to threaten the very existence of the GDR helped the East German regime to present the Soviet occupiers as "friends."[70] A photograph in a book published in Dresden on the 30th anniversary of the firebombing of the city showed young Red Army soldiers clearing the ruins of a bombed-out building. This image carried the caption, "Soldiers with the Red Star—our Liberators."[71] Additional text underneath the picture explains that "[g]one but not forgotten is that time when the men and officers of the Red Army helped us to survive the hardest period. With their personal help, rich in deeds and material assistance, with their selfless ideological support, they made the road to socialism possible for us."

This was the standard official line of the SED regime. The Red Army and the Soviet Union were "friends." The enemies, though not here specifically identified, were clearly the British and American "imperialists" whose bombers had produced the pile of rubble that the Russian troops were now so cheerfully and selflessly helping to remove. What is remarkable about this picture, apart from the fact that it was probably staged, is the way in which it invokes a common postwar symbol of German recovery—the "women of the ruins" (*Trümmerfrauen*)—who began to rebuild German cities literally with their own two hands.[72] Consciously or unconsciously, this picture appropriates the considerable symbolic capital that had been invested in the image of the *Trümmerfrau* since 1945. If "Soldiers with the Red Star" was not a "true" picture (and even perhaps if it was), it raised the question of how ordinary Germans who had experienced Russian occupation could possibly have reacted to it? This image of the Russian "friends" would certainly have clashed quite violently with the racist images of the Asiatic threat cultivated by Goebbels during the Nazi period. Probably even more important, this image pushed aside the real experiences and more widespread knowledge of mass rapes by Soviet occupying forces, forced labor, and incarceration in Soviet "special camps," all of which were officially ignored.[73]

We can see a similar official amnesia in a story published in February 1955 in the *Sächsische Zeitung* that depicted the "Soviet soldiers as the first people to help us."[74] The article claimed that as soon as it arrived in Dresden, the Red Army gave inhabitants food from their own field kitchens. Later the Soviets also sent food transports. Soviet pioneers put up emergency bridges across the Elbe. The Soviet *Stadtkommandant* also directed Soviet technicians and engineers to help restore water, power, gas, and public transport.[75] Nor was this praise limited to the more practical efforts of the Russian "friends." When it entered Dresden in 1945, the Red Army removed a number of priceless paintings from the Semper Gallery and sent them to Moscow for "safekeeping." On a tour of the newly reopened gallery in 1956, Wilhelm Pieck, the president of the GDR, wrote in the museum guestbook:

> Now that I have seen the paintings in their traditional homes, I want to thank the Soviet people from the bottom of my heart for saving, restoring and returning these works of art. Only those who know the indescribable extent of the senseless destruction of Dresden in February 1945 and the chaos of the collapse of the Hitler dictatorship can measure the full extent of this achievement. The rescue of the Dresden paintings by the Soviet Army is an exceptional cultural deed, which will remain in the German people's thankful memory.[76]

The Postwar Generations

As early as 1965, the *SZ* acknowledged the problem of making the story of the bombing of Dresden meaningful to the generation of East Germans born after the war. Max Zimmering, author of *Phosphor und Flieder*, lamented that "the remnants of the Frauenkirche meant to serve as a warning probably have the same kind of effect upon [this generation] as the old castle ruins I encountered when hiking as a young man. . . . Recently, a young boy from Prague visited me. He had heard about 13 February 1945 and wanted to see something of the destruction of Dresden. He must have expected some sort of Pompeii and was almost a little disappointed when I could only show him a few open spaces on Prager Straße and the ruins around the castle."[77] When students in Class 7a at a local *Oberschule* were asked, "What do you know about the 13th February 1945 in Dresden," they provided the politically appropriate responses. All said they were happy to be able to grow up in peace, and not be subjected to war. All expressed their hatred for those who had planned the raid and their respect for the *Trümmerfrauen* who had dug Dresden out of the ruins. All were proud that the Zwinger had been reconstructed. And all swore their commitment to continued peace by learning and working hard at school.[78] Yet most of these students were too young to have experienced the raids themselves.[79] What they knew about the destruction of Dresden came secondhand from parents or older siblings.

One way to overcome this generational gap was to run stories about children who were actually born during the raid. These articles showed that the memory of the destruction of Dresden was still alive within individual families. The newspaper's job was to make this "private" knowledge "public." On February 13, 1965, for example, the *Sächsische Zeitung* told the story of Frau Wernecke who had given birth to her son Hans-Peter as the raids were under way. The article was accompanied by several photographs, one of them showing Frau Wernecke in a blanket with which she fled through the corridor of the destroyed Women's Clinic.[80]

This woman was actually separated from her son in the chaos that followed the air attack. After several anxious days of searching for her newborn, the mother was reunited with her child. Then began the long, difficult struggle "to procure food and . . . clothing for him."[81] Although his mother often told Hans-Peter the story of his birth as he was growing up, the child was not particularly interested in the past until he became a Young Pioneer. Now his mother's stories began to fit together with what he was learning in school. Now he began to understand what war is and what he owed to his mother and to all the other comrades who had worked so hard to create a new, honest Fatherland from the desert of ruins that Germany had become by the end of the war.[82] Now, on the anniversary of the destruction of Dresden, as Hans-Peter celebrated his 20th birthday, the young man decided that he must join the SED:

> He joined that party whose highest goal was peace and which would save us from new horrors . . . in a few weeks he was going for three years to a radio communications unit in the National People's Army in order to protect what all of us, including Hans-Peter's mother, had rebuilt in the last twenty years, and to prevent those who have not yet learned anything from the Second World War and from the crimes against Dresden from instigating a third, an atomic world war. Hans-Peter's own children should not be born in a night of flames, a time of horrors, of murder.[83]

Born in destruction, this generation would redeem its parents' sacrifices and suffering through its commitment to socialism.[84]

Yet the official claims that the new socialist Dresden was "better than ever" might encourage the second generation to distance itself from the war and the bombing. A survivor of the February 1945 air attacks complained in 1975, for example, that some young people, who only knew postwar Dresden, wondered whether it was really necessary to keep talking about the past; they seemed to think that "in view of the auspicious, beautiful future of our socialist metropolis . . . perhaps some forgetting might be in order."[85] As the physical remnants of the destruction of Dresden began to disappear, it seemed all the more urgent to have the remaining living witnesses of the 1945 bombing talk to young people. In February 1985, for example, the *SZ* reported that Erika

Hohlfelde, one of the *Trümmerfrauen* who had been a model for the statue in front of the new Rathaus, had met with the young workers engaged in the reconstruction of the Semperoper.[86] Six days later, other surviving witnesses spoke at an event entitled "The 13 February 1945-Reflection-Remembering-Analysis," at which films of Dresden were also screened.[87] A woman born in 1940, whose father had been killed in the war before she could know him, said that her story was like that of many others of her generation. Her grandmother did not survive the bombing of Dresden. Her aunt suffered such a shock in the raids that she had still not recovered. Just two desires dominated this young woman's entire life after the war: to have enough to eat and to live in peace. She was clearly aware that this primitive existence might be hard for her young listeners to imagine. Although she was proud of what she saw when she looked around reconstructed Dresden, she was also worried that "[m]uch has again become taken for granted by us: good food, nice clothes, modern housing, social measures, etc., etc."[88] If all this was to be preserved for her children, "we cannot simply talk about peace but must give our best and then some each and every day."[89] The date of February 13, 1985, was for this women not just a day for commemoration of the past: "no, on this day I, along with many other citizens of Dresden, consciously vow to oppose a senseless, imperialist war and to support the continued, peaceful construction of our beautiful hometown, Dresden, 40 years of peace in the GDR—that is our common task."[90]

As surviving witnesses grew older and died, concrete connections to the experience of February 13–14, 1945, became less and less common. Dresden's authorities were well aware that the relationship of most young people to the destruction of Dresden would increasingly be an indirect contact, established not by living in the ruins or listening to family stories but by media representations, especially those presented by photographs and films. In 1965, the *Sächsische Zeitung* acknowledged the uses to which photography could be put by introducing a new photo feature. Every 14 days it would publish two photographs: one taken during the war or right after 1945 in the ruins of Dresden, the other a contemporary photograph. This "then and now" juxtaposition was of course already a standard device in the visual representation of the bombing of Dresden. The novelty of this particular version was its interactive nature. Readers were encouraged "to write out their thoughts on every pair of pictures and send them in to us. In this way, with your help, we can make a small contribution to the 20th anniversary of the liberation." The best entries would receive a cash prize. The first installment of this new feature offered one picture of the Altmarkt area in ruins and then, 20 years later, "a view from the HO-Department Store on the Altmarkt of the new buildings on the Ernst-Thälmann-Strasse."[91]

That same month the *SZ* described an exhibition entitled "Dresden—20 Years After" that had been staged by eight amateur photographers. This show presented "some 170 close-ups from all areas of the new building in Dresden, created by young amateur photographers of the Photography Work-Cooperative of the German Cultural Union (*Arbeitsgemeinschaft Fotografie des Deutschen Kulturbundes*) [which are] an optimistic documentation. See what has become of us. Only a few . . . disturbing photos of Dresden after the destruction deepen our view of what has been achieved since then."[92]

The East German official public commemoration of the 25th anniversary in 1970 of the destruction of Dresden was the last for more than a decade. Propaganda against the "militarism" of West Germany and against "international imperialism" now threatened to do more harm than good to the international political standing of the GDR.[93] But in October 1981, a group of young Dresdners organized an unofficial piece initiative and distributed handmade leaflets announcing an informal commemoration on February 13 in front of the ruins of the Frauenkirche. They told people to bring candles and flowers. The group would sing "We shall overcome" and then go home. The SED authorities threatened reprisals if this meeting took place. To protect the youths, the Evangelical-Lutheran state church (Landeskirche) offered to mediate. The group of young people finally accepted a "peace forum" in the Kreuzkirche as an alternative. On the evening of February 13, some 5,000 mostly young people assembled there and discussed with representatives of the church "controversial themes of contemporary everyday politics." Nevertheless, about a thousand youths still went to the ruins of the Frauenkirche, where they stood silently with burning candles.[94] This event gave a significant impetus to the development of an unofficial peace movement in the GDR.

The SED regime attempted to reassert its claim to the exclusive rights to use the anniversaries of the bombing of Dresden in the service of its own "peace movement" by reinaugurating large public commemorations in 1982, this time in front of ruins of the Frauenkirche so as to occupy this important public space symbolically.[95] Nevertheless, in each successive year, several hundred people, sometimes even thousands, assembled for an unofficial silent commemoration with candles at the same location. Since 1983, there were also annual ecumenical religious peace services, alternately in the Kreuzkirche and the Hofkirche. On the 40th anniversary of the bombing, 200,000 people assembled for the official commemoration with Honecker as the main speaker. But the regime was not able to control unofficial expressions of remembrance, such as an artistic happening during which actors sawed a cardboard model of the city in half for exactly 13 minutes, the duration of the first 1945 raid.

In 1986 and 1989, two simultaneous remembrance services took place in the Coventry cathedral, broadcast by the BBC, and in the Dresden Kreuzkirche.[96] The testimony of eyewitnesses soon become an integral component of these church services. Volunteers started systematic interviews with eyewitnesses and some of the results were published in 1987. An important impetus was also provided by the "Working Group Encounter with Judaism," founded in 1982 by representatives of both religions. Since 1945, the official claim that Dresden was an "innocent city" with no real military targets had allowed Dresdners not to confront any questions about their own complicity in the Nazi regime; "the dominant self-image of Dresden remained untouched by the concentration camps in the city, the 'Jewish Houses,' the barracks for forced laborers and POWs or the guillotine in the courtyard of the state court (*Landgericht*). And the SED did not question [this self-image]: the innocent city."[97] By uncovering aspects of the city's involvement in the Nazi regime and the conduct of the war, the unofficial memory work of the 1980s began to raise challenges to this notion of the innocent city; "[f]rom . . . this 'informal public sphere' [created by] individual groups and churches, a parallel culture of memory developed . . . which mobilized several thousand people on the annual anniversaries of the destruction of Dresden and which counted for many as 'the real commemoration.'"[98] By the end of the 1980s, the SED had lost its monopoly of public representation of February 13, 1945.

The political instrumentalization before 1989 by the SED of the destruction of Dresden has not prevented Dresden from becoming a supersite of national memory and commemoration since the Fall of the Wall. Despite the criticisms it faced before the end of the GDR, the official Dresden narrative has not simply disappeared. No longer embedded in Cold War propaganda, key components of the official GDR narrative have survived the end of East German communism. Dresden now symbolizes the horrors of the Anglo-American air war more powerfully than the names of any of the other major German cities—above all Hamburg, Cologne, and Berlin—which were equally, sometimes more devastated by the bombing war.[99] In post-1989 publications and films, on the Internet as well as in public commemorations, Dresden is regularly represented as the "uniquely beautiful" and "innocent" city destroyed by Allied bombers for no clear military reason at a point when Hitler had already lost the war. Clearly, this particular representation of Dresden continues to serve important needs in reunified Germany.

CHAPTER 6

After the Cold War: The Multimedia Bombing War since the 1990s

The end of the Cold War and the fall of the Berlin Wall have changed the ways the bombing war is narrated and pictured in reunified Germany. Some possibilities have been eliminated. After 1990, West German narratives could, for example, no longer claim the justification provided by the renewed threat of nuclear war in the 1980s. Yet, at the same time, the first and second Gulf wars created new possibilities for depicting Germany's experience of Allied bombing as an important cautionary tale about the dangers of air war and war in general. After the fall of the Berlin Wall, the official East German narratives disappeared as quickly as the communist state that had created them. The end of the GDR created a space for local publications about the bombing of East German cities that had previously been ignored or not allowed by the SED regime.[1] Narratives and images modeled on established West German patterns rushed in to occupy this vacated representational space in the eastern part of reunited Germany.[2] Yet it is hard to ignore the undeniable continuities with the East German official narratives that were themselves heavily influenced by Nazi propaganda, even if they refused to acknowledge this connection.

As important as the question of how the stories and the pictures have or have not changed since the end of the Cold War is the transformation of the ways in which they are now communicated to much larger audiences. The most significant alteration is the spread of narratives and images of the bombing from the local publications that served as the primary "vectors of memory" for so many decades, to national publications, film, television, and the Internet.[3] An increasing emphasis on the importance of eyewitness testimony and personal accounts has accompanied this movement of narratives and images of the bombing into the modern mass media.[4]

Moving Images: Film and Television

Film was used after 1945 to show Germans the bombing war and its effects, but until quite recently it has not been as important a medium as photography. Some of the early films represented themselves as documentaries but were simply propaganda. As early as 1946, the largest German film studio, DEFA, now located in the Russian Zone of Occupation, made four short films on Berlin, Dresden, Leipzig, and Potsdam.[5] These films showed ruins but concentrated on the revival of political life, the leadership provided by the SED, and the hard physical work of ordinary Germans who were clearing away the rubble. In 1949, a Western propaganda film, *Two Cities*, contrasted rebuilding efforts in Dresden and in Stuttgart. Dresden came off badly in the comparison.[6] German cities destroyed by the bombing also appeared in fiction films, particularly the genre of "rubble films" made in the late 1940s. These movies focused on Germans' attempts to confront or avoid confrontation with the Nazi past and to reestablish some kind of postwar moral as well as material normalcy.[7] The ruins of German cities symbolized the moral disintegration of Germany under Nazism. But "rubble films" were not directly concerned with the story of the bombing war that had produced these ruins. In other postwar fiction films, the bombing figured as an important theme, though not the central concern of the story: for example, Helma Sanders-Brahm's *Germany, Pale Mother* (*Deutschland, bleiche Mutter*), which premiered at the Berlin Film Festival in February 1980.[8]

In the 1960s and 1970s, West German television was not particularly interested in the air war. By the late 1970s, however, television documentaries about World War II had begun to compete with photographs for the attention of German audiences.[9] In 1985, the 40th anniversary of the end of the war, ARD produced the most extensive documentary of the air war to date: five 45–55 minute sequences with the title *War of the Bombers* (*Krieg der Bomber*), which followed the air war from German air raids on Warsaw in 1939 to the destruction of Dresden in February 1945. The series offered viewers the problematic interpretation that the Allied air campaign was motivated by British desire for revenge against Germany for the bombing of London and other British cities. The series also morally condemned Allied bombing attacks on German cities, at least those that took place in 1945; the attack on Dresden was described as a "massacre."[10]

Since the late 1990s, films about the bombing war have changed in three important ways. First, there are now simply many more of them. Second, the genres of films available have expanded to include "doku-dramas" and one major fictional film, as well as the more conventional documentaries. Finally, large audiences have watched some of these films. What kinds of images can German viewers see in these films? Until quite recently, German documentary films relied heavily and quite uncritically on Nazi-era film footage, especially the newsreels. Even when these Nazi images were integrated into a new narrative, "their aesthetic power remained intact."[11] In recent years, filmmakers have become more sensitive to the dangers of using these "familiar newsreel pictures" and have begun to search for different images of the Nazi past.[12] Kay Hoffman notes that "[s]ince the 1990s amateur film footage has increasingly been used, which has the advantage for TV of being in color, as opposed to the black and white newsreel pictures."[13] However, private film images of the bombing war seem to be in short supply. Amateurs appear more often to have taken photographs than to have made films.[14] As a result, documentary films about the bombing war must often rely heavily on a combination of German still photographs and Allied moving pictures.

Recent documentary films have, however, created completely new images in the form of the filmed testimonies of eyewitnesses (*Zeitzeugen*). These new pictures often constitute a large percentage of the images that viewers see in a documentary. Until the end of the 1970s, historical documentaries on the German public television networks were educational programs, aimed not at a mass audience but at an interested minority of viewers. Depicting the past on television was the province of academic experts. Eyewitnesses could seldom be seen in these television history programs because the subjective and emotional qualities of first person accounts were regarded as an unwelcome distraction from the program's educational mission.[15] But then in the mid-1980s, growing competition from the new private networks that were trying to attract a mass audience forced the public networks to reconsider their original concepts. To reach more viewers, the authors of TV documentaries began to employ popular forms of storytelling "which focused upon the life histories and stories of suffering of individuals."[16] Both the public and the private networks now began to develop "a history TV for a mass public which focused upon experiences, memories, and story-telling rather than professional scientific analysis."[17] This shift placed a premium on the filmed testimony of eyewitnesses. The increasing use of eyewitness accounts in films about the bombing war may also be a response to the growing importance and success of videotaped testimonies of survivors in documentaries about the Holocaust. Gertrud Koch points out that in recent years visual archives have moved to the very center of the discourse on the Holocaust.[18] The visual has almost become a metaphor for the real. The use of eyewitness testimony in films about the bombing war is based on similar assumptions about the authenticity of eyewitness accounts.

Filmed eyewitness testimony can be used to encourage viewers to feel that it is possible to create an immediate, emotional connection with the past. But whether eyewitness testimony privileges emotion and empathy over understanding depends on how it is presented.[19] A particularly egregious example is the use of filmed eyewitness testimony in a tendentious DVD, *The Dresden Firestorm. Air Attacks against the Undefended Hospital City Dresden*, which makes a point of focusing on one woman who cries almost every time she speaks. At one point in the film, she is so overwhelmed with emotion that she has to move out of the frame of the camera.[20] Even in films that do not try so blatantly to manipulate their viewers' feelings, the ways the witnesses are presented on camera often encourage an emotional response, especially if they appear against a black background that focuses visual attention on their facial expressions.[21] It is also unnerving to see these people in their present comfortably furnished houses or apartments talking about the complete destruction of their homes during the war. When combined with historical footage, these new images can create powerful montage effects. Sound is also important. In the 2003 film *Air Attack on Hamburg* (*Luftangriff auf Hamburg*), for example, the voice of an eyewitnesses is combined with footage of burning buildings—what we hear gives meaning to what we see.[22]

The 2003 Spiegel-TV film *Feuersturm. Der Bombenkrieg gegen Deutschland* (*Firestorm. The Bombing War against Germany*) relies on extensive footage of eyewitnesses talking about their experiences.[23] Historians are also frequently on camera, especially Jörg Friedrich, author of the controversial bestseller *Der Brand. Deutschland im Bombenkrieg 1940–1945* (*The Fire: The Bombing of Germany 1940–1945*). Friedrich's commentary plays a major role in shaping and structuring the narrative.[24] Early in the film he states that the killing of German workers was an integral component of Allied strategy, not a regrettable by-product. He observes that "from a military perspective, terror can be very sensible" but adds that "torturing Krupp workers with fire . . . is not legitimate" even if it did have a military goal. Friedrich is not the only expert who appears in the film. The filmmakers also interviewed a prominent British historian, Richard Overy, who states early in the film that he does not agree that this was a war against defenseless civilians. He does admit, however, that the Allied bombing campaign contravened the provisions of the then valid international law. The filmmakers do not openly attempt to adjudicate between these two sets of claims, but Friedrich is given considerably more time on camera than Overy.

Feuersturm includes the testimony of Michael Degen, a well-known Jewish-Israeli actor, born in 1932 in Chemnitz, who survived underground in Berlin with his mother. Degen emigrated to Israel in 1949 but returned to Germany in 1951, where he enjoyed a successful career as an actor on stage, in films, and on television. In 2006, the German television network ARD filmed his autobiography *Nicht alle waren Mörder* (*Not Everyone Was a Murderer*), which he wrote in 2002. Degen's presence reminds the viewer that not all Germans saw themselves simply as victims of the bombing. In one of his first appearances on-screen, Degen remarks that when the Allies began to bomb Berlin, "we felt someone at least was with us." Later in the film, Degen observes that several hundred Jews were trying to survive underground in Berlin; "we had to deal with two threats—Gestapo and bombs." Degen also confronts German viewers with a challenging mental image; during an air raid, his mother stands on the street in a suburban neighborhood of Berlin where they were hiding and demands that the Allied planes should hit the city "Again and again." Degen's body language and his tone as he describes this incident show that he relishes this story; "I will never forget it."

Eyewitnesses from the Allied side of the air war also appear in this film. One of them, a British pilot named John Chatterton, is now an old man living not far from the site where a Lancaster bomber has been preserved and put on display. The film shows him climbing inside the plane. The quarters are cramped. We are told that as many as 44 percent of the men who went out on a raid might not return. Chatterton was unusual; he survived 30 raids. The first part of this segment could certainly promote sympathy for the young British men who died in large numbers during the air war. But the commentary takes us in a different direction; although the losses incurred were enormous, the strategists at Bomber Command refused to call a halt to the bombing campaign. Instead, they shifted the focus to population centers that bombers could attack at night when they would be less vulnerable to German air defenses. German civilians paid the price for this stubborn British commitment to continuing the bombing, regardless of whether it could clearly be shown that it made military sense. The documentary mobilizes the testimony of an Allied air man to support this conclusion. Edwin Hays, a machine gunner on a bomber, admits that "honestly, I never saw a single target in Germany." His plane and the others in his group dropped bombs through the clouds; "I never saw a single explosion on the ground."

In black-and-white footage filmed in his office during the war, Sir Arthur ("Bomber") Harris tries to convince the British public of the power of a bombing campaign against Germany. Friedrich explains what Harris had in mind, especially with his attempts to create firestorms in German cities. Carpet bombing with explosives had already made entire cities into targets. Later in the film, Friedrich explains the "logic" of this approach: "if you want to put a Motor Works out of commission, then you destroy the entire city." Firebombing was the next step in the escalation of indiscriminate destruction. Friedrich argues that firebombing did not really have a target—its goal was to create a "space," to carve out a lethal zone in the city. But that of course meant that every living thing trapped in this deadly space would be killed. Friedrich now seems to be arguing that the Allied bombing campaign was driven forward by the technical possibilities of incendiary bombs, rather than by the possibility of destroying any justifiable military targets. Harris's bombers set German cities on fire because this is what they could do best; the combination of highly combustible ancient buildings in the centers of the cities attacked with, as Friedrich remarks, "astronomical numbers" of small incendiary bombs created deadly fires that claimed large numbers of German lives. German air defense units and civilians might be able to get rid of a few incendiaries at a time, as official instruction films showed them doing, but it was simply impossible to deal with the huge numbers that the Allies began to drop.

The film moves now to a German eyewitness, the folksinger and East German dissident, Wolf Biermann, who describes what he and his mother experienced during the July 1943 firebombing of Hamburg. His words convey the unprecedented horror of the firestorm: "The firestorm roared . . . burned and cooked the asphalt." Whatever people in the air-raid cellars decided to do—either to stay put or try to escape—could simply have been "wrong." The film intersperses color photographs of dead bodies on the street with his testimony. Yet Biermann's own words are more powerful than these images. He describes, for example, seeing an old woman who ran into asphalt on the street made so hot that it was literally cooking. She lost her shoes and then her feet became stuck in the boiling asphalt. Biermann's tone of ironic disbelief as he describes this horrible scene augments the power of the mental images that his words implant in the viewer's imagination.

The film now begins to show more of the damage done by the Allied bombing. At the end of November 1943, staff members working for Goebbels took clandestine film footage through the front window of an automobile as it moved along a bomb-damaged street in Berlin. This footage was not meant for the newsreels; it was supposed to show the reality of the bombing and gauge Berliners' reactions to it. In the clips from this secret black-and-white footage, there are no dead bodies, only Germans who are still alive trying to pick their way through the rubble-strewn street. The next images do, however, show us dead bodies. Then the camera presents Friedrich looking at this same film on the screen of an editing machine in a cutting room and describing how the survivors had to search among the dead for their relatives. This was a gruesome task. Sometimes all that was left of the victims was collected in paper sacks or in buckets. The Nazis did not allow these images to appear in the newsreels, but they did show pictures like the one we see next of a woman looking for her dead relatives in a long row of corpses. The Nazis wanted these images to fuel German civilians' desire for revenge. Other newsreel images included in the *Feuersturm* documentary show Goebbels speaking in Darmstadt at a rally with a banner in the background that reads, "Terror will be broken by counter-terror." V1 and V2 rockets would deliver a deadly payback that would force the British to their knees. In the meantime, bunkers would give the German civilians the protection they needed against Allied bombs. The documentary takes us inside a bunker. The commentator observes that Jews and forced foreign laborers were not allowed to seek refuge here. Then Friedrich describes a bunker as "like a reinforced concrete dome which would be put over the German people"—the purpose was to save the race even if everything else was lost. The consolation for the destruction of German cities was Hitler's promise that after the war, Germany would rebuild towns that would be even better than before.

The film shows that many more German cities would be destroyed as the British perfected their techniques, especially with regard to navigation. Historical black-and-white footage shows us the "historical Old City" in Braunschweig. The narrator tells us that "within a few minutes Braunschweig's center was in flames." Another German eyewitness, Günther Zwingmann, who was 16 years old at the time, tells viewers that he believed that Braunschweig would not be attacked. But Rosemarie Vogt remarks that after the raid "the old Braunschweig no longer existed." She describes what she saw during the attack: "the entire city was bright with light," the city had become "a single sea of flame." We also see pictures of dead bodies on the street (although it is not clear whether these photographs were actually taken in Braunschweig). But at this point the film does not rely solely on German eyewitnesses to convey the horror of the firestorm or to raise moral questions about the legitimacy of annihilating Braunschweig. An English airman says, for example, that from the air Braunschweig looked like the mouth of hell: "I thought 'What I am doing here? I could be back on farm looking after animals.'" Another British airman who was a pilot says that this was their job—"we thought we were contributing to the war effort—if they had told us we were to kill women, children, we would have thought differently." These British eyewitnesses may now be troubled by doubts about what they did during the war. Their German counterparts focus, on the other hand, on their own struggles to survive this catastrophe. Zwingmann describes how he was trapped in a cellar for 48 hours. As soon as he was rescued, he went to work helping to dig people and bodies out of the rubble. He did this for 14 days. Vogt emphasizes that the Germans who survived the raid did "stick it out" (*durchhalten*). And there were even some quiet days when they could do something other than sit in a shelter under the bombs, such as go to the movies. Vogt suggests that despite all the horrific sights she had seen in her devastated city, film images helped her to carry on. She describes seeing what she calls "Durchhaltefilme" (films that helped Germans "stick it out"), then immediately mentions Marika Rökk in *Die Frau meiner Träume* (*The Woman of my Dreams*). During the time they were watching films like these "we could forget."

Feuersturm lets the eyewitnesses who were Allied airmen do most of the work of raising doubts about the military significance and moral legitimacy of bombing German cities. One British eyewitness helps viewers feel that German flyers were doing all they could to protect German cities. In a segment dealing with German fighter attacks on Allied bombers, the machine gunner, Edwin Hays, remarks that "the guy that shot us down did a great job." The film shows "unique color pictures" of an attack by a German fighter taken by an American cameraman. At this point, *Feuersturm* moves back and forth between these color images of attacks on US bomber formations by German fighter planes and the filmed testimony of a German fighter pilot, Günther Sinnrecker. As we are looking at the American images, we hear his voice off-camera.

The gap between the Allied bombers in the air and the German civilians on the ground closes visually when the film starts to show us what happened to airmen, like Hays, who were shot down. If Allied airmen did manage to parachute safely to the ground, they were still in great danger. The remarks of Rosemarie Vogt accompany black-and-white footage of captured airmen, as well as pictures of dead fliers on the ground. The Germans showed these men no pity; "there was already hatred" of this enemy, according to Vogt, but then she quickly adds that Germans were also angry that "that there was no end to this appalling war." The commentator reports that more than a hundred downed airmen were lynched, but the film shows no pictures. The eyewitness Günther Zwingmann says, however, that he witnessed an incident that came close to a lynching, although in the end the airman was protected by a German. An Allied eyewitness relates that when they arrived at the POW camp, they were forced to run a gauntlet where they were beaten by the guards. The film shows a POW camp in color flyover footage and an eyewitness describes the inadequate medical conditions and poor nutrition in the camp: "I was just 19, I thought I would never get out of there."

At Yalta, the Allies decided that the air war must continue undiminished. Friedrich asserts that in the final, apocalyptic phase of the air war, between January and May 1945, the bombing of German cities was driven on by "a ceaseless desire to inflict injury" and had no real military purpose. Yet despite all of this massive destruction of German cities and towns, the Germans did not give up. Berlin was indeed transformed into a landscape of ruins. Yet another German eyewitness, who worked during the war in the Berlin Fire Department, remarks that Allied bombers were never able to deliver a decisive blow to the Nazi capital.

In this final phase of the air war, the weakened German defenses were simply unable to blunt the force of the Allied air attacks. The German fighter pilot tells us that "now we really could not do much—Americans were just everywhere—wave after wave of bombers." An American eyewitness observes that Allied bombing was "like a giant rake tearing the heart out of Berlin." In just 51 minutes, the equivalent of five trainloads of explosives were dropped on the city center. Heinz Hoene, then a member of the Berlin Fire Department, describes the Leipziger Strasse where "everything was burned out." The narrator tells us that 120,000 Berliners lost their homes. The Jewish eyewitness, Michael Degen, describes what he saw in the language so often used by non-Jewish German eyewitnesses: "it was one enormous heap of ruins." At this moment, he speaks with the same voice of disbelief as German eyewitnesses; he tells us that he and his mother knew all the streets very well but now the city was completely unreadable because there was simply "nothing more there." This segment ends with color footage of the ruined capital (probably taken by US signal corps cameramen after the war). An American eyewitness acknowledges that it is sad when such air attacks cannot help killing innocent civilians but insists that "we had to do it." The off-screen voice of the commentator does, however, ask who was innocent and who was not? Were Germans the victims of Nazi criminals, as Michael Degen believes? This segment on Berlin ends with the question "should the politicians have called a halt to their gruesome handiwork?" but it is not clear which politicians the film means: the German as well as the British and American leaders or just the Allied politicians who made the decision to continue the bombing war?

German crimes are not forgotten. Michael Degen suggests that when Germans were killed by the bombs "people knew what they were dying for, in Auschwitz or in the gas chamber people did not know." Having been mentioned once by a Jewish eyewitness (no German eyewitnesses talk about the Holocaust), Auschwitz recedes into the background. The film now focuses on the destruction of Dresden. We see photographs of bodies being stacked on pyres for incineration. We are told that even Churchill was shocked by reports of what the bombs had done to Dresden. Yet the film suggests that the bombing of Dresden may not have been the most senseless air attack of these last months of the war. Friedrich is shown again, in the streets of present-day Swinemunde, telling a horrific story that he also included in his book to illustrate what he considered to be the "blind desire for destruction" of the Allied air war in its final days. On March 12, this small Baltic port city of 22,000 inhabitants, full of refugees waiting to board ships in the harbor, was attacked by an "enormous fleet" of American planes. Fourteen thousand people were killed. What could possibly have been the justification for this attack? The United States later claimed that Swinemunde was a staging point for the *Wehrmacht* and that the raid was a response to a request from the Soviets. The film juxtaposes this claim with the testimony of a German eyewitness, Edith Schäfer, who describes the attack as quite simply a "terror attack" (*Terrorangriff*). She talks about the mass graves. Another eyewitnesses describes seeing "torn up" bodies of the victims and pieces of clothing; "I could only scream and weep." British historian Overy can only provide the fairly weak response to the challenges raised by these images that the bombers had to rely on intelligence reports that could often be faulty.

But the film is not yet finished with the horrors. It turns to the destruction of Pforzheim, which shows that the Allies were now destroying cities only because they had not yet been destroyed. This final stage of the bombing war creates the endless seas of ruins we can observe in a color flyover. Overy argues that between 1943 and 1945, bombing did hinder armaments production. Friedrich agrees that if all the factories had remained intact and all the workers unharmed, then the war certainly would have lasted longer and all sides would have lost more blood: "the air war had therefore evened out this bloody path somewhat, but really only somewhat." But he asks whether this small and uncertain benefit legitimated the horrendous costs exacted by the air war that "killed hundreds of thousands of human beings . . . whose death did not save one drop of blood." The film ends, abruptly and rather incongruously, by shifting away from the main thrust of Friedrich's argument that clearly asks viewers to be critical of the Allied air war. The narrator's final statement is that so many cities were destroyed: "this, too, was the result of 12 years of Nazi rule."

Recent films about the bombing war have created a second type of new image by including staged scenes played by actors. Guido Knopp's award-winning *Das Drama von Dresden* combines the filmed testimony of *Zeitzeugen* with reenactments in which actors play the *Zeitzeuge/in* who is often talking off-camera.[25] The film begins with color footage of the *Frauenkirche* today, then moves right away to the first eyewitness, Leandro Montor-Karoly, who observes that "I feel incredibly connected to Dresden," which in those days the locals "fondly called the Florence on the Elbe." Pictures from the 1930s follow that do, however, work against this initial impression of Dresden as the "innocent, unique metropolis of culture"; here, pictures of Nazis and the swastika challenge the notion that Dresden was simply an innocent victim of the air war. The commentator also observes that "Dresden was considered loyal to the regime." The war seems to be far away until the first refugees from the East arrive in Dresden. The camera moves to another eyewitness who was a volunteer helping refugees at the train station. This is the first time that the film includes a scene with an actor playing the role of the eyewitness while the eyewitness keeps talking off-screen. The same visual device is employed with another eyewitness who was then a young soldier, wounded and in a Dresden hospital with many others on their way back from the front. In addition to this juxtaposition of eyewitnesses with the actors who play them in reenactments, the film also combines footage of other eyewitnesses today with still photos of them as they looked then. A third eyewitness describes her experience as a refugee fleeing with her small brother from Breslau on a train to Dresden that came under attack from a low-flying Russian plane (*Tiefflieger*). Her testimony also fades into a reenactment of this experience. After these four eyewitnesses, the commentator remarks that despite the fact that the Eastern Front was approaching ever nearer to Dresden, most people in the city still felt safe. Not only was this sense of security deceptive, but it did not apply to everyone—for example, the next eyewitness, a Jewish woman, Henny Brenner (maiden name Wolff), the child of a mixed marriage whose father was "Aryan." Her family already knew that they were to be deported on February 16. Her testimony is paired with a reenactment that shows her as a young girl nervously walking home at night along a street in Dresden.

The film then shifts to the Allied side of the air war. We see pictures of Churchill, Roosevelt, and Stalin at Yalta, where the decision was taken to bomb German cities in the East, including Dresden. A reenactment depicting Bomber Command at High Wycombe is followed by black-and-white footage of "Bomber" Harris and, then, finally in this sequence, the first eyewitness from the Allied side, an RAF bombardier. The testimonies of the Jewish and the British eyewitness seem to provide balance in the film's treatment of the lead-up to the bombing. The Jewish woman's story shows that Germans had already inflicted considerable suffering and the threat of death on her family, well before Allied bombers attacked Dresden. And the British bombardier's comments show that Harris was seen even by his own men as a "butcher."

The film creates a sense of impending doom by juxtaposing footage of ordinary Germans in Dresden going about their business with other images that show British planes readying for the attack and taking off. The victims are not aware of what is coming. In Dresden, it is the eve of Shrove Tuesday (Fastnacht). Color staged footage shows German children running around the Martin Luther monument and other children in Fastnacht costumes. An eyewitness describes how she and her friend dressed up and went out on the street—she is in an elegant gown, her girlfriend in tails. An interview with RAF pilot Leslie Hay follows these pictures of innocent, unsuspecting children in Dresden just before the attack. Ken Oatley, an RAF navigator, also talks to the camera, and then his testimony is followed by actors playing an air crew getting ready to go on the mission. We hear from Alf White, a radioman, who tells the camera, "I was frightened." Like a disaster movie, the visual narrative produced by this movement back and forth between Dresden and England creates a deadly countdown (the time actually appears at the bottom of the screen at the beginning of each segment).

After several eyewitnesses describe the different ways in which they experienced the first stages of the bombing, another reenactment shows an air-raid warden knocking on the Jewish family's door to tell them that they should come down into the cellar. The Jewish eyewitness remarks that even though they were "not allowed—we were supposed to burn upstairs—perhaps he had a conscience." The film then returns to the soldiers in the hospital; the eyewitness describes the bombing as "worse than at the front." From the air, of course, the bombing of Dresden looks different. The British navigator remembers that they could see all the beautiful buildings of the city lit up by fires and admits that it "was a shame really to destroy that—but that is what we did."

Now that the first wave of the bombing is over, fire brigades consisting mostly of old men and Hitler Youth try to fight back the fires. The film shows that their task is hopeless. Back at the main train station, many refugees had not made it down into the air-raid cellar. An eyewitness tells us that this was the worst thing he had ever seen; people's bodies had been slit open by bomb fragments but they were still alive and there was blood everywhere. At this point in the film, the eyewitnesses are no longer reporting on what they saw but struggling hard to find the words and images to depict the horrors they witnessed. This attempt usually involves graphic descriptions of the mutilation of human bodies.

This section of the film relies heavily on reenactments and talking heads. It keeps returning to eyewitnesses we have already seen and heard from before, so that we can follow what happens to each of them at different stages in their stories. But the film also introduces new eyewitnesses, for example, the 14-year-old Ursula Eisner, who describes her confusion and desperate feelings of helplessness as she sat in an air-raid cellar that was being jarred by "one explosion after the other." Another eyewitness describes the effects of an air mine that fell on the main train station. The concussion propelled the steel door into their cellar and the explosion itself shredded metal as if it were tinfoil. These metal pieces flew through the cellar and killed people. The eyewitness tells us she saw people without their heads still sitting there and asks, "What did the pilots feel when they were doing this?" One British airman responds that he felt proud to have taken part in this attack. After all, the Germans had started the war. Another expresses regret that civilians were killed but insists this had to be done: "this was total war." After all, at this point in the war the Germans were also launching V-2 rockets against London.

In the cellars of Dresden, many were preparing to die. Some simply could not bear the intense sounds, concussions, and threat of death and killed themselves by cutting an artery. Another eyewitness says that he did not think but simply acted on intuition. Survival was often a matter of sheer luck. Here, the story line appears even more obviously to be borrowing directly from the genre of disaster movies. A woman describes how she survived because a "brave, old woman" clinging to a lamppost told her to hang on as well. People fight for their lives in the cellars, many are trapped under debris. On one side everyone is dead under the rubble. On the other side, there is an empty coal cellar, but in the panic to escape families are separated. The blind parents of a woman we have met before get left behind. But what is a tragedy for one family means survival for another—mirroring the description in Victor Klemperer's secret diary of what he did during the raid, the Jewish eyewitness describes how her family saw the attack on Dresden as their chance to escape deportation and tore off the identifying star. The woman wants to be clear that her family did not rejoice about Dresden's destruction—they certainly did not say "Thank God" for this raid but instead took advantage of the situation, saying they would rather have "bombs on our heads than be deported." She adds that her family could only draw this kind of distinction between two horrible possibilities because they had already been so "humiliated and tormented" by the time Dresden was destroyed.

Many of those who managed to escape the firestorm sought refuge on the banks of the Elbe. From here, they could see the Circus Sarrasini on fire. Eyewitnesses insist that they saw phosphorus running down the outside of the structure, which both fascinated and horrified them. The commentator's voice observes, however, that no one is really sure whether phosphorous was dropped on the city. A bomb expert explains, in sober technical terms, that the Allies did not actually use phosphorous but a mix of gasoline and rubber, which the narration of the film observes was later called Napalm. However, the eyewitness objects that only someone who had not lived through this raid could doubt what had happened. It appears that eyewitnesses need to insist on the use of phosphorous (and later in the film that low-flying planes, *Tieffflieger*, machine-gunned civilians on the ground) because these individual horrors are commensurate with the overall horror of the attack. Then we see the first picture of an incinerated body. A man who was a boy at the time describes being unconscious, then waking up to discover that a dead body was lying on him. He thinks that this corpse probably saved his life during the firestorm. He goes on to describe seeing his mother and siblings all dead and ends forlornly with the simple statement, "I was [all] on my own." Another eyewitness describes seeing "completely carbonized people" and noticing that the women's legs were red because their stockings had melted and fused with their skin.

The third wave of bombing was launched during the day by American planes. A US Air Force pilot, Donald Nielsen, admits that it was "clear to me that Dresden was not a military target." On the ground, we see a street full of people trying to escape. The commentator observes that some people in Dresden believe that they saw *Tieffflieger*, even though there are no indications in the archives that Allied planes fired on civilians. Another American airman claims that the weather that day had made any such low level attacks impossible. The eyewitness we have seen twice before, Leandro Manton-Karoly, insists, however, that anyone who denies that *Tieffflieger* machine-gunned civilians is just a liar.[26] Another eyewitness remembers seeing body parts that "once belonged to people." The first American pilot admits that what they did was not right; "I have asked God several times for forgiveness." The film moves then to colored footage of planes returning to England from a raid. The narration observes that the casualty rate for air crews was higher than among soldiers at the front. The widow of one of these airmen, Helen Mendenhall, tells the camera that "I didn't think I could ever get over this—I hated anyone who was just a little bit German." This segment also shows black-and-white photographs of her as a young wife with her husband and children. Later in the film, a German eyewitness tells the cameras quite simply, "I cannot hate anyone."[27] The contrast is clear; the American widow who can only hate and the forgiving German survivor.

We move directly back to Dresden where those who had survived began the very next day to bury the dead. An eyewitness describes the sharp and pervasive smell of rotting corpses. Another talks about the mass incineration of bodies by flame throwers piled up on the Altmarkt. The film then moves to the contested issue of the numbers killed. A female eyewitness tells the camera that she found out the temperature that was required in a crematorium to reduce a body to ashes. It was, she says, much hotter in Dresden during the firestorm. To her this means that thousands of bodies were turned into ashes, making it impossible to finalize the numbers killed.

Both *Feuersturm* and Knopp's Doku-Drama confront the viewer with an extended series of visual and verbal oppositions. These contrasts are intended to produce strong emotional and moral responses; they signify important differences in power and responsibility during the air war. The most significant contrast sets the Allied airmen's descriptions of what they did and felt as they were attacking Dresden against the German victims' descriptions of the suffering they experienced and observed as they were being bombed. The dialectic created by this opposition pushes the story forward emotionally. Yet these are not completely black-and-white distinctions. Some Allied airmen do admit that they regret that German civilians were maimed and killed, although they do not accept direct responsibility for the bombing of German cities.

The presence of Jewish eyewitnesses in both films produces ambiguous emotional and moral effects. Their testimony reminds viewers that the Allied planes in the air above Berlin and Dresden threatened the lives of Jews as well as non-Jews. This shared experience may encourage German viewers to identify with these Jewish eyewitnesses. Yet Jews were exposed to another threat—the danger of being arrested by the Gestapo and being shipped off to their deaths in the East—that did not endanger non-Jewish Germans and which gave the bombs a different meaning for Jews than for non-Jews. The Allied bombing of Berlin showed Michael Degen and his mother that they were not alone; perhaps the bombs would help bring Germany to its knees before they were arrested by the Gestapo. In the chaos caused by the Allied bombing of Dresden, Henny Brenner and her family were able to escape their impending deportation to an extermination camp.

At the end of Knopp's film the emotional and moral dialectic produced by the interplay of the different testimonies of Germans, Allied airmen, and Jews gives way to a new synthesis: international "reconciliation." *Das Drama von Dresden* ends in 2005 with the rebuilt Frauenkirche where survivors meet to commemorate the victims of the war. In the group, we see most of the eyewitnesses we have encountered individually in the film, including the Jewish woman and the RAF airmen. All sit together in the same congregation dedicated to "shared reconciliation."

German films on the bombing war produced after the end of the Cold War have created new images—the filmed testimony of eyewitnesses and, less commonly, reenacted scenes—to give German viewers the impression that they could, as Konrad Jarausch puts it, "leap over the barrier . . . of time."[28] Some critics have expressed concern that the use of reenactments signals a problematic movement from facts to fiction. Stefan Brauberger argues, however, "that re-enactments offer the possibility of . . . tackling themes that otherwise would be very hard or simply impossible to visualize . . . reconstruction . . . allows some events to be depicted more authentically than . . . archival material, whose authors consciously wanted to pass on to posterity their own view of their times."[29] Until 2006, however, making a film about the bombing that consisted completely of fictional images was, as Joachim Käppner put it, "still unthinkable."[30] In March of that year, the German television network ZDF aired *Dresden*, the first fully fictional film about the firebombing of the city in February 1945. Shown in two parts on March 5 and March 6, this "most expensive German made-for-television production to date,"[31] at a cost of over 10 million Euros, drew an audience of 13 million viewers on the first evening it was broadcast.

The plot of *Dresden* is dominated by a love story between a British bomber pilot, Robert Newman, whose plane has been shot down in a raid on Magdeburg, and a young German woman, Anna, daughter of a bourgeois medical family who is working as a nurse in her father's hospital in Dresden. Roland Suso Richter, the director of *Dresden*, defended the decision to make this improbable love story the centerpiece of his film by insisting that "[m]ost of the good materials deal with relationships . . . love, hate, mistrust. We thought through other models but quickly discovered that it would not work without it."[32] Making an illicit love story into a long prelude to the disaster that we all know is about to descend on Dresden certainly raises the emotional temperature when the bombs begin to fall. Will Anna and Robert both survive? Will they find one another again in the ruins of the doomed city? It is not clear, however, that this emotional investment in the fate of one unlikely couple can help us recover the experiences and feelings of Germans during the firebombing of Dresden.

Shortly before the air attack that annihilates the city, Anna Mauth is riding with her mother and sister on a streetcar through the wintry streets of Dresden. The three women are taking a short vacation from the increasingly grim reality of the war as the Eastern Front approaches ever closer to the city.

But a quick shot through the window of the streetcar shows that in Nazi Germany there are no vacations from reality. Anna sees a slave laborer who has been hung from a lamppost and is wearing around his neck a sign that declares: "I engaged in race pollution with a German woman." On the street, next to the lamppost, a German woman, obviously the woman in question, is being publicly humiliated for her racial transgression. Her hair has been chopped off and she is being made to stand in the freezing cold in nothing but her slip. Anna's mother puts up her hand to block Anna's view and spare her this unpleasant image. Very soon, however, Anna will herself be guilty of "sleeping with the enemy," yet this time the enemy will be not a Russian or a Polish slave laborer but a handsome, downed British bomber pilot, whom she initially believes is a British spy.

When the three women take their brief holiday from wartime reality they go to see a Zarah Leander film, *The Great Love* (*Die grosse Liebe*, 1942). In the scene from the film that we are shown, the screen diva sings her throaty version of "This does not mean the end of the world." Soon, however, British and American bombs will put a definitive, violent, and fiery end to the world that the inhabitants of Dresden, this baroque architectural pearl, this "Florence on the Elbe," have known and cherished. The story of a romance between a German woman and a British bomber pilot is the prelude to Dresden's destruction. Yet Anna's illicit affair with Robert also symbolizes the possibilities of another, postwar world that may be able to emerge from the ruins of both Dresden and Hitler's regime.

Three incidents cause Anna to turn away from the Third Reich (or at least from her fiancée, the Oberarzt Alexander) and to seek solace in the arms of the enemy, Robert, who is now pretending he is a wounded German soldier in a ward of the hospital where Anna works. The first incident involves a young boy and his brother who are brought to the hospital for treatment. These two children found Robert when he parachuted out of his burning plane and they took his revolver. One brother now lies dying from a severe stomach wound. Alexander decides that he cannot save the boy. Frustrated and angry, Anna criticizes Alexander for not trying harder. In front of the other hospital staff, she tells him "You are so cold!" The second incident follows quickly upon the first. Now, we see Robert trying to persuade the surviving brother who still has the gun not to kill himself. Robert tells the boy, "Do you know that I am a magician?" then performs some magic tricks with a cigarette. The boy is distracted by the magic, uncocks the revolver, which he had aimed at his own chest, and gives it to Robert. Anna sees what Robert is doing and is touched by his kindness toward the child, compared with Alexander's apparent callousness.

The third incident involves a woman who wanders dazed and confused into the hospital. Two military policemen come after her, claiming that she has helped her deserter husband to hide. Anna refuses to let the soldiers take the woman away without first speaking to her father. The next thing we see is that Anna has been put up against the same wall with the woman to be shot. At the last minute, Alexander rushes out of the hospital to save Anna. He tells the military police that he needs her for an urgent operation on a wounded soldier and asks whether they want to be responsible for a comrade dying when the Führer needs every man who can fight. The military police let Anna go, but as she is walking away with Alexander the men shoot the wife of the deserter. Soon after this traumatic incident, Anna has sex with Robert in his hospital bed. The two lovers are surrounded by a ward full of wounded German soldiers; amazingly, none of them wakes up to witness this illicit sexual encounter.

Dresden is a love story but it is also a German family melodrama that traces the dissolution of a privileged bourgeois family. The bombing of Dresden completes the destruction of this family, but it is not the main cause of its tragedy. Anna Mauth's romance with the British bomber pilot, Robert, is a symptom not the cause of the tensions within the Mauth family that will eventually destroy it. Anna is drawn to Robert as she becomes alienated not only from her fiancée, the hospital's assistant medical director, Alexander, but from her own father. Nor does the Nazi regime itself appear to be a serious cause of conflict within the family, even though Anna's sister, Eva, is an active member of the League of German Girls and is having an affair with the local Gauleiter's adjutant. Politics is usually kept at arm's length by irony. At the breakfast table one morning, after Anna has announced that Alexander has asked her to marry him, Eva reports that she has been able to use her influence with the Gauleiter's adjutant to get everything needed for Anna's engagement party. Anna wonders out loud whether it is "Strength through Joy" (with the adjutant) that has allowed her sister to obtain the scarce items needed for the party. No, Eva responds, it was a "Triumph of the Will." In a parody of the official propaganda language of the time, Anna then says, "I hope it was not too great a sacrifice?" to which Eva responds, in an equally ironic tone, that "in these times, one cannot always think only of oneself." It is true that a more sinister confrontation between the two young women does immediately follow this good-natured sisterly banter charged with sexual innuendo. When Anna starts to fill a bag with food, Eva exclaims: "I know who that food is for. Your friend [Maria, who is married to a Jewish man, Simon] should have gotten divorced long ago." Yet Anna never seems to pay a price for her friendship with the Aryan wife of a Jew.

The real problem in the Mauth family is the father. He knows that the Russians will soon be in Dresden and he has made plans for his family's escape to a new life in Switzerland, where he and his future son-in-law, Alexander, will start a clinic. To finance the move, Dr. Mauth has gone into business with the Gauleiter's adjutant to sell on the black market morphine that he has diverted from his own hospital's supply. Dr. Mauth tells Anna that one day she may hate him. This prediction comes true when Robert, now disguised as a German officer, appears at her engagement party and convinces her that her father has been dealing in stolen morphine. For his crime the father pays a horrendous price when he is caught in the air raid. Several men commandeer the ambulance in which he is trying to escape. One of them takes Dr. Mauth's case containing all of the money he plans to transport to Switzerland. As Allied bombs rain down, the two men fight, the case opens, and the money blows away into the burning buildings. Finally, Dr. Mauth is killed in the raid. From a distance, Anna sees that her father is lying on the ground in agony, bleeding to death because his legs have been crushed by a falling wall. In a painfully melodramatic scene, he tells Anna he is sorry and that she must now "Go, go your own way." Alexander drags her away. Then a burst of flame from a nearby building incinerates the dying father's body. The message appears to be that a German who deprives good German soldiers of the morphine they so desperately need deserves a horrible death.

In the section of the *Dresden* DVD that explains how the film was made ("Das Making Of"), Günther van Endert, a ZDF editor, insists that the filmmakers had no intention of painting the bombing of Dresden in simple black-and-white tones; "naturally we did not want to say that the Germans . . . were victims and the English were perpetrators." The opening scenes of the film certainly promise a balanced view. Hitler and the Nazis will shoulder their full share of the blame. As we are taken on a visual tour of the architectural wonders of the Dresden that will soon be annihilated, we hear, first of all, Hitler's voice. In a speech he threatens that for every kilogram of British bombs dropped on Germany, the Luftwaffe will drop tens, even hundreds of kilograms on British cities in return. If the British launch major attacks against our towns, Hitler warns, "we will wipe out their cities!" (and it is important that we also hear the jubilant applause of the audience in response to this threat). Then the film switches to a voice identified as "Sir Arthur Harris, the head of British Bomber Command," saying, "there are a lot of people who think you cannot win a war with bombs. Well, my answer is that this has not yet been tried. Germany . . . will make a very interesting initial experiment."

After this introduction, however, we seldom again hear Hitler or other Nazi leaders ranting about the need to hold on and fight through to the Final

Victory (*Endsieg*), whatever the cost to the German people. We learn that there are some "good men" in Bomber Command who doubt the wisdom of bombing Dresden and, indeed, of the Allies' entire bombing strategy. Yet these men still do their duty, which may perhaps make it easier for Germans to believe that these "good men," like their own "good men," were victims of their leaders (Hitler, but also Stalin and Churchill). Robert Saundby, the second-in-command to "Bomber" Harris, expresses his doubts when the decision has been taken to bomb Dresden: "There are people," he tells Harris, "who say Germany is slowly being over-bombed, we are in danger of inheriting a completely destroyed country," to which Harris responds, "The Germans wrote the rules." Yet the Harris portrayed in this film is not simply a man who "liked destruction for its own sake."[33] He clearly wants to believe that there are justifiable military reasons for continuing the bombing campaign. In another scene at the High Wycombe headquarters of Bomber Command, Harris tells his subordinates: "The last German troops have left Warsaw. The Russians are breaking through everywhere in the East. . . . The Germans will mobilize everything to stop them on the Oder. The 6th SS Panzer Army which caused us such great difficulties in the Ardennes is being moved into central Germany. Stalin expects our help. . . . We must disrupt the supplies to the German Eastern Front." Yet Harris is also well aware of the high political stakes attached to the bombing war. He tells his men that the prime minister "needs something at Yalta to show Stalin we're still in the game and part of the Allied military strategy." At the briefing held for the air crews who will lead the British attack on Dresden, an officer emphasizes that Dresden has been chosen as a target because it has "munitions factories, poison gas works, Gestapo headquarters—but, above all, it is full of German troops who are to be thrown onto the Eastern front." Yet in the same scene the air crews are told, "Gentlemen, the Prime Minister has a personal interest in Dresden's destruction. It seems the Russians do not have a high opinion of the RAF's work. It is about showing them what Bomber Command is capable of. Good luck lads. Get flying and bomb the city until it burns."

Further down the chain of command, some ordinary British airmen are troubled by the raid. Even Robert's closest friend, William, questions whether the attack on Dresden is justified. Earlier we have seen William in the officers' mess proposing a toast to Robert and the other "men of the Mona Lisa—they gave their lives for England and the peace of Europe. May they rest in peace." Yet as he gets into his plane just before the raid on Dresden, William asks his superior officer, "Where are the militarily important transport notes. We are attacking the Old City." The officer impatiently responds, "Dresden is a city near the front, we are not politicians, William, we are airmen. We are carrying out our orders."

When Nazi figures do appear in this film they come from another world. Some are depicted as muscular, steeled, cold-blooded murderers in uniform—for example, the military police who drag the wife of the deserter out of the hospital to shoot her for hiding him and also put Anna up against the wall because she has interfered. Near the end of the film, after the raid, we also see two tough-looking soldiers execute an air-raid warden for "looting." The warden is standing in the ruins with his newborn baby in one hand and a metal cooking pot he has found in the other. The soldiers take the baby from the man and give it to Anna's mother and sister who are standing nearby. They make the warden place the pot over his heart and then one of them shoots him through the pot. Other Nazi figures in the film are menacing yet a bit ridiculous. When the blustering, cigar-smoking Gauleiter puts in an appearance at Anna's engagement party, he insists that the Führer's "miracle weapons" will soon win the war. In search of the toilet, he blunders into a room where Robert, now wearing the uniform of a German second lieutenant, is waiting for Anna. Robert does not speak. The Gauleiter asks him whether he has been wounded at the front and then assures him, "Don't worry, *Leutnant*, you will get total victory." After the Gauleiter has left the room, Robert responds softly and in English, "I am sure of that." Where does this leave Germans who were not clearly Nazis? *Dresden* depicts most ordinary Germans as victims twice over: first of the Nazis, then of the Allies. When the survivors of the firestorm emerge from the shelters and cellars to confront the ruins of Dresden, complicated questions of guilt and responsibility have been swept aside by the horrors of the air raid. Whatever their previous sins, Germans have more than paid the price.[34]

The makers of *Dresden* made sure to include several references to the Holocaust in the film. Hans Janke, a ZDF manager, argues that "[the story of] 'Dresden' is not told against the background of Auschwitz, but Auschwitz is there."[35] The problem, however, is not whether *Dresden* refers to the Holocaust but how the genocide appears in this film. In *Dresden*, as well as in several recent documentary films, the relationship between the bombing and the Holocaust is established in strange ways. We are shown Jews who are persecuted. It is made very clear that these Jews would have been deported to their deaths in the East had they not been saved by the bombing. However, we are not shown what the Nazis have already done with the great majority of Dresden's Jews. In a key scene, Simon tells Maria that before the war is finished, the Germans will make sure to kill all the remaining Jews: "that is . . . the splendid thing about us Germans," he jokes bitterly, "we are so thorough!" Yet *Dresden* neglects to tell us that most of the city's Jews had long since been rounded up, deported, and murdered in Auschwitz by the time the Allied bombing saved the lives of the few who remained. In November 1942, 300 Jewish men, women, and children were evicted from the so-called Judenhäuser where they had previously been segregated from the Aryan population and were sent to the Hellerberg camp on the outskirts of the city. The Nazi authorities actually made a 27-minute-long film to document this forced move, itself a prelude to deportation to Auschwitz in March 1943. These pictures of the persecution of the Jews taken by the Nazis do not appear in *Dresden*.[36] By focusing its visual attention on the tiny remnant of Dresden's Jews who were saved by the bombing, *Dresden* avoids disquieting questions about the great majority who were murdered. Nor is it clear what German viewers are supposed to feel about the few Jews who were saved by the bombing of Dresden. Should they be glad that some Jews survived even at the cost of so many non-Jewish German dead? Is it even possible for contemporary German viewers to balance the few Jewish lives saved against the many Germans killed in the air raids? Or is this a moral arithmetic that many will prefer to avoid?

As Anna and Robert walk after the raid through the rubble to the remains of the Frauenkirche, they see dead human bodies that have been turned by the intense heat of the firestorm into painfully contorted, carbonized statues lying on the ground. These images evoke the gruesome photographs of corpses taken by Heinz Kröbel before February 20, 1945, when many of the people who had been killed on the streets of Dresden were cremated in huge piles on the Altmarkt. Kröbel's graphic photographs appeared in 1995 in a new exhibition on the destruction of Dresden sponsored by the Stadtmuseum bearing the symptomatic title "Burned beyond Recognition."[37] When Maria tries to find her husband Simon after the air raid, she looks up from the street to see a woman diligently sweeping her kitchen on the second floor of a building, even though one entire wall of the house has been completely blown out by a bomb. This image may remind viewers who have read Hans Erich Nossack's novella *The End. Hamburg 1943* of the author's description of a woman cleaning the windows of a building "that stood alone and undamaged in the middle of the desert of ruins. . . . We thought we were looking at a madwoman."[38]

These visual references help establish the film's claims to authenticity and give the last third of *Dresden* the feel of a documentary. Yet the film also tries to outbid previous documentaries emotionally by confronting the viewer with images not to be found in any existing visual archive. Only in a fiction film has it been possible graphically to simulate horrors that were left to the imagination before. In *Dresden* we are shown a demented woman pulling a burning baby carriage through the ruins of the city. In another frame, a man with a wooden leg walks through the rubble while the leg is on fire. *Dresden* also confronts us with images of the agonies suffered by people trapped in the air-raid cellars. We see an older woman ask a young soldier to shoot every one trapped in a cellar before they suffocate from carbon monoxide—he does, one by one, as the rest keep praying. One of the most powerful images in this section of the film does not actually show anyone dying but alludes indirectly to the horrific deaths the firestorm inflicted on its victims. As Alex and Anna sit out the raid in a cellar, incendiaries set the house above them on fire, making the walls of the cellar hotter and hotter. Then Alex sees that the liquid in several jars filled with preserves on a shelf against the wall is actually beginning to boil. He screams a warning just before the glass explodes. If the heat from the firestorm has this effect upon jars of preserves what is it capable of doing to the human bodies trapped outside? Although each of these images is in its own way ghastly, some of them do seem contrived, as if the filmmakers included them simply because they were technically able to produce the effects.

Dresden encourages its German viewers to believe that the time has come to reclaim their past emotionally, to feel the suffering of previous generations, and to talk openly about that pain without running the risk of being branded as right-wing extremists.[39] It is no accident that a producer of *Dresden*, Nico Hofmann, has also been responsible for two other TV blockbuster historical-disaster movies: *Die Sturmflut*, which dramatizes the catastrophic flood that inundated Hamburg in February 1962, and *Die Luftbrücke*, about the Berlin airlift of 1948–49. One of the blurbs advertizing *Die Luftbrücke* exclaims that "German history has seldom been so thrilling and emotional to see," a claim that could just as well be used to describe *Dresden*.[40] Like the other two films, *Dresden* is built on the premise that German history can be visualized in compelling images that allow German viewers to engage in strong emotional responses to their own historical past. This has caused some critics to dismiss *Dresden* as a "trashy anti-war film" (*Antikriegsschmonzette*)[41] or as "reconciliation kitsch" (*Versöhnungskitsch*).[42] Yet whatever we may think about the quality of this particular film, these are the pictures now in the minds of millions of Germans with which they will try to imagine the bombing of Dresden.

What German viewers who have seen *Dresden* will probably remember most about this particular past is how it looked. The makers of this film want viewers to believe that *Dresden* is as historically authentic as they could make it because they spared no expense to give the film the "look" of the past. This meant, first of all, shooting much of the film on location in Dresden. Many of the extras were ordinary Dresden citizens; some had even lived through the firebombing. It was particularly important to the filmmakers that they were allowed to film in the reconstructed Frauenkirche. Ironically, the fact that this film would not have been possible without the virtual world that teamWorx, the production company, was able to generate with computer graphics does not seem to contradict the film's claim to visual authenticity. The filmmakers emphasize that only the wonders of digital technology allowed them to show viewers what the swarms of Lancasters that attacked Dresden actually looked like (they were unable to find Lancaster bombers that could still fly) as well as the massive destruction that their bombs produced. Historical authenticity required building a special set of fire-resistant buildings so that the filmmakers could stage the biggest fire ever filmed for a German production (complete with four airplane engines to create the wind to simulate a firestorm). This striving for the look and feel of the past included sound as well as images—the director insisted, for example, that recordings of bomb explosions should be played very loudly while he was shooting the scenes in the air-raid cellars, so that the actors themselves would know what it felt like to be caught in a massive air raid and be able in turn to make "palpable to viewers how it must have been." If this film looks and sounds like the past, can it not then claim to be an accurate, compelling, if nonetheless fictional, representation of the past? Yet "seeing" and "feeling" the past is obviously not the same as understanding it. "Gripping and emotional" can be another way of saying that this is "history light" not designed to require viewers to do much thinking about the past, especially about its moral ambiguities and contradictions.

Writing in the *Süddeutsche Zeitung,* Joachim Käppner claimed that "the fiction-film 'Dresden' has managed to represent [both] German guilt and German pain."[43] In the end, however, *Dresden* is never able to resolve the contradictions of its own good intentions. Even though the film earnestly pays lip service to the need for a balanced view that lets all sides speak, it does not succeed in its attempt to show German guilt while at the same time depicting German suffering. Once we see the firestorm, it is these images that take over, that trump all other images and imaginings of the suffering that Germans inflicted on others.

The film provides a double-ending; one conclusion tells us what happens to the love story of Anna and Robert after the war, the other provides historical resolution of the national trauma caused by the bombing of Dresden. These two endings are connected by Anna's voice. First, we see the couple trying to find their way through the rubble that has made Dresden into an unrecognizable wasteland. Anna asks Robert, "Where should we go?" He responds: "I want to see if there is a way. Anna . . ." but then she stops him before he can finish this sentence: "Don't say anything. I love you." Robert walks over to the tower of the Frauenkirche. He climbs up to the top, as he and Anna had done just the day before. Then, she had been able to point out to him all the major architectural and historical points of interest in beautiful Dresden. Now that his buddies in Bomber Command have smashed these treasures to bits, all Robert can see is a vast expanse of ruins. He looks out over them to find a route by which he and Anna can escape the devastated city. The camera then returns to Anna sitting outside the church. As she begins to speak we learn that although she and Robert did find their way out of Dresden they were not able to follow a new path into their own future together. Robert went back to England. A few months after the war his plane went down over the North Sea and his body was never found: "He was on his way to Dresden for the birth of our daughter." At this point, some viewers may be prepared to agree with one critics' frustrated complaint that "[t]here is no escape from the *kitsch*."[44]

Anna and Robert have been denied the opportunity to put the past behind them and find a new postwar future. But the promise of reconciliation between German victims and British enemies symbolized by their relationship and by the British-German child they conceived together does become reality. As the screen goes black, a second ending begins to take shape. First we see a date, "30 Oktober 2005," then crowds of people attending the dedication of the reconstructed Frauenkirche in Dresden. The trauma of the bombing now finds resolution in the revaluation of Dresden as a site of united Germany's national memory and identity and in the reconsecration of the Frauenkirche as a symbol of international reconciliation. We see Bundespräsident Horst Köhler giving a speech at the rededication ceremony. We hear Anna's voice saying: "It is difficult to grasp what happened then in February 1945. But everyone who survived had the obligation to make something new. Those who only always look back will see nothing but their own shadows."

Dresden shows us just how difficult it is to make "a fiction film about the misery of the German civilian population during the final months of the war . . . so long as one continues to remember who . . . started the war in the first place."[45] Instead of confronting this problem head on, *Dresden* retreats into the safety of a nonjudgment; everybody was a victim of the war! Questions of guilt and responsibility are submerged in a "natural history of destruction," as W. G. Sebald has put it, which presents the war as a disaster for which no one appears to have been responsible but from which everyone eventually suffered.[46] This narrative certainly resonates with Germans' traumatic memories of the very end of the war. Of the more than 5 million German soldiers who were killed or went missing in World War II, more than a million died in just the last four months of the fighting.[47] Of the 2.7 million tons of bombs used by the Allies during the entire bombing campaign, more than 70 percent were dropped on Germany after July 1944. Cities and even small towns that had previously been spared major air attacks now became candidates for destruction. What the bombs missed, the fighting on the ground destroyed. By the end of the war, most major cities lay in ruins, and millions of civilians were dead, injured, or homeless. Too often, this suffering at the end of the war has allowed Germans to forget that just a few years earlier, before Stalingrad and before the bombing had begun to destroy Germany's cities, many of them had applauded the war that Hitler had given them. They had exulted in his Blitzkrieg victories and enjoyed the benefits of Germany's short-lived racial empire. At the end of *Dresden*, the camera pans over the faces of older Germans, some of them survivors of the bombing that destroyed the city. Which war do they remember as the president of Germany ends his speech with the earnest admonition that there should be no more war, "not in Europe, and not anywhere else in the world"?

The Bombing War on the Internet

Since the late 1990s, the Internet has developed into an important new medium for the circulation of narratives and images of the bombing war. Between 1997 and 2001, the number of Germans older than 14 using the Internet increased from 6.5 to 38.8 percent of the population. By the beginning of 2005, 55 percent of German households possessed an Internet connection.[48] The "historical knowledge" offered on the Internet has become increasingly popular because it is readily available and free.[49] The Internet permits large numbers of Germans to consume images and narratives of the bombing, but it has also allowed many others to produce their own textual and visual representations of the air war.

Most Germans looking for information about the bombing war on the Internet will go first to one of the major search engines—Google, Yahoo, Bing, or some other service. When the keyword "Luftkrieg" ("Air War") is combined with the name of a specific town, the search will normally return a list that is a mixture of public and private websites, including city archives or research centers, museums, media outlets (regional press/TV), private associations, schools, or organizations of retired people. Some keywords are politically loaded—"Bombenterror, Bombenholocaust"("Bombing Terror, Bombing Holocaust")—and produce a quite different selection of sites, often located on the far-right of the political spectrum, sometimes linked to Holocaust denial. These sites are polemical. They attempt to stimulate and exploit emotional responses to the material they present. Yet even Internet sites that are not linked to the radical right often privilege emotion and empathy over understanding. When they allow users to send in comments—as is the case with YouTube—these sites also give voice to the emotional responses of their viewers that are mainly anger and outrage. It is not surprising that other Internet sites have tried to distance themselves from these emotional appeals by constructing sober, scholarly analyses of the history of the air war—the site maintained by the Historisches Centrum (Historical Center) in Hagen is one important example, but so too are the growing numbers of sites created by the municipal archives or city administrations of individual towns. Most of these sites are text-heavy, relying upon "thick" description and analysis to establish their authority.

Wikipedia entries are at the top of the list of sites generated by the German version of Google (http://www.google.de) in response to the most obvious keywords "Luftkrieg" and "Bombenkrieg" ("Bombing War").[50] One posting on Wikipedia traces the history of the air war from World War I to the Second Gulf War. Then there is a more detailed discussion of the air war in World War II. Here, a subheading leads the reader to a discussion of "Luftangriffe gegen Städte" ("Air Raids against Cities"). This section includes information not only on German cities targeted by bombing but also cities in France, Great Britain, Japan, Yugoslavia, the Netherlands, Poland, and even Switzerland. The central argument of the section about the bombing of German cities is that "not only accepting the deaths of civilians but actually making the civilian population a . . . target and shaping the air attacks in such a way that the highest possible number of people died conformed to the explicit decision of the Churchill government. The premise was to break the morale of the population and to sap the confidence of the population in its own government." This overview includes direct links to other Wikipedia articles on such topics as "Electron-Thermitstab Brandbomben"("Electron Thermite Stick Firebombs"), "Arthur Harris," "Flaktürme" ("Flak Towers"), and "Kinderlandverschickung" ("Evacuation of Children to the Countryside"). Photographs posted on this site include an aerial picture taken from an American plane that shows below it two B-17s during a US Air Force bombing attack on Koblenz on September 19, 1944 (left-side of page), and four-barreled flak canons mounted on the flak tower in Berlin-Friedrichshain. A link connects the reader to an article on this type of weapon and its use in World War II. The rest of this section is taken up by an extensive table giving detailed information about the first air raids on a long list of German cities, the heaviest raids, the numbers of bombs dropped, and the numbers of Germans killed.

Clicking on the name of one of the individual German cities mentioned in the body of the text takes the reader to a detailed description of the air raids that targeted this city. Much of the text is devoted to explaining the Allied planning, organization, and execution of these attacks. Many of the photographs that accompany these articles are taken from Allied sources. In the article on Hamburg, viewers can play a short Allied propaganda film that has also been used in several YouTube postings, "Hamburg No.1 Nazi War Center Blasted by Bombs," which shows that Hamburg was "virtually wiped off the map" because it was a center of Nazi war production, above all submarines. The film includes a shot of a rather oafish-looking member of an American ground crew chewing gum. There is an obvious contradiction between the claims made by this Allied film (assuming, of course, that the German viewer can understand what is being said—the commentary is in English) and the clear statement made earlier in the more general article on the air war that the Allies had decided to attack civilians. The article on Dresden immediately discusses the issue of how many died. Although six-figure numbers are often cited, the article concludes that "according to the newest historical examinations . . . between 22,700 and 25,000 people died" as a result of these attacks. The article includes a detailed and considered assessment of the military situation in early 1945, giving several military reasons why Dresden was seen by the Allies as a valid target, and providing details of the role Dresden played in the Nazi war machine.[51]

The Historisches Centrum in Hagen maintains the most scholarly Internet site on the bombing war.[52] It begins with a thoughtful introduction by the historian Ralf Blank that spells out what he thinks is required for a balanced discussion of the bombing war. Blank explains historical and media interest in the air war as a response to the controversies generated by Sebald and Friedrich. He situates these debates about the bombing of German cities within the larger framework of a "new historiography" that focuses on the suffering of Germans in the last stages of the war and the immediate postwar period. Blank dismisses as a "modern legend" the claim—often made in the recent discussions—that the bombing war was subject to a taboo in postwar German society and historical research. But he acknowledges that the recent discussions have encouraged new local and regional research that has drawn attention to the need for more detailed investigation of the effects of the bombing on the home front. He also observes that the current literature on the air war concentrates on the bombing of Germany; there is still no comprehensive overview of the air war conducted by the Germans against other European countries, such as Poland, England, France, Yugoslavia, and Greece. Blank argues that more attention to such phenomena as the lynching of Allied airmen and the distribution of plundered Jewish property to Germans who lost households in the bombing would complicate attempts to present Germans simply as the victims of the bombing. He also observes that in the current German culture of remembrance and commemoration there appears to be little space for the recognition of either the victims of German V1 and V2 rockets or the tens of thousands of slave laborers, concentration camp victims, and POWs who were also exposed to Allied bombs but who were generally excluded from the air-raid shelters and bunkers.

The individual contributions on specific themes written by professional historians and other scholars reflect the growing richness of current research on the social and cultural as well as the military history of the bombing. The Hagen site includes articles on the bombing war and literature, *Kinderlandverschickung*, *Luftwaffenhelfer* ("Air Force Helpers"), the roles played by Nazi organizations after bombing raids, German air attacks on foreign cities in World War I and II, the air war in West German TV documentaries, Dresden and the "memory politics" of the GDR, the depiction of the bombing in *Feldpostbriefen* (letters between the fighting and home fronts), and the "Battle of the Ruhr" (air attacks on the Ruhr and Rhineland in the spring and summer of 1943). These discussions are followed by studies of the bombing of individual German cities—Trier, Hamburg, Mainz, Koblenz, Dresden, Swinemünde, Augsburg, Frankfurt am Main, Düsseldorf, Nürnberg, Leipzig, and Pforzheim—by some of the leading, especially younger, scholars in the field. The site also includes a detailed timeline that is "continuously expanded" along with links to two external sources of Allied statistics from the bombing campaign. The site ends with an extensive bibliography with links to reviews of relevant books and to a wide range of other Internet sites in both English and German.

Although they differ in their interpretations, both the Wikipedia and Hagen sites offer their users comprehensive discussions of the air war. They combine detailed descriptions of the destruction of individual German cities by Allied bombing with analyses of the longer-term origins of the air war against Germany. Both situate the bombing within the wider context of World War II. And both attempt to tackle the difficult questions of the morality, legality, and military effectiveness of the bombing war. The Hagen site also situates recent German discussions of the bombing war in the longer history of postwar German memory, rejecting the claim that public discussion of the bombing was subject to a taboo until the late 1990s.

Some of the websites maintained by individual cities are equally ambitious. The city of Frankfurt am Main provides an extensive website on the Nazi period.[53] If users click on the first category "Beiträge" ("Contributions") on the left-hand side of the homepage, they are taken to a "Navigationsleiste" ("Navigation Strip"). Of the eight categories that appear when the user clicks on "Krieg und Zerstörung" ("War and Destruction") four deal directly with the air war. The category "Die Stadt als Heimatfront" ("The City as the Home Front") also includes information on the air war. Subheadings in each of these sections lead the user directly to specific details and pictures of individual air raids on Frankfurt, such as the March attacks in 1944, the heaviest of the war, which "transformed large parts of the city into a desert of smoking ruins." These sections of the website are, however, more descriptive than analytic.

The site tries to bring the user closer to the lived experience of Frankfurt citizens during the bombing war by including several eyewitness accounts. Under the heading "Luftalarme in Riederwald 1941" ("Air Raid Warning in Riederwald, 1941"), the site reproduces some of the text and two of the actual pages from a notebook compiled by Johanna Tesch. She made a record of every air raid warning in her district in the course of 1941–45 and described how she and her husband responded to each alarm. In 1944, her husband kept a similar notebook. Johanna Tesch's journal from 1941 showed that it was then still possible to go on walks, visit friends, and go into the center of the city in the time between air raids. By the time her husband compiled his list in 1944, however, "the airwar . . . dominated everyday life." In that year, he recorded no fewer than 523 warnings. In the attack on March 18, 1944, Johanna and Richard Tesch, at that time almost 69 and 74 years old, respectively, were bombed out. At the bottom of this page, clicking on "Ereignisse: Tod von Johanna Tesch im KZ Ravensbrück" ("Events: Death of Johanna Tesch in Ravensbrück concentration camp") shows the reader that Johanna Tesch was a Reichstag member for Frankfurt between 1919 and 1924. After the failed attempt in July 1944 to kill Hitler, she was deported to Ravensbrück concentration camp where, in March 1945, at the age of almost 70, she died, probably from malnutrition.

The site also includes audio and video "documents" that can be played in Flash format. By clicking on the section headed "Hilfe zur Recherche" ("Research Assistance") users can consult an inventory of both written eyewitness accounts and audio and film/video recordings. However, very few of these eyewitness accounts deal with the bombing war; the great majority describes the persecution of Jews under the Nazis or the activities of the political resistance against Nazism.

The Frankfurt website also exhibits artifacts. A section on "Death/Dying in the Bockenheim Bunker" shows a picture of a porcelain cup and a ceramic sugar bowl that have been fused together with a lump of glass. The user is told that glass melts at 1,000 degrees Celsius, porcelain at 1,300 degrees. This curious object was all that was left of Margarete Ritsert's household in the Leipziger

Strasse after a particularly heavy attack. Another page shows a picture of a wooden crate used to move documents from the Stadtarchiv (Municipal Archive) out of the city to save them from the bombing. An article tells the user that in 1942 the city began to implement measures to protect important documents, cultural items, and other valuables in the city's archive and museums; as a result, "the great majority of holdings of the municipal museums survived the Second World War," but unfortunately the Stadtarchiv "began this relocation too late and thus lost considerable portions of its holdings."

Visual material can be used in a variety of different ways on the Internet, the simplest being the conversion of analog photographs that were produced before the Internet to digital versions that to the user's eye appear no different than the originals. Most municipal websites do not go beyond this conservative use of the Internet. Very few take advantage of the technical possibilities that the Internet offers to create new images or to allow users to see conventional images in new ways. In his discussion of the way that German cities represent themselves visually on their websites, Lutz Philip Günther concludes that "it comes much more to the transferal of already established conventions of representations and less to the formation of new [ones]."[54] This certainly is true of the Frankfurt website. A considerable number of the pictures have been drawn from the two books by Schmid (1965) and Krämer (1983). The most unique visual aspect of this website are the selections it has put online from "the almost 100 . . . color slide pictures, which the Historical Museum acquired from the Frankfurt photographer Paul Wolff."[55]

The eyewitness testimonies listed on the Frankfurt website—written, recorded, and filmed—are all drawn from the holdings of other archives and organizations, such as the Fritz Bauer Institute or the Frankfurter "Erzählcafe" ("Story Telling Café").[56] In 2010, another municipal archive was actively engaged in generating new textual and visual archives of the bombing war by asking eyewitnesses to provide their own accounts and photographs. The website for this research project on "Luftkrieg in Nürnberg 1942–1945," which was connected with the Stadtarchiv, offered several accounts by residents of Nuremberg who experienced the bombing, each of which was accompanied by photographs.[57] Some of these pictures were standard ruin images but others had clearly been provided by the eyewitnesses from family photo collections. This site also included personal accounts by crew members of an Allied bomber accompanied by pictures of an Australian radioman as he looked in 1944 and as an old man. Finally, the website presented the account of a Belgian forced worker along with a picture of him as an older man in 2001, a group photograph of other *Zwangsarbeiter* in 1944, and the testimony and photograph of a

Soviet POW who was forced to dig German victims out of the ruins and bury the corpses.[58]

In comparison with the Frankfurt and Nuremberg websites, Paderborn's online treatment of the bombing is sparse, consisting of a 1,336-word description of "Paderborn im Bombenkrieg" that concentrates on the major raids on this Westphalian city. The text describes Arthur Harris's strategy of "moral bombing" and remarks that it had already been tried by the German Luftwaffe and had clearly failed. The site includes no images but users can download a 40-page PDF file with numerous pictures of significant Paderborn buildings before and after their destruction and, in some cases, after their postwar reconstruction, along with detailed descriptions of each building's history.[59]

Media outlets—mainly regional TV networks or national illustrated magazines such as *Bild* and *Spiegel*—are responsible for another type of website dedicated to the bombing war. One example is the extensive website on "Kriegsende in Bayern 1945" ("End of the War in Bavaria") maintained by Bayerischer Rundfunk (BR-online).[60] The topics covered include "Liberation of Bavaria, Liberation of Concentration Camps, Terror and Resistance, Air-War in Bavaria, Everyday life during the War, Flight and Expulsion, Divided Families, Links, Tips for Readers." Although this site incorporates some of the findings of recent academic research, it also recycles obvious strands of popular local narratives from the 1950s. The inhabitants of Bavarian cities are depicted as innocent and unsuspecting; by the end of the war, most of the men were at the front and the majority of the victims of the bombing were women, children, and old people. They are depicted as the gullible victims of Nazi propaganda that promised that the measures taken would be more than adequate to protect them from the bombing. Many also believed, or wanted to believe, fantastic "urban legends" that promised that their city would be spared because Churchill once studied there or because of a family relationship with the British monarchy. Few could understand why their architecturally beautiful cities, which from their point of view offered few strategic military targets, should be destroyed.

The Holocaust is not ignored. The description of the first big attack on Augsburg on April 17, 1942, remarks that this was "the day on which the first deportation trains began to move—a coincidental juncture with cynical symbolic power: Until the end of 1943, the regime kept the growing housing shortage within limits, by housing people who had been 'bombed out' in empty 'Jewish housing.'" This acknowledgment of the direct involvement of the residents of Augsburg in the persecution of the Jews suggests that Germans were not all simply innocent victims of the air war, as the site has tried to argue in all the previous discussions of the bombing of Bavarian cities. The site also shows that significant numbers of the bombing victims were not Germans. Many forced laborers from the occupied territories were working in the local war industries at the time of the attack; they "particularly often counted among the victims of the bombing."

This section of the site ends with a discussion of "Consequences and Long-Term After Effects: The Echo of the Bombing." It juxtaposes two quite different traces of the bombing war. On the left-hand side of the page, the user sees a photograph of a grave on which a wreath has been laid; unexpectedly, this "Stilles Andenken" ("Silent Remembrance") honors one of the 2,934 Allied pilots buried in Dürnbach war cemetery. This is the first time that this section of the site has talked about Allied airmen. Farther down the page, the site describes a photograph of one of 10 dud Allied bombs as an "Explosive Souvenir" of the war. On the other side of the page the user hears the stories of two German eyewitnesses, but their accounts focus on the long-term psychological effects of the bombing war rather than directly talking about their experiences during the war itself. For these Germans, the bombing war is not over; it continues to manifest itself in physical and mental symptoms.

This website is critical of the postwar reconstruction of German cities, arguing that the word itself "glosses over . . . the often fundamental alteration of the localities, to which [buildings that survived the war] also often fell victim." Although the hectic pace of new building was necessary to respond to the housing crisis, postwar urban architecture soon drew criticism from conservatives and liberals alike. Wolf Jobst Siedler and Alexander Mitscherlich lamented the aesthetic as well as social deficits of postwar buildings along with the damage done by cutting wide new streets through urban areas to produce the "city suited to the automobile." In contrast with Pforzheim, Darmstadt, Kassel, and many East German cities, local governments in Bavaria opted for historical reconstruction. But the website suggests that reconstructing historic buildings has not produced an authentic urban environment. With a photograph on the right-hand side of the "resurrected" Hofbräuhaus in Munich, the user is reminded that many of the supposedly historic buildings now to be seen in Bavarian cities are in fact not genuine; "One guesses more than sees it: . . . what looks historic in Munich, Nuremberg, Würzburg is often not more than 50 years old." Repeating a criticism of historical reconstruction already expressed in the 1950s,[61] the site suggests that rebuilding historic structures has produced a "Life as a 'Remake'" that lacks the aura of the original.

The overall effect of this collage of strands of older and newer narratives, conventional and newer visual motifs, is contradictory. The tensions are most evident in the site's depiction of the victims of the bombing war in Bavaria. On the one hand, they are to be seen as innocent—largely because they are women, children, and old people. The suffering of those who survived continues long after the war is over in the form of mental and even physical symptoms of anxiety and trauma, although these problems were not generally acknowledged at the time, nor were their symptoms treated. The Germans who lived through the bombing were left to deal with the aftermath by themselves and until recently, so the site claims, were denied even the opportunity to speak publicly about their suffering. Yet this site also shows that these German victims sometimes profited from the persecution of Jews—when they were bombed out they were given the apartments of Jews who had been deported to ghettoes or to their deaths in the East. And the site shows that Germans were not the only victims—the Allies also dropped their bombs on POWs, slave laborers, and concentration camp prisoners.

Right-Wing Websites

"Virtuelles Museum gegen das Vergessen" ("Virtual Museum against Forgetting") is a website maintained by the publication *Junge Freiheit*, a weekly newspaper, which has been categorized by the German domestic intelligence agency as right-wing.[62] This site is text-heavy. Photographs are featured, including some grisly pictures of the incinerated remains of Germans killed in bombing raids, but the bulk of the site is devoted to long transcripts of eyewitness testimonies. The testimonies that appear on this website were sent to *Junge Freiheit* in response to an appeal the paper made in January 2003 to older readers to tell their personal stories of the air war. The newspaper claimed that it was overwhelmed by the number of letters received: "This topic appears to have touched a nerve of the generation who experienced the war. For years, even decades, many clearly repressed the memory, because the experience was so terrible. Now, however, they are talking." But this website is not content simply to reproduce eyewitness accounts. It also makes a point of pitting eyewitnesses against experts. In an interview with the magazine, Wolfgang Schaarschmidt, who is identified only as a "historian," reports that citizens of Dresden were outraged by a book written by the historian Helmut Schnatz that claimed to disprove a long-standing popular belief that American *Tiefflieger* had machine-gunned civilians. When Schnatz presented his book in Dresden in 2000,

> Outrage reigned in the room (where he spoke), some visitors showed that they were furious . . . and were close to tears . . . There are simply too many eyewitnesses in Dresden, who experienced, believed they experienced, or imagined they experienced such attacks. In innumerable other cases, attacks by Allied fighter planes on German civilians are undeniable, so to that degree it is also possible they happened in Dresden.

Feeling that debate had been suppressed for 40 years in the GDR, many Dresdners were humiliated once again to be deprived of the right to speak by "outsiders," historians, and politicians who felt they should enlighten the eyewitnesses about "how it really was." Schaarschmidt's remarks suggested that authentic memory of the destruction of Dresden should be the property of the eyewitnesses in Dresden itself. Historians and politicians who offered narratives of the bombing that conflicted with popular memories deprived ordinary Dresdners of their past and their local identity, a charge that might gain traction at a time when many East Germans may have felt that unification had amounted to no more than colonization by the West. By putting so many of the personal testimonies it had received on its website, "Virtuelles Museum" defended the right of these dispossessed eyewitnesses to be heard. In addition to Dresden, Berlin, and Hamburg, the site includes eyewitness accounts from 50 other towns or regions in the former West and East Germany.

YouTube

The visual representation of the bombing war on YouTube postings is generally quite derivative, taking film footage from recent documentaries or wartime Allied propaganda films sometimes combined with German newsreel (*Wochenschau*) reports. Sometimes these are not even moving images but sequences of still photographs in black and white or color. More interesting than the visual elements of these YouTube postings are the voice-over commentaries that accompany them, the music, and the comments sent in by users. YouTube also keeps track of the number of visitors to each posting, which allows us to see which ones get the most attention. Some of these postings are international with comments in German, English, Dutch, even Russian. Some of the users who send in comments are very active and comment on a number of other sites—their activities can be followed by clicking on the profile attached to their YouTube user name. If they have their own channel on YouTube, the user can go to the videos they have posted.

YouTube postings are usually short (less than 10 minutes).They seldom try to show or explain the wider historical context of the bombing war. They concentrate almost exclusively on the moment of destruction and its immediate aftermath. Users' remarks are often emotionally charged and can be politically provocative. Commentators may engage in vitriolic arguments with one another. The comments can become so extreme that they must be removed. One YouTube posting carried a warning that "comments which defame other human beings will be deleted."[63] On other postings, the comment function has simply been disabled.

The far right-wing is well represented on YouTube both as producers and commentators. Dresden attracts particularly extreme postings. "Dresden—der geplante Massenmord," for example, is a 2:01 minute sequence consisting entirely of color footage of burning buildings (probably from Brunswig's film of Hamburg). A woman's voice describes the horrors caused by the firestorm, including the burning of corpses on the Altmarkt.[64] Then the following words appear on the screen in capital letters while *Schindler's List*-type violin music plays in the background: "WE SELDOM CONSOLE OURSELVES ABOUT GREAT SUFFERING BUT SEEK TO HIDE IT FROM VIEW. 13. FEBRUARY, DRESDEN LEAGUE FOR ACTION AGAINST FORGETTING WWW.AKTIONSBUENDNIS-GDV.DE." The text written by 5paul23 to explain this posting (which, by October 11, 2010, had been seen by 30,424 users since January 7, 2008) depicts the attack as the senseless killing of "above all women, children, old people and wounded soldiers who had been taken into the hospitals" and had no way of defending themselves. Many of these victims had already suffered at the hands of the invading Soviet army; "the Red Army advanced toward eastern Germany, plundered, raped, murdered, forced the population to flee—a large number fled towards Dresden." 5paul23 also repeats the story that has been part of the popular Dresden narrative of the bombing since 1945, namely that "during the third wave of attacks, the fliers used their machine guns to hunt those trying to flee and seek shelter . . . on the Elbe meadow alone, [they] mowed down hundreds." Wildly exaggerated numbers reinforce 5paul23's message that the attack on Dresden was an unprecedented catastrophe: "of the 1.2 million people who at that point in time were staying in Dresden, at least 300,000 died—only 30,000 of them could be identified . . . by . . . 20.3.1945 202,041 dead had been counted, overwhelmingly women and children. Because it was impossible to remove these dead bodies from the city, they had to be incinerated on the spot—that is why a confirmed number of the dead could never be determined." To support the claim that the Allied bombing of Dresden was a crime against humanity, 5paul23 cites R. Crossman, "head of the political conduct of the war against Germany during the war," who published an article in the *New Statesman* in May 1963, which argued that those responsible for the air war "would have been put on trial at Nuremberg, had this trial not been perverted into purely an instrument of Allied revenge." The website argues that Churchill should have been charged with war crimes: "the attack on Dresden was no mistake on the part of the English air force, but premeditated murder, because the goal was to break 'the morale of the population' . . . it has been firmly established that in Dresden hundreds of thousands had to die because Winston Churchill, either on his own initiative or on the urging of his adviser Lord Cherwell, whose real name was Lindemann, gave the order for the bombing of the city."

By October 11, 2010, users had sent 509 comments to this site. Eight months earlier SPIELHAUSkniffo asked, "have the English not caused enough misery in the world?" Six months later edaurdelet wrote in English, "I am Flemish . . . for me Dresden always stands out as a war crime. There was no reason to destroy such a beautiful city and it only increased the misery. The British were cowards and couldn't win the war on their own." Krautkiller1969 disagreed, registering a minority opinion: "[THE GERMANS] WERE THEMSELVES RESPONSIBLE, NO ASS IN THE WORLD HAS_ SYMPATHY [FOR THEM]." However, the authors of some comments did accuse other users of being Nazi sympathizers or simply outright Nazis.

Even a more sober and considered posting can produce extremely combative responses, especially with regard to the question of how many people were actually killed in Dresden. A short clip (3:59 minutes) posted on February 12, 2010, had drawn 8,827 views by October 11, 2010.[65] The posting shows a video of a story taken from the online version of *Focus Magazin*, a legitimate, mainstream publication started in 1993 and based in Munich. The report tells the story of Hans-Joachim Dietze who, as a 15-year–old boy, had taken photographs of the firestorm in the center of Dresden. At one point in the filmed interview, the commentator observes that "between 18,000 and 24,000 people died during the attacks on Dresden, a number that has often abusively been falsified by raising it up to ten times higher, first by the Reich Propaganda Ministry, then by the GDR regime, and today by the NPD [a right-wing political party], as Dietze observes. The eighty-year old thinks this instrumentalization of suffering is one of the saddest chapters of postwar German history." These remarks provoked Elberiver11, a frequent contributor of comments to this site, to exclaim, "Attention, listen to this: 'A number that has often been abusively falsified by raising it,' so the narrator claims at the end. Sorry, I actually only hear every day how the number has been falsified by deceitful politicians_and Multiculti do-gooders [who] abusively lower it."

This YouTube posting gave some users the chance to voice grievances and resentments that did not relate directly to the bombing of Dresden. In another comment, Elberiver11 jumbled together refusal to accept the number of deaths mentioned in the film clip with grievances about the introduction of the Euro, an attack on American foreign policy, and perhaps even traces of dissatisfaction with German reunification. Elberiver11 insisted, "The 25,000 is a lie—everyone in Dresden knows that. Just as much a lie as the claim by Frau Merkel and Herr Kohl that 'the Euro would be just as strong as the D-Mark.' Obviously, we see right off, how strong the 'Teuro' is, ha ha ha. Politicians LIE, above all when, like Merkel & Kohl, they are the handmaidens of criminal occupation powers . . . in Iraq, we can see the 'desire for peace' of the 'guiltless' Anglo-Americans."

Anti-American and anti-British rhetoric, nourished by the Iraq war but perhaps also reflecting the post-1990 afterlife of official GDR Cold War propaganda, also found its way into the comments of some other users. @DDkatrin argued, for example, that "Germany is still under the US and British occupation law. That was also the reason why . . . the USA and England declared war on us: not so as 'to save the Jews,' but rather to engage in the mass murder of Germany, to plunder it and to bomb it off the planet. The subjugation of Germany was the reason for WWII, nothing else." Another user, @Deeforcer, agreed: "Since 1945 occupation law has been valid in Germany . . . the Americans call the shots . . . Germany . . . is a colony of the USA whose President decides what happens to us, and the_ Germans=slaves. The Law of the Occupier=SHAEF laws." The war in Iraq fueled these anti-American outbursts. In response to another user's comments, Krafat asked whether "[a] ccording to your logic, one can unscrupulously kill all Iraqi citizens, because_ they support Saddam?!"

Other users attempted to move the tone of the comments to more neutral ground. Beoland100 wrote, for example, that "I have read these comments here and as a Dresdner I understand your emotions, [we need to] learn [from this experience] and live in peace." Dreasebert added the simple statement that "I can only feel grief about this_piece of [the history] of my home town, I believe that this is a feeling that only someone who has seen this beautiful city can feel." But Geril1969 insisted that users must realize that "here, Germany was liberated—of its art, culture and beauty. And Dresden was not even the worst stage. It is such a shame that the substance of this topic has been left to the right-wing parties and discussion in German society has been placed under taboos and [saddled with] untruths. The bombing war against Germany was a war against German culture in general—that comes out of the statements of the politicians who were responsible. War never produces anything good."

YouTube postings on Dresden sometimes demonize Sir Arthur Harris as a war criminal.[66] One, put up on April 23, 2009, which had attracted 6,515 viewers by October 13, 2010, begins with a still photograph of the former chief of Bomber Command who died in 1984. On the right-hand side of this picture the caption reads, "In memory of the great British mass murderer." After a lengthy text describing the attacks on Dresden in February 1945, the posting displays two well-known still photographs of the incineration of bodies on a Dresden square, followed by a ruin picture. The posting ends with the following text on screen: "may such terror and wrong to the civilian population never happen again! We commemorate the victims who 64 years ago . . . had to die senselessly in Dresden." Another posting by the right-wing Nationale Bewegung Deutschland shows a still picture of the monument to Harris in London with burning skies in the background and a sea of skulls at the foot of the monument. It then focuses on the inscription that says: "This monument was erected to thank Sir A. 'Bomber' Harris for his service to the United Kingdom," to which the posting has added the comments "(and last but not least also for having roasted the 135,000 civilians in Dresden and destroyed the majority of German cities with his 'liberating' bombers)."[67]

YouTube users who identify themselves as "Anti-Fascists" sometimes contest the messages of postings like these two. In response to the first posting on Arthur Harris, xXxAntifascistAction insisted, for example, that "Dresden simply cannot be ripped out of its context! Grief for relatives? Yes. Collective mourning and exploitation as the 'Allied Bombing Holocaust' for right-wing propaganda? NO!" In a second comment that same month, xXXAntifascistAction encouraged other users to "battle against the German victim myth! Dresden is the result of the war of annihilation that Germany began, in which the Russian population was extinguished and English _cities bombed into rubble and ashes . . . for decades Dresden was a military center and until 1945 served the deployment of large military detachments."

"Anti-Fascists" also have their own postings on YouTube. "Dresden 1945—Mythos und Realität (2/2)," put up on October 9, 2008, by DresdenRealitaet, starts with footage of protesters in Dresden who are trying to prevent what they call a "Nazi" procession on the occasion of the commemoration of the bombing of Dresden.[68] Users then see two young women from behind who are talking about the demonstration to an unidentified man. The film moves next to scenes of the "Memorial Square at the Heath Cemetery." One of the two young women claims that this monument was originally conceived under the Nazis as a memorial to the dead of World War I and is laid out in the form of a *Thingsstätte*, a Germanic cult site. After the war, under the communists, the stele arranged in a circle around the central open space were dedicated to both concentration camps, such as Auschwitz, and German cities destroyed by the bombing, such as Dresden. Words now appear on the screen taking us to February 13, 2006, followed by footage of demonstrators and police. Next, the camera moves to the commemoration that day at the cemetery. Captions inserted into the frame identify the minister president of Saxony and members of the right-wing "NPD-Fraktion," who are later shown to be among those laying wreaths at the memorial. Off camera, the young woman's voice criticizes the "absurd standpoint to which the Dresden politics of mourning adheres," which talks a great deal about "reconciliation" but ignores the larger context of World War II that produced the destruction of Dresden. She continues: "the thirteenth of February, a symbol for the status of the Germans as victims which is a hallucination, may well be the most unsuitable date to demonstrate this struggle with [our] own history. Instead of thanking the Allies for the destruction of Nazi Germany, and confronting the role Germans played as perpetrators, [Germans] present themselves as victims who, in a magnanimous fashion, have managed to bring themselves to the point of (re)conciliation."

YouTube postings about cities that are less symbolically important than Dresden are not as political as these, but they too can attract emotional responses. A posting on Kiel showed unusual film footage of the city before and after the bombing, accompanied by the sound of a clock ticking and dramatic guitar music.[69] From Canada, sprichbeeke wrote that "I was born in Kiel in 1945 . . . and this film shows not only the devastation of war . . . but also visualizes . . . what for my generation and that of our parents are deeply rooted impressions which continue to shape us even today. I have lived for 40 years in Canada . . . and see clearly that this war arouses other emotions in me than in the North Americans." The comments by other users focused on Kiel's architectural losses. Hannes Beckmann lamented that "before the war_Kiel was still beautiful." Poochykiel observed, "When today you go through Kiel it is scarcely to be believed that Kiel once _had been such a beautiful city." Staudtwerner asked sarcastically "which city [ever] became more beautiful after the firestorms_of the English?" Another user remarked that "Kiel certainly was a_beautiful city before the war, today Kiel is really ugly." MartinaBC1963 agreed, commenting that "I have lived for over 30 years in Kiel and _find the hotchpotch of buildings in the Kiel city center sad." Some other users preferred to draw attention to the achievements of postwar reconstruction. Silentlouis recommended "complete respect for all_those who raised this city from the rubble!" Seroison agreed: "Wow, you only properly gain respect for those people who rebuilt everything when you see such pictures. Until now, I only knew about this_from the stories I heard."

Conclusion

From the 1940s to the 1990s, Germans who tried to imagine the bombing of their cities during World War II had to rely on local publications as the primary "vectors of memory." In the 1990s, the rapid spread of narratives and images of the bombing into the visual/virtual mass media—particularly film and the Internet—made the bombing war accessible to much larger audiences. But which bombing war(s) could Germans now see in film or online? In recent years, films have given their audiences new images of the bombing war: filmed eyewitness testimony, staged reenactments, and fictional images. These new pictures appear to offer emotional and imaginative connections to the past that viewers may feel they cannot find with other images or narratives.[70] Yet the most common of these new images—filmed eyewitness testimony—-often run the risk of narrowing rather than enriching the imaginative possibilities of film. The stories told by German eyewitnesses can easily become "a narrative of guiltless ensnarement and helplessness" at the "mercy of forces beyond their control."[71] German eyewitnesses generally have little to say about their own behavior and attitudes earlier in the war and they seldom draw attention to the fate of Jews or other victims of the Nazi regime. Recent films frequently combine the testimony of German eyewitnesses with the accounts of Allied airmen and of German Jews. Yet the stories told by these other eyewitnesses must operate within economies of feeling and morality that promote empathy with the German victims but more ambivalent attitudes toward the Allied airmen or Jews. Even though Allied airmen also died in large numbers (and this high mortality rate is mentioned in some of these films), their moral status does not allow them to be represented simply as victims. How they talk about what they did—whether they express regret or sorrow or whether they insist that they were just doing their job or even that the Germans started all of this—will undoubtedly influence German viewers' reactions to their testimony.

At the same time that the Jewish eyewitnesses in these films were trying to survive the bombing they were also attempting to avoid denunciation by Germans, evade the Gestapo, and save themselves from deportation. This double threat gave the Jewish experience of the bombing war a meaning it could not have in German eyes. Although Jewish lives were certainly threatened by air attacks, Allied bombs could also save Jews from being murdered in Auschwitz. Some attempts have been made recently to depict Germans and Jews (as well as Russian POWs and forced foreign laborers, who are not allowed to speak in these films) as members of a "victim collective" on whom Allied bombs rained down indiscriminately.[72] Yet the very real differences between the Jewish and the German experiences of the bombing war cannot be erased and may make it harder for German audiences to empathize with the Jewish than with the German eyewitnesses they see on the screen.[73]

Unlike film, the Internet provides new opportunities for ordinary Germans to create as well as to consume narratives and images of the air war.[74] This potential for popular creativity is not reflected in the images used on most Internet sites about the bombing, which are generally drawn from the publicly available visual repertoire that has been established by the print media since 1945. What makes Internet sites on the bombing war unusual is the way in which they allow users to create their own individual collages of images, words, and sound as well as to comment on the narratives and images posted by others. Although some Internet sites attempt to provide comprehensive, measured, and multiperspectival discussions of the bombing war, numerous websites depend on inflammatory rhetoric, shock images, emotional appeals, and narrow perspectives to focus users' attentions exclusively on German suffering. These sites provide public outlets for emotional responses—primarily anger and outrage—that, before the end of the Cold War, were seldom overtly expressed in mainstream West German local publications and were only allowed in East Germany, so long as they remained within the boundaries of the official Cold War propaganda.

This new emphasis on anger and outrage is reflected in the way that these websites use images. Pictures of desolate ruins and gruesome corpses stand alone, confronting the viewer "more and more drastically with the experience of the senselessness and futility . . . than in the first postwar years."[75] In the 1950s and 1960s, ruin pictures helped Germans lament what they had lost but were also the necessary visual counterparts to the images that celebrated the achievements of postwar rebuilding. By the 1990s, the function of ruin pictures had become increasingly distilled into outrage, anger, and accusation. Viewers were now generally denied the consolation provided by the pictures of postwar reconstruction, of "life after death," that so often appeared in the early local publications.[76] This way of using images does not encourage viewers to think about the differences between the moral valence and the emotional impact of an image or series of images. No one would even begin to suggest that pictures of bodies incinerated by a firestorm are not absolutely horrific, even heartbreaking. But can these images, by themselves, really help viewers arrive at a moral judgment? What would happen if images of the German victims of Allied bombing were placed on these websites next to equally dreadful photos of the victims of the German bombing of Warsaw, of the London Blitz,[77] of the siege of Leningrad, or of the extermination camps? Most of these websites clearly do not expect or want their users to ask this question.

Conclusion

The power of the local master narrative established in the 1950s depended on its ability to compress the local memory of the war and the Nazi past into the experience of the bombing. This version of local history depicted the inhabitants of individual towns and cities as innocent, unsuspecting victims of both Allied bombs and the Nazi regime that had deceived and misled them. By the late 1990s, this narrative had become intensely problematic. New scholarship, the activities of local History Workshops, and public controversies about the traveling exhibition "Crimes of the Wehrmacht" (1995–99) and about Daniel Jonah Goldhagen's book *Hitler's Willing Executioners: Ordinary Germans and the Holocaust* (1996) had all focused public attention on the participation of ordinary Germans in the crimes of the Nazi regime.[1] At the end of the 20th century, it seemed no longer possible to decontaminate local history.

Yet the most recent visual and textual representations exhibit no clear agreement on the "right" narratives and the "right" images that should be used to depict the bombing of German cities.[2] A range of different voices and pictures now compete for the attention of German audiences. This "pluralization" of bombing narratives and images both reflects and enables the competing, sometimes contradictory ways that Germans imagine the air war. It is certainly still possible to produce a book on the bombing of a German city that does not differ in essentials from a 1950s publication. In 2003, Egbert A. Hoffmann published a volume comprising a series of articles that had previously appeared in the Hamburg *Abendblatt*.[3] He focused narrowly on Hamburg, ignoring the wider contexts of the bombing campaign or of the Nazi conduct of the war. His narrative relied on a typical motif already established in the late 1940s that juxtaposes the centuries-long history of the Hansestadt with its abrupt annihilation by British bombers in 1943.[4] Readers who want to focus on German suffering and loss in World War II are likely to find books like Hoffmann's appealing. But although this older kind of narrative has certainly not disappeared altogether, it has become more unusual. Two other books on Hamburg, published at about the same time as Hoffmann's, adopted the wider historical perspectives that distinguish many, if certainly not all, of the recent publications from their predecessors in the late 1940s and 1950s. These two books embed their stories in the broader history of the war and the Nazi regime, and they support this widened historical context with pictures of the Nazi dictatorship and the destruction of other European cities by German bombing. Yet even books that discuss the cities Germans bombed, or the fate of Jews, slave laborers, and Russian POWs, may do so not to raise in their readers' minds questions about German guilt, responsibility, and complicity but rather to show that everyone suffered during the war.

Since 1945, authors of local publications have been well aware that language was incapable of conveying the full horror of the bombing war. But did this mean that images could do the work that words could not? Attempts to visualize the story of the bombing war have continued to struggle with the dilemma that some photographs showed too little, while others showed too much. On the one hand, photography was unable to document some of the most extreme experiences and horrors of the air war. Pictures of the ruins of devastated German cities and, to a lesser extent, horrific photographs of mutilated or incinerated German bodies could only serve as surrogates for the impossible, absent images of the actual moment of destruction. At the same time, other photographs might show too much. Photographs of Germans in the ruins were meant, for example, to invoke sympathy for their suffering and loss but also admiration for their courage and perseverance. Yet they might also encourage viewers to ask what these Germans had done and felt before these photographs were taken. Had they, perhaps, played some role in the production of their own suffering through their support of Hitler's war when the Nazis had been winning? Photographic images can certainly be presented in ways that raise questions about Germans' involvement in the Nazi regime. Malte Thiessen draws attention, for example, to a series of Hamburg newspaper articles published in 1993 that "make clear the causes and the effects of 'Operation Gomorrha' with the juxtaposition of two photographs: Next to a picture of Hitler being cheered during his visit to Hamburg in 1938 is a photograph of people killed by the bombing. This sequence concludes that the bombing attacks were certainly madness, although insanity that Germany itself had begun."[5] Yet photographs can still be employed in a very conventional manner. Like the nostalgic picture books produced right after the war, a volume also published in 1993 shows Dresden as it was before the bombing. Only three photographs at the end of the book show the ruins left behind by the Allied bombers in February 1945.[6]

Images certainly play a more important role today in the depiction of the bombing war than they did in the 1950s.[7] The results of this new visual attention to the bombing of German cities are paradoxical. On the one hand, recent films have expanded and enriched the visual possibilities for imagining the air war. Despite the criticisms that can be made of the intensive use of eyewitness testimony, staged reenactments, and even completely fictional images, these new films do make it possible for Germans to see the bombing war in new ways. At the same time, however, many Internet postings have diminished and impoverished the imaginative possibilities by oversimplifying and coarsening both the textual and the visual representation of the bombing war. Greater emphasis on the visual may also encourage Germans to conflate seeing with understanding. Talking about photographs of another war, Vilem Flusser suggests that "we . . . prefer to stick to the photograph that . . . absolves us from the bother of going into the causes and consequences of the war. . . . In the image we see with our own eyes what the war looks like. The text simply consists of instructions as to how we are to see."[8]

Unlike the local publications of the 1940s and 1950s, contemporary textual and visual representations of the bombing war must contend with "the hegemony of the Holocaust-centered memory regime" that structures contemporary German public discourse about World War II and the Nazi past.[9] Few current depictions of the bombing war ignore the Holocaust altogether. Today, mainstream publications, popular films, and websites incorporate direct references and indirect allusions to the Holocaust into their larger textual and visual strategies. The crucial issue is how they do this. In 1993, for example, the Museum of the History of Hamburg (Museum für Hamburgische Geschichte) mounted an exhibition on the occasion of the 50th anniversary of the firebombing of the city.[10] The displays included a number of photographs that drew attention to the persecution of Jews in Hamburg. A well-known picture showed SA men with smiles on their faces boycotting a Jewish business on the Grindelallee in April 1933. On the right-hand side of the photograph we can also see several ordinary Germans—a man, a young girl who is looking into the camera, and a woman behind her. Two other photographs show a park bench bearing the sign "Nur für Arier" ("For Aryans Only") and a smashed shop display window. One of the most challenging exhibits combines a photograph of a Hamburg train station (Hannoversche Bahnhof) with a well-known picture of the gatehouse at Auschwitz. The text accompanying this juxtaposition makes clear that "The Path to Auschwitz" began with the first deportation of Hamburg Jews to Lodz from this train station on October 25, 1941. It was followed by 16 more transports to Minsk, Riga, Theresienstadt, and Auschwitz. The 1993 exhibition also included a Nazi propaganda poster that blamed the war on the Jews. Yet even though the 1993 Hamburg exhibition included images that would not have appeared in most local publications from the 1940s to the 1990s, the relationship this exhibition wanted to establish between the Holocaust and the bombing remains unclear. This becomes evident when we look at the larger display, the "Pendulum of Destruction," which included several of the photographs that drew attention to the persecution and murder of the Jews. This pendulum "symbolically connected the sites of the air war that Hitler began with his program of mass murder of the 'racially less valuable' which was methodically carried out right up to 1945." Are these all to be seen simply as different examples of the unprecedented violence of Nazi Germany and World War II? Or does the exhibition want to suggest that there is a link between the persecution and annihilation of Jews or other victims considered by the Nazis to be racially inferior and the eventual destruction of Hamburg and other German cities by Allied bombing? If so, why does the pendulum of destruction also include the names of cities attacked by German bombers as well as Nagasaki, which was destroyed by an American atomic bomb?

An issue of *Spiegel-special* on the bombing war published in 2003 included two articles related to the Holocaust. One described how it was possible, due to the chaos in German cities increasingly generated by the effects of the bombing, for many Jews to evade capture by the police and the SS. The article draws on a well-established distinction between the Nazi authorities and ordinary Germans by arguing that "[t]hrough the help of brave citizens about 1,500 Jews survived amidst the ruins of Berlin alone."[11] The other article draws attention directly to Auschwitz, yet in a curious way. Rather than focusing, as did the 1993 Hamburg exhibition, on the road that led from German cities like Hamburg to the extermination centers, this piece asks whether the Allies could not or did not want to bomb Auschwitz, thereby suggesting that there were better targets than German cities for Allied bombs.[12]

Even when the Holocaust is ignored, it may still be present as an implied visual or rhetorical point of reference. In the 1950s, the danger of producing associations with the bodies of Jewish victims of the Holocaust may have discouraged the authors of local publications from using gruesome pictures of the Germans killed in the bombing war. Today, the fact that the Holocaust is a central element of German public memory and identity and that most Germans are familiar with pictures of the bodies of murdered Jews appears, paradoxically, to have made it possible to display more photographs of Germans killed by Allied bombs without concern that these pictures will conjure up unwelcome associations with dead Jewish bodies. In a picture book published in

2003, for example, Jörg Friedrich included no fewer than 30 pictures of German civilian corpses.[13]

Until recently, any suggestion of a moral equivalence between the Holocaust and the bombing war was the exclusive province of the radical right wing. Now it appears to have gone mainstream. Friedrich has, for example, appropriated the language that has come to be associated with the Holocaust to describe German suffering in the bombing war. He repeatedly uses the term *Vernichtung* (annihilation), which will remind many readers of the term *Vernichtungskrieg* to describe the Nazis' racial war of annihilation in the Soviet Union that claimed the lives of millions of Jews and Slavs.[14]

A pessimistic reading of some of the recent developments in the representation of the bombing war might lead to the conclusion that "the new preoccupation with German victims has come, explicitly, at the expense of the Nazis' victims."[15] Yet there are two reasons to disagree with this assessment. First, it is clear that by the mid-1990s the landscape of German public remembering of World War II was populated by a broad range of victims: German victims of the bombing, German refugees and expellees from the East, but also Jews and other racial or political victims of the Nazis.[16] It may well be true, as Klaus Neumann has argued, that the proliferation of these victim discourses has produced a growing fragmentation and compartmentalization of the public remembering and commemoration of World War II. Although lip service may be paid to the importance of acknowledging that a wide range of both Germans and non-Germans were victims of the war, the suffering that really seems to count is the suffering of the individual "memory community" with which individual Germans, young or old, identify.[17] Yet although these fragmented, self-referential forms of public memory may hinder emotional identification with the suffering of others, they certainly do not ignore or deny that suffering.

Second, Germans have been arguing with one another about the meaning of the air war more in the early 21st century than at any other time since 1945. The new interactive public spaces created by the Internet make it possible for (potentially) thousands of ordinary Germans to participate directly in these disagreements. In Schweinfurt, on the 70th anniversary in August 2013 of the first air raid, for example, one speaker at the commemoration ceremony noted that almost a third of the 1,194 people killed in all the air raids on the city were foreigners "who had been forced to work here." The air war against Germany was depicted "as a response to previous wrongs." Another speaker told a story about a Schweinfurt woman who predicted after Kristallnacht 1938 that Germany would have to atone for the persecution of the Jews. A disgruntled reader who posted a comment on the newspaper's website on August 19, 2013, insisted, however, that it was not the German people but the American and British pilots and their superiors who needed to atone. They did not drop their bombs on residential areas by mistake, as the newspaper story had claimed, "and it was also no mistake that foreign workers were not spared by these killings . . . with their deaths the Germans could later be blackmailed."[18] From 1945 to 1990, the local master narrative of the air war proved to be remarkably durable.[19] Disagreements such as this one in Schweinfurt should ensure that, in the foreseeable future at least, no single interpretation of the air war is likely to achieve that kind of power again.

Notes

INTRODUCTION

1. Stefan Glienke, "The Allied Air War and German Society," in Claudia Baldoli, Andrew Knapp, and Richard Overy, eds., *Bombing, States and Peoples in Western Europe, 1940–45* (London and New York: Continuum, 2011), 186.

2. Robert G. Moeller, "Remembering the War in a Nation of Victims: West German Pasts in the 1950s," in Hanna Schissler, ed., *The Miracle Years: A Cultural History of West Germany 1949–1968* (Princeton: Princeton University Press, 2001), 88.

3. W. G. Sebald, *Luftkrieg und Literatur. Mit einem Essay zu Alfred Andersch* (München: Carl Hanser Verlag, 1999), 12.

4. Jörg Friedrich, *Der Brand. Deutschland im Bombenkrieg 1940–1945* (München: Propyläen, 2002).

5. Lothar Kettenacker, ed., *Ein Volk von Opfern? Die neue Debatte um den Bombenkrieg 1940–1945* (Berlin: Rowohlt, 2003).

6. *Spiegel Special. Das Magazin zum Thema*, "Als Feuer vom Himmel fiel. Der Bombenkrieg gegen die Deutschen," Nr. 1/2003; "Feuersturm. Der Bombenkrieg gegen Deutschland," DVD-Edition (Hamburg: Spiegel TV, 2003).

7. See especially Gert Ledig, *Die Vergeltung. Ein Roman* (Frankfurt am Main: Suhrkamp Taschenbuch, 2001).

8. Spiegel Online, February 13, 2006; http//www.spiegel.de/international/0,1518,400691,00.html (accessed February 28, 2006). Unless otherwise indicated, all translations are my own.

9. Joachim Käppner, "Kommentar. Das deutsche Leid," *Sueddeutsche Zeitung* (March 16, 2006); http://www.sueddeutsche.de/,tt2m3/deutschland/artikel/479/71408 (accessed April 1, 2006).

10. On the German media and "economies of attention" see Erik Meyer, "Problematische Popularität? Erinnerungskultur, Medienwandel und Aufmerksamkeitsökonomie," in Barbara Korte and Sylvia Paletschek, eds., *History Goes Pop. Zur Repräsentation von Geschichte in populären Medien und Genres* (Bielefeld: Transcript Verlag, 2009) [Historische Lebenswelten in populären Wissenskulturen. History in Popular Cultures, Band I], 267–88.

11. Nicola Lambourne, *War Damage in Western Europe: The Destruction of Historic Monuments During the Second World War* (Edinburgh: Edinburgh University Press, 2001), 42.

12. Friedrich, *Deutschland im Bombenkrieg 1940–1945*, 290.

13. Meyer, "Problematische Popularität?" 267–88. On the history of depictions of German victimhood see Bill Niven, ed., *Germans as Victims* (New York: Palgrave Macmillan, 2006).

14. Klaus Rainer Röhl, *Verbotene Trauer. Ende der deutschen Tabus* (München: Universitas Verlag, 2002), 9.

15. Malte Thießen, *Eingebrannt ins Gedächtnis. Hamburgs Gedenken an Luftkrieg und Kriegsende 1943 bis 2005* (Hamburg: Dölling und Galitz Verlag, 2007); Jörg Arnold, *The Allied Air War and Urban Memory: The Legacy of Strategic Bombing in Germany* (Cambridge: Cambridge University Press, 2011); Neil Gregor, "Trauer und städtische Identitätspolitik. Erinnerungen an die Bombardierung Nürnbergs," in Jörg Arnold, Dietmar Süss, and Malte Thiessen, eds., *Luftkrieg. Erinnerungen in Deutschland und Europa* (Göttingen: Wallstein Verlag, 2009), 131–45; Dietmar Süß, *Tod aus der Luft. Kriegsgesellschaft und Luftkrieg in Deutschland und England* (München: Siedler Verlag, 2011). For an important overview of the recent research see Arnold, Süss, and Thiessen, eds., *Erinnerungen in Deutschland und Europa*, and Dietmar Süß, ed., *Deutschland im Luftkrieg. Geschichte und Erinnerung* (München: R. Oldenbourg Verlag, 2007).

16. Geoff Eley, *Nazism as Fascism: Violence, Ideology, and the Grounds of Consent in Germany* (London: Routledge, 2013), 156–57.

17. Michael Rothberg, "Between Auschwitz and Algeria: Multidirectional Memory and the Counterpublic Witness," *Critical Inquiry* 33, no. 1 (Autumn 2006): 161.

18. Gregor, "Trauer und städtische Identitätspolitik," 140. See also Gilad Margalit, *Guilt, Suffering, and Memory: Germany Remembers Its Dead of World War II* (Bloomington: Indiana University Press, 2010), 184–85.

19. Süß, *Tod aus der Luft,* 502.

20. Ibid., 502.

21. Hans Rumpf, *The Bombing of Germany*, translated from the German by Edward Fitzgerald (New York: Holt, Rinehart and Winston, 1963).

22. Ibid., 6.

23. Nancy Wood, *Vectors of Memory: Legacies of Trauma in Postwar Europe* (Oxford: Berg, 1999).

24. Frank Bösch and Constantin Goschler, eds., *Public History. Öffentliche Darstellungen des Nationalsozialismus jenseits der Geschichtswissenschaft* (Frankfurt am Main: Campus Verlag, 2009).

25. Süß, *Tod aus der Luft*, 90. On Nazi "memory politics," see Dirk Rupnow, *Vernichten und Erinnern. Spuren nationalsozialistischer Gedächtnispolitik* (Göttingen: Wallstein Verlag, 2005).

26. For stimulating discussions of the importance of thinking about how archives are created and used see Sebastian Jobs and Alf Lüdtke, eds., *Unsettling History: Archiving and Narrating in Historiography* (Frankfurt: Campus Verlag, 2010).

27. Süß, *Tod aus der Luft*, 502.

28. Paul B. Jaskot and Gavriel D. Rosenfeld, "Introduction: Urban Space and the Nazi Past in Postwar Germany," in Gavriel D. Rosenfeld and Paul B. Jaskot, eds., *Beyond Berlin: Twelve German Cities Confront the Nazi Past* (Ann Arbor: University of Michigan Press, 2007), 1.

29. Ibid., 1.

30. Ibid., 1.

31. Süß, *Tod aus der Luft*, 513.

32. *Dokumente deutscher Kriegsschäden. Evakuierte. Kriegsgeschädigte. Währungsgeschädigte. Die geschichtliche und rechtliche Entwicklung* (Band V. Bibliographie), Herausgegeben vom Bundesminister für Vertriebene, Flüchtlinge und Kriegsgeschädigte Bonn (Stuttgart:Zentraldruckerei, Ackermann & Honold, 1964), 26–53.

33. *Dokumente deutscher Kriegsschäden: Evakuierte, Kriegssachgeschädigte, Währungsgeschädigte; die geschichtliche und rechtliche Entwicklung*, Band I. (Bonn: Bundesministerium des Innern, Abt. Vertriebene, Flüchtlinge und Kriegsgeschädigte, 1958).

34. Among the still quite rare exceptions are Wolgang Hesse, "Der 'Engel von Dresden. Trümmerfotografie und visuelles Narrativ der Hoffnung," and Marita Krauss, "Trümmerfrauen Visuelles Konstrukt und Realität," both in Gerhard Paul, ed., *Das Jahrhundert der Bilder 1900 bis 1949* (Göttingen: Vandenhoeck and Ruprecht, 2009), 730–37 and 738–45. See also Jörg Arnold, "'In wächserner Blässe wie Schaufensterpuppen.' Leichenbilder aus dem Lufkrieg und ihr sozialen Gebrauch (1940–1960)," *Fotogeschichte* 32, no. 125 (2012): 27–38, and, most recently, Anne Fuchs, *After the Dresden Bombing: Pathways of Memory, 1945 to the Present* (Basingstoke: Macmillan, 2012).

35. Julia Adeney Thomas, "The Evidence of Sight," *History and Theory* 48 (December 2009): 152–55, here page 151. See also Michael S. Roth, "Why Photography Matters to the Theory of History," *History and Theory* 49 (February 2010): 86.

36. Thomas, "Evidence of Sight," 159–64.

37. Ibid., 168.

38. Joan Neuberger, "Past and Presence," Sheffield (UK) Photography Conference May 16–17, 2013. My thanks to my colleague Joan Neuberger for permission to cite this unpublished article.

39. Jörn Glasenapp, "Vergangenheit und Zukunft. Wie fotografische Sinn entsteht," *Fotogeschichte* 32, no. 143 (2012): 5.

40. Ibid.

41. Thomas Heimann, *Bilder von Buchenwald. Die Visualisierung des Antifaschismus in der DDR (1945–1990)* (Köln: Böhlau Verlag, 2005), 17.

42. Armin Schmid, *Frankfurt im Feuersturm. Die Geschichte der Stadt im Zweiten Weltkrieg* (Frankfurt: Verlag Frankfurter Bücher, 1965), foreword.

43. Josef Fischer, *Köln '39-'45. Der Leidensweg einer Stadt. Miterlebt von Josef Fischer* (Köln: Verlag J. P. Bachem, 1970), 5.

44. Ludger Derenthal, *Bilder der Trümmer- und Aufbaujahre. Fotografie im sich teilenden Deutschland* (Marburg: Jonas Verlag, 1999), 87–98.

CHAPTER 1

1. Adelheid von Saldern, ed., *Inszenierter Stolz. Stadtrepräsentationen in drei deutschen Gesellschaften (1935–1975)* (Stuttgart: Franz Steiner Verlag, 2005).

2. Adelheid von Saldern, "Stadtgedächtnis und Geschichtswerkstätten," *Werkstatt-Geschichte* 50 (March 2008): 54–68.

3. Armin Schmid, *Frankfurt im Feuersturm. Die Geschichte der Stadt im 2. Weltkrieg* (Frankfurt am Main: Frankfurter Bücher, 1965).

4. See Andrew Bergerson, "Reconstructing the Self: The Uses of Alt Hildesheim after Its Destruction," in Georg Wagner Kyora, ed., *Wiederaufbau europäischer Städte/ Rebuilding European Cities. Rekonstruktionen, die Moderne und die lokale Identitätspolitik seit 1945/Reconstructions, Modernity and the Local Politics of Identity Construction since 1945* (Stuttgart: Franz Steiner Verlag, 2014), 272–310, and Elizabeth Harvey, *Women and the Nazi East: Agents and Witnesses of Germanization* (New Haven: Yale University Press, 2003), as well as Wendy Lower, *Hitler's Furies: German Women in the Nazi Killing Fields* (Boston: Houghton Mifflin Harcourt, 2013).

5. Stefan Glienke, "The Allied Air War and German Society," in Baldoli, Knapp, and Overy, eds., *Bombing, States and Peoples*, 184–205.

6. Jörg Arnold, "Sammelrezension: Bombenkrieg," H-Soz-Kult: http://hsozkult.geschichte.hu-berlin.de/rezensionen/2004-2-062 (accessed July 29, 2009).

7. Georg Seiderer, "Würzburg, 16 März 1945. Vom 'kollektiven Trauma' zur lokalen Sinnstiftung," in Arnold, Süss, and Thiessen, eds., *Erinnerungen in Deutschland und Europa*, 150.

8. Alois Stadtmuller, *Aschaffenburg im Zweiten Weltkrieg. Bombenangriffe-Belagerung-Übergabe* (Aschaffenburg: In Kommission bei Paul Pattloch Verlag, 1970; Veröffentlichung des Geschichts-und Kunstvereins Aschaffenburg e.V.12).

9. Jörg Arnold, "Sammelrezension: Bombenkrieg," H-Soz-Kult; http://hsozkult.geschichte.hu-berlin.de/rezensionen/2004-2-062 (accessed July 29, 2009).

10. Jeffry Herf, *Divided Memory: The Nazi Past in the Two Germanys* (Cambridge, MA: Harvard University Press, 1997), 267.

11. Robert G. Moeller, "War Stories: The Search for a Usable Past in the Federal Republic of Germany," *American Historical Review* 101, no. 4 (October 1996): 1008–48.

12. Jörn Glasenapp, *Die deutsche Nachkriegsfotografie. Eine Mentalitätsgeschichte in Bildern* (Paderborn: Wilhelm Fink, 2008), 100.

13. Süß, *Tod aus der Luft,* 505.

14. Ibid., 505.

15. Neil Gregor, *Haunted City: Nuremberg and the Nazi Past* (New Haven: Yale University Press, 2008), 10.

16. Ibid., 3.

17. Klaus Hesse and Philipp Springer, *Vor aller Augen. Fotodokumente des nationalsozialistischen Terrors in der Provinz* (Essen: Klartext, 2002); Michael Wildt, "Gewalt gegen Juden in Deutschland 1933 bis 1939," *WerkstattGeschichte* 18 (1997): 59–80, and "Gewaltpolitik, Volksgemeinschaft und Judenverfolgung in der deutschen Provinz 1932 bis 1935," *WerkstattGeschichte* 35 (2003): 23–43.

18. Klaus-Michael Mallmann and Gerhard Paul, "Omniscient, Omnipotent, Omnipresent? Gestapo, Society and Resistance," in David F. Crew, ed., *Nazism and German Society, 1933–1945* (New York: Routledge, 1994), 173.

19. Ibid., 185.

20. Ulrich Herbert, "Good Times, Bad Times: Memories of the Third Reich," in Richard Bessel, ed., *Life in the Third Reich* (Oxford: Oxford University Press, 1987), 97.

21. Malte Thiessen, "Gedenken an die 'Operation Gomorrha.' Hamburgs Erinnerungskultur und städtiche Identität," in Süss, ed., *Deutschland im Luftkrieg*, 122–23.

22. See Frank Biess, "'Everybody has a Chance': Nuclear Angst, Civil Defence, and the History of Emotions in Postwar West Germany," *German History: The Journal of the German History Society* 27, no. 2 (April 2009): 236; "the emotions of fear and anxiety linked the 'horizon of expectation' of ordinary Germans during the Cold War with their real and imagined experiences and memories of War II."

23. Rumpf, *The Bombing of Germany*, 13.

24. Schmid, *Frankfurt im Feuersturm*, foreword.

25. Bas von Benda-Beckmann, "Eine deutsch-deutsche Katastrophe? Deutungsmuster des Bombenkriegs in der ost-und westdeutschen Geschichtswissenschaft," in Arnold, Süß, and Thiessen, eds., *Erinnerungen in Deutschland und Europa*, 301.

26. Ibid., 301.

27. Ibid., 303.

28. Ibid., 311.

29. Malte Thiessen, *Eingebrannt ins Gedächtnis. Hamburgs Gedenken an Luftkrieg und Kriegsende 1943 bis 2005* (Hamburg: Dölling und Galitz Verlag, 2007).

30. Max-Braun Rühling, *Eine Stadt im Feuerregen. Die Zerstörung der Stadt Kaiserslautern* (Unveränderter Nachdruck der Originalausgabe von 1953, Ergänzt durch weitere Bilder. Beiträge von Hansgeorg Bassler, Roland Paul und Jürgen Keddigkeit) (Kaiserslautern: Reinhold Gondrom Verlag, 1991), 54.

31. *Paderborn. Werden. Untergang. Wiedererstehen.* Im Auftrage der Stadt Paderborn. Herausgegeben von Dr. Rudolf Kiepke. Künstlerische Gestaltung Heinrich Niedieck (Paderborn: Verlag Bonifacius-Druckerei, 1949) [Faksimile-Nachdruck der Orginalausgabe, 1949, 1976], 67.

32. Ibid., 67.

33. Ibid., 17.

34. Ibid., 30.

35. Ibid., 32.

36. Ibid., 26.

37. Ibid., 31.

38. Ibid., 37, 33.

39. Ibid., 44.

40. Ibid., 43.

41. Ibid., 49.

42. Ibid., 104.

43. Ibid., 58.

44. Ibid., 112.

45. Ibid., 166–67.

46. Ibid., 167.

47. Ibid., 180.

48. Ibid., 57, 66.

49. Ibid., 132.
50. Rudolf Wilms, *14. März. Zweibrückens Zerstörung und Wiederaufbau. Eine Erinnerungsschrift zum 10. Jahrestag der Zerstörung der Stadt Zweibrücken* Herausgegeben mit Unterstützung der Stadtverwaltung Zweibrücken (Zweibrücken: Zweibrücker Druckerei und Verlagsgesellschaft m.b.H, 1955), 11.
51. Ibid., 12.
52. Ibid., 12.
53. Ibid., 13.
54. Ibid., 15.
55. Ibid., 23.
56. Ibid., 28.
57. Ibid., 30.
58. Ibid., 30.
59. Ibid., 32.
60. Ibid., 35.
61. Ibid., 34.
62. Schmid, *Frankfurt im Feuersturm*, 77.
63. Ibid., 50.
64. Thiessen, *Eingebrannt ins Gedächtnis*, 82.
65. Max Domarus, *Der Untergang des alten Würzburg und seine Vorgeschichte* (Gerolshofen: Franz Teutsch, 1955), 28.
66. Ibid., 29.
67. Ibid., 30
68. Ibid., 33.
69. Ibid., 35.
70. Ibid., 36.
71. Ibid., 46.
72. Ibid., 47–48.
73. Ibid., 48–49.
74. Ibid., 49.
75. Ibid., 83.
76. Ibid., 84.
77. Georg Seiderer observes that although this argument was first challenged in 1980 by the municipal archivist (Stadtarchivar) Heinrich Dunkhase on the basis of research in the British Public Records Office, it continued to be repeated by other authors for some years to come. In 1994, Ursula R. Moessner's research on the bombing of Pforzheim decisively refuted the claim that Würzburg was destroyed because it was on a list of targets with populations of 100,000 or more; see Seiderer, "Würzburg, 16 März 1945," 152.
78. Domarus, *Der Untergang des alten Würzburg*, 84.
79. Ibid., 84.
80. Ibid., 106.
81. Ibid., 109.
82. Ibid., 110.
83. Ibid., 148.

84. Fritz Nadler, *"Ich sah wie Nürnberg unterging . . . !" Tatsachenberichte und Stimmungsbilder aus bittersten Notzeiten nach Tagebuchaufzeichnungen* (Nürnberg: Fränkische Verlagsanstalt und Buchdruckerei GMBH, 1955), 197–98.

85. Ibid., 42

86. Ibid., 51.

87. Ibid., 59.

88. Hans Brunswig, *Feuersturm über Hamburg. Die Luftangriffe auf Hamburg im Zweiten Weltkrieg und ihre Folgen* (Stuttgart: Motorbuch Verlag, 1978), 7.

89. Rudolf Prescher, *Der rote Hahn über Braunschweig. Luftschutzmassnahmen und Luftkriegsereignisse in der Stadt Braunschweig 1927 bis 1945* [Braunschweiger Werkstücke aus Archiv, Bibliothek und Museum der Stadt, Band 18] (Braunschweig: Waisenhaus Buchdrückerei, 1955).

90. Ibid., 11.

91. Ibid., 15.

92. Ibid., 16.

93. Ibid., 16.

94. Ibid., 34.

95. Ibid., 35.

96. Ibid., 50.

97. Ibid., 67.

98. Ibid., 67.

99. Ibid., 90.

100. Ibid., 91.

101. Ibid., 91.

102. Ibid., 94.

103. Ibid., 100.

104. Ibid., 103.

105. Ibid., 103.

106. Ibid., 103.

107. Thiessen, *Eingebrannt ins Gedächtnis*, 87 and 157–58.

108. Braun Rühling, *Eine Stadt im Feuerregen*, 96.

109. Dietmar Süss, "Nationalsozialistische Deutungen des Luftkrieges," in Dietmar Süss, ed., *Deutschland im Luftkrieg. Geschichte und Erinnerung*, 107.

110. Ibid., 67.

111. Ibid., 67.

112. Ibid., 67.

113. Braun-Rühling, *Eine Stadt im Feuerregen*, 60.

114. *Paderborn. Werden.Untergang. Wiedererstehen*, 112.

115. Braun-Rühling, *Eine Stadt im Feuerregen*, 95–96.

116. Ibid., 96.

117. See Wilms, *Zweibrückens Zerstörung und Wiederaufbau*, 23; Bardua, *Stuttgart im Luftkrieg 1939–1945. Mit Dokumentaranhang und 67 Abbildungen* (Stuttgart: Ernst Klett Verlag, 1967), 52, 76, 124.

118. Dietmar Süß, "Wartime Societies and Shelter Politics in National Socialist Germany and Britain," in Baldoli, Knapp, and Overy, *Bombing, States and Peoples*, 23–42.

119. Nadler, *"Ich sah wie Nürnberg unterging . . . !" Tatsachenberichte und Stimmungsbilder*, 121.

120. Thiessen, *Eingebrannt ins Gedächtnis*, 87.

121. Ibid., 246.

122. Wilms, *Zweibrückens Zerstörung und Wiederaufbau*, Geleitwort.

123. Ibid., 185–86.

124. Ibid., 203.

125. Braun-Rühling, *Eine Stadt im Feuerregen*, 102.

126. See Maria Höhn, *GIs and Fräuleins: The German-American Encounter in 1950s West Germany* (Chapel Hill: University of North Carolina Press, 2002).

127. Wilms, *Zweibrückens Zerstörung und Wiederaufbau*, 37.

128. Ibid., 37.

129. Ibid., 44.

130. Ibid., 45.

131. Thiessen, *Eingebrannt ins Gedächtnis*, 58.

132. Jeffrey Herf, *The Jewish Enemy: Nazi Propaganda during World War II and the Holocaust* (Cambridge, MA: The Belknap Press of Harvard University Press, 2006), 157.

133. Nicholas Stargardt, *Witnesses of War: Children's Lives Under the Nazis* (New York: Alfred A.Knopf, 2006), 252.

134. Ibid., 253.

135. On the importance of rumors in World War II see, for example, Hans-Joachim Neubauer, "In der 'Zone der Legendenbildung.' Zu einigen Kontexten der amerikanischen *rumor clinics* im Zweiten Weltkrieg," *WerkstattGeschichte* 15, no. 5 (December 1996): 33–40. See also Gerhard Jochem, "Der Luftkrieg im Urteil der Zeitzeugen heute," in Michael Diefenbacher and Wilhelm Fischer-Pache, eds., *Der Luftkrieg gegen Nürnberg Der Angriff am 2. Januar 1945 und die zerstörte Stadt* [Quellen und Forschungen zur Gechichte und Kultur der Stadt Nürnberg. Herausgegeben von Michael Diefenbacher and Wiltrud Fischer-Pache im Auftrag der Stadt Nürnberg. 33. Band (Neustadt an der Aisch: Schmidt, 2004), 497.

136. Karl-Heinz Mistele , "Kriegsgerüchte," in *Lebendige Volkskultur. Festgabe für Elisabeth Roth zum 60. Geburtstag* (Bamberg: In Kommission bei Meisenbach, 1980), 151, quoted in Helmut Schnatz, *Tiefflieger über Dresden. Legenden und Wirklichkeit* (Köln: Böhlau Verlag, 2000), 145–46.

137. Saul Friedlander, *The Years of Extermination: Nazi Germany and the Jews, 1939–1945* (New York: Harper Collins, 2008), 514.

138. Stargardt, *Witnesses of War*, 250.

139. Ibid., 250.

140. Christopher R. Browning, "One Day in Jozefow. Initiation to Mass Murder," in David F. Crew, ed., *Nazism and German Society 1933–1945* (London and New York: Routledge, 1994), 306.

141. Arnold, "'In Wächserner Blässe wie Schaufensterpuppen' . . . ," 27.

142. Marion A. Kaplan, *Between Dignity and Despair: Jewish Life in Nazi Germany* (Oxford: Oxford University Press, 1998).

143. Habbo Knoch, "Das mediale Gedächtnis der Heimat. Krieg und Verbrechen in

den Erinnerungsräumen der Bundesrepublik," in Habbo Knoch, ed., *Das Erbe der Provinz. Heimatkultur und Geschichtspolitik nach 1945* (Göttingen: Wallstein Verlag, 2001), 290.

144. Omer Bartov, "'Seit die Juden weg sind . . .': Germany, History and Representations of Absence," in Scott Denham, Irene Kacandes, and Jonathan Petropoulos, eds., *A User's Guide to German Cultural Studies* (Ann Arbor: University of Michigan Press, 1997), 209–26.

145. Philip Gassert and Alan E. Steinweis, "Introduction," in Philip Gassert and Alan E. Steinweis, eds., *Coping with the Nazi Past: West German Debates on Nazism and Generational Conflict, 1955–1975* (New York: Berghahn Books, 2006), 2.

146. Ibid., 4.

147. Robert Sackett, "Pictures of Atrocity: Public Discussion of *Der gelbe Stern* in Early 1960s West Germany," *German History: The Journal of the German History Society* 24, no. 4 (2006): 526–61. See also Cornelia Brink, "Nach Bildern suchen—fotografische Erinnerung," in Peter Reichel, Harald Schmid, and Peter Steinbach, eds., *Der Nationalsozialismus-Die Zweite Geschichte. Überwindung-Deutung-Erinnerung* (München: Verlag C. H. Beck, 2009), 339.

148. Marc von Miqucl, "Explanation, Dissociation, Apologia: The Debate over the Criminal Prosecution of Nazi Crimes in the 1960s," in Gassert and Steinweis, eds., *Coping with the Nazi Past*, 50–63.

149. Jörg Arnold, *The Allied Air War and Urban Memory: The Legacy of Strategic Bombing in Germany* (Cambridge: Cambridge University Press, 2011).

150. Schmid, *Frankfurt im Feuersturm*, foreword.

151. Ibid., foreword.

152. Ibid., foreword.

153. Ibid., foreword.

154. Ibid., foreword.

155. Ibid., foreword.

156. Ibid., 50–51.

157. Ibid., 61.

158. Ibid., 62–64.

159. Ibid., 62–64.

160. Ibid., foreword.

161. Ibid., foreword.

162. Ibid., 16–17.

163. Ibid., 31, 39.

164. Ibid., 20.

165. Ibid., 54–55.

166. Ibid., 55–56.

167. Ibid., 54.

168. Ibid., 123.

169. Ibid., 16–17.

170. Ibid., 20.

171. Ibid., 149.

172. Ibid., 155.

173. Ibid., 167.
174. A. C. Grayling, *Among the Dead Cities: The History and Moral Legacy of the WWII Bombing of Civilians in Germany and Japan* (London: Bloomsbury, 2007).
175. Ludwig Wiener, *Schweinfurt sollte sterben. Untergang und Wiedergeburt einer Stadt* (Schweinfurt: Verlag Neues Forum, 1961).
176. Bardua, *Stuttgart im Luftkrieg 1939–1945*, 7.
177. Ibid., 7.
178. Ibid., 7.
179. Ibid., 151.
180. Ibid., 151.
181. Ibid., 7.
182. Ibid., 7.
183. Ibid., 7–8.
184. Ibid., 151.
185. Ibid., 33.
186. Ibid., 33.
187. Ibid., 119.
188. Ibid., 120.
189. Ibid., 142.
190. Ibid., 53.
191. See, for example, Michael Greve, "Täter oder Gehilfen? Zum strafrechtlichen Umgang mit NS-Gewaltverbrechern in der Bundesrepublik Deutschland," in Ulrike Weckel and Edgar Wolfrum, eds., *"Bestien" und "Befehlsempfänger." Frauen und Männer in NS-Prozessen nach 1945* (Göttingen: Vandenhoeck and Ruprecht, 2003), 194–221.
192. Bardua, *Stuttgart im Luftkrieg 1939–1945*, 43.
193. Ibid., 110.
194. Ibid., 45.
195. Ibid., 42.
196. Nicole Kramer, "Lynchmorde an allierten Fliegern im Zweiten Weltkrieg," in Dietmar Süß, ed., *Deutschland im Luftkrieg*, 71–84.
197. Bardua, *Stuttgart im Luftkrieg 1939–1945*, 48.
198. Ibid., 48.
199. Ibid., 155.
200. Ibid., 155.
201. Ibid., 48.
202. Ibid., 156
203. Ibid., 173.
204. Fischer, *Köln '39-'45. Der Leidensweg einer Stadt*, 98.
205. Ibid., 97.
206. Ibid., 95.
207. Ibid., 149.
208. Ibid., 183.
209. Ibid., 145.
210. Ibid., 145.

211. Ibid., 143.
212. Ibid., 195.
213. Ibid., 198–99.
214. Ibid., 59.
215. Ibid., 61.
216. Ibid., 63–64.
217. Ibid., 64.
218. Ibid., 66.
219. Ibid., 66.
220. Ibid., 107–8.
221. Ibid., 188. Fischer had already introduced readers to some of these darker elements of his 1970 narrative in a series of Cologne newspaper articles published in 1949.
222. Ibid., 45.
223. Ibid., 45.
224. Alf Lüdtke, "'Coming to Terms with the Past': Illusions of Remembering, Ways of Forgetting Nazism in West Germany," *Journal of Modern History* 65, no. 31 (September 1993): 545, footnote 10.
225. Friedrich Knilli and Siegfried Zielinski, eds., *Betrifft "Holocaust" Zuschauer schreiben an den WDR* (Berlin: Verlag Volker Spiess, 1983).
226. Anton Kaes, *From Hitler to Heimat: The Return of History as Film* (Cambridge, MA: Harvard University Press, 1989), 184.
227. Ibid., 184.
228. Ibid., 163.
229. Ibid., 164.
230. Ibid., 185.
231. Ibid., 187.
232. Ibid., 185.
233. Ibid., 186.
234. Geoff Eley, "Nazism, Politics and the Image of the Past: Thoughts on the West German Historikerstreit 1986–1987," *Past & Present*, no. 121 (November 1988): 171–208. Here, 173.
235. Adelheid von Saldern, "Stadtgedächtnis und Geschichtswerkstätten," *Werkstatt-Geschichte* 50 (2008): 63.
236. Eckart Conze, *Die Suche nach der Sicherheit. Eine Geschichte der Bundesrepublik von 1949 bis in die Gegenwart* (München: Siedler Verlag, 2009), 536.
237. Jörg Arnold, Dietmar Süss, and Malte Thiessen, "Tod, Zerstörung, Wiederaufbau, Zu einer europäischen Erinnerungsgeschichte des Luftkrieges," in Arnold, Süss, and Thiessen, eds., *Erinnerungen in Deutschland und Europa*, 16.
238. Karl Krämer, *"Christbäume" über Frankfurt 1943. Ein Bericht von Karl Krämer* (Frankfurt: Buchergilde Gutenberg, 1983), 13. Foreword by Gerhard Beier.
239. Ibid., 13.
240. Ibid., 6.
241. Ibid., 14.
242. Ibid., 22.
243. Ibid., 14.
244. Ibid., 30–32.

245. Ibid., 39.
246. Ibid., 52.
247. Ibid.
248. Ibid., 48.
249. Ibid., 48.
250. Ibid., 148.
251. Dieter Busch, *Der Luftkrieg im Raum Mainz während des Zweiten Weltkrieges 1939–1945* (Mainz: v.Hase and Kohler Verlag, 1988). Im Auftrage der Kommission des Landtages herausgegeben bei der Landesarchivverwaltung Rheinland-Pfalz von Franz-Josef Heyen. Veröffentlichung der Kommission des Landtages für die Geschichte des Landes Rheinland-Pfalz Band 2.
252. Ibid., v.
253. Ibid., 359.
254. Ibid., 360.
255. Ibid., 359.
256. Ibid., 360.
257. Ibid., 359.
258. Ibid., 360.
259. Süß, *Tod aus der Luft*, 90.
260. Busch, *Luftkrieg im Raum Mainz*, vi.

CHAPTER 2

1. See Susanne Vees-Gulani, *Trauma and Guilt: Literature of Wartime Bombing in Germany* (Berlin and New York: Walter de Gruyter, 2003).
2. *Dokumente deutscher Kriegsschäden. Evakuierte. Kriegsgeschädigte. Währungsgeschädigte. Die geschichtliche und rechtliche Entwicklung. 1. Beiheft. Aus den Tagen des Luftkrieges und des Wiederaufbaues. Erlebnis-und Erfahrungsberichte.* Herausgegeben vom Bundesminister für Vertriebene, Flüchtlinge und Kriegsgeschädigte (Bonn: Bundesministerium des Innern, Abt. Vertriebene, Flüchtlinge und Kriegsgeschädigte, 1960), 65.
3. The title of the Dresden exhibition; *Verbrannt bis zur Unkenntlichkeit. Die Zerstörung Dresdens 1945.* Hg. Stadtmuseum Dresden. Redaktion Friedrich Reichert (Altenburg: DZA Verlag für Kultur und Wissenschaft, 1994).
4. Derenthal, *Bilder der Trümmer-und Aufbaujahre*, 55.
5. Jörn Glasenapp, "Vergangenheit und Zukunft," 6.
6. See Karin Hartewig, *Wir sind im Bilde. Eine Geschichte der Deutschen in Fotos vom Kriegsende bis zur Entspannungspolitik* (Leipziger: Universitätsverlag, 2010), 18–21.
7. See also Thiessen, *Eingebrannt ins Gedächtnis*, 84.
8. C. U. Schmink-Gustavus, ed., *Bremen-Kaputt. Bilder vom Krieg 1939–1945. Berichte. Dokumente. Erinnerungen* (Bremen: Brockkamp Verlag, 1983), 10 and 12.
9. Helmut Beer, "'Luftkrieg und Zerstörung' 1942–1945 in den Fotobeständen des Stadtarchivs Nürnberg," in Michael Diefenbacher und Wilhelm Fischer-Pache, eds.,

Der Luftkrieg gegen Nürnberg. Der Angriff am 2.Januar 1945 und die zerstörte Stadt [Quellen und Forschungen zur Geschichte und Kultur der Stadt Nürnberg. Herausgegeben von Michael Diefenbacher und Wiltrud Fischer-Pache im Auftrag der Stadt Nürnberg. 33. Band (Neustadt an der Aisch: Schmidt, 2004), 599.

10. Mark Lehmstedt, ed., *Leipzig brennt. Der Untergang des alten Lepizig am 4. Dezember 1943 in Fotografien und Berichten* (Leipzig: Lehmstedt Verlag, 2003), 264.

11. Hugo Schmidt-Luchs and Werner Schmidt-Luchs, *Hamburg. Phönix aus der Asche. Ein dokumentarischer Bildband mit Texten von Werner Sillescu* (Hamburg: Harry v.Hoffmann Verlag, 1967), 9.

12. Ibid.

13. Beer, "'Luftkrieg und Zerstörung' 1942–1945," 601.

14. Schmink-Gustavus, ed., *Bremen-Kaputt*, 10 and 12.

15. Kay Hoffmann, "Die Deutsche Wochenschau. Die Bildersprache des Krieges im Film," in Paul, ed., *Das Jahrhundert der Bilder.1900 bis 1949*, 579.

16. Scott Denham, "Erich Andres: Photographs," in Hans Erich Nossack, *The End: Hamburg 1943*. Translation and foreword by Joel Agee (Chicago: University of Chicago Press, 2004), 66. Erich Andres (1905–1992) was already well known locally in Hamburg in the 1920s for his series of human interest photos of the Hamburg docks and of children on the streets of the Hansestadt; http://www.bui.haw-hamburg.de/projekte/billers/fotoandr/htm/fotoand1.html (last accessed January 31, 2015).

17. http://www.youtube.com/watch?v=QvLX96G-ucY; Feuersturm in Hamburg 06:05 From: HeadHunter131

18. http://www.lauritzen-hamburg.de/hh_bombenkrieg.html (last accessed January 31, 2015).

19. Rita Bake, ed., *"Aber wir müssen zusammenbleiben" Mütter und Kinder in Bombenkriegen 1943 bis 1993. Gespräche*. Landeszentrale für politische Bildung (Hamburg: Dölling und Galitz Verlag, 1993).

20. Lehmstedt, ed., *Leipzig brennt*, 264.

21. Cord Pagenstecher, "Privatfotos ehemaliger Zwangsarbeiterinnen und Zwangsarbeiter—eine Quellensammlung und ihre Forschungsrelevanz," in Winfried Meyer and Klaus Neitmann, eds., *Zwangsarbeit während der NS-Zeit in Berlin und Brandenburg. Formen, Funktion, Rezeption* (Potsdam: Verlag für Berlin und Brandenburg, 2001), 223–46.

22. Martin Rüther, "Die Fotografen—Zur Entstehungsgeschichte ihrer Bilder," in Thomas Deres and Martin Rüther, eds., *Fotografieren Verboten! Heimliche Aufnahmen von der Zerstörung Kölns* (Köln: Emons, 1995), 98.

23. Ibid., 103.

24. Thomas Deres, "Vom Umgang mit den Fotos," in Deres and Rüther, eds., *Fotografieren Verboten!*, 129–30.

25. Wilhelm Steinhilber, *Heilbronn. Die schwersten Stunden der Stadt* (Heilbronn am Neckar: Druckerei und Verlagsanstalt Heilbronn GMBH, 1961), 36.

26. Schmidt-Luchs, *Hamburg. Phönix aus der Asche*, 9. See also Thiessen, *Eingebrannt ins Gedächtnis*, 426.

27. Frankfurt am Main: http://www.ffmhist.de/ffm33-45/portal01/portal01.php (accessed July 28, 2009).

28. Frankfurt am Main. Krieg und Zerstörung, Luftkrieg 1944, Am Römerberg: http://www.ffmhist.de/ffm33-45/portal01/portal01.php (accessed July 28, 2009).

29. Martin Rüther, "Die Fotografen—Zur Entstehungsgeschichte ihrer Bilder," in Deres and Rüther, eds., *Fotografieren Verboten!*, 106–9.

30. Thomas Deres, "Vom Umgang mit den Fotos," in Deres and Rüther, eds., *Fotografieren Verboten!*, 127.

31. Martin Rüther, in Deres and Rüther, eds., *Fotografieren Verboten!*, 109.

32. Thomas Deres, in Deres and Rüther, eds., *Fotografieren Verboten!*, 129.

33. Ibid., 129.

34. Rolf Sachsse, "Es wird nochmals ausdrücklichst darauf hingewiesen . . .". Aspekte der Bildzensur im NS-Staat und im Zweiten Weltkrieg," in Deres and Rüther, eds., *Fotografieren Verboten!*, 47.

35. Wiener, *Schweinfurt sollte sterben*, 11.

36. Martin Rüther, in Deres and Rüther, eds., *Fotografieren Verboten!*, 96–104.

37. Thomas Deres, in Deres and Rüther, eds., *Fotografieren Verboten!*, 123.

38. Scott Denham, "Erich Andres: Photographs," 66.

39. Beer, "'Luftkrieg und Zerstörung' 1942–1945," 605.

40. Friedrich Reichert, "Rundgang durch die zerstörte Dresdner Innenstadt im Februar und März 1945," in *Verbrannt bis zur Unkenntlichkeit. Die Zerstörung Dresdens 1945*. Begleitbuch zur Ausstellung im Stadtmuseum Dresden. Februar bis Juni 1995 (Dresden: DZA Verlag für Kultur und Wissenschaft, 1994).

41. Ibid., 63.

42. Beer, "'Luftkrieg und Zerstörung' 1942–1945," 605–6.

43. Richard Peter sen., *Erinnerungen und Bilder eines Dresdener Fotografen* (Leipzig: VEB Fotokinoverlag, 1987), 57–59.

44. Ibid., 57–59. See, for example, the photograph by Richard Peter sen. of 243 corpses in an air-raid cellar taken in April 1946, 14 months after the attack on Dresden; Sächsische Landes-, Staats- und Universitäts Bibliothek, Deutsche Fotothek Dresden, Nachlaß Peters, PS 48.

45. *Verbrannt bis zur Unkenntlichkeit,* 63.

46. Ursula Müller, "Der unbekannte Fotograf Tiedemann und das Bildarchiv der Ostberliner Bauverwaltung," in Florian Ebner and Ursula Müller, eds., *So weit kein Auge reicht. Berliner Panoramafotografien aus den Jahren 1949–1952 Aufgenommen vom Fotografen Tiedemann Rekonstuiert und interpretiert von Arwed Messmer* (Berlin: Berlinische Galerie/Dumont Buchverlag, 2008), 13.

47. Ludger Derenthal, "Trümmerbilder. Fotografien der Kriegszerstörungen von Walter Frentz (1939–1947)," in Hans Georg Hiller von Gaertringen, ed., *Das Auge des Dritten Reiches. Hitlers Kameramann und Fotograf Walter Frentz* (Berlin: Deutscher Kunstverlag München, 2007), 226–47.

48. Ries left Germany in 1938, emigrated to the United States, became a US citizen, and served with an aerial photographic unit in India. He returned to Berlin in August 1945; Janos Frecot, "Der Historiker mit der Kamera," in *Henry Ries Berlin Photographien 1945–1949* (Berlin: Nicolaische Verlagsbuchhandlung, 1998), 11.

49. Pisarek was born in Poland in 1901. He came to Germany in 1919 and trained as a press photographer. Although only allowed by the Nazi regime to photograph Jew-

ish organizations and sports events after 1933, Pisarek also took secret pictures of Max Liebermann's funeral and of Reichskristallnacht. Pisarek survived the Holocaust. After 1945, he used his camera to document the Soviet occupation and the emergence of the GDR. From the 1950s, he concentrated upon stage photography; http://www.akg-images.com/akg_couk/_customer/london/collections/pisarek.html (accessed August 24, 2010).

50. See Beer, "'Luftkrieg und Zerstörung' 1942–1945," 606.

51. Christopher Pinney, "Introduction. 'How the other half . . .'," in Christopher Pinney and Nicholas Peterson, eds., *Photography's Other Histories* (Durham: Duke University Press, 2003), 9.

52. See, for example, Leora Auslander, "Archiving a Life: Post-Shoah Paradoxes of Memory Legacies," in Jobs and Lüdtke, eds., *Unsettling History*, 127–48. For an example of a contemporary local picture archive, see http://www.kiel.de/kultur/stadtarchiv/medienarchiv.php (accessed November 9, 2010).

53. Barbara Grimm, "*Lynchmorde an alliierten Fliegern im Zweiten Weltkrieg*," in Dietmar Süß (Hrsg.): *Deutschland im Luftkrieg. Geschichte und Erinnerung* (Munich: Oldenbourg Wissenschaftsverlag, 2007), 71–84.

54. Frank Bajohr, *'Aryanisation' in Hamburg: The Economic Exclusion of Jews and the Confiscation of their Property in Nazi Germany* (New York: Berghahn Books, 2002), 278. For photographs of furniture stolen from Jews that was destined for Germans in the Ruhr whose households had been damaged or destroyed by the bombing see Klaus Hesse and Philipp Springer, *Vor aller Augen. Fotodokumente des nationalsozialistischen Terrors in der Provinz* (Essen: Klartext, 2002), 182–83.

55. Katherine Pence, "'A World in Miniature': The Leipzig Trade Fairs in the 1950s and East German Consumer Citizenship," in David F. Crew, ed., *Consuming Germany in the Cold War* (Oxford: Berg Publishers, 2003), 29.

56. Ibid., 29.

57. Erhard Schütz, "Der 'Käfer.' Die Ikone des Wirtschaftswunders," in Paul, ed., *Das Jahrhundert der Bilder*, 122–29.

58. Eckart Dietzfelbinger and Gerhard Liedtke, *Nürnberg-Ort der Massen. Das Reichsparteigelände. Vorgeschichte und schwieriges Erbe* (Berlin: Chr. Links Verlag, 2004) and Stephen Brockmann, *Nuremberg: The Imaginary Capital* (Rochester, NY: Camden House, 2006). See also Neil Gregor, *Haunted City: Nuremberg and the Nazi Past* (New Haven: Yale University Press, 2008).

59. Ibid., 1.

60. Hermann Hasenclever, *Die Zerstörung der Stadt Remscheid.* Herausgegeben von der Ehrenhain-Stiftung mit freundlicher Unterstützung der Stadtverwaltung und der Stadtsparkasse Remscheid (Remscheid: Verlag Loose-Durach, 1964).

61. Bardua, *Stuttgart im Luftkrieg*, Plates 48 and 49.

62. Ibid., 8.

63. Bardua, *Stuttgart im Luftkrieg*, 272.

64. Ibid., 60.

65. Ibid., 271.

66. Ibid., 271.

67. Ibid., 48–49.

68. See Inge Marszolek and Marc Buggeln, eds., *Bunker: Kriegsort, Zuflucht, Erinnerungsraum* (Frankfurt: Campus Verlag, 2008).

69. Fischer, *Köln '39-'45. Der Leidensweg einer Stadt*, 98. These graphic descriptions in postwar publications appear not to have characterized public commemorations of the bombing; see Thiessen, *Eingebrannt ins Gedächtnis*, 177.

70. Nadler, *"Ich sah wie Nürnberg unterging . . . !"Tatsachenberichte und Stimmungsbilder*, 16.

71. Domarus, *Der Untergang des alten Würzburg*, 106–7.

72. Ibid., 106–7.

73. Fischer, *Köln '39-'45. Der Leidensweg einer Stadt*, 72.

74. Ibid., 95.

75. *Dokumente deutscher Kriegsschäden* (1960), 65.

76. Domarus, *Der Untergang des alten Würzburg*, 106.

77. Ralf Blank, review of Jörg Friedrich, *Brandstätten. Der Anblick des Bombenkrieges*, H/Soz/Kult (October 22, 2003); http://hsozkult.geschichte.hu-berlin.de/rezensionen/2003-4-044 (last accessed January 31, 2015).

78. Axel Rodenberger, *Der Tod von Dresden. Bericht vom Sterben einer Stadt in Augenzeugenberichten* (Dortmund: Landverlag, 1951).

79. Eva Vieth, "Die letzte 'Volksgemeinschaft' -das Kriegsende in den Bildern einer deutschen Illustrierten," in Jörg Hillmann and John Zimmermann, eds., *Kriegsende 1945 in Deutschland* (München: R.Oldenbourg Verlag, 2002), 271.

80. Thiessen, *Eingebrannt ins Gedächtnis*, 46.

81. Ibid., 45.

82. Gerhard Paul, *Bilder des Krieges. Krieg der Bilder. Die Visualisierung des modernen Krieges* (Paderborn: Schöningh, 2004), 231.

83. Vieth, "Die letzte 'Volksgemeinschaft,'" 273–74.

84. Malte Thiessen, "Von der 'Heimstätte' zum Denkmal. Bunker als städtische Erinnerungsorte-das Beispiel Hamburgs," in Inge Marszolek and Marc Buggeln, eds., *Bunker: Kriegsort, Zuflucht, Erinnerungsraum*, 45–60.

85. Schmidt-Luchs, *Hamburg. Phönix aus der Asche*, 85.

86. Ibid., 85.

87. Thiessen, "Von der 'Heimstätte' zum Denkmal," 51.

88. Ibid., 60.

89. Aus dem "Bericht des Polizeipräsidenten in Hamburg als örtlicher Luftschutzleiter über die schweren Großluftangriffe auf Hamburg im Juli/August 1943," in *Dokumente deutscher Kriegsschäden* (1960), 60–61.

90. Ibid., 63.

91. Ibid., 63.

92. Wilhelm Steinhilber, *Heilbronn. Die schwersten Stunden der Stadt*, 56–57.

93. Heinrich Johannsen, Aus dem "Bericht des Polizeipräsidenten in Hamburg als örtlicher Luftschutzleiter über die schweren Grossluftangriffe auf Hamburg im Juli/August 1943" Anlagenband 10: "Augenzeugenberichte," Blatt 16, in *Dokumente deutscher Kriegsschäden* (1960), 83.

94. Erika Wilken, Aus dem "Bericht des Polizeipräsidenten in Hamburg als örtlicher Luftschutzleiter über die schweren Grossluftangriffe auf Hamburg im Juli/August

1943" Anlagenband 10: "Augenzeugenberichte," Blatt 12, in *Dokumente deutsche Kriegsschäden* (1960), 80.

95. Aus dem "Bericht des Polizeipräsidenten in Hamburg als örtlicher Luftschutzleiter über die schweren Grossluftangriffe auf Hamburg im Juli/August 1943."In *Dokumente deutscher Kriegsschäden* (1960), 64.

96. Aus dem "Bericht des Polizeipräsidenten in Hamburg als örtlicher Luftschutzleiter über die schweren Grossluftangriffe auf Hamburg im Juli/August 1943" Anlagenband 10: "Augenzeugenberichte," Blatt 29, in *Dokumente deutsche Kriegsschäden* (1960), 94.

97. Ralf Blank, review of *Kucklick, Christoph: Feuersturm. Der Bombenkrieg gegen Deutschland. Hamburg 2003*, H-Soz-Kult (October 22, 2003); http://hsozkult.geschichte.hu-berlin.de/rezensionen/2003-4-043 (accessed July 29, 2009).

98. Brunswig, *Feuersturm über Hamburg*, 7. For his biography see http://fhh.hamburg.de/stadt/Aktuell/behoerden/inneres/feuerwehr/wir-ueber-uns/amtsleiter/hans-brunswig/start.html

99. Brunswig, *Feuersturm über Hamburg*, 264.

100. Ibid., 265.

101. Ibid., 270.

102. Ibid., 230.

103. Hans Ulrich Gumbrecht, *In 1926: Living at the Edge of Time* (Cambridge, MA: Harvard University Press, 1997), 425. See also Gerhard Paul, "Der Fluchtlingstrek. Bilder von Flucht und Vetreibung als europäische *lieux de memoire*," in Paul, ed., *Das Jahrhundert der Bilder*, 668.

104. See Jens Jäger, "Fotografie als historisches Dokument," *Fotogeschichte. Beiträge zur Geschichte und Ästhetik der Fotografie* 32, no. 124 (2012): 14–15 and also Julia Adeney Thomas, "The Evidence of Sight," 151–68.

105. Joachim Paech, "Der Krieg als Form im Medium der Fotografie und des Films," in Waltraud "Wara" Wende, ed., *Krieg und Gedächtnis. Ein Ausnahmezustand im Spannungsfeld kultureller Sinnkonstruktionen* (Würzburg: Königshausen and Neumann, 2005), 329.

106. Anton Holzer, "'Going Over the Top': Neue Perspektiven aus dem Schützengraben," in Paul, ed., *Das Jahrhundert der Bilder*, 196–203.

107. Paech, "Der Krieg als Form," 328.

108. Ibid., 336 and 338. See also Andreas Elter, "Tod eines Kameramannes. Fotografen und Kameraleute zwischen den Fronten," in Paul, ed., *Das Jahrhundert der Bilder*, 450–57.

109. Aus dem "Bericht des Polizeipräsidenten in Hamburg als örtlicher Luftschutzleiter über die schweren Grossluftangriffe auf Hamburg im Juli/August 1943," in *Dokumente deutscher Kriegsschäden* (1960), 60.

110. James Stern, *The Hidden Damage* (New York: Harcourt, Brace and Company, 1947), 122.

111. Aus dem "Bericht des Polizeipräsidenten in Hamburg als örtlicher Luftschutzleiter über die schweren Grossluftangriffe auf Hamburg im Juli/August 1943" Anlagenband 10: "Augenzeugenberichte," Blatt 29, in *Dokumente deutsche Kriegsschäden* (1960), 94 and 95.

112. Jens Jäger, "Zwischen Bildkunde und Historischer Bildforschung-Historiker und visuelle Quellen 1880–1930," in Jens Jäger and Martin Knauer, eds., *Bilder als historische Quellen? Dimension der Debatten um historische Bildforschung* (München: Wilhelm Fink Verlag, 2009), 64.

113. Elizabeth Heinemann, "The Hour of the Woman.Memories of Germany's 'Crisis Years' and West German National Identity," in Hanna Schissler, ed., *The Miracle Years: A Cultural History of West Germany, 1949–1968* (Princeton: Princeton University Press, 2001), especially 34.

114. Marita Krauss, "Trümmerfrauen Visuelles Konstrukt und Realität," in Paul, ed., *Das Jahrhundert der Bilder*, 740. See also Leonie Treiber, *Mythos Trümmerfrauen. Von der Trümmerbeseitigung in der Kriegs-und Nachkriegszeit und der Entstehung eines deutschen Erinnerungsortes* (Essen: Klartext, 2014).

115. *Unvergängliches Nürnberg*. Aufgenommen und beschrieben von Eugen Kusch (Nürnberg: Verlag Hans Carl, 1953), 13.

116. *Nürnberg 1945 Bilddokumente* (Weimar: Verlag W. A. Beckert, 1947).

117. Christoph Hamann, "Der Junge aus dem Warschauer Ghetto. Der Stroop-Bericht und die globalisierte Ikonographie des Holocaust," in Paul, ed., *Das Jahrhundert der Bilder*, 620.

118. Holzer, "'Going Over the Top,'" 325.

119. Christopher Pinney, "Introduction: 'How the other half . . . ,' in Christopher Pinney and Nicholas Peterson, eds., *Photography's Other Histories* (Durham: Duke University Press, 2003), 7.

120. Schmid, *Frankfurt im Feuersturm*, 117–18.

121. Ibid., 117.

122. Ibid., 118.

123. Klaus Hesse, "Deportation. Die offiziöse Dokumentation des NS-Terrors im Bild," in Paul, ed., *Das Jahrhundert der Bilder*, 602.

124. Robert Sackett, "Pictures of Atrocity: Public Discussion of *Der gelbe Stern* in Early 1960s West Germany," *German History: The Journal of the German History Society* 24, no. 4 (2006): 526–61.

CHAPTER 3

1. Jörg Arnold, "'In wächserner Blässe wie Schaufensterpuppen.' Leichenbilder aus dem Luftkrieg und ihr sozialen Gebrauch (1940–1960)," *Fotogeschichte. Beiträge zur Geschichte und Ästhetik der Fotografie* 32, no. 125 (2012): 31.

2. Ibid., 34, 35–36.

3. Peter Geimer, "Fotos, die man nicht zeigt. Problem mit Schockbildern," in Katharina Sykora, Ludger Derenthal, and Esther Ruelfs, eds., *Fotografische Leidenschaften* (Marburg: Jonas Verlag, 2006), 245–60.

4. Arnold, "'In wächserner Blässe wie Schaufensterpuppen,'" 34, 35–36.

5. Brunswig, *Feuersturm über Hamburg*, 7–8.

6. See "Tod im Luftangriff—Ergebnisse pathologisch-anatomischer Untersuchun-

gen anlässlich der Angriffe auf Hamburg in den Jahren 1943–1945," by Siegfried Gräff, H. H. Nölke Verlag, Hamburg, 1955, in "Erlebnisse-und Erfahrungsgeschichte," *Dokumente Deutscher Kriegsschäden* (1960), 109.

7. Fischer, *Köln '39-'45. Der Leidensweg einer Stadt*, just before page 49. This was presumably the Hilfskrankenhaus der Universitätsklinik (Gagernkrankenhaus).

8. Ibid., just before page 161.

9. See also Karola Fings, "The Public Face of the Camps," in Jane Caplan and Nikolas Wachsmann, eds., *Concentration Camps in Nazi Germany: The New Histories* (London and New York: Routledge, 2010), 108.

10. Arnold, "'In wächserner Blässe wie Schaufensterpuppen,'" 27.

11. Ibid., 28.

12. Habbo Knoch, "Die Grenzen des Zeigbaren. Fotografien der NS-Verbrechen und die westdeutsche Gesellschaft 1955–1965," in Sven Kramer, ed., *Die Shoah im Bild* (München: Edition text+kritik, 2003), 93.

13. Ibid., 93.

14. Susan Sontag, *Regarding the Pain of Others* (New York: Farrar, Straus and Giroux, 2003), 84.

15. See Heinz-Peter Preußer, "Regarding and Imagining: Contrived Immediacy of the Allied Bombing Campaign in Photography, Novel and Historiography," in Helmut Schmitz, ed., *A Nation of Victims? Representations of German Wartime Suffering from 1945 to the Present* (Amsterdam and New York: Rodopi, 2007), 146.

16. Jens Jäger, "Fotografie-Erinnerung-Identität. Die Trümmeraufnahmen aus deutschen Städten 1945," in Jörg Hillmann and John Zimmermann, eds., *Kriegsende 1945 in Deutschland* (München: R. Oldenbourg, 2002) [Beiträge zur Militärgeschichte, Bd. 55], 288. See also Benjamin Städter, *Verwandelte Blicke Eine Visual History von Kirche und Religion in der Bundesrepublik 1945–1980* (Frankfurt: Campus Verlag, 2011), 37.

17. Glasenapp, *Die Deutsche Nachkriegsfotografie*, 100–132.

18. Fuchs, *After the Dresden Bombing*, 26.

19. Ibid., 39.

20. Stefan Glienke, "The Allied Air War and German Society," in Baldoli, Knapp, and Overy, eds., *Bombing, States and Peoples*, 193. Security Service (SD) reports show, however, that some Germans did not accept this official focus on buildings. One industrial worker in Suhl remarked, "Better the destruction of Cologne cathedral than 100 people dead," and a female worker in Halle complained that "the poor people who have lost their lives were not mentioned; passed over in silence. The individual apparently has no more value in today's Germany!"; Ibid., 193.

21. Kurt Schaarschuch, *Bilddokument Dresden 1933–1945* (Dresden: Rat der Stadt Dresden, 1945). On the genre of postwar "ruin photography" see Derenthal, *Bilder der Trümmer-und Aufbaujahre*, 44–91.

22. For example, *Paderborn. Werden. Untergang. Wiederstehen*, 9–26.

23. B. Heusenberg und Frau. Aus dem "Bericht des Polizeipräsidenten in Hamburg als örtlicher Luftschutzleiter über die schweren Grossluftangriffe auf Hamburg im Juli/August 1943" Anlagenband 10: "Augenzeugenberichte," Blatt 21, in *Dokumente*

deutsche Kriegsschäden. 1. Beiheft, Aus den Tagen des Luftkrieges und des Wiederaufbaues Erlebnis-und Erfahrungsberichte (Bonn: Bundesministerium des Innern, Abt. Vertriebene, Flüchtlinge und Kriegsgeschädigte, 1960), 85.

24. Fuchs, *After the Dresden Bombing*, 37.

25. Valentine Cunningham, "Zerbombte Städte-Die vorzeitigen Ruinen des Zweiten Weltkriegs," in Aleida Assmann, Monika Gomille, and Gabriele Rippl, eds., *Ruinenbilder* (München: Wilhelm Fink Verlag, 2002), 108.

26. Ibid., 109.

27. Karl F. P. Moll, *Ludwigshafen in Trümmern. Ein vergleichendes Bildwerk über die Zeit vor und nach der Zerstörung der Stadt im zweiten Weltkrieg 1939–1945* (Neustadt: Neustadter Druck and Verlagsanstalt, 1949).

28. W. G. Sebald, *On the Natural History of Destruction* (New York: Random House, 2003), 6–7.

29. On postwar rebuilding, see Jeffry M. Diefendorf, *In the Wake of War: The Reconstruction of German Cities After World War II* (Oxford: Oxford University Press, 1993).

30. Olivier Dumoulin has found that churches regularly featured in newsreels as symbols of the destruction caused by the bombing not just in Germany but in France and Britain as well; Olivier Dumoulin, "A Comparative Approach to Newsreels and Bombing in the Second World War: Britain, France, Germany," in Baldoli, Knapp, and Overy, eds., *Bombing, States and Peoples*, 298–314.

31. Fischer, *Köln '39-'45. Der Leidensweg einer Stadt*, 164.

32. Hermann Claasen, *Gesang im Feuerofen; Köln; Überreste einer alten deutschen Stadt* (Düsseldorf: L. Schwann, 1947).

33. Gerhard Stade, "Hannovers alte Kirchen," in Heinz Lauenroth and Gustav Lauterbach, *Tod und Leben Hannovers 9 Oktober* (Hanover: Heimatbund Niedersachsen, 1953), 81.

34. Heinz Lauenroth and Gustav Lauterbach, *Tod und Leben Hannovers 9 Oktober* (Hanover: Heimatbund Niedersachsen, 1953).

35. Ibid., 76.

36. Vera Frohwein-Ziroff, *Die Kaiser Wilhelms-Gedächtniskirche. Entstehung und Bedeutung* (Berlin: Gebr. Mann Verlag, 1982), 336–40.

37. Ludwig Wiener, *Schweinfurt sollte sterben.Untergang und Wiedergeburt einer* Stadt mit Beiträgen von Budd J. Peaslee and Erik Friedheim (Schweinfurt: Verlag Neues Forum, 1961), 9.

38. Nadler, *Tatsachenberichte und Stimmungsbilder*, 61.

39. Horst Urbschat, *Berlin im Jahre Null. Fotoreportagen 1945–1949* (Berlin: B&S Siebenhaar Verlag, 2002).

40. Paul Virilio, *War and Cinema: The Logistics of Perception* (London: Verso, 1989). See also *Das XX. Jahrhundert. Fotografien zur deutschen Geschichte aus der Sammlung des Deutschen Historischen Museums* (Berlin: DHM. Edition Braus, 2004), 58–59 and review of Jörg Friedrich, *Brandstätten*, by Ralf Blank, Historisches Centrum Hagen; http://hsozkult.geschichte.hu-berlin.de/rezensionen/id=3483 (last accessed February 27, 2015).

41. Friedrich Reichert, "Rundgang durch die zerstörte Dresdner Innenstadt im Feb-

ruar und März 1945," in *Verbrannt bis zur Unkenntlichkeit. Die Zerstörung Dresdens 1945*, 61. See also Esther Schmalacker-Wyrick, ed., *Pforzheim 23.Februar 1945. Der Untergang einer Stadt in Bilder und Augenzeugenberichten* (Pforzheim: Verlag J. Eßlinger, 1980), 26.

42. Hugo Schmidt-Luchs and Werner Schmidt-Luchs, *Hamburg. Phönix aus der Asche. Ein dokumentarischer Bildband mit Texten von Werner Sillescu* (Hamburg: Harry v.Hofmann Verlag, 1967), 14. See also the 1947 Berlin show "Value beneath the Rubble: An Exhibition about the Recovery of Valuable Economic Goods" geared toward helping survivors identify things buried beneath the rubble that might be salvaged and made over as usable personal items; Paul Betts, *The Authority of Everyday Objects: A Cultural History of West German Industrial Design* (Berkeley: University of California Press, 2004), 83.

43. Schmidt-Luchs, *Hamburg. Phönix aus der Asche*, 90.

44. Ibid., 74.

45. Habbo Knoch, "Das mediale Gedächtnis der Heimat," 279.

46. Fischer, *Köln '39-'45. Der Leidensweg einer Stadt*, 101.

47. Jürgen Lillteicher, "National Socialist Expropriation: The Restitution of Jewish Property, 1947–1964," in Phillip Gassert and Alan Steinweis, eds., *Coping With the Nazi Past: West German Debates on Nazism and Generational Conflict, 1955–1975* (New York: Berghahn Books, 2007); Kindle Edition. Location 2360.

48. Ralf Blank, review of *Kucklick, Christoph: Feuersturm. Der Bombenkrieg gegen Deutschland. Hamburg 2003*, H-Soz-Kult (October 22, 2003); http://hsozkult.geschichte.hu-berlin.de/rezensionen/2003-4-043 (accessed July 29, 2009).

49. Jörg Bernig, "Phantomschmerzen. Die Gegenwärtigkeit des Bombenkrieges gegen die Deutschen," in Walter Schmitz, ed., *Die Zerstörung Dresdens. Antworten der Künste* (Dresden: Thelem, 2005), 15.

50. See Annemarie Tröger, "German Women's Memories of World War II," in Margaret Randolph Higonnet, Jane Jensen, Sonya Michel, and Margaret Collins Weitz, eds., *Behind the Lines: Gender and the Two World Wars* (New Haven: Yale University Press, 1987), 285–99; Margarete Dörr, "Wer die Zeit nicht miterlebt hat . . . ." *Frauenerfahrungen im Zweiten Weltkrieg und in den Jahren danach.* Band 2: *Kriegsalltag* (Frankfurt: Campus Verlag, 1998), especially Kapitel 5; Rita Bake, ed., *"Aber wir müssen zusammenbleiben" Mütter und Kinder in Bombenkriegen 1943 bis 1993. Gespräche* [Landeszentrale für politische Bildung] (Hamburg: Dölling and Galitz, 1993).

51. Elizabeth Heinemann, "The Hour of the Woman: Memories of Germany's 'Crisis Years' and West German National Identity," in Hanna Schissler, ed., *The Miracle Years: A Cultural History of West Germany, 1949–1968* (Princeton: Princeton University Press, 2001), 21–56, but especially 34.

52. Krauss, "Trümmerfrauen Visuelles Konstrukt und Realität," 740.

53. Ibid., 740.

54. Ibid., 744.

55. Hannes Kilian, *Die Zerstörung Stuttgart 1944 und danach.* Mit einem Vorwort von Peter Lahnstein (Berlin: Quadriga Verlag J. Severin, 1984), photograph after page 88. For Kilian's biography, see http://www.hannes-kilian.de

56. Stargardt, *Witnesses of War*, 244.

57. Dörr, *Frauenerfahrungen im Zweiten Weltkrieg*, 260.

58. Stargardt, *Witnesses of War*, 234–36.

59. For example Abb. 64: Fliegeralarm in Bingen. Die Bevölkerung flüchtet in die Luftschtuzräume. Foto; Stadtarchiv Bingen," in Busch, *Der Luftkrieg im Raum Mainz*, 197. This photograph shows six identifiable figures who are women from behind so that we cannot see the expressions on their faces. One figure on the right-hand side is a man in uniform.

60. Alois Stadtmüller, *Aschaffenburg im Zweiten Weltkrieg. Bombenangriffe-Belagerung-Übergabe* (Aschaffenburg: In Kommission bei Paul Pattloch Verlag, 1970), Abb. 90.

61. Christoph Hamann, "Der Junge aus dem Warschauer Ghetto. Der Stroop-Bericht und die globalisierte Ikonographie des Holocaust," in Paul, ed., *Das Jahrhundert der Bilder*, 620.

62. C. U. Schminck-Gustavus, ed., *Bremen-Kaputt. Bilder vom Krieg 1939–1945. Berichte. Dolumente. Erinnerungen* (Bremen: Brockkamp Verlag, 1983), 201.

63. "A Boy on his 'Slide'" (Berlin, 1947); http://germanhistorydocs.ghi-dc.org/print_document.cfm?document_id=1235 (last accessed February 27, 2015).

64. Urbschat, *Berlin im Jahre Null*, 96.

65. Marc Hansen, "'Wirklichkeitsbilder' Der Erste Weltkrieg in der Farbfotografie," in Paul, ed., *Das Jahrhundert der Bilder*, 192.

66. Gerhard Paul, "'Mushroom Clouds.' Enstehung, Struktur und Funktion einer Medienikone des 20. Jahhrunderts im interkulturellen Vergleich," in Ibid., 249.

67. Klaus Naumann, *Der Krieg als Text. Das Jahr 1945 im kulturellen Gedächtnis der Presse* (Hamburg: Hamburger Edition, 1998), 36.

68. Eve Rosenhaft, "At Large in the 'Gray Zone': Narrating the Romani Holocaust," in Jobs and Lüdtke, eds., *Unsettling History*, 155.

69. Hasenclever, *Die Zerstörung der Stadt Remscheid*, 86.

70. Ibid., x.

71. See James Elkins, *Pictures & Tears: A History of People Who Have Cried in Front of Paintings* (New York: Routledge, 2004).

72. Angus Calder, *The Myth of the Blitz* (London: J. Cape, 1991).

73. "'Bürger, Luftalarm' Der Moskauer Historiker Lew Besymenski über den deutschen Bombenangriff auf Stalingrad im August 1942," in *Als Feuer vom Himmel fiel. Der Bombenkrieg gegen die deutchen. Spiegel special. Das Magazin zum Thema*, no. 1 (2003): 28–29.

CHAPTER 4

1. Jörn Glasenapp, "Vergangenheit und Zukunft," 6, 11.

2. Daniel Magilow, *The Photography of Crisis: The Photo Essays of Weimar Germany* (University Park: Pennsylvania State University Press, 2012), 35.

3. On the history and importance of photo books, more generally, see Peter Pfrundner, "Fragen an das Fotobuch. Gedruckte Fotografien—eine unterschätzte Dimension der Fotogeschichte," *Fotogeschichte* 124 (2012): 42–49. Pfrundner draws attention to

the importance of the physical artifact itself and the way that it "delivers" the photographs to the reader.

4. Alon Confino, *Germany as a Culture of Remembrance: Promises and Limits of Writing History* (Chapel Hill: University of North Carolina Press, 2006).

5. Werner Gauss, *Alt-Heilbronn. Wie wir es kannten und liebten. Ein Bildband der Erinnerung*. Mit einem Geleitwort von Oberbürgermeister Paul Meyle (Heilbronn am Neckar: Gauss-Verlag, 1950). Zum Geleit.

6. Ibid.

7. Ibid.

8. Ibid., Vorwort des Herausgebers.

9. Ibid., Vorwort des Herausgebers.

10. Ibid., Vorwort des Herausgebers.

11. Ibid., Vorwort desHerausgebers.

12. Ibid., Vorwort des Herausgebers.

13. Ibid., Vorwort des Herausgebers.

14. Roland Barthes, *Camera Lucida: Reflections on Photography* (New York: Hill and Wang, 1982).

15. Lauenroth, Heinz and Gustav Lauterbach, eds., *Tod und Leben Hannovers 9. Oktober* (Hanover: Heimatbund Niedersachsen, 1953).

16. *Paderborn. Werden. Untergang. Wiedererstehen*, 203.

17. See also Georg Wagner-Kyora, "Die neue City in der kriegszerstörten Altstadt. Das 'Wiederaufbau' -Image in Bremen (1946–1964)," in Daniela Münkel and Lu Seegers, eds., *Medien und Imagepolitik im 20. Jahrhundert. Deutschland, Europa, USA* (Frankfurt am Main: Campus Verlag, 2008), 293–318.

18. Lutz Philipp Günther, *Die bildhafte Repräsentation deutscher Städte. Von den Chroniken der Frühen Neuzeit zu den Websites der Gegenwart* (Köln: Böhlau Verlag, 2009), 226.

19. *Heilbronn. Blüte, Untergang, Wiedererstehen einer Stadt* (Heilbronn: Druckerei and Verlagsanstalt, 1954).

20. Ibid.

21. Hugo Schmidt-Luchs and Werner Schmidt-Luchs, *Hamburg. Phönix aus der Asche. Ein dokumentarischer Bildband mit Texten von Werner Sillescu* (Hamburg: Harry v.Hofmann Verlag, 1967). This popular picture book went through two editions in the year it was published and two more in 1979 and 1985; see Thiessen, *Eingebrannt ins Gedächtnis*, 246.

22. Schmidt-Luchs, *Hamburg. Phönix aus der Asche*, 21.

23. Ibid., 22.

24. Ibid., 23.

25. Ibid., 49.

26. My observation here follows the line of argument developed by Jonathan Wiesen that the West German "economic miracle" was imagined, scripted, and staged well before it actually happened; S. Jonathan Wiesen, "Miracles for Sale: Consumer Displays and Advertising in Postwar Germany," in Crew, ed., *Consuming Germany in the Cold War*, 151–78.

27. Schmidt-Luchs, *Hamburg. Phönix aus der Asche*, 14.

28. Alexander Mitscherlich, *Die Unwirtlichkeit unserer Städte. Anstiftung zum Unfrieden* (Frankfurt am Main: Suhrkamp Verlag, 1965), 16.

29. Ibid., 14–16.

30. Ibid., 15.

31. See, for example, Jörn Glasenapp's discussion of "Chargesheimer's Spätwerk: *Köln 5 Uhr 30* und *Hannover*," in Glasenapp, *Die Deutsche Nachkriegsfotografie*, 322–36.

32. Viktoria Schmidt-Linsenhoff, "Die Verschlußzeit des Herzens. Zu Hilmar Pabels Fotobuch *Jahre unseres Lebens* (1954)," in *Fotogeschichte. Beiträge zur Geschichte und Ästhetik der Fotografie* 12, no. 44 (1992): 54.

33. Cunningham, "Zerbombte Städte-Die vorzeitigen Ruinen des Zweiten Weltkriegs," 108.

34. Steinhilber, *Heilbronn. Die schwersten Stunden der Stadt*, 46–47.

35. The series of nine photographs which begin on page 67 were deposited in the Stadtarchiv. Steinhilber does not identify the photographer specifically other than to say, on page 71, that the pictures were taken by someone whose train unexpectedly stopped in Heilbronn.

36. Steinhilber, *Heilbronn. Die schwersten Stunden der Stadt*, 70–71.

37. Paech, "Der Krieg als Form," 328. See also Andreas Elter, "Tod eines Kameramannes. Fotografen und Kameraleute zwischen den Fronten," in Paul, ed., *Das Jahrhundert der Bilder*, 450–57.

38. Prenzlauer Berg Museum. Annett Gröschner, ed., *"Ich schlug meiner Mutter die brennenden Funken ab." Berliner Schulaufsätze aus dem Jahr 1946* (Berlin: Rowohlt Taschenbuch Verlag, 1996).

39. Steinhilber, *Heilbronn. Die schwersten Stunden der Stadt*, 120.

40. Ibid., 120.

41. Ibid., 122. Even today unexploded bombs are still being uncovered in German cities. See, for example, http://www.dw.de/thousands-evacuated-in-german-city-for-wwii-bomb-disposal/a-17201409 (last accessed February 1, 2015).

42. Errell was a German-Jewish photographer whose real name was Richard Levy. He made up the name Errell by combining the German pronunciations of the letters "R" and "L" to form a new surname. In the 1920s, he was a member of the avant-garde of Weimar photography. He fled Germany for Czechoslovakia in 1933 when the Nazis came to power. See also http://www.photorevue.com/phprs/view.php?cisloclanku=2005010403 (last accessed February 27, 2015).

43. Richard Errell, *Bilderbuch für Nachdenkliche* (Frankfurt am Main: Europäische Verlangsanstalt, 1962), 40–41.

44. See also Jürgen Neven und Michael Mansfeld, *Denke ich an Deutschland.Ein Kommentar in Bild und Wort* (München: Verlag Kurt Deutsch, 1956).

45. Thomas Grabe, Reimar Hollmann, Klaus Mlynek, and Michael Radtke, *Unter der Wolke des Todes leben . . . Hannover im Zweiten Weltkrieg* (Hamburg: Ernst Kabel Verlag, 1983).

46. See Ibid., Bildnachweis.

47. Ibid., 132.

48. Ibid., 151.

49. Ibid., 86.
50. Ibid., 19.
51. Ibid., 119.
52. F. Lueddecke, *Hannover Einst und Jetzt. Bilder aus der Hauptstadt Niedersachsens* (Hanover: Adolf Sponholtz Verlag, 1951).
53. Grabe, Hollmann, Mlynek, Radtke, *Unter der Wolke des Todes leben*, 101.
54. Ibid., 104.
55. C. U. Schmink-Gustavus, ed., *Bremen-Kaputt*. Born in 1942, Schmink-Gustavus was a Professor of Legal History who began teaching in 1973 at the newly founded Bremen University. His research interests included fascism and the Second World War and he engaged in extended research on German war crimes committed in occupied Greece and in Italy. See http://de.wikipedia.org/wiki/Christoph_Schminck-Gustavus. Last accessed February 27, 2015.
56. Schmink-Gustavus, ed., *Bremen-Kaputt*, 90.
57. Ibid., 92.
58. Ibid., 101.
59. Ibid., 98.
60. Ibid., 100.
61. Ibid., 102.
62. Ibid., 109.
63. Ibid., 110.
64. Ibid., 126.
65. Ibid., 137.
66. Anton Holzer, *Die andere Front. Fotografie und Propaganda im Ersten Weltkrieg* (Darmstadt: Primus Verlag, 2007), 323.
67. Cunningham, "Zerbombte Städte-Die vorzeitigen Ruinen des Zweiten Weltkriegs," 105–30.
68. F. Lueddecke, *Hannover Einst und Jetzt*, 13.
69. Matthias Neutzer, "Vom Anklagen zum Erinnern. Die Erzählung vom 13. Februar," in Oliver Reinhard, Matthias Neutzner, and Wolfgang Hesse, eds., *Das rote Leuchten. Dresden und der Bombenkrieg* (Dresden: Edition Sächsische Zeitung, 2005), 147.
70. Bernhard Haagen, "Das neue Hildesheim," in *Hildesheim 1945–1955. 22 März.* Zusammengestellt und bearbeitet von Dr. Hans Kayser und Gustav Lauterbach.Herausgegeben vom Heimatbund Niedersachsen in Zusammenarbeit mit der Stadt Hildesheim (Hanover: Verlag Heimatland, 1955), 129.
71. Paech, "Der Krieg als Form," 333.
72. See Thiessen, *Eingebrannt ins Gedächtnis*, 318.
73. Roland Barthes, *Camera Lucida*, 59.
74. Habbo Knoch, *Die Tat als Bild. Fotografien des Holocaust in der deutschen Erinnerungskultur* (Hamburg: Hamburger Edition, 2001), 468 f. On the changing memory politics of the 1960s see Gassert and Steinweis, eds., *Coping with the Nazi Past.*
75. Schmink-Gustavus, ed., *Bremen-Kaputt*, 126.
76. Norman Davies, *No Simple Victory: World War II in Europe, 1939–1945* (New York: Penguin Books, 2006), 69.

77. Lawrence L. Langer, *Holocaust Testimonies: The Ruins of Memory* (New Haven: Yale University Press, 1991), 189–98.

78. Ulrich Baer, "Revision, Animation, Rescue: Color Photographs from the Lodz Ghetto and Darius Jablonski's Holocaust Documentary *Fotoamator*," in Ulrich Baer, *Spectral Evidence: The Photography of Trauma* (Cambridge, MA: MIT Press, 2005), 141–47.

79. Ibid., 141.

80. A. C. Grayling, *Among the Dead Cities: Is the Targeting of Civilians in War Ever Justified?* (London: Bloomsbury, 2007).

81. Dieter Forte, *In der Erinnerung. Roman* (Frankfurt am Main: Fischer Taschenbuch Verlag, 2001), 75.

CHAPTER 5

1. Albrecht Wiesener, "Halle an der Saale—Chemiemetropole oder 'Diva in Grau'?," in Karin Hartewig and Alf Lüdtke, eds., *Die DDR im Bild. Zum Gebrauch der Fotografie im anderen deutschen Staat* (Göttingen: Wallstein Verlag, 2004), 58.

2. Jörg Arnold, *The Allied Air War and Urban Memory: The Legacy of Strategic Bombing in Germany* (Cambridge: Cambridge University Press, 2011).

3. Süß, *Tod aus der Luft*, 553.

4. Matthias Neuntzner, "Vom Anklagen zum Erinnern. Die Erzählung vom 13. Februar," in Reinhard, Neutzner, and Hesse, eds., *Das rote Leuchten*, 146.

5. *Sächsische Zeitung* (henceforth *SZ*) (February 9–10, 1985): 3, "Inferno Dresden" by Olaf Groehler.

6. Neutzner, "Vom Anklagen zum Erinnern," 137.

7. Ibid., 137.

8. See, for example, Max Seydewitz, *Zerstörung und Wiederaufbau von Dresden* (Berlin: Kongress Verlag, 1955), 161–78.

9. *SZ*, February 12, 1965.

10. *SZ*, February 12, 1965; February 13, 1965.

11. *SZ*, February 12, 1965.

12. *SZ*, January 18, 1955.

13. *SZ*, February 13, 1965; "Hiroshima grüsst Dresden."

14. Neuntzer, "Vom Anklagen zum Erinnern," 150.

15. Ibid., 151.

16. Ibid., 153.

17. Ibid., 156.

18. Ibid., 156.

19. *SZ*, February 7, 1975.

20. *SZ*, February 9–10, 1985, Seite 3: "Inferno Dresden" by Olaf Groehler.

21. Derenthal, *Bilder der Trümmer-und Aufbaujahre*, 63.

22. Ibid., 66.

23. In 1937, Schaarschuch had illustrated another picture book with his photographs, Kurt Herzog's *Wir marschieren nach Nürnberg. Ein Bilderbuch vom Marsch der politischen Leiter, Werkscharmänner und DAF-Walter von Hof nach Nürnberg und vom Leben in Lager*; see Derenthal, *Bilder der Trümmer-und Aufbaujahre*, 67.

24. Derenthal, *Bilder der Trümmer-und Aufbaujahre*, 65.
25. Ibid., 65.
26. Ibid., 66.
27. Ibid., 67.
28. Richard Petersen, *Erinnerungen und Bilder eines Dresdener Fotografen* (Leipzig: VEB Fotokinoverlag, 1987).
29. Michael Neumann, "Genealogie einer Geste: '. . . eingebrannt in das Bildbewusstsein der modernen Menschheit.' Ikone, Ritual und Gedächtnis," in Schmitz, ed., *Die Zerstörung Dresdens*, 159–69.
30. Anne Fuchs, *After the Dresden Bombing*, 41.
31. Susanne Vees-Gulani, "'Phantomschmerzen' Durs Grünbeins Porzellan und neue Wege in der Literatur über den Luftkrieg," in Arnold, Süss, and Thiessen, eds., *Erinnerungen in Deutschland und Europa*, 287.
32. Derenthal, *Bilder der Trümmer-und Aufbaujahre*, 71.
33. Ibid.
34. Ibid.
35. Richard Peter, *Eine Kamera klagt an* (Dresden: Dresdener Verlags-Gesellschaft, 1949).
36. Quoted in Derenthal, *Bilder der Trümmer-und Aufbaujahre*, 73.
37. *SZ*, February 13, 1975.
38. Bundesarchiv-DA4/604, Präsidialkanzlei (v.a.Protokollabt.), Rede des Präsidenten in Dresden am 19.9.56.
39. *Dresde Aujourd'hui/Dresden Today/Dresden Heute.* Panorama DDR. 1.1978, 22 Jahrgang (Dresden: Verlag Zeit im Bild), 12.
40. *SZ*, February 7, 1985.
41. *SZ*, February 7, 1985.
42. Max Zimmering, *Phosphor und Flieder. Vom Untergang und Wiederaufstieg der Stadt Dresden* (Berlin: Dietz Verlag, 1954). On Zimmering (pseudonyms: Mix, Max Lorbeer) see Karin Hartewig, *Zurückgekehrt. Die Geschichte der jüdischen Kommunisten in der DDR* (Köln: Böhlau Verlag, 2000), 81, 338.
43. Even the reviewer in the *SZ* admitted that Zimmering's book was not really a novel but rather a chronicle of the destruction and rebuilding of Dresden combined with stories of a variety of characters: an antifascist freed from a police prison by the Allied air raids, a bourgeois-liberal art professor, and so on. The review criticized Zimmering for failing properly to develop these characters; *SZ*, January 25, 1955.
44. Zimmering, *Phosphor und Flieder*, 314.
45. Ibid., 317. See also *Dresde Aujourd'hui/Dresden Today/Dresden Heute*, 74.
46. Susanne Vees-Gulani, "The Politics of New Beginnings: The Continued Exclusion of the Nazi Past in Dresden's Cityscape," in Rosenfeld and Jaskot, eds., *Beyond Berlin*, 30.
47. Ibid., 29.
48. Matthias Lerm, "'Der Bombenterror hat freie Bahn geschaffen, sie ist zu nützen' Reaktionen, Aktionen, Visionen von Architekten, Stadtplanern, Politikern," in Schmitz, ed., *Die Zerstörung Dresdens*, 385.
49. Alfred Hahn and Ernst Neef, *Dresden. Ergebnisse der heitmatkundlichen Bestandsaufnahme* (Berlin: Akademie Verlag, 1984), Plates 18 and 19.

50. "Wiedereröffnung der Semperoper wird in 19 Länder übertragen. Heute 20 Uhr im DDR-Fernsehen/Stationen in Europa und übersee senden Berichte," *Neues Deutschland* (February 13, 1985): 2.

51. *SZ*, February 13, 1975.

52. Neuntzer, "Vom Anklagen zum Erinnern," 142.

53. Ibid., 147.

54. Susanne Vees-Gulani, "The Politics of New Beginnings," 35.

55. Christoph Klessmann, *Zwei Staaten, eine Nation. Deutsche Geschichte 1955–1970* (Göttingen: Vandenhoeck and Ruprecht, 1988), 68–70.

56. *SZ*, January 18, 1955. See also SED-Bezirksleitung Dresden. Kommission zur Erforschung der Geschichte der örtlichen Arbeiterbewegung Staatsarchiv Dresden, ed., *Der Beitrag des Bezirkes Dresden zum Werden und Wachsen der Deutschen Demokratischen Republik. Dokumentensammlung zur Geschichte der DDR.* Teil II [1952–63] (Dresden: Staatsarchiv Dresden, 1971).

57. *SZ*, January 19, 1955.

58. *SZ*, January 28, 1955.

59. *SZ*, January 10, 1955.

60. *SZ*, January 28, 1955.

61. *SZ*, January 29, 1955, "Die Elbestadt mahnt alle Deutschen. Oberbürgermeister Weidauer zum 10. Jahrestag der Zerstörung Dresdens."

62. *SZ*, February 2, 1955.

63. On partnerships and "twinning" in West Germany see Johannes Sticker, *Kommunale Aussenpolitik. Jumelage, Verschwisterung, Twinning, Gemelagio, Verbroedering* (Köln: Deutscher Gemeindeverlag, 1975), and *Twinning. Deutsch-Britische Partnerschaften* (London: Oswald Wolff, 1974).

64. Neutzner, "Vom Anklagen zum Erinnern," 147.

65. Zimmering, *Phosphor und Flieder*, 457.

66. *SZ*, February 15, 1965.

67. Neuntzer, "Vom Anklagen zum Erinnern," 153.

68. Bundesarchiv Filmarchiv -Berlin, Max Jaap, "Dresden-Erinnerung und Mahnung" (1965).

69. Ibid.

70. Jan C. Behrends, "Freundschaft, Fremdheit, Gewalt. Ostdeutsche Sowjetunionbilder zwischen Propaganda und Erfahrung," in Gregor Thum, ed., *Traumland Osten. Deutsche Bilder vom östlichen Europa im 20.Jahrhundert* (Göttingen: Vandenhoeck and Ruprecht, 2006), 157–80.

71. Rat d. Stadt Dresden, ed., *Dresden—30 Jahre nach der Befreiung* (Dresden: Verlag Rat der Stadt Dresden, 1975).

72. Elizabeth Heinemann, *What Difference Does a Husband Make?: Women and Marital Status in Nazi and Postwar Germany* (Berkeley: University of California Press, 1999).

73. See Norman M. Naimark, *The Russians in Germany: A History of the Soviet Occupation, 1945–1949* (Cambridge, MA: Belnap Press of Harvard University Press, 1995), 69–140; Regina Mühlhauser, "Vergewaltigungen in Deutschland 1945. National Opferdiskurs und individualles Erinnern betroffener Frauen," in Klaus Naumann, ed., *Nachkrieg in Deutschland* (Hamburg: Hamburger Edition, 2001), 384–408; and, especially, Sabine Moller, *Vielfache Vergangenheit. Öffentliche Erinnerungskulturen und*

Familienerinnerungen an die NS-Zeit in Ostdeutschland (Tübingen: Edition Discord, 2003), IV.4. "Die Russen" in Ostdeutschland, 165–75.

74. *SZ*, February 12–13, 1955; more generally, see Jan C. Behrends, "Freundschaft, Fremdheit, Gewalt. Ostdeutsche Sowjetunionbilder zwischen Propaganda und Erfahrung," in Gregor Thum, ed., *Traumland Osten*, 157–80.

75. *SZ*, February 12–13, 1955.

76. Bundesarchiv-DA4/604. Präsidialkanzlei (v.a.Protokollabt). Eintragung des Präsidenten in das Gästebuch. Dresden, den September 19, 1956.

77. *SZ*, February 12, 1965.

78. *SZ*, February 13, 1965.

79. On the ways that children experienced bombing raids see Annett Gröschner, ed., *Berliner Schulaufsätze aus dem Jahr 1946*, and the novels by Dieter Forte, *Das Haus auf meinen Schultern. Romantrilogie* (Frankfurt am Main: S. Fischer Verlag, 1999).

80. *SZ*, February 13, 1965.

81. *SZ*, February 13, 1965.

82. *SZ*, February 13, 1965.

83. *SZ*-Sonnabend, February 13, 1965; see also "Geboren: 13 Februar 1945. Geburtsort: Dresden," *Neues Deutschland*, February 13, 1975.

84. On this theme, see Dorothee Wierling, "Nationalsozialismus und Krieg in den Lebens-Geschichten der ersten Nachkriegsgeneration der DDR," in Elisabeth Domansky and Harald Welzer, eds., *Eine offene Geschichte. Zur kommunikativen Tradierung der nationalsozialistischen Vergangenheit* (Tübingen: Edition Discord, 1999), 35–56.

85. *SZ*, February 7, 1975.

86. *SZ*, February 6, 1985.

87. *SZ*, February 8, 1985.

88. *SZ*, February 8, 1985.

89. *SZ*, February 8, 1985.

90. *SZ*, February 8, 1985.

91. *SZ*, February 2, 1965.

92. *SZ*, February 11, 1965.

93. Neuntzer, "Vom Anklagen zum Erinnern," 157.

94. Ibid., 158.

95. Ibid., 158.

96. Ibid., 160.

97. Ibid., 143.

98. Ibid., 161.

99. Olaf B. Rader, "Dresden," in Etienne Francois and Hagen Schulze, eds., *Deutsche Erinnerungsorte III* (München: Verlag C. H. Beck, 2001), 452–55. See also Jörg Friedrich, *Der Brand. Deutschland im Bombenkrieg 1940–1945* (München: Propyläen Verlag, 2002).

CHAPTER 6

1. Margalit, *Guilt, Suffering, and Memory*, 165–69.

2. See, for example, Mark Lehmstedt, ed., *Leipzig brennt. Der Untergang des al-*

ten Leipzig am 4. Dezember 1943 in Fotografien und Berichten (Leipzig: Lehmstedt Verlag, 2003).

3. Nancy Wood, *Vectors of Memory: Legacies of Trauma in Postwar Europe* (Oxford: Berg, 1999).

4. Malte Thiessen, "Der 'Feuersturm' im kommunikativen Gedächtnis. Tradierung und Transformation des Luftkriegs als Lebens-und Familiengeschichte," in Arnold, Süss, and Thiessen, eds., *Erinnerungen in Deutschland und Europa*, 312.

5. "Aufbau Ost 1946. Berlin, Dresden, Leipzig, Potsdam in ersten Friedensjahr," DVD,"Die grossen DEFA-Dokumentarfilme," Icestorm.

6. Bundesarchiv-Filmarchiv, "Zwei Städte" (1949). For East German criticism of this American "propaganda film" see Walter Weidauer, *Inferno Dresden. Über Lügen und Legenden um die Aktion "Donnerschlag"* (Berlin: Dietz Verlag, 1965), 156.

7. Robert R. Shandley, *Rubble Films: German Cinema in the Shadow of the Third Reich* (Philadelphia: Temple University Press, 2001).

8. Anton Kaes, *From Hitler to Heimat: The Return of History as Film* (Cambridge, MA: Harvard University Press, 1989), 137–60.

9. Sönke Neitzel, "'Wer Wind sät, wird Sturm ernten.' Der Luftkrieg in westdeutschen Fernsehdokumentationen"; http://www.historicum.net/themen/bomben krieg/themen-beitraege/aspekte/art/Wer_Wind_saet/html/ca/f86c9e440f/?tx_mediadb_pi1%5BmaxItems%5D=5 (last accessed March 1, 2015).

10. Ibid.

11. Bösch, Frank, and Constantin Goschler, eds. *Public History*, 324.

12. Ibid., 324.

13. Kay Hoffmann, "Die Deutsche Wochenschau. Die Bildersprache des Krieges im Film," in Paul, ed., *Das Jahrhundert der Bilder*, 581 and http://www.wochenschau-archiv.de (accessed July 31, 2014).

14. Although see, for example, the unusual footage included in the YouTube posting, "Kiel im Bombenkrieg," http://www.youtube.com/watch?v=2SG-MvQ49pc (accessed February 26, 2010), which includes color as well as black-and-white moving pictures of the aftermath of bombing raids on this city. The source of these images is not identified, but it is possible that these films were made by local authorities. See also Gesellschaft für Kieler Stadtgeschichte. DVD Kiel im Bombenkrieg 9, -13, 50 (Historische Filmdokumente 6) and http://www/kiel.de (accessed February 26, 2010).

15. Thomas Fischer, "Ereignis und Erlebnis: Enstehung und Merkmale des Zeitgenössischen Dokumentarischen Geschichtsfernsehens," in Korte and Paletschek, eds., *History Goes Pop*, 194.

16. Ibid., 193.

17. Ibid., 191.

18. Gertrud Koch, "Affekt oder Effekt. Was haben Bilder was Worte nicht haben?," in Harald Welzer, ed., *Das soziale Gedächtnis. Geschichte, Erinnerung, Tradierung* (Hamburg: Hamburger Edition, 2001), 123.

19. Stefan Brauberger, "Fiktionalität oder Fakten: Welche Zukunft hat die zeitgeschichtliche Dokumentation?," in Korte and Paletschek, eds., *History Goes Pop*, 195.

20. Produced by History Films. Dokumente der Zeit. AV Medien Produktion. Am Schelm 8. D-919629 Weihenzell.

21. James Elkins, *Pictures and Tears: A History of People Who Have Cried in Front*

of Paintings (New York and London: Routledge, 2001), 64. See also Katharina Sykora, Ludger Derenthal, and Esther Ruelfs, eds., *Fotografische Leidenschaften* (Marburg: Jonas Verlag, 2006).

22. Series: Zeitgeschichte-"Deutsche Städte in Flammen"; Luftangriff auf Hamburg (2003 e-m-s new media AG).

23. DVD-Edition Spiegel TV history. *Feuersturm. Der Bombenkrieg gegen Deutschland.*

24. Brauberger, "Fiktionalität oder Fakten," 208.

25. "Das Drama von Dresden." Ein Film von Sebastian Deinhardt Leitung Guido Knopp. ZDF broadview.tv GmbH. c.2005. This film was the International Academy of Television Arts & Sciences 2005 International Emmy Award Winner for Documentary.

26. One of the most durable popular legends about the bombing of Dresden claims that Allied fighter-bombers had strafed civilians with their machine guns as they cowered, without any cover, on the banks of the Elbe, having fled there to escape the flames. A detailed study by Helmut Schnatz has revealed "that while such strafing incidents had taken place in other cities, none had taken place in Dresden." Helmut Schnatz, *Tiefflieger über Dresden? Legenden und Wirklichkeit* (Köln: Böhlau Verlag, 2000), 158. Anne Fuchs also observes that a recent exhaustive investigation, the results of which were reported in 2010, "refutes some of the most tenacious myths . . . such as the claim by many eyewitnesses that American bombers carried out strafing attacks along the river Elbe." This report also establishes that no more than 25,000 were killed in the bombing; Fuchs, *After the Dresden Bombing*, 6.

27. See Richard Bessel, "Hatred after War: Emotion and the Postwar History of East Germany," in Alon Confino, ed., *Histories and Memories of Twentieth-Century Germany,* special issue of *History and Memory* 17, nos. 1/12 (Fall 2005): 195–216, and also Richard Bessel and Dirk Schumann, eds., *Life after Death: Approaches to a Cultural and Social History of Europe during the 1940s and 1950s* (Washington, DC: German Historical Institute and Cambridge University Press, 2003).

28. Konrad H. Jarausch, "Zeitgeschichte und Erinnerung. Deutungskonkurrenz oder Interdependanz," in Konrad H. Jarausch and Martin Sabrow, eds., *Verletzes Gedächtnis. Erinnerungskulktur und Zeitgeschichte im Konflikt* (Frankfurt: Campus Verlag, 2002), 16–17.

29. Brauberger, "Fiktionalität oder Fakten," 204–5.

30. Joachim Käppner, "Kommentar. Das deutsche Leid," *Süeddeutsche Zeitung* (March 16, 2006); http://www.sueddeutsche.de/,tt2m3/deutschland/artikel/479/71408

31. Spiegel Online, February 13, 2006; http//www.spiegel.de/international/0,1518,400691,00.html

32. "Dresden" Historiker und Zeitzeugen sind begeistert. Abgelegt unter: TV-Kritisch—Tim @ 1:25 pm. March 7, 2006; http://www.tv-tipps.net/267/dresden-historiker-und-zeitzeugen-sind-begeistert

33. Sebald, *On the Natural History of Destruction*, 19. Sebald is here citing Solly Zuckerman, *From Apes to Warlords* (London: H. Hamilton, 1978), 352.

34. Evelyn Finger, "Der englische Pilot. 'Dresden,' das ZDF-Katastrophen-Rührstück über die Zerstörung der Stadt 1945," *Die Zeit*, no. 10 (March 2, 2006); http://www.zeit.de/2006/10/Dresden

35. Interview in "Das Making Of."

36. These pictures and the context of their production are analyzed in detail in Norbert Haase, Stefi Jersch-Wenzel, and Hermann Simon, eds., *Die Erinnerung hat ein Gesicht. Fotografien und Dokumente zur nationalsozialistischen Judenverfolgung in Dresden 1933–1945* (Leipzig: Gustav Kiepenheuer Verlag, 1998).

37. *Verbrannt bis zur Unkenntlichkeit. Die Zerstörung Dresdens 1945. Begleitbuch zur Ausstellung im Stadtmuseum Dresden. Februar bis Juni 1995*. Herausgegeben von der Landeshauptstadt Dresden (Dresden: DZA Verlag für Kultur und Wissenschaft, 1994).

38. Hans Erich Nossack, *The End: Hamburg, 1943* (Chicago: University of Chicago Press, 2006), 220.

39. Norbert Seitz, "Geschichtspolitik und deutsche Opferkultur," Deutschlandradio Kultur, Politisches Feuilleton, March 25, 2006. http://www.dradio.de/dkultur/sendungen/politischesfeuilleton/483094/

40. Quote from TV movie in an advertisement for "Die Luftbrücke. Nur der Himmel war frei" included with the DVD of "Die Sturmflut."

41. Evelyn Finger, "Der englische Pilot. Dresden, das ZDF-Katastrophen-Rührstück über die Zerstörung der Stadt 1945," Die Zeit, March 2, 2006, nr. 10; http://www.zeit.de/2006/10/Dresden

42. Ibid.

43. Joachim Käppner, "Kommentar. Das deutsche Leid," Sueddeutsche.de, March 16, 2006, http://www.sueddeutsche.de/,tt2m3/deutschland/artikel/479/71408/

44. Joachim Güntner, "Bomben-Kitsch. Dresdens Untergang im Fernsehen," March 8, 2006, *Neue Zürcher Zeitung*, NZZ Online, http://www.nzz.ch/2006/03/08/fe/articleDN9CM.print.html

45. Finger, "Der englische Pilot."

46. Sebald, *On the Natural History of Destruction.*

47. Nicholas Stargardt, *Witnesses of War: Children's Lives under the Nazis* (New York: Alfred A. Knopf, 2006), 15.

48. Axel Schildt and Detlef Siegfried, *Deutsche Kulturgeschichte. Die Bundesrepublik-1945 bis zur Gegenwart* (München: Carl Hanser Verlag, 2009), 489–90.

49. Erik Meyer, "Problematische Popularität? Erinnerungskultur, Medienwandel und Aufmerksamkeitsökonomie," in Korte and Paletschek, eds., *History Goes Pop*, 277.

50. Maren Lorenz, "Repräsentation von Geschichte in Wikipedia oder: Die Sehnsucht nach Beständigkeit im Unbeständigen," in ibid., 308.

51. http://de.wikipedia.org/wiki/Luftangriffe_auf_Dresden (last accessed January 15, 2015).

52. http://www.historicum.net/themen/bombenkrieg (last accessed January 15, 2015).

53. http://www.frankfurt1933-1945.de/ (last accessed January 15, 2015). Since 2005, the Institut für Stadtgeschichte has been responsible for this site.

54. Lutz Philipp Gunther, *Die bildhafte Repräsentation deutscher Städte von den Chroniken der frühen Neuzeit zu den Websites der Gegenwart* (Köln: Böhlau Verlag, 2009), 261–62.

55. For a discussion of this photographer's work see Schmid, *Frankfurt im Feuersturm*, 24–26.

56. http://www.stadtgeschichte-ffm.de/veranstaltungen/erzaehlcafe.html

57. http://www.clio-online.de/site/lang__en/ItemID__15599/mid__10304/94/default.aspx (last accessed January 15, 2015).

58. http://www.luftkrieg.nuernberg.de/zwangsarbeiter/folge2.html (accessed October 4, 2010).

59. http://www.paderborn.de/microsite/adam_eva/stadtgeschichte/109010100000031217.php (last accessed January 15, 2015).

60. http://www.br-online.de/bayern/einst-und-jetzt/kriegsende-in-bayern-1945-DID1188598133/index.xml archived at http://archive.is/X5oCE (last Accessed January 15, 2015).

61. Hermann Deckert, "Verlorenes Alt Hannover," in Lauenroth and Lauterbach, *Tod und Leben Hannovers 9 Oktober*, 60.

62. http://www.bombenkrieg.net (last Accessed January 15, 2015).

63. http://www.youtube.com/watch?v=UCk6G2rNcQ4 "Die 'Befreiung' deutscher Städte"—9,113 views (October 6, 2010), https://www.youtube.com/user/Natstattrad (accessed October 17, 2008).

64. https://www.youtube.com/watch?v=UgTb8XionVU, "Dresden-der geplante Massenmord" (last accessed July 18, 2016).

65. http://www.youtube.com/watch?v=-Nfsstlc6QM, user focusonline (last accessed January 15, 2015).

66. https://www.youtube.com/watch?v=cag8gUYS26Y, ASCHE DEUTSCH LAND1945—Part/Teil 9 (2,213 views, October 6, 2010); https://www.youtube.com/user/wehrwulf1944 (last accessed July 18, 2016).

67. Ibid. (last accessed July 18, 2016).

68. http://www.youtube.com/watch?v=VW1OHqvcMwQ, 3,999 views (5:20 minutes) (last accessed January 15, 2015).

69. http://www.youtube.com/watch?v=2SG-MvQ49pc (last accessed January 15, 2015).

70. Konrad H. Jarausch, "Zeitgeschichte und Erinnerung. Deutungskonkurrenz oder Interdependanz," in Jarausch and Sabrow, eds., *Verletzes Gedächtnis*, 16–17.

71. Arnold, "Sammelzension: Bombenkrieg." See also Ulrike Jureit, "Generations-Gedächtnis. Überlegungen zu einem Konzept kommunikativer Vergemeinschaftungen," in Lu Seegers and Jürgen Reulecke, eds., *Die "Generation der Kriegskinder" Historische Hintergründe und Deutungen* (Giessen: Psychosozial-Verlag, 2009), 135.

72. Bill Niven, ed., *Germans as Victims: Remembering the Past in Contemporary Germany* (New York: Palgrave Macmillan, 2006), 13.

73. Ibid., 13.

74. Daniel Miller and Don Slater, *The Internet: An Ethnographic Approach* (Oxford: Berg, 2000), 192.

75. Klaus Neumann, *Der Krieg als Text. Das Jahr 1948 im kulturellen Gedächtnis der Presse* (Hamburg: Hamburger Edition, 1998), 323.

76. Bessel and Schumann, eds., *Life after Death.*

77. Compare, for example, the images in *Dresden* with those in the BBC docudrama about the Nazis' failed attempt to create a firestorm in the center of London at the end of December 1940: *The Blitz. London's Longest Night* (PBS Home Video DVD 2006).

CONCLUSION

1. Geoff Eley, ed., *The "Goldhagen Effect": History, Memory, Nazism—Facing the German Past* (Ann Arbor: University of Michigan Press, 2000); Bill Niven, *Facing the Nazi Past: United Germany and the Legacy of the Third Reich* (London: Routledge, 2001), 227.

2. Arnold, "Sammelrezension: Bombenkrieg."

3. Egbert A. Hoffmann, *Als der Feuertod vom Himmel stürzte. Hamburg Sommer 1943* (Gudensberg-Gleichen: Wartberg Verlag, 2003).

4. Arnold, "Sammelrezension: Bombenkrieg."

5. See, for example, "Der Feuersturm in Hamburg" (6.Teil), *Morgenpost* (July 6, 1993). Cited in Thiessen, *Eingebrannt ins Gedächtnis*, 323.

6. *Dresden. Ein verlorenes Stadtbild.* Zusammengestellt und bearbeitet von Heike Liebsch und Uwe Schieferdecker (Gudensberg-Gleichen: Wartberg Verlag, 1993).

7. See also Arnold, "Sammelrezension: Bombenkrieg."

8. Vilem Flusser, *Towards a Philosophy of Photography* (London: Reaktion Books, 2007), 62.

9. Eric Langenbacher, "Moralpolitik versus Moralpolitik: Recent Struggles over the Construction of Cultural Memory in Germany," *German Politics and Society* 23, no. 3 (Fall 2005): 106.

10. "Hamburgs Weg in den Feuersturm," *Memo. Museum für Hamburgische Geschichte-Illustrierte Zeitgeschichte*, no. 1 (October 1993).

11. "Als Feuer vom Himmel fiel. Der Bombenkrieg gegen die Deutschen," *Spiegel special. Das Magazin zum Thema*, no. 1 (2003): 96–98.

12. Ibid., 40–41. "'Was für eine Idee!' Konnten oder wollten die Alliiertern Auschwitz nicht bombardieren?"

13. Jörg Friedrich, *Brandstätten. Der Anblick des Bombenkrieges* (München: Propyläen, 2003), 108–55. See also *Verbrannt bis zur Unkenntlichkeit.*

14. Niven, ed., *Germans as Victims*, 14.

15. Margalit, *Guilt, Suffering, and Memory*, 292.

16. Klaus Neumann, *Der Krieg als Text. Das Jahr 1945 im kulturellen Gedächtnis der Presse* (Hamburg: Hamburger Edition, 1998).

17. Ibid., 322.

18. http://www.mainpost.de/regional/schweinfurt/Gedenkfeier-70-Jahre-Bombenkrieg-Wenn-mir-des-buess-muessn;art742,7631605. Story published in the *Main Post* in August 2013. Comment from bacigalupo (326 Kommentare) am 19.08.2013 20:27 (last accessed January 15, 2015).

19. Dietmar Süß, "Review article, *Memories of the Air War*," *Journal of Contemporary History* 43, no. 2 (2008): 333–42.

Selected Bibliography

ARCHIVES

Bildarchiv preußischer Kulturbesitz (now known as Bildagentur für Kunst,Kultur und Geschichte), Berlin.

Bundesarchiv-DA4/604, Präsidialkanzlei (v.a.Protokollabt.), Rede des Präsidenten in Dresden am 19.9.56.

Bundesarchiv Filmarchiv-Berlin, Max Jaap, "Dresden-Erinnerung und Mahnung" (1965).

Sächsische Landes-, Staats- und Universitäts Bibliothek, Deutsche Fotothek Dresden, Nachlaß Peters, PS 48.

PUBLISHED WORKS, FILMS, AND WEBSITES

Arnold, Jörg. *The Allied Air War and Urban Memory: The Legacy of Strategic Bombing in Germany* (Cambridge: Cambridge University Press, 2011).

Arnold, Jörg. "Sammelrezension:Bombenkrieg," in H-Soz-Kult, http://hsozkult.geschichte.hu-berlin.de/rezensionen/2004-2-062

Arnold, Jörg. "'In Wächserner Blässe wie Schaufensterpuppen' Leichenbilder aus dem Luftkrieg und ihr sozialer Gebrauch (1940–1960)," in *Fotogeschichte* 32, no. 125 (2012): 27–38.

Arnold, Jörg, Dietmar Süss, and Malte Thiessen, eds. *Luftkrieg: Erinnerungen in Deutschland und Europa* (Göttingen: Wallstein Verlag, 2009).

Assmann, Aleida, Monika Gomille, and Gabriele Rippl, eds. *Ruinenbilder* (München: Wilhelm Fink Verlag, 2002).

Baer, Ulrich. *Spectral Evidence: The Photography of Trauma* (Cambridge: MIT Press, 2005).

Bake, Rita, ed. *"Aber wir müssen zusammenbleiben" Mütter und Kinder in Bombenkriegen 1943 bis 1993. Gespräche* [Landeszentrale für politische Bildung] (Hamburg: Dölling und Galitz, 1993).

Bardua, Heinz. *Stuttgart im Luftkrieg 1939–1945*, Veröffentlichungen des Archivs der Stadt Stuttgart, Band 23. (Stuttgart: Ernst Klett Verlag, 1967).

Barthes, Roland. *Camera Lucida. Reflections on Photography* (New York: Hill and Wang, 1982).

Bartov, Omer. "'Seit die Juden weg sind . . .' Germany, History and Representations of Absence." In Scott Denham, Irene Kacandes, and Jonathan Petropoulos, eds., *A User's Guide to German Cultural Studies* (Ann Arbor: University of Michigan Press, 1997), 209–26.

Behrends, Jan C. "Freundschaft, Fremdheit, Gewalt.Ostdeutsche Sowjetunionbilder zwischen Propaganda und Erfahrung." In Gregor Thum, ed., *Traumland Osten. Deutsche Bilder vom östlichen Europa im 20.Jahrhundert* (Göttingen: Vandenhoeck & Ruprecht, 2006), 157–80.

Bergerson, Andrew. "Reconstructing the Self: The Uses of Alt Hildesheim after its Destruction." In Georg Wagner-Kyora, ed., *Wiederaufbau europäischer Städte: Rekonstruktionen, die Moderne und die lokale Identitätspolitik seit 1945 / Rebuilding European Cities: Reconstructions, Modernity and the Local Politics of Identity Construction since 1945* (Stuttgart: Franz Steiner Verlag, 2014), 272–310.

Bessel, Richard. "Hatred after War: Emotion and the Postwar History of East Germany." In Alon Confino, ed., *Histories and Memories of Twentieth-Century Germany*. Special Issue of *History and Memory* 17, nos. 1/12 (Fall 2005): 195–216.

Bessel, Richard, and Dirk Schumann, eds. *Life after Death: Approaches to a Cultural and Social History of Europe during the 1940s and 1950s* (German Historical Institute, Washington, DC, and Cambridge University Press, 2003).

Betts, Paul. *The Authority of Everyday Objects. A Cultural History of West German Design* (Berkeley: University of California Press, 2004).

Blank, Ralf. Review of Jörg Friedrich, *Brandstätten*, Historisches Centrum Hagen, http://hsozkult.geschichte.hu-berlin.de/rezensionen/id=3483

Blank, Ralf. Rezension zu *Kucklick, Christoph: Feuersturm. Der Bombenkrieg gegen Deutschland. Hamburg 2003*, in H-Soz-Kult (October 22, 2003); http://hsozkult.geschichte.hu-berlin.de/rezensionen/2003-4-043

Der Bombenkrieg gegen die Deutschen: Als Feuer vom Himmel Fiel. DVD (Hamburg: Spiegel TV, 2003).

Bösch, Frank, and Constantin Goschler, eds. *Public History. Öffentliche Darstellungen des Nationalsozialismus jenseits der Geschichtswissenschaft* (Frankfurt am Main: Campus Verlag, 2009).

Brunswig, Hans. *Feuersturm über Hamburg. Die Luftangriffe auf Hamburg im Zweiten Weltkrieg und ihre Folgen* (Stuttgart: Motorbuch Verlag, 1978).

Busch, Dieter. *Der Luftkrieg im Raum Mainz während des Zweiten Welkrieges 1939–1945*. Veröffentlichungen der Kommission des Landtages für die Geschichte des Landes Rheinland-Pfalz, Band 9. (Mainz: v.Hase & Koehler Verlag Main, 1988).

Caplan, Jane, and Nikolas Wachsmann, eds. *Concentration Camps in Nazi Germany: The New Histories* (London and New York: Routledge, 2010).

Confino, Alon. *Germany as a Culture of Remembrance: Promises and Limits of Writing History* (Chapel Hill: University of North Carolina Press, 2006).

Conze, Eckart. *Die Suche nach der Sicherheit. Eine Geschichte der Bundesrepublik von 1949 bis in die Gegenwart* (München: Siedler Verlag, 2009).

Crew, David F. "Mourning, Denial, Celebration: The Visual Work of West German Reconstruction after 1945," In Georg Wagner-Kyora, ed., *Wiederaufbau europäischer Städte.Rekonstruktionen, die Moderne und die lokale Identitätspolitik seit 1945 /*

Rebuilding European Cities. Reconstructions, Modernity and the Local Politics of Identity Construction since 1945 (Stuttgart: Franz Steiner Verlag, 2014), 232–49.

Crew, David F. "Sleeping with the Enemy? A Fiction Film for German Television about the Bombing of Dresden," in *Central European History* 40, no. 1 (2007): 117–32.

Das XX. Jahrhundert. Fotografien zur deutschen Geschichte aus der Sammlung des Deutschen Historischen Museums (Berlin: DHM. Edition Braus im Wachter Verlag, 2004).

Davies, Norman. *No Simple Victory: World War II in Europe, 1939–1945* (New York: Penguin Books, 2006).

Derenthal, Ludger. *Bilder der Trümmer-und Aufbaujahre.Fotografie im sich teilenden Deutschland* (Marburg: Jonas Verlag, 1999).

Didi-Hubermann, Georges. *Bilder trotz allem* (München: Wilhelm Fink Verlag, 2007).

Diefenbacher, Michael, and Wilhelm Fischer-Pache, eds. *Der Luftkrieg gegen Nürnberg Der Angriff am 2.Januar 1945 und die zerstörte Stadt*, Quellen und Forschungen zur Geschichte und Kultur der Stadt Nürnberg. Herausgegeben von Michael Diefenbacher und Wiltrud Fischer-Pache im Auftrag der Stadt Nürnberg. 33. Band (Neustadt an der Aisch: Schmidt, 2004).

Diefendorf, Jeffry M. *In the Wake of War: The Reconstruction of German Cities After World War II* (Oxford: Oxford University Press, 1993).

Dokumente deutsche Kriegsschäden. 1 . Beiheft, Aus den Tagen des Luftkrieges und des Wiederaufbaues Erlebnis-und Erfahrungsberichte, Herausgegeben vom Bundesminister für Vertriebene, Flüchtlinge und Kriegsgeschädigte Bonn (Bonn: Bundesministerium des Innern, Abt. Vertriebene, Flüchtlinge und Kriegsgeschädigte, 1960).

Dokumente deutscher Kriegsschäden. Evakuierte. Kriegsgeschädigte.Währungsgeschädigte.Die geschichtliche und rechtliche Entwicklung (Band V. Bibliographie), Herausgegeben vom Bundesminister für Vertriebene, Flüchtlinge und Kriegsgeschädigte Bonn (Stuttgart: Zentraldruckerei, Ackermann & Honold, 1964).

Domarus, Max. *Der Untergang des alten Würzburg und seine Vorgeschichte* (Gerolshofen: Franz Teutsch, 1955).

Dörr, Margaret. *"Wer die Zeit nicht miterlebt hat . . .": Frauenerfahrungen im Zweiten Weltkrieg und in den Jahren danach. Band 2: Kriegsalltag* (Frankfurt: Campus Verlag, 1998).

Dresde Aujourd'hui/Dresden Today/Dresden Heute. Panorama DDR. 1.1978, 22 Jahrgang (Dresden: Verlag Zeit im Bild), 74.

Dresden. Ein verlorenes Stadtbild. Zusammengestellt und bearbeitet von Heike Liebsch und Uwe Schieferdecker (Gudensberg-Gleichen: Wartberg Verlag, 1993).

Dumoulin, Olivier. "A Comparative Approach to Newsreels and Bombing in the Second World War: Britain, France, Germany." In Claudia Baldoli, Andrew Knapp, and Richard Overy, eds., *Bombing, States and Peoples in Western Europe 1940–1945* (London and New York; Continuum International Publishing Group, 2011), 298–314.

Echternkamp, Jörg, and Stefan Martens, eds. *Der Zweite Weltkrieg in Europa.Efarhung und Erinnerung* (Paderborn: Ferdinand Schöningh, 2007).

Eley, Geoff, ed. *The 'Goldhagen Effect': History, Memory, Nazism—Facing the German Past* (Ann Arbor: University of Michigan Press, 2000).

Eley, Geoff. *Nazism as Fascism: Violence, Ideology, and the Grounds of Consent in Germany* (London: Routledge, 2013).

Eley, Geoff. "Nazism, Politics and the Image of the Past: Thoughts on the West German Historikerstreit 1986–1987," in *Past & Present*, no. 121 (November 1988), 171–208.

Elkins, James. *Pictures and Tears: A History of People Who Have Cried in Front of Paintings* (New York: Routledge, 2001).

Elter, Andreas. "Tod eines Kameramannes. Fotografen und Kameraleute zwischen den Fronten." In Gerhard Paul, ed., *Das Jahrhundert der Bilder.1949 bis heute* (Göttingen: Vandenhoeck & Ruprecht, 2008), 450–57.

Errell, Richard. *Bilderbuch für Nachdenkliche* (Frankfurt am Main: Europäische Verlagsanstalt, 1962).

Feuersturm. Der Bombenkrieg gegen Deutschland. Special ed. DVD. Directed by Michael Kloft (Hamburg: Spiegel TV, 2003).

Finger, Evelyn. "Der englische Pilot. 'Dresden,' das ZDF-Katastrophen-Rührstück über die Zerstörung der Stadt 1945," in *Zeit Online*, no.10 (March 2, 2006); http://www.zeit.de/2006/10/Dresden

Fischer, Josef. *Köln '39-'45. Der Leidensweg einer Stadt. Miterlebt von Josef Fischer* (Köln: J.P. Bachem, 1970).

Flusser, Vilem. *Towards a Philosophy of Photography* (London: Reaktion Books, 2007).

Forte, Dieter. *Das Haus auf meinen Schultern.Romantrilogie* (Frankfurt am Main: S. Fischer Verlag, 1999).

Forte, Dieter. *In der Erinnerung. Roman* (Frankfurt am Main: Fischer Taschenbuch Verlag, 2001).

Friedrich, Jörg. *Brandstätten. Der Anblick des Bombenkrieges* (München: Propyläen, 2003).

Friedrich, Jörg. *Der Brand. Deutschland im Bombenkrieg 1940–1945* (München: Propyläen, 2002).

Fuchs, Anne. *After the Dresden Bombing: Pathways of Memory, 1945 to the Present* (London: Palgrave Macmillan Memory Studies, 2011).

Gassert, Philip, and Alan E. Steinweis, eds. *Coping with the Nazi Past: West German Debates on Nazism and Generational Conflict, 1955–1975* (New York: Berghahn Books, 2006).

Gauss, Werner. *Alt-Heilbronn. Wie wir es kannten und liebten. Ein Bildband der Erinnerung.* (Heilbronn am Neckar: Gauss-Verlag, 1950).

Geimer, Peter, "Fotos, die man nicht zeigt. Probleme mit Schockbildern." In Katharina Sykora, Ludger Derenthal, and Esther Ruelfs, eds., *Fotografische Leidenschaften* (Marburg: Jonas Verlag, 2006), 245–60.

Glasenapp, Jörn. *Die deutsche Nachkriegsfotografie. Eine Mentalitätsgeschichte in Bildern* (Paderborn: Wilhelm Fink, 2008).

Glienke, Stefan. "The Allied Air War and German Society." In Claudia Baldoli, Andrew Knapp, and Richard Overy, eds., *Bombing, States, and Peoples in Western Europe 1940–45* (London and New York: Continuum, 2011), 184–205.

Grabe, Thomas, Reimar Hollmann, Klaus Mlynek, and Michael Radtke. *Unter der Wolke des Todes leben . . . Hannover im Zweiten Weltkrieg* (Hamburg: Ernst Kabel Verlag, 1983).

Grayling, A. C. *Among the Dead Cities: The History and Moral Legacy of the WWII Bombing of Civilians in Germany and Japan* (London: Bloomsbury, 2007).

Gregor, Neil. *Haunted City: Nuremberg and the Nazi Past* (New Haven: Yale University Press, 2008).

Greve, Michael. "Täter oder Gehilfen? Zum strafrechtlichen Umgang mit NS-Gewaltverbrechern in der Bundesrepublik Deutschland." In Ulrike Weckel and Edgar Wolfrum, eds., *"Bestien" und "Befehlsempfänger." Frauen und Männer in NS-Prozessen nach 1945* (Göttingen: Vandenhoeck & Ruprecht, 2003), 194–221.

Gröschner, Annett, ed. *"Ich schlug meiner Mutter die brennenden Funken ab." Berliner Schulaufsätze aus dem Jahr 1946* (Berlin: Rowohlt Taschenbuch Verlag, 1996).

Günther, Lutz Philipp. *Die bildhafte Repräsentation deutscher Städte. Von den Chroniken der Frühen Neuzeit zu den Websites der Gegenwart* (Köln: Böhlau Verlag, 2009).

Haase, Norbert, Stefi Jersch-Wenzel, and Hermann Simon, eds. *Die Erinnerung hat ein Gesicht. Fotografien und Dokumente zur nationalsozialistischen Judenverfolgung in Dresden 1933–1945* (Leipzig: Gustav Kiepenheuer Verlag, 1998).

Hahn, Alfred, and Ernst Neef. *Dresden. Ergebnisse der heitmatkundlichen Bestandsaufnahme* (Berlin: Akademie Verlag, 1984).

Hannover Einst und Jetzt. Bilder aus der Hauptstadt Niedersachsens (Hanover: Adolf Sponholtz Verlag, 1951).

Hartewig, Karin. *Wir sind im Bilde. Eine Geschichte der Deutschen in Fotos vom Kriegsende bis zur Entspannungspolitik* (Leipzig: Leipziger Universitätsverlag, 2010).

Hartewig, Karin. *Zurückgekehrt. Die Geschichte der jüdischen Kommunisten in der DDR* (Köln: Böhlau Verlag, 2000).

Harvey, Elizabeth. *Women and the Nazi East: Agents and Witnesses of Germanization* (New Haven: Yale University Press, 2003).

Hasenclever, Hermann. *Die Zerstörung der Stadt Remscheid.* Herausgegeben von der Ehrenhain-Stiftung mit freundlicher Unterstützung der Stadtverwaltung und der Stadtsparkasse Remscheid (Remscheid: Verlag Loose-Durach, 1964).

Heilbronn. Blüte, Untergang, Wiedererstehen einer Stadt (Heilbronn: Druckerei und Verlagsanstalt Heilbronn G.m.b.H., 1954).

Heimann, Thomas. *Bilder von Buchenwald. Die Visualisierung des Antifaschismus in der DDR (1945–1990)* (Köln: Böhlau Verlag, 2005).

Heinemann, Elizabeth D. *What Difference Does a Husband Make? Women and Marital Status in Nazi and Postwar Germany* (Berkeley: University of California Press, 1999).

Hoffmann, Egbert A. *Als der Feuertod vom Himmel stürzte. Hamburg Sommer 1943.* (Gudensberg-Gleichen: Wartberg Verlag 2003).

Höhn, Maria. *GIs and Fräuleins: The German-American Encounter in 1950s West Germany* (Chapel Hill: University of North Carolina Press, 2002).

Holzer, Anton. *Die andere Front. Fotografie und Propaganda im Ersten Weltkrieg* (Darmstadt: Primus Verlag, 2007).

Jarausch, Konrad H., and Martin Sabrow, eds. *Verletzes Gedächtnis. Erinnerungskulktur und Zeitgeschichte im Konflikt* (Frankfurt: Campus Verlag, 2002).

Jobs, Sebastian, and Alf Lüdtke, eds. *Unsettling History. Archiving and Narrating in Historiography* (Frankfurt: Campus Verlag, 2010).

Kaes, Anton. *From Hitler to Heimat: The Return of History as Film* (Cambridge, MA: Harvard University Press, 1989).

Käppner, Joachim. "Kommentar. Das deutsche Leid," in *Sueddeutsche Zeitung* (March 16, 2006); http://www.sueddeutsche.de/,tt2m3/deutschland/artikel/479/71408

Kaule, Martin. *Faszination Bunker. Steinerne Zeugnisse der europäischen Geschichte* (Berlin: Christoph Links Verlag, 2014).

Kettenacker, Lothar, ed. *Ein Volk von Opfern? Die neue Debatte um den Bombenkrieg 1940–1945* (Berlin: Rowohlt, 2003).

Kiel im Bombenkrieg. (Historische Filmdokumente 6). DVD. Directed by Kay Gerdes. http://www.kiel.de (last accessed February 26, 2010).

Kilian, Hannes. *Die Zerstörung Stuttgart 1944 und danach. Mit einem Vorwort von Peter Lahnstein* (Berlin: Quadriga Verlag J. Severin, 1984).

Kilian, Katrin. "'Mir hat es jedenfalls wieder gereicht, aber wir hatten alle Glück': Die Bombardierung der Heimat, dargestellt in deutschen Feldpostbriefen," in historicum.net, Geschichtswissenschaften im Internet (March 28, 2006); http://www.historicum.net/no_cache/persistent/artikel/1788 (last accessed July 22, 2016).

Klessmann, Christoph. *Zwei Staaten,eine Nation.Deutsche Geschichte 1955–1970* (Göttingen: Vandenhoeck & Ruprecht, 1988).

Knilli, Friedrich, and Siegfried Zielinski, eds. *Betrifft "Holocaust" Zuschauer schreiben an den WDR* (Berlin: Verlag Volker Spiess, 1983).

Knoch, Habbo. "Das mediale Gedächtnis der Heimat. Krieg und Verbrechen in den Erinnerungsräumen der Bundesrepublik." In Habbo Knoch, ed., *Das Erbe der Provinz. Heimatkultur und Geschichtspolitik nach 1945* (Göttingen: Wallstein Verlag, 2001), 275–300.

Knoch, Habbo. *Die Tat als Bild. Fotografien des Holocaust in der deutschen Erinnerungskultur* (Hamburg: Hamburger Edition, 2001).

Korte, Barbara, and Sylvia Paletschek, eds. *History Goes Pop. Zur Repräsentation von Geschichte in populären Medien und Genres* [Historische Lebenswelten in populären Wissenskulturen / History in Popular Cultures] Band I (Bielefeld: Transcript Verlag, 2009).

Krämer, Karl. *"Christbäume" über Frankfurt 1943. Ein Bericht von Karl Krämer. Mit einem Vorwort von Gerhard Beier* (Frankfurt: Büchergilde Gutenberg, 1983).

Kramer, Nicole. "Lynchmorde an allierten Fliegern im Zweiten Weltkrieg." In Dietmar Süss, ed., *Deutschland im Luftkrieg.Geschichte und Erinnerung* (München: R. Oldenbourg Verlag, 2007), 71–84.

Kramer, Sven, ed. *Die Shoah im Bild* (München: edition text+kritik, 2003).

Lambourne, Nicola. *War Damage in Western Europe: The Destruction of Historic Monuments During the Second World War* (Edinburgh: Edinburgh University Press, 2001).

Langer, Lawrence L. *Holocaust Testimonies: The Ruins of Memory* (New Haven: Yale University Press, 1991).

Lauenroth, Heinz, and Gustav Lauterbach. *Tod und Leben Hannovers 9 Oktober* (Hanover: Heimatbund Niedersachsen, 1953).

Ledig, Gert. *Die Vergeltung.Ein Roman* (Frankfurt am Main; Suhrkamp Taschenbuch, 2001).

Lehmstedt, Mark, ed. *Leipzig brennt. Der Untergang des alten Leipzig am 4. Dezember 1943 in Fotografien und Berichten* (Leipzig: Lehmstedt Verlag, 2003).

Lower, Wendy. *Hitler's Furies: German Women in the Nazi Killing Fields* (Boston: Houghton Mifflin Harcourt, 2013).

Lüdtke, Alf, and Michael Wildt, eds. *Staats-Gewalt: Ausnahmezustand und Sicherheitsregimes; Historische Perspektiven* (Göttingen: Wallstein-Verlag, 2008).

Magilow, Daniel. *The Photography of Crisis: The Photo Essays of Weimar Germany* (University Park: Pennsylvania State University Press, 2012).

Margalit, Gilad. *Guilt, Suffering, and Memory: Germany Remembers Its Dead of World War II* (Bloomington: Indiana University Press, 2010).

Miller, Daniel, and Don Slater. *The Internet. An Ethnographic Approach* (Oxford: Berg, 2000).

Mitscherlich, Alexander. *Die Unwirtlichkeit unserer Städte. Anstiftung zum Unfrieden* (Frankfurt am Main: Suhrkamp Verlag, 1965).

Moeller, Robert. *War Stories: The Search for a Usable Past in the Federal Republic of Germany* (Berkeley: University of California Press, 2003).

Moll, Karl F. P. *Ludwigshafen in Trümmern.Ein vergleichendes Bildwerk über die Zeit vor und nach der Zerstörung der Stadt im zweiten Weltkrieg 1939–1945* (Neustadt: Neustadter Druck und Verlagsanstalt, 1949).

Moller, Sabine. *Vielfache Vergangenheit. Öffentliche Erinnerungskulturen und Familienerinnerungen an die NS-Zeit in Ostdeutschland* (Tübingen: Edition Discord, 2003).

Mühlhauser, Regina. "Vergewaltigungen in Deutschland 1945. Nationaler Opferdiskurs und individuelles Erinnern betroffener Frauen." In Klaus Naumann, ed., *Nachkrieg in Deutschland* (Hamburg: Hamburger Edition, 2001), 384–408.

Nadler, Fritz. *"Ich sah wie Nürnberg unterging . . . !" Tatsachenberichte und Stimmungsbilder aus bittersten Notzeiten nach Tagebuchaufzeichnungen* (Nürnberg: Fränkische Verlagsanstalt und Buchdruckerei, 1955).

Naimark, Norman M. *The Russians in Germany: A History of the Soviet Occupation, 1945–1949* (Cambridge, MA: Belnap Press of Harvard University Press, 1995).

Naumann, Klaus. *Der Krieg als Text. Das Jahr 1945 im kulturellen Gedächtnis der Presse* (Hamburg: Hamburger Edition, 1998).

Neitzel, Sönke. "'Wer Wind sät, wird Sturm ernten.' Der Luftkrieg in westdeutschen Fernsehdokumentationen," in historicum.net.Geschichtswissenschaften im Internet https://www.historicum.net/de/themen/bombenkrieg/themen-beitraege/aspekte/artikel/Wer_Wind_saet_wird_Sturm_ernten_Der_Luftkrieg_in_westdeutschen_Fernsehdokumentationen (last accessed July 22, 2016).

Neubauer, Hans-Joachim. "In der 'Zone der Legendenbildung.' Zu einigen Kontexten der amerikanischen *rumor clinics* im Zweiten Weltkrieg," in *WerkstattGeschichte* 15, no. 5 (December 1996): 33–40.

Neumann, Michael. "Genealogie einer Geste: '. . . eingebrannt in das Bildbewusstsein der modernen Menschheit.' Ikone, Ritual und Gedächtnis." In Walter Schmitz, ed., *Die Zerstörung Dresdens. Antworten der Künste* (Dresden: Thelem, 2005), 159–69.

Neven, Jürgen, and Michael Mansfeld. *Denke ich an Deutschland. Ein Kommentar in Bild und Wort* (München: Verlah Kurt Deutsch, 1956).

Niven, Bill, ed. *Germans as Victims* (New York: Palgrave Macmillan, 2006).

Nossack, Hans Erich. *The End: Hamburg 1943* (Chicago: University of Chicago Press, 2006).

Pabel, Hilmar. *Jahre unseres Lebens. Deutsche Schicksalsbilder* (Stuttgart: Constantin Verlag, 1954).

Paderborn. Werden. Untergang. Wiedererstehen. Im Auftrag der Stadt Paderborn. Herausgegeben von Dr. Rudolf Kiepke. Künstlerische Gestaltung Heinrich Niedieck (Paderborn: Verlag Bonifacius-Druckerei, 1949) [Faksimile-Nachdruck der Orginalausgabe, 1949, 1976].

Paul, Gerhard, ed. *Das Jahrhundert der Bilder 1900 bis 1949* (Göttingen: Vandenhoeck & Ruprecht, 2009).

Paul, Gerhard, ed. *Visual History. Ein Studienbuch* (Göttingen: Vandenhoeck & Ruprecht, 2006).

Petersen, Richard. *Eine Kamera klagt an* (Dresden: Dresdener Verlags-Gesellschaft, 1949).

Petersen, Richard. *Erinnerungen und Bilder eines Dresdener Fotografen* (Leipzig: VEB Fotkinoverlag, 1987).

Pfrundner, Peter. "Fragen an das Fotobuch.Gedruckte Fotografien—eine unterschätzte Dimension der Fotogeschichte," in *Fotogeschichte* 124 (2012): 42–49.

Prescher, Rudolf. *Der rote Hahn über Braunschweig. Luftschutzmassnahmen und Luftkriegsereignisse in der Stadt Braunschweig 1927 bis 1945* [Braunschweiger Werkstücke aus Archiv, Bibliothek und Museum der Stadt, Band 18] (Braunschweig: Waisenhaus Buchdrückerei, 1955).

Rat d. Stadt Dresden, ed. *Dresden—30 Jahre nach der Befreiung* (Dresden: Rat der Stadt Dresden, 1975).

Reichel, Peter, Harald Schmid, and Peter Steinbach, eds. *Der Nationalsozialismus-Die Zweite Geschichte. Überwindung-Deutung-Erinnerung* (München; Verlag C. H. Beck, 2009).

Reinhard, Oliver, Matthias Neutzner, and Wolfgang Hesse, eds. *Das rote Leuchten. Dresden und der Bombenkrieg* (Dresden: Sächsische Zeitung, 2005).

Rosenfeld, Gavriel D., and Paul B. Jaskot, eds. *Beyond Berlin: Twelve German Cities Confront the Nazi Past* (Ann Arbor: University of Michigan Press, 2007).

Rühling, Max-Braun. *Eine Stadt im Feuerregen. Die Zerstörung der Stadt Kaiserslautern* [Unveränderter Nachdruck der Originalausgabe von 1953, Ergänzt durch weitere Bilder. Beiträge von Hansgeorg Bassler, Roland Paul und Jürgen Keddigkeit] (Kaiserslautern: Reinhold Gondrom Verlag, 1991).

Rumpf, Hans. *The Bombing of Germany*. Translated from the German by Edward Fitzgerald (New York: Holt, Rinehart and Winston, 1963).

Rumpf, Hans. *Das war der Bombenkrieg. Deutsche Städte im Feuersturm. Ein Dokumentarbericht* (Oldenburg: G. Stalling, 1961).

Rupnow, Dirk. *Vernichten und Erinnern. Spuren nationalsozialistischer Gedächtnispolitik* (Göttingen: Wallstein Verlag, 2005).

Sackett, Robert. "Pictures of Atrocity: Public Discussion of *Der gelbe Stern* in Early 1960s West Germany," in *German History: The Journal of the German History Society* 24, no. 4 (2006): 526–61.

Schaarschuch, Kurt. *Bilddokument Dresden 1933–1945* (Dresden: Rat der Stadt Dresden, 1945).

Schildt, Axel, and Detlef Siegfried. *Deutsche Kulturgeschichte. Die Bundesrepublik-1945 bis zur Gegenwart* (München: Carl Hanser Verlag, 2009).

Schissler, Hanna, ed. *The Miracle Years. A Cultural History of West Germany, 1949–1968* (Princeton: Princeton University Press, 2001).

Schmalacker-Wyrick, Esther, ed. *Pforzheim 23.Februar 1945. Der Untergang einer Stadt in Bilder und Augenzeugenberichten* (Pforzheim:Verlag J. Eßlinger, 1980).

Schmid, Armin. *Frankfurt im Feuersturm. Die Geschichte der Stadt im Zweiten Weltkrieg* (Frankfurt: Verlag Frankfurter Bücher, 1965).

Schmidt-Luchs, Hugo, and Werner Schmidt-Luchs. *Hamburg. Phönix aus der Asche. Ein dokumentarischer Bildband mit Texten von Werner Sillescu* (Hamburg: Harry v.Hofmann Verlag, 1967).

Schminck-Gustavus, C. U., ed. *Bremen-Kaputt. Bilder vom Krieg 1939–1945. Berichte. Dokumente. Erinnerungen* (Bremen: Brockkamp Verlag, 1983).

Schmitz, Walter, ed. *Die Zerstörung Dresdens. Antworten der Künste* (Dresden: Thelem, 2005).

Schnatz, Helmut. *Tiefflieger über Dresden?Legenden und Wirklichkeit* (Köln: Böhlau Verlag, 2000).

Schramm, Georg Wolfgang. *Bomben auf Nürnberg Luftangriffe 1940–1945*, Stadt im Bild. Dokumentationen zur neueren Stadtgeschichte. Herausgegeben von Richard Bauer (München: Hugendubel, 1988).

Schwarzfelder, Herbert. *Bremen und Nordwestdeutschland am Kriegsende 1945/1. Die Vorbereitung auf den "Endkampf"*, Bremer Veröffentlichung zur Zeitgeschichte. Herausgegeben im Auftrage des Senators für Bildung, Wissenschaft und Kunst der Freien Hansestadt Bremen von Karl H. Schwebel und Herbert Schwarzwälder Heft 5 (Bremen: Carl Schünemann Verlag, 1972).

Sebald, W. G. *Luftkrieg und Literatur. Mit einem Essay zu Alfred Andersch* (München: Carl Hanser Verlag, 1999).

Sebald, W. G. *On the Natural History of Destruction* (New York: Random House, 2003).

SED-Bezirksleitung Dresden. Kommission zur Erforschung der Geschichte der örtlichen Arbeiterbewegung Staatsarchiv Dresden, ed. *Der Beitrag des Bezirkes Dresden zum Werden und Wachsen der Deutschen Demokratischen Republik.Dokumentensammlung zur Geschichte der DDR.* Teil II [1952–63] (Dresden: Bezirksleitung der SED Dresden, 1971).

Seegers, Lu, and Jürgen Reulecke, eds. *Die "Generation der Kriegskinder" Historische Hintergründe und Deutungen* (Giessen: Psychosozial-Verlag, 2009).

Shandley, Robert R. *Rubble Films. German Cinema in the Shadow of the Third Reich* (Philadelphia: Temple University Press, 2001).

Städter, Benjamin, *Verwandelte Blicke Eine Visual History von Kirche und Religion in der Bundesrepublik 1945–1980* (Frankfurt: Campus Verlag, 2011).

Stadtmüller, Alois. *Aschaffenburg im Zweiten Weltkrieg. Bombenangriffe-Belagerung-Übergabe* Veröffentlichungen des Geschichts-und Kunstvereins Aschaffenburg e.V, 12. (Aschaffenburg: Im Kommission bei Paul Pattloch Verlag Aschaffenburg, 1970).

Stargardt, Nicholas. *Witnesses of War. Children's Lives under the Nazis* (New York: Alfred A. Knopf, 2006).

Steinhilber, Wilhelm. *Heilbronn. Die schwersten Stunden der Stadt* (Heilbronn am Neckar: Druckerei und Verlagsanstalt Heilbronn, 1961).

Sticker, Johannes. *Kommunale Aussenpolitik. Jumelage, Verschwisterung, Twinning, Gemelagio, Verbroedering* (Köln: Deutscher Gemeindeverlag, 1975).

Süss, Dietmar. *Death from the Skies: How the British and Germans Survived Bombing in World War II* (Oxford: Oxford University Press, 2013).

Süß, Dietmar. Review of *Memories of the Air War*, in *Journal of Contemporary History* 43, no. 2 (2008): 333–42.

Süß, Dietmar. *Tod aus der Luft. Kriegsgesellschaft und Luftkrieg in Deutschland und England* (München: Siedler Verlag, 2011).

Thiessen, Malte. *Eingebrannt ins Gedächtnis. Hamburgs Gedenken an Luftkrieg und Kriegsende 1943 bis 2005* (Hamburg: Dölling und Galitz Verlag, 2007).

Thomas, Julia Adeney. "The Evidence of Sight," in *History and Theory* 48, no. 4 (December 2009): 151–68.

Thum, Gregor, ed. *Traumland Osten. Deutsche Bilder vom östlichen Europa im 20. Jahrhundert* (Göttingen: Vandenhoeck & Ruprecht, 2006).

Tröger, Annemarie. "German Women's Memories of World War II." In Margaret Randolph Higonnet, Jane Jensen, Sonya Michel, and Margaret Collins Weitz, eds., *Behind the Lines. Gender and the Two World Wars* (New Haven: Yale University Press, 1987), 285–99.

Twinning. Deutsch-Britische Partnerschaften (London: Oswald Wolff, 1974).

Urbschat, Horst. *Berlin im Jahre Null. Fotoreportagen 1945–1949*. Herausgegeben von Steffen Damm (Berlin: Bostelmann & Siebenhaar, 2002).

Vees-Gulani, Susanne. "The Politics of New Beginnings: The Continued Exclusion of the Nazi Past in Dresden's Cityscape," in Gavriel Rosenfeld and Paul Jaskot, eds., *Beyond Berlin: Twelve German Cities Confront the Nazi Past* (Ann Arbor: University of Michigan Press, 2008), 25–47.

Vees-Gulani, Susanne. *Trauma and Guilt: Literature of Wartime Bombing in Germany* (Berlin: Walter de Gruyter, 2003).

Verbrannt bis zur Unkenntlichkeit. Die Zerstörung Dresdens 1945. Begleitbuch zur Ausstellung im Stadtmuseum Dresden.Februar bis Juni 1995. Herausgegeben von der Landeshauptstadt Dresden (Dresden: DZA Verlag für Kultur und Wissenschaft, 1994).

Virilio, Paul. *War and Cinema. The Logistics of Perception* (London: Verso, 1989).

von Saldern, Adelheid, ed. *Inszenierter Stolz. Stadtrepräsentationen in drei deutschen Gesellschaften (1935–1975)* (Stuttgart: Steiner, 2005).

von Saldern, Adelheid. "Stadtgedächtnis und Geschichtswerkstätten," in *WerkstattGeschichte* 50 (2008): 54–68.

Wagner-Kyora, Georg. "Die neue City in der kriegszerstörten Altstadt. Das 'Wiederaufbau'-Image in Bremen (1946–1964)." In Daniela Münkel and Lu Seegers, eds., *Medien und Imagepolitik im 20. Jahrhundert. Deutschland, Europa, USA* (Frankfurt am Main: Campus Verlag, 2008), 293–318.

Wagner-Kyora, Georg, ed. *Wiederaufbau europäischer Städte. Rekonstruktionen, die Moderne und die lokale Identitätspolitik seit 1945* (Stuttgart: Franz Steiner Verlag, 2014).

Weckel, Ulrike, and Edgar Wolfrum, eds. *"Bestien" Befehlsempfänger. Frauen und Männer in NS-Prozessen nach 1945* (Göttingen: Vandenhoeck & Ruprecht, 2003).

Weidauer, Walter. *Inferno Dresden. Über Lügen und Legenden um die Aktion "Donnerschlag"* (Berlin: Dietz Verlag, 1965).

Welzer, Harald, ed. *Der Krieg der Erinnerung. Holocaust, Kollaboration und Widerstand im europäischen Gedächtnis* (Frankfurt am Main: Fischer Taschenbuch Verlag, 2007).

Welzer, Harald. *Das soziale Gedächtnis. Geschichte, Erinnerung, Tradierung* (Hamburg: Hamburger Edition, 2001).

Wende, Waltraud "Wara," ed. *Krieg und Gedächtnis. Ein Ausnahmezustand im Spannungsfeld kultureller Sinnkonstruktionen* (Würzburg: Königshausen & Neumann, 2005).

Wiener, Ludwig. *Schweinfurt sollte sterben. Untergang und Wiedergeburt einer Stadt mit Beiträgen von Budd J. Peaslee und Erik Friedheim* (Schweinfurt: Verlag Neues Forum, 1961).

Wierling, Dorothee. "Nationalsozialismus und Krieg in den Lebens-Geschichten der ersten Nachkriegsgeneration der DDR." In Elisabeth Domansky, and Harald Welzer, eds., *Eine offene Geschichte. Zur kommunikativen Tradierung der nationalsozialistischen Vergangenheit* (Tübingen: Edition Discord, 1999), 35–56.

Wiesen, S. Jonathan. "Miracles for Sale: Consumer Displays and Advertising in Postwar Germany." In David F. Crew, ed., *Consuming Germany in the Cold War* (Oxford: Berg, 2003), 151–78.

Wildt, Michael. "Gewalt gegen Juden in Deutschland 1933 bis 1939," in *WerkstattGeschichte* 18 (1997): 59–80.

Wildt, Michael. "Gewaltpolitik,Volksgemeinschaft und Judenverfolgung in der deutschen Provinz 1932 bis 1935," in *WerkstattGeschichte* 35 (2003): 23–43.

Wilms, Rudolf. *14. März. Zweibrückens Zerstörung und Wiederaufbau. Eine Erinnerungsschrift zum 10. Jahrestag der Zerstörung der Stadt Zweibrücken* (Zweibrücken: Zweibrücker Druckerei u. Verlagsges, 1955).

Wood, Nancy. *Vectors of Memory: Legacies of Trauma in Postwar Europe* (Oxford: Berg, 1999).

Zeitgeschichte-Deutsche Städte in Flammen / *Luftangriff auf Hamburg* (DVD, e-m-s new media AG, 2003).

Zimmering, Max. *Phosphor und Flieder. Vom Untergang und Wiederaufstieg der Stadt Dresden* (Berlin: Dietz Verlag, 1954).

Illustration Credits

I would like to offer thanks to the publishers and archives who have given permission for the use of these photographs.

Fig 1. Photo by Erich Andres. Courtesy of Denkmalschutz Hamburg Bildarchiv.

Figs. 2, 3, 11, and 12. Photos from Fritz Nadler, *"Ich sah wie Nürnberg unterging . . . !": Tatsachenberichte und Stimmungsbilder aus bittersten Notzeiten, nach Tagebuchaufzeichnungen* (Nürnberg: Fränkische Verlagsanstalt und Buchdruckerei GmbH, 1955).

Fig. 4. Photo from Heinz Bardua, *Stuttgart im Luftkrieg 1939–1945* (Stuttgart: Ernst Klett Verlag, 1967). Veröffentlichungen des Archivs der Stadt Stuttgart, Band 23., 1967. Courtesy of Stadtarchiv Stuttgart.

Figs. 5 and 6. Photos from Alois Stadtmüller, *Aschaffenburg im Zweiten Weltkrieg. Bombenangriffe-Belagerung-Übergabe* (Aschaffenburg: Im Kommission bei Paul Pattloch Verlag Aschaffenburg, 1970). Veröffentlichungen des Geschichts-und Kunstvereins Aschaffenburg e.V, 12. Courtesy of Stadt- und Stiftsarchiv Aschaffenburg.

Figs. 7–10. Photos from Hans Brunswig, *Feuersturm über Hamburg. Die Luftangriffe auf Hamburg im Zweiten Weltkrieg und ihre Folgen* (Stuttgart: Motorbuch Verlag, 1978). Source: Hans Brunswig. © Berlin/Hans Brunswig/Art Resource, NY.

Figs. 13–14. Photos from Armin Schmid, *Frankfurt im Feuersturm. Die Geschichte der Stadt im Zweiten Weltkrieg* (Frankfurt: Verlag Frankfurter Bücher, 1965). Source: Sammlung Richard Rudolph, Stadtarchiv Wiesbaden. Courtesy of Stadtarchiv Wiesbaden.

Figs. 15–16. Photos from Josef Fischer, *Köln 39–45: Der Leidensweg einer Stadt Miterlebt von Josef Fischer* (Köln: Verlag J. P. Bachem, 1970).

Figs. 17–18. Photos from Karl F. P. Moll, *Ludwigshafen in Trümmern. Ein vergleichendes Bildwerk über die Zeit vor und nach der Zerstörung der Stadt im zweiten Weltkrieg 1939–1945* (Neustadt: Neustadter Druck und Verlagsanstalt, 1949). Courtesy Stadtarchiv Ludwigshafen.

Fig. 19. Photo from Horst Urbschat. *Berlin im Jahre Null. Fotoreportagen 1945–1949. Herausgegeben von Steffen Damm* (Berlin: Bostelmann & Siebenhaar, 2002). Source: Puck 29129, Bildarchiv, Deutsches Historisches Museum. © Deutsches Historisches Museum. Courtesy of Bildarchiv, Deutsches Historisches Museum.

Fig. 20. Photo from Heinz Lauenroth and Gustav Lauterbach, *Tod und Leben: Hannovers 9. Oktober* (Hanover: Heimatbund Niedersachsen, 1953).

Fig. 21. Source: M 75/1, Stadtarchiv Freiburg. Courtesy of Stadtarchiv Freiburg.

Fig. 22. Photo from Walter Weidauer, *Inferno Dresden. Über Lügen und Legenden um die Aktion "Donnerschlag"* (Berlin: Dietz Verlag, 1965). Source: Richard Peter, df_ps_0000070, © Deutsche Fotothek. Courtesy of Deutsche Fotothek

Fig. 23. Photo from C. U Schminck-Gustavus, ed., *Bremen-Kaputt. Bilder vom Krieg 1939–1945. Berichte.Dokumente. Erinnerungen* (Bremen: Brockkamp Verlag, 1983). © Staatsarchiv Hansestadt Bremen. Courtesy of Staatsarchiv Bremen.

Fig. 24. Photo by Fritz Geist from Alois Stadtmüller, *Aschaffenburg im Zweiten Weltkrieg.Bombenangriffe-Belagerung-Übergabe*. Veröffentlichungen des Geschichts-und Kunstvereins Aschaffenburg e.V, 12. (Aschaffenburg: Im Kommission bei Paul Pattloch Verlag Aschaffenburg, 1970). Source:Fritz Geist/Stadt- und Stiftsarchiv Aschaffenburg. Courtesy of Stadt- und Stiftsarchiv Aschaffenburg.

Fig 25. Photo from C. U Schminck-Gustavus, ed., *Bremen-Kaputt. Bilder vom Krieg 1939–1945. Berichte.Dokumente. Erinnerungen* (Bremen: Brockkamp Verlag, 1983). © Staatsarchiv Hansestadt Bremen. Courtesy of Staatsarchiv Hansestadt Bremen.

Figs. 26–29. Photos by Hilmar Pabel from *Jahre unseres Lebens: Deutsche Schicksalbilder* (Stuttgart, Constantin-Verlag, 1954). Courtesy Bildarchiv Preußischer Kulturbesitz, Berlin.

Fig. 30. Photo from Wilhelm Steinhilber, *Heilbronn. Die schwersten Stunden der Stadt* (Heilbronn am Neckar: Druckerei und Verlagsanstalt Heilbronn, 1961).Source: Fotosammlung Stadtarchiv Heilbronn. Courtesy of Stadtarchiv Heilbronn.

Figs. 31–32. Photos by Richard Errell from *Bilderbuch für Nachdenkliche*

(Frankfurt am Main: Europäische Verlagsanstalt, 1962). Source: © Ullstein Bild/Granger, NYC. All rights reserved.

Figs. 33–34. Photo from *Unter der Wolke des Todes Leben: Hannover im Zweiten Weltkrieg* by Thomas Grabe, Reimer Hollmann, and Klaus Mlynek (Hamburg: Kabel Ernst Verlag, 1983).

Figs. 35–39. Photos from C. U Schminck-Gustavus, ed., *Bremen-Kaputt. Bilder vom Krieg 1939–1945. Berichte.Dokumente. Erinnerungen* (Bremen: Brockkamp Verlag, 1983. © Staatsarchiv Hansestadt Bremen. Courtesy of Staatsarchiv Hansestadt Bremen.

Figs. 40–43. Photo by Richard Peter, from *Dresden: Eine Kamera klagt an* (Dresden: Dresdener Verlags-Gesellschaft, 1949). Source: Richard Peter, df_ps_0000010, © Deutsche Fotothek. Courtesy of Deutsche Fotothek.

Figs. 44–45. Photo from Alfred Hahn and Ernst Neef, *Dresden. Ergebnisse der heitmatkundlichen Bestandsaufnahme* (Berlin: Akademie Verlag, 1984). Source: df_hauptkatalog_0063588. © Deutsche Fotothek. Courtesy of Deutsche Fotothek.

Index

Aachen, 7
Achim, 50
Adenauer, Konrad, 14–15
Aerial overview, 96
"air gangsters," 5, 54, 55
"air pirates," 162
air-raid shelters, 2, 14, 23, 24, 26, 32, 33, 34, 60, 62, 69, 70–72, 152, 197
Alex, Dietmar, 151
Allied air attacks, 26, 30, 36, 46, 53, 57, 71, 119, 177
Allied bombers, 14, 19, 30, 45, 66, 67, 68, 97, 99, 113, 158, 161, 168, 176, 177, 180, 214
Allies, 4, 5, 7, 15, 23, 27, 30, 38, 42–48, 59, 67–68, 87, 90, 91, 95, 106, 146–47, 148, 162–63, 173–74, 177, 178, 182, 188, 189, 194, 196, 202, 208, 216
Alte Stadt, 92, 115, 142
Altstadt, 116
amateur films and photographs, 60, 62, 167, 171
Amnesty Law (1949), 15
Andres, Erich, 57, 60, 62, 77, 151
anger, 36, 151, 195, 210
"Anti-fascists," 207–8
anti-nuclear campaign(s), 18, 55, 141
anti-Semitism, 38
architectural heritage, 3, 19, 96, 113, 156–58
armaments, 129, 135, 178
Arnold, Jörg, 4, 6, 39, 87–90, 97
Aschaffenburg, 26, 72
atomic bomb, 147, 162, 216
Augsburg, 197, 200
Auschwitz, 38, 39, 49, 91, 147, 177–78, 189–90, 208, 210, 215–16
authenticity, 132, 172, 190, 192

Baer, Ulrich, 143
Bajohr, Frank, 64
Bardua, Heinz, 43–46
Barthes, Roland, 115
before and after pictures, 141, 142, 200, 208
Berlin, 7, 24, 27, 29, 33, 50, 60, 62, 63, 76, 95–96, 100, 106, 109, 129, 132, 148, 168, 170, 173–74, 177, 183; air-lift, 191; Wall, 1, 148, 168–69
Bernig, Jörg, 99
Biermann, Wolf, 174
Bild magazine, 200
Blank, Ralf, 196
Blitzkrieg, 16, 20, 41, 194
bodies, 10–11, 21, 25, 39–40, 47, 57, 58–59, 60, 62, 64, 68, 75–76, 78, 87, 88–91, 94, 97, 98, 108–9, 125–27, 129, 132, 136, 138, 142, 152, 174–75, 176, 178, 181, 183, 190–91, 204, 207, 211, 214, 216
Bomber Command (RAF), 44, 173, 187–88, 193, 207
Boog, Horst, 18
Brauberger, Stefan, 184
Braun-Rühling, Max, 19, 33, 35, 102, 175
Braunschweig, 29–31, 71
Bremen, 7, 59, 104, 106, 136–40, 143
Britain, air war against, 4, 48, 55, 82, 111, 195
Buchenwald, 41, 147
bunkers, 14, 26, 30–31, 34, 42–43, 52, 69–72, 74, 137, 175, 197
Busch, Dieter, 53, 54

catastrophe, 3, 15, 19, 24–25, 27, 31, 41, 47, 83, 176, 204
Cherwell, Lord, 205
children, 1, 37, 43, 47, 55, 69, 75, 84, 87, 90, 99–100, 102, 129, 132–36, 155, 164–66, 175, 180, 182, 185, 190, 195, 200, 202, 204
Churchill, Winston, 26, 27, 44, 48, 178–79, 188, 195, 200, 205
Circus Sarrasini, 181
city planners, 35, 117
Claasen, Hermann, 81, 83, 95, 149
Cold War, 1, 11, 15, 18, 31, 50, 56, 65, 95, 141, 145–46, 148, 168–69, 184, 206, 210
Cologne, 9, 13, 24, 38, 44, 46, 47–48, 56, 59, 60–61, 63, 69, 70–71, 81, 83, 90, 95–96, 99, 105, 149, 168
concentration camps, liberation of (1945), 4, 15, 91, 142–43, 200
Congo, 147
corpses, 14, 21, 40, 51, 57, 61–62, 75, 88–90, 129, 132, 138, 152, 175, 183, 190, 200, 204, 210, 217; mass incineration of, 178, 183, 207
Coventry, 3, 5, 48, 56, 161–62, 168
Crimes of the Wehrmacht Exhibition, 2, 213
Czechoslovakia, 147, 157, 161

Darmstadt, 27, 57, 95, 175, 201
Deckert, Hermann, 115
DEFA (film studios), 170
Degen, Michael, 173, 177, 183
Derenthal, Ludger, 11
Deres, Thomas, 59, 61
documentaries (film), 162, 170–71, 173, 175, 189, 190
"doku-dramas," 170, 183
"dollar imperialism," 147
Domarus, Max, 14, 25–28, 70
Dörr, Margarete, 104
Dortmund, 29, 118
Dresden, 2, 11, 13, 25, 29, 62–63, 87, 91–92, 95, 100, 102, 145–68, 170, 172, 178–84; *Altmarkt*, 62, 152, 166, 183, 190, 204; "Blue Wonder" Elbe bridge, 161; *Brühlsche Terrasse*, 157; "code" (*Chiffre*), 147; "doku-drama" (*Das Drama von Dresden*), 179, 183; (eye)witness, 165–66; feature film (*Dresden*), 2, 184–94; *Frauenkirche*, 152, 158, 164, 167, 179, 183, 190, 192–93; narrative, 145–48; Prager Straße, 158; Semper Gallery, 163–64; *Semperoper*, 158, 166; Zwinger, 157, 162, 164

"Economic Miracle" (*Wirtschaftswunder*), West Germany, 142–43
economies of feeling and morality, 209
Eichmann trial, 4, 38
Elbe, 11, 145, 149, 155, 156, 160, 161, 163, 179, 181, 185, 204
emotion, 15, 29, 45, 49, 81, 84, 97, 117, 141–42, 151, 171–72, 183–84, 190–91, 192, 204, 206, 208–9, 219, 217
emotional functions of picture books, 11, 115
emotional responses, 8, 49, 110, 111, 183, 195
Endsieg (Final Victory), 188
Errell, Richard, 128–32, 142
Eschen, Fritz, 62
Essen, 129
eyewitness(es), 5, 18, 39, 41, 58, 71, 75–76, 80, 92, 126, 132, 168, 171–84, 198–99, 201–3, 209, 215

fascism, 49, 152, 162
Faulhaber, Cardinal Michael von, 90
Federal Republic, of Germany, 15, 17, 38, 39, 91, 116, 160
Feldpostbriefe, 197
Feuersturm, 4, 13, 76, 172–73, 175–76, 183
film(s), 2, 12, 41, 49, 59, 60–61, 74, 80, 87, 124–25, 142, 162, 166, 168, 169, 184–85, 187–93, 196, 199, 203–10, 215
firebombs, 26, 80, 125, 195
firestorms, 2, 31, 57, 74–78, 174, 208
First World War, 80
Fischer, Josef, 46–48, 90, 99
Flak helpers, 133
Florea, John, 105
Flusser, Vilem, 215
forced laborers, 22, 33, 143, 168, 201
foreign workers, 20, 24, 33–34, 47, 53, 66, 138–39, 143, 218

Forte, Dieter, 143
Frankfurt am Main, 7, 13, 18, 38–39, 41–42, 50–53, 61, 84, 86, 128, 197–99, 200
Frankfurter "Erzählcafe," 199
Freiburg 63, 87
Frentz, Walter, 63
Friedrich, Jörg, 2–5, 172–75, 177–78, 195–96
Fritz Bauer Institute, 199
Fuchs, Anne, 91–92, 151
furniture: in ruins, 98, 99, 109, 119; stolen from Jews, 64, 99

gas masks, 134, 136
Gauss, Werner, 115
GDR (German Democratic Republic), 1, 4, 11, 87, 116, 145, 147–48, 156, 158, 160, 162–64, 167–68, 169, 197, 203, 295, 206
gender, 99, 152
genocide: of German/European Jews, 4, 10, 15, 38, 49, 91, 111, 189–90, 210, 216, 217
Gestapo, 2, 16, 41, 61, 84, 86, 173, 183
Glasenapp, Jörn, 113
Glienke, Stefan, 13
Goebbels, Joseph, 5, 11, 16, 36–37, 59, 87, 146, 163, 174–75
Goldhagen, Daniel Joseph, 213
Göttingen, 7
Greece, 196
Gregor, Neil, 4, 6, 16
Groehler, Olaf, 18, 148
Guernica, 111, 136
Gumbrecht, Hans Ulrich, 78
Günther, Lutz Philip, 199

Habermas, Jürgen, 50
Hahn, Walter, 148
Hamann, Christoph, 106
Hamburg, 4, 7, 13, 24, 45, 57, 59–60, 62, 64, 71–72, 74–78, 80, 90, 92, 95, 98–99, 104, 116–18, 168, 172, 174, 190–91, 196–97, 203–4, 213–16; Sport Club, 118; Museum of the History of, 215
Hanover, 7, 13, 22, 64–66, 95, 100, 115, 132–36; Export Trade Fair, 65
Harris, Air Marshal Arthur ("Bomber Harris"), 44, 53–54, 173–74, 179–80, 187–88
Hasenclever, Hermann, 66–67, 110
Heilbronn, 7, 26, 37, 60, 63, 114–15, 116, 124–27
Heimat, 49–50, 114, 116, 118, 198
Herbert, Ulrich, 17
Herf, Jeffrey, 36
High Wycombe, 179, 188
Hildesheim, 222n4
Hiroshima, 147–48, 160
Historisches Centrum (Hagen), 195–97
History Workshops (*Geschichtswerkstätten*), 13, 50, 55, 213
Hitler, Adolf, 2, 3, 11, 13, 16–17, 20, 27–29, 39–41, 45, 50, 59, 63, 66, 68, 110, 111, 128, 132, 136, 142, 145, 157, 161–64, 168, 175, 185, 187–88, 194, 198, 213–14, 216
Hitler Youth, 98, 129, 139, 180
Hoffmann, Egbert A., 213–14
Hoffmann, Kay, 17
Hoffmann, Nico, 191
Höhne, Erich, 148
Holocaust, 3, 4, 38, 49–50, 63, 84, 143, 171, 178, 189, 194, 200, 207, 213, 215–17
Holzer, Anton, 141
Honecker, Eric, 167
household goods, 64, 98–99, 109, 119, 197–98
Hungarian Jewish women, 139, 143

identity, 1, 4, 17, 95–96, 109, 114–15, 118, 151, 193, 203, 216
imagination, 11, 38, 71, 81, 84, 118, 174
Imperial War Museum, London, 63
Internet, 12, 168–69, 209–10, 215, 217; coverage of bombing war on, 194–202; Iraq, 1, 206
Irving, David, 44, 147

Jaap, Max, 162
Janke, Hans, 189
Japan, 161, 195
Jarausch, Konrad, 184
Jaskot, Paul, 5

Jews, 2–4, 10, 13, 16, 21, 28, 33, 36–38, 41–42, 49, 52, 55, 64, 84, 91, 111, 132, 138, 142–43, 173, 175, 183, 189, 190, 198, 202, 206, 209, 210, 215–17; deportation of, 86, 99
Jozefow (Poland), 37
juxtaposition(s), 64–65, 125–26, 128–32, 166

Kaiser Wilhelm Memorial Church, 95
Kaiserslautern, 19, 23, 31, 33, 35, 64, 92, 102
Käppner, Joachim, 184, 192
Kassel, 4, 7, 13, 39, 67, 201
Kiel, 208
Kiepke, Rudolf, 19, 20
Kinderverschickung (child evacuation), 195
Klemperer, Victor, 181
Knoch, Habbo, 91
Knopp, Guido, 178, 183
Koblenz, 7, 195, 197
Koch, Gertrud, 49, 171
Köhler, Horst (*Bundespräsident*), 193
Krämer, Karl, 51–53
Krauss, Marita, 81, 100
Kriegsalltag, 133–34, 136
Kristallnacht, 28, 84, 217
Kröbel, Heinz, 62, 190
Kröber, Paul, 59
Krupp, 128–29, 172

Lancaster bomber(s), 45, 146, 173, 192
language, 8, 25, 40, 57–58, 67, 75, 77, 177, 185, 214, 217
Leander, Zarah, 185
Leipzig, 29, 59, 60, 62, 65, 170, 197
Lenin, Vladimir, 157
Leningrad, 162, 211
Lidice, 162
Life (magazine), 63
Lodz ghetto, 143, 215
London, 5, 44, 48, 56, 63, 111, 162, 170, 181, 207, 211
Lüdtke, Alf, 84
Ludwigshafen, 93, 118
Luftwaffe, 43, 47–48, 60, 87, 136, 187, 200
lynching of Allied airmen, 64, 176, 196

Magdeburg, 4, 13, 145, 184
Mainz, 7, 9, 53–54, 197
Mallmann, Klaus-Michael, 16
memory cultures, 5–6, 14, 55
Meyle, Paul, 114
militarism, German, 145, 160–61, 167
Minsk, 215
Misberg, 135–36
Mitscherlich, Alexander, 118
moment of destruction, 204
moral equivalence, 43, 214
Moscow, 163
mourning, 11, 17, 40, 95, 98, 113–14, 141, 207, 208
multimedia bombing war, 169–211

Nadler, Fritz, 28–29, 32, 34, 64–66, 70, 81
Nagasaki, 148, 160, 162, 216
napalm, 141, 182
narrative(s): local master narrative, 10, 39, 48, 213, 218; Nazi narratives of the air war, 5–6
National People's Army (GDR), 165
NATO, 51, 160
Neuberger, Joan, 8
Neumann, Klaus, 217
Neumann, Michael, 150–51
newsreels (*Wochenschauen*), 203
Nolte, Ernst, 50
nuclear rearmament, 162
nuclear war, 51, 141, 147, 160, 162
Nuremberg, 4, 7, 15, 26, 28–29, 32, 34, 39, 59–60, 62–66, 70, 81, 83, 199, 201, 205

Operation Gomorrah, 214
Operation Thunderclap, 145
Ostarbeiter, 33
outrage, 44, 195
Overy, Richard, 172, 178

Pabel, Hilmar, 119–24, 127
Paderborn, 19–22, 33–35, 57, 63–64, 102, 115, 200
Paech, Joachim, 80, 126
panorama(s), 57, 83, 96–97, 157
Paris Treaties, 160–61
Paul, Gerhard, 16
peace and socialism (GDR), 160–62

"peace movement" (GDR), 160, 167
Peter, Richard, 62, 91, 148–55
Pforzheim, 7, 13, 24–25, 161, 178, 197, 201
phosphorus, 182
picture books, 9, 11, 83, 102, 113–43, 214
Pieck, Wilhelm, 156, 164
Pinney, Christopher, 84
Pisarek, Abraham, 63
plundered Jewish property, 2, 196–97
pluralization of bombing images and narratives, 213
Poland, 161–62, 195, 196
Pompeii, 164
Potsdam, 170
POWs, 13, 22, 34, 139, 168, 197; French, 53; German, 15; Russian, 111, 142–43, 210, 214
Prague, 164
Preußer, Heinz-Peter, 91

RAF, 20, 27, 44, 47, 53–54, 179–80, 184, 188
Ravensbrück concentration camp, 198
reconciliation, 183–84, 191, 193, 208
reconstruction, 7, 10, 11, 34–36
Red Army, 3, 24, 50, 87, 143, 146–47, 149, 161–64, 204
refinery, 136
refugees, ethnic German, 7, 15, 60, 74, 146, 155, 178–80, 217
Reitz, Edgar, 49
Remscheid, 29, 66–67, 110
Ries, Henry, 62, 63
Riga, 215
right-wing websites, 202–3
Rökk, Marika, 176
Roosevelt, Franklin Delano, 179
Rosenfeld, Gavriel, 6
Rossner, Willy, 151
Rothberg, Michael, 4
Rotterdam, 5
"rubble films," 170
Rudolph, Wilhelm, 148
ruins, 2, 10–11, 15, 17, 19–21, 26, 30–31, 33, 35, 36, 39, 40–42, 46–48, 57–65, 70, 72, 81, 83, 87–111, 114, 116–19, 122–23, 127–29, 132–36, 141, 142–43, 148–53, 158, 162–64, 166–67, 170, 177–78, 184–85, 189–91, 193, 194, 198, 200, 210, 214, 216; churches (ruined), 36, 94–96; furniture in, 98, 99, 109, 119; people in, 64, 97–99; pictures of, 11, 58, 64, 91–92, 109, 111, 118, 145, 156, 210, 214, 216; premature, 93, 141; self-help in, 102–6
Rumpf, Hans, 4–5, 7–8
Russian "friends," 162–64
Rüther, Martin, 59, 60, 61

Sachsenhausen (concentration camp), 128
Sächsische Zeitung, 146, 158, 161, 163–66
Sanders-Brahms, Helma, 170
Saundby, Robert, 188
Schaarschuch, Kurt, 102, 148–49
Schmid, Armin, 18, 39–42, 51, 53, 59, 84, 86, 90, 199
Schmidt-Luchs, Hugo, 59–60, 98, 99, 117
Schmidt-Luchs, Werner, 98, 117
Schmidt, Ernst, 151
Schnatz, Helmut, 202
Schoenberner, Gerhard, 38, 86
Schweinfurt, 26, 43, 96, 217–18
Sebald, W. G., 2–4, 93, 193, 196
Seidenstücker, Friedrich, 62, 109
Seydewitz, Max, 146
shock images, 75, 87, 210
Siedler, Wolf Jobst, 201
Sontag, Susan, 91
Spiegel: magazine, 200; *Spiegel-special*, 216; *Spiegel-TV*, 172
Stalin, 50, 143, 148, 179, 188
Stalingrad, 17, 41, 111, 161, 194
Stargardt, Nicholas, 36
Steinhilber, Wilhelm, 124–27
Stern, James, 80
Strasbourg, 162
Stuttgart, 7, 26, 43–45, 63, 68, 71, 104, 170
Süß, Dietmar, 4, 6, 33
Swinemunde, 178, 197
Switzerland, 187, 195

tanks, 135
television, 2, 12, 49, 74, 162, 169, 170–71, 173, 184

terror: (alleged) Jewish "air terror," 36, 37; Allied "air terror," 11, 45; bombing terror, 14, 54–55, 67, 147–48, 172, 175, 178, 194, 207; weapon of, 36–37, 42
textuality, 58
Theresienstadt, 84, 215
Thießen, Malte, 4, 6
Thomas, Julia Adeney, 7–8
Tiedemann, Emil, 63
Tiefflieger, 178, 182, 202
Topography of Terror Foundation, 16
Treiber, Leonie, 81
Trier, 197
Trümmerfrau(en) (women of the ruins), 81, 100, 105, 163, 164, 166

Ulm, *Einsatzgruppen* trial (1958), 4, 38
Ulm, 4, 63
Urbschat, Horst, 62, 96, 109

Van Endert, Günther, 187
"vectors of memory," 5, 12, 169, 209
Vees-Gulani, Susanne, 156
Vernichtung, 217
V1 and/or V2 rockets, 48, 175, 181, 197
"victim collective," 210
"victim discourses," 217
Vietnam War, 141, 148, 162
virtual city, 113
visual archive(s), 9, 10, 58–63, 156, 171, 199
visual canon, 10, 142
visual escape, 114, 116
visual repertoire(s), 9, 12, 64, 66, 109, 142, 210
visuality, 58
Volksgemeinschaft, 32, 33
Vonnegut, Kurt, 148

war industry, German, 44–45, 60, 134–35
Warsaw, 3, 111, 136, 161–62, 170, 188, 211
Weber, Hermann, 60, 62
Wehrmacht, 2, 17, 28, 41, 52, 67, 129, 132, 133, 135, 157, 161, 178, 213
Weidauer, Walter, 147, 161
Westwall, 22, 23
Wiener, Ludwig, 43
Wikipedia, 195, 197
Wildt, Michael, 16
Wilms, Rudolf, 22–24, 34, 36, 64
Wolff, Paul, 199
words and images, 57–58
Würzburg, 7, 14, 25–28, 37, 70, 201

Yalta, 177, 179, 188
YouTube, 195–96, 203–9
Yugoslavia, 195–96

"Zero Hour" (*Stunde Null*), 143
Zimmering, Max, 149, 157, 161, 164
Zweibrücken, 22–24, 34–36, 64